ONE-TO-ONE
for Sales Professionals

Scripts for Achieving
Success in the Marketplace

DR. MARLENE CAROSELLI

ALPHA

A Pearson Education Company

One-to-One for Sales Professionals
Scripts for Achieving Success in the Marketplace

International Standard Book Number: 0-02-864070-5
Library of Congress Catalog Card Number: 2001089694

03 02 01   8 7 6 5 4 3 2 1

Interpretation of the printing code: The rightmost number of the first series of numbers is the year of the book's printing; the rightmost number of the second series of numbers is the number of the book's printing. For example, a printing code of 01-1 shows that the first printing occurred in 2001.

Printed in the United States of America

This is a CWL Publishing Enteprises Book developed for Alpha Books by CWL Publishing Enterprises, John A. Woods, President. For more information contact CWL Publishing Enterprises, 3010 Irvington Way, Madison, WI 53713, www.cwlpub.com.

Trademarks

Contents

Prologue vii

1 Your Single Most Important Script: Selling Yourself 1

The Short "Self-Script" 3
The Longer "Self-Script" 6
Win with Wit 8
Handling Awkward Situations 11
Take the Blame 14
Thinking on Your Feet 17
Become a Problem-Solving Pro 20
Building Long-Term Relationships..24

2 Cold Calling 29

Establish a Relationship..31
Create Credibility...35
Flex Your Flexibility 38
Demonstrate Confidence..42
Uncover Needs 45
Generate Leads 49
End on a Positive Note 53
You Must Leave a Message...57

3 Overcoming Objections 61

"The Price Is Too High" 63
"We're Happy with Our Current Supplier" 66
"I Need to Think About It" 69
"We Have Everything We Need Right Now" 73
"I Have to Talk It Over With …" 76
"We Haven't Budgeted for This"...79
"Could You Send Something in the Mail?" 82
"I'll Get Back to You"...85

4 Questioning 89

Ask Knowledge Questions..92
Ask Comprehension Questions...95
Ask Application Questions 98
Ask Analysis Questions 102
Ask Synthesis Questions 105

Ask Evaluation Questions 109

Ask Attitude Questions 113

Ask Divergent Questions 116

5 Listening

121

Listen to Yourself 123

Listen for Opportunities Embedded in Challenges 125

Let Those at the Top Hear from You 128

Hear "Possible" When Others Say "Never" 131

Listen to What Moves You and Your Prospect 134

Guide the Sales Exchange 137

Get and Give Definitions...139

When the Customer Speaks, the Employee Listens 142

6 Moving Past the Stall

147

Forestalling Objections 149

Directing the Sales Interaction 152

Circumventing Obstacles...155

Empathize..159

Turn Around the Objection 161

Leading the Way to a Successful Sale 164

Offset Negatives in the Selling Equation 167

Substantiate Your Product-Claims 170

7 Recognizing Signals

173

"This Is Taking Too Long"..176

"You're Talking Too Much" 179

"I'm Bored" 182

"I'm Scared" 185

"I Don't Believe This" 188

"I'm Lost" 191

"I'm Not Getting My Questions Answered" 194

"I'm Ready to Buy" 198

8 Making Your Pitch

201

Hook the Prospect 203

Build Trust 207

Position Your Product 210

Develop Rapport 213

Tell a Story 216

Keep Their Interest 219

Plan for Spontaneity 222

Sell Steak and Sizzle 225

9 Motivating Yourself and Others

229

Goal Setting Through One-Person Dialogs 231
Embrace Challenges..235
Let Exemplars Inspire You 239
Use Rejection as a Spur 242
Know the Motivators 245
Empower Employees 249
Perk Up Your Sales Staff 253
Motivate Your Customers 257

10 Employing Atypical Methods

261

Prospect for Prospects 263
Adore the Gatekeeper 266
Get Your Foot in the Door 269
Deliver Drama 272
Harness Humor 276
Use Unconventional Wisdom 280
Do Well by Doing Good 283
Go Virtual...286

11 Closing

291

Use Trials, Avoid Tribulations 293
Think of No as Maybe 296
Empathize..299
Make a Promise 302
Respond to a Question with a Question 305
Use an Example 308
Offer Reassurance 311
Ask for the Order..313

12 Following Through

317

Practice "Picturing" 319
Regard Closings as Openings 322
Add a Personal Touch 326
Make Unexpected Calls 330
Dealing with Problems 334
Handle Complaints Personally 338
Sell After the Sale 342
Study After the Sale 346

13 Letting Other Sources Sell You   **349**

Ask for Internal Business...351
Ask for External Business 355
Put Out Material 359
Take In Material..363
Turn to Your Competitors..366
Turn to Your Complementors...370
Develop a Network 374
Develop an "Internet-Work"...378

Index   **381**

Prologue

What do these men have in common: Lee Iacocca, Ronald Reagan, Bill Clinton, Bill Gates, and Michael Dell? According to a recent survey of sales professionals, these are the greatest salespeople of our time. Their very selection reinforces the concept that each of us must sell to survive. Whether you're selling a promise to the federal government, faith to the American people, or a computer to quality-conscious consumers; whether you're selling the importance of learning to schoolchildren or the need for soul-salvation to parishioners or the need for better teamwork to your co-workers, you're employing sales behaviors. In *One-to-One for Sales Professionals: Scripts for Achieving Success in the Marketplace*, you'll learn how to sharpen your persuasive skills, how to do what the best salespeople do—whether they're automotive engineers, politicians, software or hardware entrepreneurs.

If, on the other hand, your title relates to sales as a profession, you'll find in these pages a whole new array of selling techniques. The principles illustrated in these scripts apply to any situation in which a buyer and seller are exchanging words. You'll find references to the tried-and-true—the Ben Franklin closing, for example. But you'll also find some cutting-edge closings, ones that'll prompt you to try something new. ("A foolish consistency," as Emerson warned, "is the hobgoblin of little minds." I'm endorsing *big*-minded thinking here.)

The Need for Change

You'll no doubt feel comfortable when you encounter the old-standbys, like the concept of translating features into benefits. But this is a book designed to challenge, not to comfort. After all, if you always do what you're already doing, you'll always have what you've already got. Explore. Experiment. Examine your current practices and revise as necessary. Adopt the motto of Sparky Anderson, former manager of the Detroit Tigers: "I've got my faults, but living in the past isn't one of them. There's no future in it."

The death of Willy Loman (the protagonist in Arthur Miller's play, *Death of a Salesman*) gave birth to a whole new salesman. In fact, the traveling salesman still travels, but today, "he" is just as likely to be a "she." (For this reason, we've alternated gender-references chapter by chapter.) And, he or she is just as likely to be speeding down an electronic highway as down the road to the next appointment.

The world of sales has been transformed. And if you're not continuously improving, you're running the risk described by Louis Ross, former vice-chairman and Chief Technical Officer of Ford Motor Company:

> "In your career, knowledge is like milk. It has a shelf life stamped right on the carton. The shelf life of a degree in engineering is about three years. If you're not replacing everything you know by then, your career is going to turn sour fast."

As some experts assert, if you've always done something a particular way in the past, it's probably the wrong way for the present and the worst way for the future.

You may not have to re-invent yourself but you probably will have to re-fashion some of your basic approaches.

Organization of the Book

One-to-One for Sales Professionals: Scripts for Achieving Success in the Marketplace is divided into 13 chapters. As you can tell by glancing at the table of contents, these are familiar faces at the table of sales contents. But, beneath the well-known facades are innovative interiors— ideas you've not heard before, ideas that pulsate with the energy of the new, the creative, the modern. Put your pioneering spirit to work as you forge into new strategic territory.

Throughout this book, you're encouraged to change your mind-set as well as some of your sales strategies. If you belong to the group described in one book on selling—"Selling is hand-to-hand combat. Only the toughest, smartest, and best-prepared sales 'killers' excel in today's kill-or-be-killed business climate"—you'll be encouraged to adopt a more adversarial viewpoint. However, we don't agree with this. We believe you need to think consultatively—i.e., how can your product or service best solve your customer's problem?

Why? Because customers today are savvy. They've been exposed to enough knowledge to recognize artifice when they see it. They are like Chairman Mao Tse-tung, who rebuffed what he regarded as insincerity on the part of former Secretary of State Henry Kissinger. The Chairman came right out and asked Kissinger what he wanted from the Chinese.

With the diplomacy for which he was famed, Kissinger responded, "We seek nothing but your friendship." This smooth remark prompted a much rougher one from the head of the People's Republic: "If you want nothing, you shouldn't be here. If I sought nothing from you, I would not have invited you to come here."

Like suspects who can see right through the good-cop/bad-cop tactics, today's buyer is sophisticated enough to see through ploys that have worked in the past. That's why we've collected extensive original material, fresh slants from the masters, and new twists on old methods. And they work—whether you're selling a two-dollar widget or a two-million-dollar system.

Organization of the Chapters

Each chapter begins with a *Scenario*, which sets up the situation on which the dialog is based. An overview of the *Strategies* that we will employ is presented next, followed by the opening lines of the script.

Typically, these scripts are one-to-one exchanges between the salesperson and the prospect or client. On occasion, though, the dialogs are more like monologs that successful sellers use when they self-talk.

The opening script lines are then analyzed in the *Notes*. Dialogs illustrating the various strategies come next. In the *Further Considerations* section, you'll find suggestions encouraging further thought or activities for you to engage in to sharpen your skills still more.

Sidebars are scattered throughout, highlighting relevant ideas in the form of ...

- **Insights.** Relevant quotations from famous individuals, applied to the world of sales

- **Experience Shows.** Tips to help you internalize and make habitual best practices employed by best-practitioners

- **Be Careful.** Cautions to take under advisement before undertaking certain actions

- **What the Exemplars Do.** Insider secrets and admirable techniques used by individuals and organizations alike

- **What the Experts Say.** Not all of these quotables are salespeople, but all are recognized for the excellence they've attained in their respective fields

- **What the Research Shows.** Studies, surveys, and tested theories are reported on in this section. Correlations to the selling field are made abundantly clear.

Finally, if you're serious about ongoing learning, you can continue your growth as a salesperson via questions in the *Ask Yourself* section that concludes each chapter. Think about the answers you'd give and then discuss those answers with friends, colleagues, and sales managers.

The Salesperson as a Prism

The one-dimension sales figure who, like Willie Loman, could get by in the past "riding on a smile and a shoeshine" is an anachronism in today's high-demand world. Today's successful seller needs technology skills, leadership skills, communication skills, and time-management skills. He or she is a diplomat, a comedian, a politician, a showman or show-woman. In short, if you are to "make it" in this competitive world, you'll have to:

- **Break it.** Break an outmoded style

- **Shake it.** Shake your perspective

- **Fake it.** Address the abrasive prospect with respect

- **Forsake it.** Use manipulative strategies

- **Overtake it.** Overtake rapidly advancing technology

- **Undertake it.** Make new plans

- **Take it.** Take the available opportunities

- **Wake it.** Wake the sleeping giant of potential lying dormant within you

- **Slake it.** Slake your thirst for success

In Conclusion ...

To paraphrase philosopher Soren Kierkegaard, "Selling without bias is like love without passion." The best salespeople have convictions. They are committed to ethical exchanges, to sales that genuinely aid the buyer, to post-sale service. They have firm beliefs but are willing to amend them as they learn about the beliefs of master persuaders.

Maintain your zeal: Expect to learn as you proceed through these pages. Intensify and extensify your current sales persona. Expect to alter some of your strategies. Expect to make the sale. After all, "A salesman has got to dream," Willie Loman would have told you. "It comes with the territory."

Acknowledgments

The idea for this book came from Renee Wilmeth, senior acquisitions editor at Alpha Books, working with John Woods, head of CWL Publishing Enterprises, who first approached me about writing it. John, along with his colleague at CWL, Bob Magnan, worked on the manuscript before it reached the hands of the publisher. There, Tom Stevens, Billy Fields, and Diana Francoeur helped turn this into the book you now hold. I appreciate their help.

About the Author

After earning her doctorate in education at the University of Rochester, **Marlene Caroselli** left the public classroom and her native New York State in 1980 and headed to the West Coast. She soon began working as a manager for Trizec Properties, Inc., and as an adjunct professor for UCLA, Clemson University, Michigan State University, and National University. Her university work led to training contracts with the Department of Defense and with such *Fortune 100* firms as Lockheed Martin, Northrop Grumman, and Allied-Signal.

In 1984, she founded the Center for Professional Development and began adding books to her list of professional achievements. Her first book, *The Language of Leadership,* was chosen a main selection by Newbridge's Executive Development Book Club. Since that publication, she has written 44 additional books, including *Quality Care,* being offered as a three-day workshop by the American Society for

Quality. Her latest book, *Principled Persuasion: Influence with Integrity, Sell with Standards,* was recently named a Director's Choice by Doubleday Book Club. She is also author of *Leadership Skills for Managers,* a title in the *Briefcase Books* series.

In addition to books, Dr. Caroselli writes frequently for Stephen Covey's *Executive Excellence,* for the *International Customer Service Association Journal,* and for the *National Business Employment Weekly,* as well as for numerous other print and electronic publications.

She has conducted training in more than half the states in the United States and has presented programs as well in Guam, Singapore, Montreal, and Sao Paolo, Brazil. Her corporate clients include Eastman Kodak, Xerox, Bausch & Lomb, Mobil, Chevron, Rockwell, Hughes Aircraft, and Magnavox. Numbered among the federal agencies with which she has worked are the Departments of Labor, Transportation, Agriculture, Interior, the General Services Administration, and the Bureau of Indian Affairs.

Further, she makes presentations for organizations such as The Executive Committee, the Mortgage Bankers Association, The Institute for International Research, the American Society for Training and Development, Public Relations Society of America, Professional Secretaries International, and a variety of other associations.

Gender Equity Note

For the sake of gender equity, pronouns in the dialogues have been alternated by gender, chapter by chapter.

Before you can sell your product or service, you have to sell yourself—to yourself and to others. Confidence in one's self and in one's product/service is integral to successful selling.

Chapter 1

Your Single Most Important Script: Selling Yourself

As a sales professional, you know the importance of making yourself presentable. You take care to be well-groomed, well-attired, and well-accessorized. But there's more to being a successful sales pro than having an attractive appearance. You must also sell yourself. In this chapter we examine ways to do that, starting with how you present yourself through your words. For example, in describing yourself and what you do, are your words well chosen? Do they reflect your strengths? Do they draw upon the power of humor?

We also explore ways of handling difficult situations—those times when, instead of selling yourself, you embarrass yourself. Awkward moments are part of everyone's professional life at some time or other. Having prepared some well-thought-out responses for such moments can provide you with a valuable asset—a positive means for dealing with a negative situation and an ability to summon grace under pressure. By thinking on your feet and having a ready reply, you sell yourself with self-confidence.

Problem-solving skills are also examined. They are valuable tools, whether applied to your own career issues or to the problems that your customers might be facing in business. Problem-solving skills help you sell yourself by putting your best foot forward in terms of how you handle your professional life and what you can offer to those you serve. The final dialog examines the whys and hows of building long-term relationships.

In addition to using the dialogs and strategies presented in this chapter, you might want to look at other ways to sell yourself. The following might be appropriate for you:

- **Newspaper articles that mention you.** These are valuable not only at the time they're written but also later on, because they can be copied and sent out to new prospects as a way to introduce yourself.

- **Your own Web page.** Once you've created a Web page, you can refer prospects to it. The page could detail the highlights of your career and could include illustrations of all your achievements and honors. This might be an especially useful tool if you're uncomfortable tooting your own horn in a face-to-face setting.

- **Public service work.** If you stand out in the community because you do public service work for a cause near-and-dear to your heart, one by-product may be that additional business comes your way because of what this work reveals about your character.

Keep in mind that the more you develop your unique assets and the better you reveal them, the more likely you'll be to reach your career goals. The material that follows will help you sell yourself successfully—rather than sell yourself short.

Dialog 1

The Short "Self-Script"

Scenario

You're meeting people. You're telling them about yourself on the phone, in one-on-one chance encounters, or in group settings. Whenever you're selling yourself, you're using a "self-script." Self-scripts can be long or short, spontaneous or prepared, unrefined or polished. In this scenario, you are selling yourself in a situation where you have only a few moments to speak.

Strategies

When you must talk about yourself for a brief period of time, try to use the fewest number of words to convey the most information. Using potent words is the essence of the High-Octane-Words strategy. Referencing numbers can also be a powerful way of conveying information. The Strength-in-Numbers strategy focuses on that fact. Finally, the technique called Another-Life strategy allows you to weave impressive but seemingly unrelated information into your self-script. All these strategies illustrate ways in which you can define and sell yourself in just a few moments.

> **INSIGHTS**
>
> "The more words you know, the more clearly and powerfully you will think and the more ideas you will invite into your mind."
>
> —Wilfred Funk

Further Considerations

- Book jackets usually contain brief author biographies. Study some for inspiration. They're typically concise and complimentary, and often conclude with a humorous punch.

- Strangers will generally be more receptive to you if you can say something flattering about them at the start of a conversation.

The Short "Self-Script"

> **You:** *(In a chance meeting, you're introduced to the president of a company with whom you'd love to do business.)* Hello. My name is Nancy Cathcart. It's very nice to meet you. Our company was started in 1982. We provide software services. Are you familiar with us?

Notes: This script lacks pizzazz. There is nothing interesting, enticing, or captivating about it. It wastes words and even wastes a question: "Are you familiar with us?" It would be better at this point to be asking for a meeting, as in the following illustration.

High-Octane-Words Strategy

> **You:** What a pleasure to meet you, Mr. Galen. I've followed your work ever since a Harvard course introduced me to your company in a case study. I run a software service that could be of real benefit to you. May I contact your office to set up a meeting?

> **Mr. Galen:** Of course.

Notes: In the preceding example you asked whether you might contact Mr. Galen's office to set up a meeting. Most individuals would not refuse that request. When you follow up by calling his assistant, you'll reference the fact that "Mr. Galen said to call to set up a meeting."

Include highlights of your academic and professional history. Can you reference any well-known companies, titles, people, or places? "High-octane" also applies to verbs such as chosen, awarded, earned, selected, appointed, elected, created, designed, developed, or authored.

Another-Life Strategy

> **You:** *(To a fellow passenger in a courtesy van.)* Yes, I've just started out in pharmaceutical sales. In another life, I ran my own business, which I've since sold off.

Notes: In the Another-Life strategy, you reference past glories by prefacing them with the phrase "In another life ...." This sets up the listener to know that you're referencing a part of your past. It allows you to stake a claim in the present for a previous success.

Strength-in-Numbers Strategy

> **You:** *(Seeking a new publisher for a new book idea.)* Well, I've written 50 books on business practices. I'm looking to make my fifty-first a business novel.

> *Or (trying to start a new career)* After selling 2,500 new cars, I decided I wanted to start driving them instead. I love the idea of being a traveling salesman.

> *Or (looking to set up an e-zine)* After making half a million cold calls in my career, I decided I could write the book, or rather the e-zine, on the subject.

Notes: To use the Strength-in-Numbers strategy, examine your past to see if there are any meaningful numbers you can tout.

- Consider your voice and whether it is an asset or a liability. Try to be conscious of your rate of speech as well as the volume of your voice, and adjust accordingly.

BE CAREFUL

Don't turn your self-script dialog into a "dialong." Aim to keep comments about yourself brief.

- Good posture benefits you in several ways. Not only can it present a positive image of who you are, it can also give you a lift and help you feel more centered.

- Be aware of your posture and other aspects of body language.

- Perhaps more than any other single factor, your vocabulary can help or hurt your image. Decide whether you need to improve your vocabulary by studying books or tapes on vocabulary building.

EXPERIENCE SHOWS

Tap into the power of love. Whenever suitable, consider including the word "love" in your communications, for example, "We'd love to have your business!"

Ask Yourself

- Is my self-script clear and concise?

- Does the script reflect my strengths?

- Does it contain elements of humor, charm, character, or whatever elements I think are important to include in it?

- Do I try to prepare different self-scripts for different purposes?

- Do I revise them regularly?

Dialog 2

The Longer "Self-Script"

Scenario

During a radio appearance, baseball great Dizzy Dean replied to a listener who had accused him of not knowing the king's English. "Ol' Diz knows the king's English," he assured her. "And not only that, I also know the queen is English!" When you have the opportunity to make your case—whether it's about your product or your knowledge—try to do so without embarrassing yourself.

In this scenario, you're able to present a longer self-script, one that has a conversational tone and a carefully crafted intent: to present yourself and your company as high-quality competitors. You're attempting to expand an existing account.

Strategies

You'll use the X-L (excel) strategy: Without being overbearing, you'll speak of the pride you take in your firm's excellence. Then you'll link that feeling to the kind of pride your client takes in his own firm.

Further Considerations

The same principles you used in this script can be applied to any resumé or cover letter you write. Remember that you sell yourself on paper as well as in person.

Americans are a nation of underdog champions. If yours is a small firm struggling to get big, you can use that fact to your advantage.

INSIGHTS

"Who thinks an inch, but talks a yard, needs a kick in the foot." This ancient Chinese proverb is an effective reminder of the need to hone your remarks so they convey the most information in the least amount of time. Let them do double duty as you did with the reference to Colin Powell.

EXPERIENCE SHOWS

Do all you can to remember a prospect's name. This is especially true in a situation where an unexpected sales opportunity presents itself. To illustrate, you're at a social function and you've paid little attention to the names of the people around you. But you suddenly hear someone wish, "If I could only find a top-quality widget, most of my problems would be solved." If you sell those very widgets, you can make a much better impression on the would-be prospect if you address her by name. How to remember names? Challenge yourself. Make a game of it and aid your memory. As the person speaks, visualize a stream of purple paint leaving her lips and spelling her name.

The Longer "Self-Script"

You: I read that great article about your company, Mr. Amin. I didn't realize you'd been in business for 19 years.

Prospect: And the point is?

Notes: This is going to be a hard sell. Few things are more difficult than trying to sell to someone who's not buying, not even buying a courteous compliment. But the very pride that got you and your company to your current level of success is the pride that keeps you going. You swallow hard and continue.

"X" Strategy

You: The point is that your twentieth anniversary is coming up soon. We'd like to help you celebrate that achievement.

Prospect: What company did you say you were with?

You: The Seal of Approval. We've been in business for only eight years ourselves, but during that time we've won the Chamber of Commerce Entrepreneurial Excellence Award three years in a row. You may be wondering what we do to gain such recognition." *(Rushing before Mr. Amin can insert "No, I'm not.")* The answer is simple: We're willing to work both harder and smarter to get new accounts like yours.

Prospect: What makes you think you'll get mine?

You: You know, Mr. Amin, when I was getting my MBA, we were told repeatedly of the power of positive perspectives. My faculty advisor had served with General Colin Powell, and he was always quoting him: "Perpetual optimism is a force-multiplier." Whenever I start to get discouraged, I just remember those words.

Notes: You've achieved exactly the right tone: You've mentioned you have business training, you've cited a possible (military) connection to the prospect, and you've quoted an individual who's very highly regarded—all in one swell swoop.

"L" Strategy

Prospect: This is all very interesting. But I have work to do.

You: Is part of that work building your business? Does it include making more money?

Prospect: Of course!

You: Well, our anniversary seals help you do all of this and more. It's hard for me to keep the enthusiasm out of my voice, Mr. Amin. But the pride you take in your accomplishments is the same pride I take in ours. And I know these inexpensive seals will let you make a powerful visual statement about what you do and who you are.

Notes: Does that work involve taking advantage of promotional opportunities? Does it focus on letting your existing customers know you have a presence in the community and that you'll be around for a long time to come?

This is also a nation that values families. If your organization is family-run, you'll be able to strike a responsive chord in your prospect quite easily. If it's not family-run, try to bring in a familial anecdote that will appeal.

Ask Yourself

- Do I know how to "brag" without being offensive?

- Am I regularly scouring newspapers to find sales opportunities?

- Do I think carefully before mentioning my education—knowing it can be impressive to some people and offensive to others?

- Am I good at separating gruff-exterior executives from true ogres?

- Can I deal effectively with both types?

Dialog 3

Win with Wit

Scenario

People love to laugh, so you try to add a little levity to your dialogs and your dealings. Especially when you're serving up your own accolades to others, consider including a dash of self-deprecation to make the offering more palatable. The idea is not to demean yourself, but to humanize yourself. You're not trying to make yourself less likable, but more likable. In this scenario, you're a former lawyer who has gone into business for yourself. You're now selling computer systems that you've helped design.

Win with Wit

You: *(At a networking event where each person is asked to stand up and introduce himself.)* Hi, my name is Ian McMillan. I graduated from law school in 1985 but now I design software.

Recovering-Attorney Strategy

You: Hi! My name is Ian McMillan and I'm a recovering attorney. *(Pause for a nanosecond to encourage any laughter that might erupt.)* I now run my own company that designs interoffice computer systems for companies like High-Profile Company.

Notes: You made a stab at humor by using the Recovering-Attorney strategy. Obviously, you could fill in any profession here: police officer, lab technician, social worker, librarian, and so on. You also made a point of using high-octane verbs in this self-script, including "run" and "design." By referencing a well-recognized company, you gave yourself a powerful endorsement. People might likely conclude, "If a big company like that uses him, he must be pretty good."

Denial Strategy

Prospect: *(To whom you're selling your catering services.)* Do you have any references?

You: Well, my children think I'm the world's best cook because I can make even broccoli taste good, but what do kids know? Here's a list of my *adult* references.

Or (referencing your spouse who's a well-known chef at a local restaurant) Judith James says she'd buy my line of cookware even if I *weren't* her husband.

Or My mother insists that my recipes are the best thing since sliced bread, and we all know how objective mothers are!

Notes: When you want to reference your talents in a palatable way, name a person who clearly would be biased in your favor. State the person's opinion of you or your work and then deny it—the Denial strategy. You thereby hint at the truth of what that individual is saying, while appearing to repudiate it. while appearing to repudiate it.

"Stop It Some More" Strategy

Associate introducing you to someone new: And this is Bill McKenzie, our all-time best superstar salesperson.

You: Oh, stop it some more!

Associate: Really, Sue, this guy's sales figures last year were in the millions. And his customers love him.

Notes: Of course, you really do want to encourage the course of this conversation because you want this stranger to know more about you, but you felt you had to appear to downplay it for the sake of humility. You used the "Oh Stop It Some More" strategy effectively.

Strategies

Even though the legal system and computer systems don't have much to do with each other, you'd like to reference the fact that you used to practice law. It's something you're proud of, and you think it speaks well of your abilities. So, you'll seek an oblique way to get that fact into your self-scripts, through the Recovering-Attorney strategy. You'll also utilize some other techniques to highlight compliments, while ostensibly denying them through the Denial strategy and the "Stop It Some More" strategy.

Further Considerations

Try to keep a growing file of amusing statements or phrases that you might include in your self-scripts.

Practice humorous lines so they sound natural and spontaneous. Try to avoid repeating the same line to the same person.

As you make humor more of a focus in your life, you'll get better at noticing and expressing it.

Ask Yourself

- Do I regularly try to see the humorous side of situations in my everyday life, knowing that doing so helps me keep my perspective and also sharpens my "humor skills"?

- Do I make a deliberate effort to ensure that I get a taste of humor on a regular basis by reading books or seeing shows that make me laugh?

- What do I do to try to coax a laugh out of others?

- Do I notice what makes me (and others) laugh? Do I try to understand the principles behind the phenomenon? Do I try to apply those principles to my personal and professional life?

- Do I keep a running list of the lines I find funny?

- Do I keep humor in my environment by displaying quotes, pictures, and objects that give me a good laugh?

Dialog 4

Handling Awkward Situations

Scenario

It's a salesperson's worst nightmare: You've inadvertently insulted a prospect with an unfortunate choice of words. You wish a trapdoor would open beneath you and sweep you away in the sewer of stupidity. Unfortunately, it won't. Instead of selling yourself, you've embarrassed yourself. Now you have to make your apologies. You're certain you'll lose the account, but that pales in comparison to the loss of both respect and self-respect your words have caused.

WHAT THE EXEMPLARS DO

Professional humorist Art Gliner has consulted on humor to organizations such as the United States Department of Commerce, AT&T, and the World Bank, among others. He says that humor can be developed by following a few techniques. He assures us that everyone has a sense of humor and that exercising certain qualities can help strengthen it. Visit the Web site of the Art Gliner Center for Humor Studies at the University of Maryland by logging on to www.otal.umd.edu/amst/humorcenter.

EXPERIENCE SHOWS

If you haven't spent any time lately reading about political correctness, now's the time to remedy that. Without even realizing it, you may be using some phrases that others find offensive. You could even ask people you know fairly well what terms they (and others) regard as improper. Many women, for example, resent being referred to as "girls." Many secretaries prefer to be called "administrative assistants."

BE CAREFUL

"Clearly, no one regrets more than I do the appearance of impropriety ...." This opening from a political figure accused of using taxpayer monies for personal travel left some people wondering about the sincerity of his apology. If not carefully worded, your apology may do more harm than good.

Handling Awkward Situations

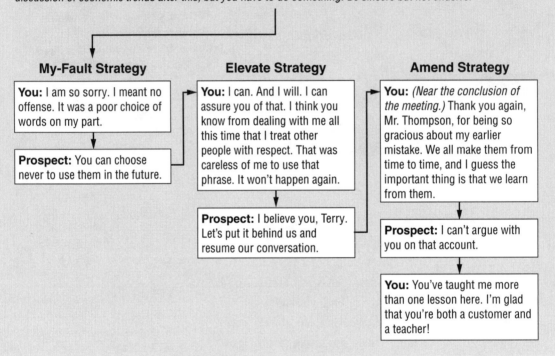

You: You're correct in saying that the economic trends are obvious. Someone would have to be deaf and dumb not to realize them.

Prospect: *(After a frozen pause.)* My son lost his hearing as the result of an infection when he was two. The term we use in referring to such a loss is "hearing-impaired."

Notes: The fact that you meant no harm pales in relation to the harm you've caused. It'll be hard to return to a discussion of economic trends after this, but you have to do something. Be sincere but not effusive.

My-Fault Strategy

You: I am so sorry. I meant no offense. It was a poor choice of words on my part.

Prospect: You can choose never to use them in the future.

Elevate Strategy

You: I can. And I will. I can assure you of that. I think you know from dealing with me all this time that I treat other people with respect. That was careless of me to use that phrase. It won't happen again.

Prospect: I believe you, Terry. Let's put it behind us and resume our conversation.

Amend Strategy

You: *(Near the conclusion of the meeting.)* Thank you again, Mr. Thompson, for being so gracious about my earlier mistake. We all make them from time to time, and I guess the important thing is that we learn from them.

Prospect: I can't argue with you on that account.

You: You've taught me more than one lesson here. I'm glad that you're both a customer and a teacher!

Strategies

The initial letters of the **My**-Fault, **E**levate, and **A**mend strategies combine to spell the first word of the Latin phrase *mea culpa*, which literally means "my fault." "My fault" is the reference you'll convey with words that acknowledge you were in error. Then you'll elevate the conversation to a level that leaves the unfortunate remark well behind you. Finally, you'll try to make amends with a brief reference to the problem.

Further Considerations

Awkward situations, of course, can be caused by others as well. As a general rule, if you find yourself in an awkward situation—another employee comes into the room and starts shouting and swearing at the prospect because of a mistake the person has made—simply excuse yourself quickly ("I think I'll get a cup of coffee") and remain in a neutral area such as the lounge or reception area for 10 minutes or so. If no one comes to retrieve you, leave word that you'll call for another appointment.

If your prospect or client has a reputation for creating awkward moments, come to meetings prepared for them. For example, if he uses language you find offensive, use a line such as, "Joe, let's see if we can get through the next five minutes without four-letter words."

Choices about whether to take a stand are always personal ones. If you're offended by the prospect's remarks, you can say so in language that is firm but still professional. It *may* cost you the account, but you'll save your honor.

Ask Yourself

- Am I known for opening my mouth and inserting my foot?

- If so, what can I do about it?

- Is it ever appropriate to get in the middle of an awkward situation in which two others are involved?

- Do I know the warning signals that mean "anger" is about to become "danger"?

BE CAREFUL

Careless phrases can have a negative impact on you and your career. Tim Jackson, writing in *Inside Intel*, reveals that Intel leaders conduct raids from time to time. Raiders come into executives' offices unannounced, cart away files, and hunt through them for careless phrases that could be damaging in a court of law. Although your organization need not go to this extreme, it's wise to consider the potential consequences of the written word.

WHAT THE EXEMPLARS DO

We can learn from people like General Norman Schwarzkopf who has had to eat humble pie in public on at least one occasion. In a television interview during Desert Storm, he recommended that the march against Iraqi forces be continued, implying that he disagreed with then-President George H. Bush about bringing an end to the war between the two nations.

Schwarzkopf's subsequent apology was simple, straightforward, and professional: "I am extremely sorry that a poor choice of words on my part in any way would result in dishonor cast upon you," he told the president. (Note that he didn't retract his opinion regarding military strategy.)

Dialog 5

Take the Blame

Scenario

Unless the customer's clearly wrong, the customer's clearly right. You'd correct an erroneous impression, of course, on the customer's part, but otherwise you'd assume the blame, even if it were not really yours. Here, you're attempting to sell by phone. The prospect is a small business that does a lot of business and thus writes a lot of checks.

Strategies

Depending on the severity of the problem, you'll take a *hard-line,* a *soft-line,* or a line that's somewhere *in-between.* In choosing a strategy, your aim is always to keep and grow the account. In the process, you want to maintain dignity—your own and the customer's. Even if you take the blame, you can still enforce company policy and allude to its reputation for accuracy.

Further Considerations

There's no such thing as the perfect job. One thing that may trouble you about yours is having to treat customers who are in the wrong as if they were in the right. If doing so truly troubles you, if it seems hypocritical, for example, take some steps. Perhaps you could speak to your sales manager about the internal conflict. Or, speak to others in a similar capacity to yours to see how they handle such conflicts. If you still can't resolve the conflict, you may be in the wrong field.

INSIGHTS

Mark Ruettgers, CEO of EMC Corporation, a computer storage company just outside Boston, was asked why anyone would want to be a sales rep for his company. He gave this passionate reply: "You get to sell the world's best product in its class, you get to work with a team that is driven to succeed, and you get really well compensated. And customers believe that you're really helping them." How would the CEO or sales managers in your company answer the very same question? Where would the emphasis on helping customers appear in their reply?

WHAT THE EXPERTS SAY

Author and expert on customer relations Ron Willingham says we should "ask for customers' ideas." But with a national mindset that prizes self-reliance, we often fall into the trap of thinking we have to come up with all the answers to all customer problems ourselves. Often, customers themselves will offer the solution if asked.

Take the Blame

Client: You have to send me a whole new batch of checks. The first time you took my order, everything was fine. But then when I called to reorder, the lady didn't put a period after the letter *T* in our company name.

↓

You: I'm very sorry about the mistake. Our reorder operators don't often make them. But we'll be happy to replace the checks, Mrs. Smith. Just return the ones with the wrong imprint, and we'll replace them with the correct ones.

Client: Oh, no. I'm not going to pay for the shipping charges when this was clearly your mistake.

Notes: You're in a bit of a bind here. If you offer to pay for the shipping charges, you're really eating into your profits. On the other hand, if you tell the client to keep the checks, you're in effect giving her twice the volume she ordered at only half what she would pay. (With only a period missing, the checks are still quite usable.) You'll choose either the Hard-Line, the Soft-Line, or the In-Between strategy, depending on a number of factors, such as whether this has happened before, how large the account is, what your relationship has been in the past, and so on.

Hard-Line Strategy

You: You can send them parcel post, Mrs. Smith. You don't need to return them by priority mail or by an express carrier.

↓

Prospect: It'll cost me more to return them than they're worth.

↓

You: *(Ignoring the seeming insult.)* Well, you have a choice actually. You can return them and get the correct ones shipped out right away. Or you can keep the ones you have. You can probably still use them. Just add a period. Most people won't even notice.

↓

Prospect: Why should I do that when you people made the mistake?

↓

Soft-Line Strategy

You: We usually don't run into this problem. Our order-takers are trained to repeat the name and address by spelling out each letter, punctuation mark, and space very carefully. We pride ourselves on our accuracy. We couldn't have remained in business for two decades if we weren't careful.

↓

Prospect: Well, they weren't careful enough in my case.

↓

You: I'm really sorry about that, Mrs. Smith. Why don't you tell me exactly how you want the information to appear and I'll ship a new batch to you right away? You've worked with me before. You know I do what I say I'll do.

↓

In-Between Strategy

You: Let's not worry about the shipping charges, Mrs. Smith. I can have our sales rep pick up the incorrect checks the next time he's in the area. In the meantime, I can take the new order and get them out to you within a week. That way, I won't get in trouble for violating our company policy about having the incorrect checks returned.

↓

Prospect: Well, I hate to trouble the rep. Why don't I just keep them and stick in a period? That way I can still use them.

↓

continues

15

Take the Blame (continued)

You: When customers return things, as a general rule, Mrs. Smith, the customer takes care of the return charges. If you bought a suit and then decided you didn't want it, the store wouldn't come and pick it up for you. They'd expect you to take the time and minor expense of bringing it back to the store. It's really the same principle here.

Prospect: Do I have to send these back?

↓

You: No, of course not.

You: Well, if you want to do that, it's fine with us, of course. You know, ours is a company that appreciates its customers. To thank you for excusing this mistake, why don't I send you a coupon for $5 off your next order?

↓

Prospect: That would be great.

INSIGHTS

"If anything goes bad, I did it. If anything goes semi-good, then we did it. If anything goes real good, then you did it."

—Coach Paul "Bear" Bryant

BE CAREFUL

Comedian Jane Wagner has given thought to having a distrustful nature. "I worry no matter how cynical you become, it's never enough to keep up," she reveals. Although her remark is tongue-in-cheek, it does typify the perspective that some salespeople hold: Customers typically try to get something for nothing. Don't let such thinking poison your view. The average customer just wants to be treated respectfully while she gets what she paid for.

Make sure there's alignment between your verbal language and your body language. If the words are saying "you're right" to the customer, but your tone implies suspicion or your face betrays your skepticism, then the words will carry little weight.

Examine the order-taking process. If mistakes are occurring more often than they should, some scrutiny is probably in order.

Ask Yourself

- How often have I felt a customer was "trying to get away with something"?

- Does our company have a policy about bending the rules?

- When can "being right" actually be the wrong thing to do?

- Have I checked with other reps to learn what they do when the customer is clearly wrong but the corporate policy says she's not?

Dialog 6

Thinking on Your Feet

Scenario

According to a man who many regard as the "salesperson of the century," developing the skill of thinking well on your feet is "the best thing you can do for your career." Lee Iacocca knows how often businesspeople—whether they're at the buying or the selling end—are called upon to respond verbally to unanticipated events. In this scenario you'll see that instead of opening your mouth and inserting your foot, you're going to open your mouth and find words of diplomacy streaming out. By having a ready reply, maybe even a clever one, you'll sell yourself via your evident self-confidence.

Strategies

You'll use two techniques here. The first is the Associated-Word strategy. To use it, though, you must be a good listener because you'll need the word(s) the other person has spoken as the trigger for your own reply. The second technique is known as the Memorized-Line strategy. If you have a few situation-specific comments ready in your metaphorical hip pocket, you can handle virtually any challenge that presents itself.

Further Considerations

With the help of a friend, you can gain practice in responding quickly and easily to unexpected verbal thrusts. Once a week, have your friend toss out a far-out question. Without missing a beat, reply to it and, if you can, find a way to make a connection to the product or service you sell.

INSIGHTS

"Leaders who are inarticulate make us all uneasy."

—James Hayes, former head of the American Management Association

---

EXPERIENCE SHOWS

In the Associated-Word strategy, the word you hear in the prospect's reply is the same word you use in your response. In the "Thinking on Your Feet" script, the word was "endorse." You merely changed the direct object of "endorse" from "products" to "health." On other occasions, you could use an associated, but different word altogether. For example, a word related to "husband" is the word "wife."

Thinking on Your Feet

You: Good morning, Dr. Cambell. This is Dennis Ersoll from Sound Bites. I'm calling about our new plaque remover.

Prospect: I already have one. Thank you. Good-bye.

You: It's not for you. It's your patients I'm calling about.

Prospect: We don't endorse products.

Notes: It's pretty clear the dentist just wants to get off the line. So, you'll have to think and react fast to keep her there. You need to get her interested instead of just continuing with the verbal volley.

Associated-Word Strategy

You: It's not for you. It's your patients I'm calling about.

Prospect: We don't endorse products.

You: But you *do* endorse good dental health?

Prospect: Of course!

You: We'd just like a chance to introduce our product to your patients with a short video. We'd loan you the VCR and the tape for one whole month. Your patients can watch it in the waiting room. Then, if they ask you about purchasing the water-pick, you could give them a coupon for $5 off the purchase price.

Prospect: I don't have to do anything?

You: Nothing at all—directly. Indirectly, you'll be encouraging thorough plaque removal with an oscillating brush, one that works at an amazing 3,000 strokes a minute. As you know, these electric toothbrushes are much more efficient than manual toothbrushes.

Memorized-Line Strategy

You: It's not for you. It's your patients I'm calling about.

Prospect: We don't endorse products.

You: Have you ever heard what Joseph Cook said: "Minor surgery is surgery that someone else is having"? If you have patients that are facing oral surgery, it's major surgery for them.

Prospect: That's true.

You: Well, our new tooth-cleaner enhances oral hygiene in the simplest possible way. Won't you give us a chance to show your patients how they can lessen the chance of having oral surgery—major or minor?

You'll have better control of your nerves if, just before an important meeting, you spend one minute, not in reviewing your notes, but in engaging in a mental activity. Do some high-level math or work on a crossword puzzle, for example.

If you're thrown by a prospect's statement or question, gain some time by asking a question in return. The question "Why is that important to you?" for example, puts the burden of response back on the prospect's shoulders and gives you time to collect your thoughts.

WHAT THE EXPERTS SAY

To sell convincingly, you have to immerse yourself in every aspect of your product. Listen to the words of wine salesman William Wren, "You have to look, walk, and talk like a wine person. You have to be able to say, 'I just spoke with the wine maker. We just crushed the last of the cabernet.'" As a salesperson, do you give the impression of having cutting-edge knowledge of your product?

Ask Yourself

- Do I make people uneasy because I mumble, stumble, or fumble when quick-witted responses are called for?

- What can I do to improve my ability to think well on my feet?

- How can I learn more about what the most articulate people do?

- Does nervousness sometimes freeze my brain?

- Do I have a collection of favorite quotations?

Dialog 7

Become a Problem-Solving Pro

Scenario

Like everyone else, you encounter problems everywhere: at home, at work, or at play. You're also exposed to the problems of your customers, clients, and co-workers. In this scenario, you're looking at a problem not as an obstacle but rather as a means for honing your creative problem-solving skills. You begin to see a problem as more of an element in a problem-solving game. Treating problems as an opportunity for creativity will not only help you come up with better solutions, but also help you boost business, because customers see you as a valuable consultant and not simply a salesperson.

INSIGHTS

"A problem clearly stated is a problem half-solved."

—Dorothea Brande

EXPERIENCE SHOWS

The Internet is a valuable resource for solving problems. Use a search engine (such as www.google.com, www. altavista.com, or www.excite.com) and enter a relevant word or phrase. The search engine is bound to locate some resources that you can go to for answers.

WHAT THE EXPERTS SAY

In his latest book, *Rethinking the Sales Force,* author Neil Rackham (who also wrote *Spin Selling*) speculates that in the future a sale done face-to-face (as opposed to using the Internet or some other means) will be essentially a consultative sale, wherein the salesperson adds value by coming up with solutions to a customer's problems.

Strategies

In this scenario you're applying creative problem-solving techniques to your customers' problems. The strategies used here can be summarized by the acronym SOLVER. When faced with a problem, you'll consider one or more of the following strategies. Use the questions and perspectives to help generate creative solutions.

- **S**ave strategy. What should be kept? What works best? What is "baby" and what is "bathwater"? Can valuables be used in a different form, media, setting? Rolled over? Can they be morphed into something else?

- **O**ppositize strategy. Could the top be put to the bottom, or vice-versa? Front to back? In to out? Past to future? Push to pull? Old to young? First to last? Up to down? Fall to spring? Winter to summer?

Become a Problem-Solving Pro

You: Well, it sounds to me like you're saying that if you could just push up the production schedule, you could justify buying our sheet metal in bulk and reap the savings.

Customer: Yes, but I just don't see how that can be done.

Lessen Strategy

You: I know that the Big Manufacturing Company was in a similar situation. Their solution was to outsource some of the steps in their production process.

Customer: That's an interesting solution, but I don't think that our management would go for it. They want absolute control of quality.

Volumize Strategy

You: Have you looked into running the facility when it's normally shut down and adding a shift to work at that time?

Customer: Unfortunately, it's cost prohibitive. And in this tight labor market, probably difficult to staff.

Exchange Strategy

You: What if you switched the order of the production process? It seems to me there's a lag time while the people at point C await the parts from the people at point D. What if you switched the order in which those two parts were produced and let the process branch off at point B?

Customer: Now that's interesting. Let's explore that further.

Notes: You employed tools from the Solver strategy to help you come up with creative solutions for a customer. (You could apply the same technique to a problem that comes up for you.)

continues

Become a Problem-Solving Pro (continued)

You: I want to improve the performance and morale of my sales staff as a whole.

Save Strategy

You: Joe and Cindy are my best performers. I don't want to change anything they're doing. In fact, I'm going to make them my models. In terms of morale, our monthly team luncheon works well. I want to keep that going in some form.

Oppositize Strategy

You: Maybe I'll switch roles with the staff for a week. Instead of sitting in my office, I'll go out on sales calls. Yeah, that kind of contact will be good for customers, and it will provide valuable information for me. And maybe we'll institute a training practice whereby the newest members of the team get paired with the most experienced for a month. That might help even out some of this variability in performance.

Rid Strategy

You: I'm going to drop my weekly paperwork requirement. I think it takes too much time for the sales staff. I'll eliminate half of the reports by requiring them only every two weeks instead of weekly. That should help boost morale!

Notes: You carry on with this sort of examination, using the Solver strategies or any other problem-solving tools you like, to get a fresh perspective on problems and their possible solutions.

- **L**essen strategy. What could be decreased, minimized, outsourced, stored, divided up, or made faster, lighter, thinner? Offered in a reduced size? Done in a shorter time period? Should something be done on a trial basis or under a temporary arrangement?

- **V**olumize strategy. What could be emphasized, repeated, done in-house, or made slower, heavier, wider? What could be included, promoted, taken on? Offered in a larger size? Done over a longer time period? Made into a mandate or prerequisite? Made permanent?

- **E**xchange strategy. Could one thing be substituted for another? Could different people, places, or elements serve as a temporary or permanent replacement for the original?

Could something be done at a different time? From a different place? Under a different label? In a different medium or format? On a different timetable?

- **R**id strategy. What should be cut out, gotten rid of, destroyed, made to lapse or expire? What should be edited out, sold off, or donated elsewhere?

Further Considerations

Of course, a problem must be accurately defined before a satisfactory solution can be found. Slight variations in wording can yield different problem statements, and therefore different results. Be sure you identify a given problem as accurately as possible before attempting to solve it, whether it's your own problem or your customer's.

> **WHAT THE EXEMPLARS DO**
>
> Author, speaker, and consultant Charles "Chic" Thompson, in his book *What a Great Idea,* suggests using the "Dear Abby" technique as a problem-solving tool. "In my creativity seminars, I encourage participants to write a 'Dear Abby' letter describing a problem needing either their organization's or their own attention. The technique works wonders. The letter, I point out, should read just like a 'Dear Abby' letter you'd find in the newspaper. It should state what the problem is and should include as many examples of the problem as possible." Visit Thompson's Web site at www.whatagreatidea.com for more information.

Ask Yourself

- Do I cite solutions that have worked for other individuals or other businesses when dealing with problems?

- Do I make note of good solutions whenever and wherever I see them?

- Do I try to apply such solutions to the problems I encounter?

- Do I practice brainstorming with others?

- As a regular mental activity, do I try to observe problems and come up with solutions?

- Even if no one identifies something as a problem, do I try to note ways in which things all around me could be improved knowing that doing so may help me identify opportunities in my personal and professional life, as well as in the lives of others?

- What are some problem-solving techniques that have worked well for me in the past?

Dialog 8

Building Long-Term Relationships

Scenario

You've decided that the best way for you to operate in your sales career is to build long-term relationships with your colleagues as well as with your customers. You're not the type to make a one-time sale and then ride out of town. You believe in great customer service, and you know that the idea of building solid relationships reflects your basic values. You also know the practical side of good customer service: It can positively impact your reputation, your referral list, and the cumulative amount of business you'll do with each customer over the life of your sales career. Therefore, you're seeking ways to improve your ability to build long-term relationships.

Strategies

Staying up to date with customers and the important events in their lives is one of the key ways to build long-term relationships. By utilizing the elements of the Keep-Current strategy, you'll help strengthen your bonds with customers.

Another way to build bonds is by using the Nonsales-Call strategy: In business relationships, just as in other relationships, people don't want to hear from you *only* when you want something from them (that is, a sale!). If you check in on customers "just to say hello" from time to time (and completely avoid any discussion about sales), you'll certainly strengthen your ties.

Building Long-Term Relationships

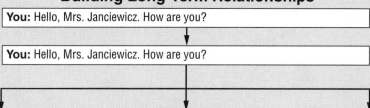

You: Hello, Mrs. Janciewicz. How are you?

You: Hello, Mrs. Janciewicz. How are you?

Keep-Current Strategy

You: Great, thank you. And how's your mother doing? Last time we spoke she was just about to undergo surgery.

Customer: She's made a remarkable recovery and is as good as new! Thanks for asking.

You: That's great. When we spoke last, I mentioned that we'd be coming out with a new product line shortly. Well, it's complete and I'd love to stop by to show it to you.

Notes: You utilized a Keep-Current strategy in this dialog with your longtime customer. This strategy requires two parts—unless you have a fail-safe memory. First, you must keep a log wherein you make notes of what to follow up on in your next conversation with your customer. Any pending event that the customer mentions should be noted on an index card or a call list or in any other way that will allow you easy reference when you call next. Trips, the kids, or any other issues that are mentioned can be followed up on. The second step is to actually refer to the notes before you make your sales call so that you'll be prepared to mention these items when speaking to your customer.

Nonsales-Call Strategy

You: Hi, Lacey. I just wanted to touch base and see how things are with you.

Customer: How nice! Yadda. Yadda. Yadda.

You: Yadda. Yadda. Yadda. Okay then, take care.

Notes: The Nonsales-Call strategy works well not only in dialogs, but also in other forms of communication, including notes or postcards sent by mail or e-mail, relevant articles that you forward, something humorous that you fax, and so on.

Future-Focus Strategy

Prospect: I'm sorry. We just don't need your products or services at this time. We're really satisfied with our current supplier.

You: That's okay, Kenesha. If we don't do business today, I'll look forward to the possibility of doing business together some time in the future. I believe in building long-term relationships. I admire your loyalty, though, and I hope I'm the beneficiary of it one day. When I finally earn enough trust for you to give us a try with a small order, I hope you'll become that loyal to us, too.

WHAT THE EXEMPLARS DO

Jacques Maison-Rouge, an executive at IBM, had this to say about the company's orientation toward its customers: "IBM always acts as if it were on the verge of losing every customer."

Now suppose that instead of dealing with a current customer, you're talking with a prospect. You might try to establish the fact that you're looking for long-term relationships with your customers—by employing the Future-Focus strategy.

Further Considerations

When you're feeling stumped about how to build better relationships in your professional life, look to your personal life for cues. Consider what practices you employ in your personal relationships that might apply to your professional ones as well.

Now reverse the exercise. Consider what practices have drawn you into a relationship, whether personal or professional, with others? What principles can you apply from those experiences?

Think about how you might inject more fun into your business relationships. Consider the element of humor. Also consider taking clients to activities they enjoy—from the ballet to baseball.

Be sensitive to cultural or religious observances and celebrations that differ from your own. Show respect by acknowledging them in a verbal or written form.

Ask Yourself

- How would I treat each of my individual customers if I knew I was on the verge of losing them?

- How far am I willing to go to provide great service to my customers? How do I communicate that strength to my customers?

- Do I keep my eyes open for news that would be of interest to my customers? Do I make a point of passing it along?

- Do I mention effective solutions I've seen elsewhere that might be applicable to my customers?

- Am I interested in seeing my customers succeed? How do I let them know that?

- Am I attuned to what my customers value—personally and professionally? Do I keep those values in mind when interacting with my customers?

- Do I make a point of finding out and acting on dates that are significant to my customer—for example, her birthday, or the anniversary of the date when we starting doing business together?

- In what other ways could I let my customers know that I don't take them or their business for granted?

Chapter 2

Cold Calling

You pick up the phone and start calling strangers to try to make a sale. Or you walk into an office without an appointment—again seeking sales. You've thereby entered the realm of cold calling, and it's not called cold calling for nothing! Sometimes the calling gets ice-cold. It's pure arctic blizzard as you trudge along a frozen terrain where no seed will sprout. But there are things that can be done to thaw the icy landscape of cold calling and make it more hospitable. Several techniques can turn your path from futile to fertile, making that polar terrain look more and more like a tropical paradise.

The three most important steps you can take on the road to successful cold calling are these: gathering good information, creating impelling solutions, and using effective scripts. We'll look at each in turn.

Study your prospects: The more you know, the better your chances for success. Visit their Web sites. Get copies of their annual reports, or go to sites such as www.wsj.com, www.reportgallery.com, and www.prars.com.

Check newspapers and magazines for articles about a company, or visit news sites such as www.cnn.com, www.prnewswire.com, and www.newshub.com.

Seek information on ways to connect with the prospects in a given firm. These connections can be either personal or professional. Go to sites such as www.google.com and type in the name of your prospect. You'll get a list of articles and other sources that mention the prospect.

Find any personal links you might have with your contacts and use them as cold-call conversation starters. A connection of any sort that gives you and your prospect a shared reference point will increase your success rate for cold calling. On the professional side, learn particulars about the company and work them into your dialog with the prospect.

Based on your research, determine how the products and services you offer can help a company solve a problem or improve operations. Establish beforehand what your particular advantage is over the competition, and convey those specifics when you contact your prospect.

In the world of cold calling, your words will either make or break your overtures. Using the right words in the delivery of your message will make your efforts at gathering information and crafting solutions pay off. The dialogs presented in this chapter are designed to help you hone your choice of words and supply you with a cache of cold-calling strategies that will boost your ability to achieve sales success.

INSIGHTS

"It is not the quantity, but the pertinence of your words that does the business."
—Seneca

Dialog 1

Establish a Relationship

Scenario

You've prepared a list of companies you think might qualify as good prospects, and you're eager to start calling.

Strategies

Before making any calls, you need to do the research described at the beginning of this chapter. In addition, talk to the people associated with the company so that you can identify your own connections with the organization and its people. Try to have conversations with the firm's customers, suppliers, competitors, current and former employees, and so on. For each business, draw a rough organizational chart, including any names, contact numbers, and e-mail addresses you have. Add to your chart as you gather more information about the company. Make a set of notes indicating any and all connections you have with each prospect so that you can mention those connections at the start of the conversation. For example, you and he might share ...

- Membership in the same organization

- A mutual acquaintance

- Related family circumstances

- The same ethnicity

- A geographic connection

- Similar interests

- Comparable career circumstances

EXPERIENCE SHOWS

Make sure you pronounce your contact's name correctly. If in doubt, make a call to the receptionist for confirmation.

INSIGHTS

"Remember that a man's name is, to him, the sweetest and most important sound in any language."

—Dale Carnegie

Establish a Relationship

You: Hi, Peter! Joe Fredericks here. I saw your biographical sketch on your company's Web site and noticed that you're a member of the Nature Conservancy. I am, too. *(Carry on a little small talk to establish your connection: people you both may know; events you both may have attended; and so on; but don't take too much time before getting to the point of your call.)* Well, Peter, the reason I'm calling today is that I want to show you a product that is consistently providing increased sales for its users ....

Or Tony Petrillo! And I thought I was the only Italian within a 50-mile radius of this town! I'm Dominick LaBella and it's nice to talk to a fellow paisano ....

Or Hello, Susan. I'm Tracy Clark. I think I may have seen you at our children's school ....

Prospect: (Rather cold and impatient.) May I ask why you're calling?

Notes: You've referenced any personal connections you have with your contact, but you may still be met with resistance. If that's the case, shift your focus to professional connections by mentioning information you've discovered about the company and the ways your products and services tie in.

Reference-Recent-Events Strategy

You: Well, I saw your statement in *The Wall Street Journal* and wanted to let you know how impressed I was with it. Your innovative line of thinking is completely consistent with that of my company, and I believe we should be doing business together. We offer ...

Reference-Corporate-Material Strategy

You: Certainly. I read your annual report and saw that your company is starting to move into software development. My firm can help you in that realm, just as we've helped such companies as Macrosoft.

Even if you can't find a personal connection with your prospect, you can still customize your call so that it doesn't sound like a canned presentation. Let the work you've done on gathering information and crafting solutions lead you toward conversational material that is specific and relevant and that shows you've done your homework. Use a Reference-Recent-Events strategy that mentions current goings-on at the company or use a Reference-Corporate-Material strategy that draws upon information gleaned from company literature, including annual reports and Web site material.

Further Considerations

Make notes after your conversation with a prospect. The next time you contact that person, your notes will assist you in making meaningful conversation and will help in developing your relationship further.

Although your initial conversation may have come to a dead end for the moment, you may sense that this prospect will turn into a customer eventually. If so, make a follow-up contact, but consider doing it in another format. For example, if you first spoke by phone, you might want to send your prospect an e-mail a day or two later, simply stating how much you enjoyed talking with him. Or, if you find a magazine article related to the conversation you had on the phone, drop it in the mail along with a brief note. An ad specialty with your company's name and Web site address may be a welcome gesture as well. Maintain this sort of light contact every so often in order to develop your relationship in between sales calls.

Remember to follow up on the connections that you've discovered. For example, if you found that you and your prospect are both members of the same organization, seek out this person at the next meeting so that you can make face-to-face contact. Or, if you've found that you have a mutual acquaintance, consider asking that person to put in a good word for you.

EXPERIENCE SHOWS

The public library can help you use online services such as Infotrack to locate any printed articles that have been written about almost anyone. Call your local branch for more information.

BE CAREFUL

Although time spent on research usually pays off, there is a risk of doing too much of a good thing. Make sure you're not spending too much time on research and too little time on selling.

WHAT THE EXPERTS SAY

Should you immediately call a prospect by his first name when making a cold call? Experts disagree. Some say that prospects might resent such attempts at "instant intimacy." Others say that using first names helps establish a relaxed rapport and makes it more likely that receptionists will put your calls through. It's a judgment call, so use your best instincts in each case.

WHAT THE EXEMPLARS DO

Wendy Hubbard helped build an $18 million technology company, iNova Corporation (www.inovacorp.com), largely through cold calling. She recommends making cold calls late in the day when you might actually catch a prospect at his desk with no one screening calls. An added benefit is that because you, too, are working late, your call conveys a positive message about your work ethic to someone who is like-minded.

Ask Yourself

- Do I make a practice of gathering good information before my initial contact with a prospect, and do I continue to add relevant information to my files for future reference?

- Do I try to convey a warmth and openness in my attitude and tone of voice in order to help nurture a positive relationship?

- Do I continually try to identify compelling solutions for potential customers?

- Do I convey a genuine enthusiasm for the products and services I offer?

- Do I want to help my customers succeed? Do I communicate that to them?

- Am I constantly on the lookout for personal and professional connections?

- Do I follow up on the connections I discover?

- Do I define my own personal competitive advantage and that of my company for my prospects?

- Do I try to strengthen that advantage in a variety of ways? (Obviously, if you're reading this book, you can give yourself one pat on the back! Can you give yourself any other pats?)

Dialog 2

Create Credibility

INSIGHTS

"Character is the real foundation of all worthwhile success."

—John Hays Hammond

Scenario

You're on the phone with your prospect or meeting in person, and you know that you have only a few moments in which to establish credibility. This is true for virtually every cold call, but especially so when your prospect reveals himself to be a doubting Thomas.

EXPERIENCE SHOWS

Consider asking your contact for his fax number so you can send him some relevant printed materials right after your call ends. Put some attractive pieces of corporate literature in the mail, too (especially if they show that your company has been in business a long time). Tangibles help establish credibility.

Strategies

What's the single best way to establish credibility? Let someone else do it for you! Since you're an unknown commodity to your prospect, you must find a commodity known to him that will serve as a positive reference for you. Using a 3-P strategy (*products, people,* and *places* of business) you'll reference well-known people, products, and places of business that speak for you in some way.

For example, if a well-known person or company uses your products or services, tout that fact to your prospect up front. (Note that "well-known" doesn't necessarily mean famous.) If your company makes a well-respected product and is venturing into a brand-new line, reference the former to help you establish credibility with the latter. Whenever possible, use the known to recommend the unknown.

When you don't have the luxury of knowing which references might be meaningful to your contact, you can turn to the 5-P strategy and utilize two additional techniques to help you establish credibility: referencing *personal proficiency* and utilizing *polarization*. For example, you'll cite your own achievements to help establish your credibility. And when you're met with a generalized negative perception you'll employ polarization to establish the ways in which you're different.

Create Credibility

You: … The reason I'm calling today, Ms. Liston, is that we're launching a new product line—soda dispensers.

Prospect: We already have soda dispensers that work just fine, thank you.

3-P Strategy (Products, People, Places of Business)

You: Well, I'm sure you're familiar with the Stardust chain of coffee shops. They thought their espresso machines were working just fine, too, until they tried ours. They saw the superior results our equipment produced and how it contributed to increased sales. We know you'll have the same experience with our soda dispensers. Tom Silatta of Papa Tom's Pizza did! Now he's offering our dispensers to all his franchises.

Prospect: Well, our operation doesn't come close to the size of those superstars. How would we get service from your company when you're so busy with big accounts like that?

You: Ms. Liston, we think all of our customers are important—not just the big ones. In fact, we just got a contract with the restaurant over on Fifth Street. They operate in a single location now, but we believe they're poised to grow. Those are the kinds of clients I seek out—ones who run their businesses well and have a good potential. Look, I know from the biography on your Web site that you volunteer at the soup kitchen downtown. I've already asked our company to see whether they could donate some of our used but usable equipment to the kitchen. I did that because your example inspired me to do a good deed, and I did it because I want to have your business.

5-P Strategy (Personal Proficiency)

You: … I want you to know I've been with this company for eight years, and I believe this is the single best product we've ever produced. I'm certain you'll be happy with it. I also want you to know that I was named Salesman of the Year last year, so you can count on me to serve you well. I've got a reputation to uphold.

Or I want you to know I've been with this company for eight years, and I believe this is the single best product we've ever produced. I think you'll agree once I demonstrate it for you. And when we talk more about your specific needs, I'll tell you whether or not I think this equipment is right for you.

Prospect: I don't know about making a change. I've been reading those articles in the newspaper lately.

Notes: The variation in the script for this strategy emphasizes your personal proficiency but allows for the possibility that what you have to offer may not work for your contact. By not overselling your product and by acknowledging its potential limitations, you can boost your credibility.

continues

Create Credibility (continued)

Prospect: Well, that was nice of you. But listen, I need to know that I can get service. If my machines go down, so do my profits.

Notes: You've used the 3-P strategy and cited well-known people, products, and places of business that reflect well on you and what you're offering. You realized your prospect might respond better to a more personal approach, along with some reassurances about service and your personal credibility. Having done your homework, you've gathered good information and crafted compelling solutions, and you've woven them into your response.

5-P Strategy (Polarization)

You: I want to assure you that my company isn't like the one you've been reading about. We couldn't have stayed in business for 55 years if we were! And I want you to know that I don't go after just the biggest accounts like some salespeople do. I like to establish relationships with people who impress me—personally and professionally. I believe that's what pays off in the long run, and that's how small accounts become big accounts. My record proves that my approach makes sense. After five years of nurturing my accounts, I had the top sales figures out of my entire company this year.

Further Considerations

Credibility is established through dialog, of course. However, don't forget that printed materials can speak volumes for you, too. Consider preparing a list of clients who use your products or services. Include as much information as the client is comfortable revealing, such as how long they've been with you, the different categories of products they purchase from you, whether they use your company exclusively, and perhaps a testimonial quote about your company. Lay out the information in a visually appealing format, and keep copies in your briefcase for distribution.

Remember that credibility isn't just about connecting the unknown with the known. It's also about personal integrity. Always operate in an honorable manner, and never promise something you can't deliver. Your sterling reputation will grow along with your sales.

EXPERIENCE SHOWS

Remember to not only promote your product's assets but also to be honest about its limitations. Doing so will help create credibility.

EXPERIENCE SHOWS

If your company's Web site includes written customer testimonials or ones that can be heard on audio playback, remember to reference those sorts of credibility builders so that your prospect can see and hear them for himself.

BE CAREFUL

Never cite an individual or a company as a reference without prior permission.

WHAT THE EXEMPLARS DO

The value of credibility and integrity cannot be overstated in terms of their importance in an individual's career or the success of an entire company. Consider the words of Andrew Carnegie, one of America's most successful businessmen, who began life with nothing and ended it as the world's richest man: "A great business is seldom if ever built up, except on lines of strictest integrity."

Ask Yourself

- Do I stay on top of any corporate connections to well-known people and places of business so that I can use them as easy references in my cold calls? Do I mention any corporate honors in my calls? (For example, "We were just given the Malcolm Baldrige award for quality.")

- Do I continue to strive for professional accomplishments that I can mention as testaments to my own credibility and creditableness, such as length of service, professional recognitions, or awards?

- Do I do everything I can to keep my personal integrity and credibility intact?

- Do I do my homework on prospects by gathering good information and crafting compelling solutions so that I can customize my presentation with material that's meaningful to them?

- Do I use printed materials that are up to date and fresh-looking?

Dialog 3

Flex Your Flexibility

Scenario

Flexibility is manifested in a variety of ways, large and small. It can consist of something as simple as rephrasing a statement, or it can be as complex as overhauling an entire corporate policy. Successful cold calling requires that you be on the alert for expressed and unexpressed resistance from your contacts. In order to handle such resistance deftly, you must have a trove of options at your fingertips to offer as alternatives. In this scenario, the prospect presents a variety of roadblocks during your cold call to him.

Flex Your Flexibility

Prospect: Sam Wilson. *(He sounds rushed to you, but you can't be sure since you've never spoken to him before. Maybe he always sounds like this?)*

You: Hello, Sam. This is Marshall of XYZ Corp. Bob Rodriguez suggested I call you because we've got a new product line that he raves about, and he said you would, too.

Prospect: Look, I'm really busy right now.

Detect and Inspect Strategies

You: *(His response confirms your instinct that he was rushed. Instead of pushing on with your pitch, you take the cue and flex your flexibility with a shift of gears.)* I'm sorry I caught you at a bad time. I can try you again tomorrow.

Prospect: *(His speech slows down a notch.)* No. I'm in the middle of corporate budgeting, and I'm afraid I'll be tied up every day for several weeks.

Notes: In the first few seconds of your call, you found a problem and offered a solution. But resistance is usually recurrent and multifaceted, reflecting a wide variety of issues. As your conversation continues, you'll likely be met with additional resistance. For example, even though this prospect appreciates that you're being sensitive to his situation by offering to call back the next day, this isn't a solution to his bigger problem.

Select Strategies

You: *(You sense this is a genuine problem and not just a brush-off. Again, you flex your flexibility to come up with a creative solution. Instead of saying, "Okay, I'll call back in a few weeks," you suggest the following.)* Well, we do have an introductory offer going on right now that I'd hate to have you miss out on. If you'll give me your e-mail address, I'll send you some basic information along with a link to our Web site that gives more details. I'll also put some brochures in the mail for you. You can look at the materials whenever it's convenient for you. Based on what Bob said, you're going to love what you see. Then I can stop by for a few minutes before our introductory offer ends and explain how it works so that you don't miss out on the deal.

Prospect: That's great. You can reach me at …

Strategies

Your strategy consists of identifying a "problem" (roadblocks, difficulties, or resistance of any sort) and offering an appropriate "solution" (alternatives that are truly more appealing to your contact, but still meet your needs). When it's not clear what the real issues are, you'll need other strategies in order to dig deeper and offer more creative alternatives.

When you sense that you need to know more or need to offer additional alternatives, try the following strategies:

Detect strategy. Acknowledge (silently, to yourself) that you've sensed implicit resistance or heard explicit resistance.

Inspect strategy. Study the verbal and nonverbal clues and cues of the conversation to confirm your suspicions and to ascertain that you've identified the real issues.

Select strategy. Consider alternatives that address the issues. Then choose those that best meet the needs of your prospect and yourself, and offer them as solutions.

Further Considerations

Remember to listen not just to the words that are said when people talk. Take into account nonverbal signals as well, such as tone of voice and speed of delivery. Try to ascertain mood, and then use all this information to help guide your dialog.

Unless you correctly identify genuine problems, the alternatives you offer, no matter how creative, won't solve them. Try to probe until you get at real issues.

Consider how far you're willing to *flex your flexibility.* Think outside the box and offer novel solutions, if you're so inclined. For example, if your contact says something like, "I'm so busy these days, I'll even be here on Saturday morning," respond with, "Great! I can stop by then with some donuts and coffee, and we can have a 10-minute chat. How's 9:00?"

Ask Yourself

- Do I constantly try to add to my trove of solutions for the objections I'll encounter?

- Do I review those solutions and responses regularly so they're at my fingertips?

- Do I practice listening well in everyday contexts so I can hone my ability to read between the lines and discern what people are really saying?

- Am I flexible with myself? Do I try to find fresh perspectives and new solutions to my own problems? Do I give myself credit not just for the big sales, but also for any ventures that were really well-executed (even if they lead nowhere for the moment)?

- Is my company flexible in terms of empowering me to do what it takes to entice new customers or maintain an old one? If not, perhaps such a suggestion is in order.

WHAT THE EXPERTS SAY

Isn't it a waste of time to follow up a cold call by sending out material when what's really needed is a face-to-face meeting? As usual, experts disagree. That's because there are times when this practice will be fruitful and times when it will be futile. At the very least, the practice can be used as a way to obtain e-mail addresses or fax numbers, which themselves can be used to advance the sales process to the next step. You can always follow up with a message like, "I sent out the brochures you requested last week. Unfortunately, brochures really can't convey the whole story on this product. But a 15-minute demonstration can! I'd be happy to show you all the different things this product can do for your company."

WHAT THE EXEMPLARS DO

Many of the most successful people in business talk about the value of embracing problems. They even express a certain gratitude for how problems helped them and their businesses grow. Consider the words of J.C. Penney: "I am grateful for all my problems. After each one was overcome, I became stronger and more able to meet those that were still to come. I grew in all my difficulties."

Dialog 4

Demonstrate Confidence

Scenario

You're conversing with a contact on the phone or in person, and want to do your best to demonstrate confidence—in yourself, your product, your company. If you do so successfully, you'll likely inspire your contact to feel confident about you and what you're offering. Inspiring such confidence on a regular basis will certainly improve your cold-calling success rate.

<table>
<tr><td>

INSIGHTS

"All that is necessary to break the spell of inertia and frustration is this: Act as if it were impossible to fail."

—Dorothea Brande

</td></tr>
</table>

<table>
<tr><td>

EXPERIENCE SHOWS

Good posture plays an important role in conveying confidence—both in person and on the phone. Pay attention to your posture.

</td></tr>
</table>

<table>
<tr><td>

EXPERIENCE SHOWS

Remember that a rejection from one person in a company isn't a rejection from the whole company. Unless you're dealing with the actual head of the company, a company never has just one decision-maker—there are many! So, if one person rejects your overtures, don't let that rejection make a dent in your confidence. Simply move down to the next person on your list.

</td></tr>
</table>

Strategies

Demonstrate confidence through your tone of voice, your attitude, and the words you choose. Reference your personal competencies and the features of your products or your company that inspire confidence. When you're met with resistance, utilize a "Been There Before" strategy that illustrates how someone who is now a good customer initially demonstrated the same sort of resistance as your current contact. Employ a Remarkable-Results strategy by offering some specifics on the results that you and your product or service have been able to produce.

Further Consideration

Consider surrounding yourself with all that inspires confidence in you. Is it awards? Diplomas? Charts showing your sales record? Photos of those who encourage you, such as family and friends? Quotes and pictures of business leaders who inspire you? Put yourself in constant contact with these confidence builders.

Demonstrate Confidence

You: Hello, Mrs. McDonough. I'm Samantha Rodino of Calls Incorporated. We sell phone systems and related equipment to call centers like yours. I'd like to set up an appointment to show you what our cutting-edge products can do for you.

Prospect: I've never heard of your company.

You: The name may be new, but the people who run the company aren't. Our president ran PhoneTel for 25 years, and our head of operations was with Ball Telephone for 27 years. As for me, I've sold communications equipment for over 12 years. U-Know-Who Company was one of my accounts for that entire time.

"Been There Before" Strategy

Prospect: Well, you and your company may be great, but the fact is, we just don't need any new equipment.

You: Mrs. McDonough, that's exactly what the people at Well-Known-Company said until I demonstrated what our products could do for them. Now they're one of our best customers.

Notes: You demonstrate confidence by making reference to the fact that you've heard a similar rebuff before from someone who ultimately turned into a valued customer.

Remarkable-Results Strategy

Prospect: There's no money in the budget right now.

You: Well, we have no-money-down financing plans available. But more importantly, our customers report on average that our equipment results in a 25 percent increase in productivity. That translates into huge savings for their companies. How would your superiors feel if you were responsible for a 25 percent increase in productivity at your company?

Prospect: Great, obviously.

You: Well, we should meet then. I'm free all Wednesday afternoon or Thursday at 10:00.

Notes: Calculate ahead of time some specifics regarding the results that your products or services have produced. For example, how much money or time did your products save your average customer last year; how much did your products help your customers increase sales; in what other ways did your products contribute to your customers' successes? Then reference those results in your conversations to emphasize that what you've done for others, you can do for this company.

BE CAREFUL

Confidence does not mean cockiness. Watch your tone of voice and your manner to be sure your confidence is tempered with humility. Remember that you can be confident in your abilities even when you don't have all the answers. For example, "Susan, I honestly don't know if our services are right for you because I'd need some more information from you to determine that. But I've been in this business long enough to know that I can give you an answer to that question after a 10-minute meeting. How's Thursday at 4:00?"

WHAT THE EXPERTS SAY

Psychologist Martin Seligman of the University of Pennsylvania has studied the subject of optimism extensively and found that, with people of comparable abilities, optimists are more successful than pessimists. Related studies on salespeople showed that optimistic ones consistently outsold their pessimistic counterparts—sometimes by as much as 50 percent.

Try writing a list of the reasons why you're a confident salesperson, and study the list before you begin making cold calls. It may include reasons such as: because I've been doing this so many years; because I really believe in our products; because I've seen how much they can help my customers; because I'm proud of the service we provide; because we deal with problems in a way that produces many satisfied customers; because I know we can get the job done right; because I've been trained well; and so on.

Practice affirmations. Decide on a big goal and write it at the top of a sheet of paper. For example: "I will triple my sales totals this year." Then write out the statement another 20 times. Do this exercise daily.

Practice visualization. Take a few minutes and close your eyes. Relive your past successes, such as getting the news that you made a big sale or received a big bonus. Think about all your different accomplishments and the times that people have praised you. Focus on reexperiencing past successes and imagining future ones. (Read more about visualization in Chapter 9, "Motivating Yourself and Others.")

Ask Yourself

- Do I always try to look my best, knowing how that can boost my confidence?

- What things do I do to try to maintain an optimistic outlook on life?

- Do I try to take on new personal and professional challenges regularly?

- Do I practice visualization or affirmations often enough?

- Do I have a trusted friend or colleague who's able to help me discard any seeds of self-doubt that I may be feeling from time to time?

- What would I attempt to do if I could be assured in advance that it would be impossible to fail in this endeavor?

Dialog 5

Uncover Needs

Scenario

You're having a conversation. It could be any conversation anywhere—in person or on the phone, with the head of operations or with the receptionist. You use the opportunity to gather information about how the company operates and thus uncover its needs.

Strategies

Needs are often unexpressed, even to the person who has them. Try to uncover needs by asking probing, open-ended questions that encourage people to elaborate. Strategies such as the following will help you to do so: Opinion-Seeking strategy, What's That Like? strategy, Tell Me More strategy, and the Similar-Solution strategy.

Further Considerations

Employ "the art of wishing" to help uncover needs. It can point the way to innovations, identify problems, and boost employee morale and performance. Wishes represent rich possibilities for any company.

INSIGHTS
"Imagination is the only source of real value in the new economy."
—Tom Peters

Ask questions such as these to try to ascertain wishes:

- "If money were no object, what products or services would you get for your company right now to make things better?"

- "If there were one thing you could change about the products/ services you're currently using, what would that be?"

Uncover Needs

Receptionist: No, Mr. Wong's away on vacation.

↓

You: *(As you're jotting down information to fill in the blanks on your organizational chart.)* Oh! Some tropical paradise, I hope!

↓

Receptionist: *(She may not reveal anything at this point, but if she does, you'll have some personal information that you can reference when you call back Mr. Wong.)* Actually, he headed for Alaska.

↓

You: Well, I was going to send him some information on our office products. Who else in your company makes those sorts of decisions?

Receptionist: Well, he's the only one at this location. Our three different sites make their own choices on office products because each has different needs.

↓

You: How are their needs different?

Or What are the names of the people at your two other locations?

↓

Receptionist: I can't give out that information.

Notes: You've tried to glean as much information as you can, and you've succeeded to some degree. When you seem to reach a dead end, you may need to dig deeper to identify the itch that needs to be scratched.

Opinion-Seeking Strategy

You: I wonder if you would give me your opinion on something. The three best features of our office products are the cost, the quality, and the convenience of same-day delivery. Which of those three features do you think would be most valued at your location? Do you think Mr. Wong would have the same opinion? And what about at the other two locations? Which of those three features would be most valued there?

Notes: People love to give opinions, especially those whose opinions may not be sought very often.

↓

What's That Like? Strategy

You: That must be difficult. What's it like for you and your department (or you and the office) when the copier goes down? What do people do?

↓

Receptionist: Blah, blah, blah.

You: What are some of the best achievements of your *(department, company)*? What part did you play in them?

Or What are your greatest satisfactions in the work you do?

Or What's it like for you when you're able to achieve something like that?

Notes: Even more than giving opinions, most people love to vent about their difficulties and brag about their successes. If a contact has acknowledged a problem ("Yes, our copier goes down often"), ask him to elaborate. Also, if appropriate, give your contact an opportunity to talk about his successes. Take notes as your prospect replies. His answers will help you uncover needs, priorities, and motivations.

continues

Uncover Needs (continued)

Tell Me More Strategy

You: Tell me more.

Or Why do you think that is so?

Or What else is important?

Or What else?

Notes: *Asking questions such as these encourages people to elaborate.*

Similar-Solution Strategy

You: Oh, so that's how your call center functions! You know, ABC Corporation used to work that way as well until we provided them with this real-time display unit to help them direct their incoming calls. They found that it really streamlined operations. I'm sure it would work equally well for you. I can show it to your managers in a five-minute demonstration. How's tomorrow at 10:00?

Notes: *Here you reference a solution that you provided for a customer in a similar situation.*

- "What would the ideal product (or service) consist of for you?"

- "If you could wave a magic wand, what changes would you make in the way your company works to produce its products or services?" (A more neutral way to ask this would be to substitute "employees" for "you.")

- "How about in the way your company delivers customer service or other functions?"

- "If you knew that there would be no obstacles, what would you like to see as the next step for your (department, company, industry)?"

- "What would the long-range steps be?"

Don't forget about the needs of current customers. Current customers may be more forthcoming in revealing information because they have an established relationship with you. Consider sending them a questionnaire of sorts that states something like this:

> "We are inspired by the thought that 'reality can be beaten with enough imagination.' If we could make the impossible possible for you, what would you ask us to do? We encourage you to enter the world of fantasy here. Don't be limited by reality. Let your imagination fly. We're not asking you for realistic solutions; we're asking you to state problems, frustrations, wishes, and desires. We may not be able to satisfy them all, but we'd like to try to define your idea of the ideal. As Albert Einstein said, 'Imagination is more important than knowledge.'"

Then set up a meeting to discuss the results with them. At the very least, such a questionnaire demonstrates that you care about your customers and how best to serve them.

Consider making a "Wish List" notebook that identifies the wishes of your various customers, and keep it for reference. If you should come across something in the future that might help them turn a wish into a reality, you can inform them accordingly. They'll appreciate your looking out for them and may come to see you as a valuable resource for their company.

Ask Yourself

- Do I make a practice of trying to glean the wishes, hopes, and dreams of my friends, my family, and myself? Doing so will help you get better at identifying those of your customers.

- Do I try to see how things could be improved on a regular basis? Make a game of seeing how you might do things differently. Say to yourself, "If this (operation, department, company, service) were left completely up to me, here is how I'd change things." It could be something as simple as how a waiting room is set up or something as complex as how an entire organization is run. Practicing this exercise will hone your abilities to see things as they could be.

- Do I make good use of my imagination in all areas of my life?

WHAT THE EXEMPLARS DO

Richard Branson is a master at uncovering needs. A dyslexic high school dropout, he's the self-made multibillionaire head of over 200 businesses in his Virgin empire. He constantly seeks out the wishes of customers and employees alike. The result is great products and great service. Branson writes to his 25,000 Virgin employees regularly and asks about their ideas and dreams—and their problems as well. According to Virgin's Web site (www.virgin.com), "... we review the industry and put ourselves in the customer's shoes to see what could make it better. ... Is the customer confused or badly served? ... We look for opportunities where we can offer something better, fresher, and more valuable; and we seize them. We often move into areas where the customer has traditionally received a poor deal, and where the competition is complacent. ... We also look to deliver 'old' products and services in new ways ...."

Dialog 6

Generate Leads

Scenario

You're in your office making cold calls from your list of prospects. You'll try to get those prospects to generate additional leads.

INSIGHTS

"Small opportunities are often the beginning of great enterprises."

—Demosthenes

Generate Leads

You: Thanks for the appointment, Ms. Wilson! You know, I'd like to provide the same useful products to others in your company. Who is in a position like yours at your other locations?

Prospect: Well, let's see. There's Joe at …

Notes: When you're having a positive exchange with another person (perhaps a prospect who's excited about meeting you and seeing your products, or a customer who's given you a compliment along with a reorder), you can capitalize on the goodwill that's coming your way by seeking additional leads. In other words, when you're having a conversation that's leading somewhere, use the Leading-Somewhere Leads strategy, as just shown in the preceding exchange.

Leading-Nowhere Leads Strategy

You: Well, Ms. Wilson, thanks for that information. It's clear that your company won't need any of this kind of paper product now that you've gone completely digital. It would really help me out, though, if you would tell me the names of others in the industry. Whom would you call about these products if you were me?

Notes: Even if you're making a cold call that seems to be leading nowhere, you can still seek leads. Most people don't enjoy rejecting others and may be inclined to give you referrals at that moment—even if only out of sheer guilt. However, be careful how you phrase inquiries. Watch what sort of response you're inviting: A yes-or-no question invites a "Yes" or "No" response (usually a "No!").

Who/What/Where Strategy

Prospect: Well, there's David Smith over at XYZ Corporation.

You: Great! I'll give him a call. Who else can you think of in the industry?

Prospect: Susan Cartwright's secretary is a friend of mine. I'm sure she wouldn't mind getting a call.

You: Terrific! What other offices in your building might I be able to help?

Prospect: Come to think of it, the office right above mine is still on a paper system. Their number is 555-6457.

You: You've been so helpful, I really appreciate it. Where in your chain of suppliers could services like these be utilized?

Notes: By starting your questions with "who," "what," or "where," you're inviting the respondent to provide a list of names. While it's possible you'll still get a negative response to such questions, you've improved your chances for getting a positive one. Rephrasing your questions by employing the preceding strategies will improve your success rate when seeking referrals. If who/what/where questions feel too direct to you, soften them by starting your sentence with "I was wondering …." Then carry right on with questions such as, "What other departments in your company use these kinds of office products?"

continues

Generate Leads (continued)

Give-a-Group Strategy

You: One last question, Ms. Wilson, what groups are you affiliated with that might have members in need of products like mine? I'm thinking of groups such as the Chamber of Commerce and the Marketing Association.

Prospect: Gee, I can't think of anyone there.

You: How about other organizations you're in?

Prospect: Well, I am a member of Toastmasters. Jon Thompson is our president and he might make a good prospect for you.

You: Ms. Wilson, I am grateful for all your input. Thank you for taking this time with me.

Notes: Here are examples of various groups you could mention in your questions:
- *Colleagues at other local companies*
- *Contacts at companies on the Internet*
- *Other businesses sharing this office space*
- *Friends in other businesses*
- *Suppliers*
- *Customers/clients*
- *Vendors*
- *Co-workers who have a similar position*
- *Members of the same organization (for example, Chamber of Commerce, SCORE, industry associations, Toastmasters)*

Strategies

Generating leads should be a constant mindset—almost a way of life rather than an activity that is done only at a particular time. So, in addition to talking to virtually everyone you come into contact with about what you do and what you have to offer, you'll also use your cold calls, no matter what direction they're taking, to try to generate leads. If the call is "leading somewhere" you'll use a Leading-Somewhere Leads strategy. If you sense the call is "leading nowhere," you'll employ a Leading-Nowhere Leads strategy. Additional strategies can be utilized to maximize your lead-generating potential, including the Who/What/Where strategy and the Give-a-Group strategy.

Further Considerations

If a source has been kind enough to give you a referral, be sure to keep him apprised of the developments. Doing so will serve many purposes:

- A follow-up thank you (preferably in written form) will demonstrate your courtesy and build the bond you have with your source.

- It always feels good to be able to take some credit for a successful transaction.

- Such feelings may serve as a reinforcement that inspires your source to offer you more leads.

- Even when referrals lead nowhere, contact your source with a thank you. It might inspire him to suggest other leads that have come to mind since your last contact.

- The follow-up contact you have with your source regarding referrals may lead to additional sales with the source himself: "Well, I'm glad it worked out well with Juanita. I haven't thought of any other leads, but we're running low ourselves on some office supplies right now."

Ask Yourself

- Do I look at the sources I have in my personal life for generating leads, including the following?

- Friends

- Family

- Schools

- Church or other religious groups

- Neighborhood contacts such as other families or nearby businesses

- Anyplace where I'm "a regular," such as restaurants, dry cleaners, and gas stations

- Community groups

- Hobby groups

- Recreational sports groups

- People who provide services to me, such as doctors, lawyers, accountants, realtors, brokers, bankers, barbers, hairdressers, manicurists, travel agents

- People I know from "another life," such as former high school or college contacts

BE CAREFUL

Never use the name of the person who has given you the referral unless you have explicit permission.

EXPERIENCE SHOWS

To look for leads, go to www.excite.com and click on "business finder." This site boasts 11 million company profiles that can be searched by company name, location, telephone number, or even stock exchange ticker symbol. At www.yahoo.com, you can click on "business and economy" and then "directories" for similar information. Other search engines offer comparable data. You can also go to www.sellingpower.com and click on "prospecting" or visit www.zapdata.com for information on leads.

Dialog 7

End on a Positive Note

Scenario

It's time to end your call. By this time your prospect has responded somewhere between buying your product and hanging up on you.

End on a Positive Note

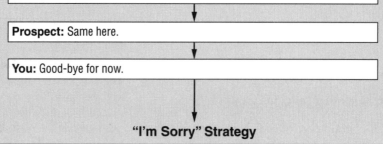

You: Well that's great, Nia! I'll look forward to coming to your office on Tuesday, the 12th, at 9:00 A.M. In the meantime, I'll e-mail you that chart you wanted. Thanks again for your interest, and I hope to see you at the next Chamber meeting.

Prospect: Same here.

You: Good-bye for now.

"I'm Sorry" Strategy

Prospect: Will you sales people just quit? I'm sick of getting calls all the time!

You: I'm sorry. It's clear this isn't a good time to have called you, so I'll just say good-bye now.

Notes: It's impossible to know your contact's context, since this is a cold call. He may have just received the news that he has been downsized out of a job. So don't take rudeness personally, and don't respond in kind. Use the "I'm Sorry" strategy by taking the high ground and politely end the conversation. Make sure your tone is warm and positive, without a trace of sarcasm. After you hang up, pat yourself on the back, knowing that you retained your dignity. Know, too, that because no one could ever find fault with such a response, you're keeping your reputation intact and leaving the slate clean if you should decide to contact this company again. End all calls on a positive note in order to build, not burn, bridges.

Strategies

In this scenario, you'll be using a group of strategies called RECAP, the letters of which stand for **R**estate, **E**xpress, **C**onfirm, **A**dd, and **P**olite. Assuming you still have a live person and not just a dial tone on the other end of the line, end your conversation by doing a RECAP of the following strategies and, if necessary, addressing any negatives so that the conversation ends on a positive note.

INSIGHTS

"Tact is the art of making a point without making an enemy."

—Jon Olson

- **Restate strategy.** Recall any promise you made in the conversation. In doing so, you are reminding yourself to carry out the promise and reminding your prospect that it's going to be done (for example, "I'll fax that article to you right away," or "I'll put that sample in the mail today"). Then, of course, follow through on your promises.

- **Express strategy.** Convey positive emotions such as gratitude, appreciation, or excitement (for example, "I'm glad we talked today," or "I'll look forward to speaking with you next month," or "I appreciate your taking time to talk today").

- **Confirm strategy.** Restate the details of your next contact, whether that's a specific meeting time and place or whether it's a general "in a few weeks."

- **Add strategy.** Mention again any connection you may have referenced at the start of your call (for example, "I'll look for you at the school picnic," or "If you see Linda before I do, please send her my regards"). Or, if appropriate, reference a humorous statement or a meaningful moment from your conversation. Such practices help cement the bond you're beginning to build.

- **Polite strategy.** Politely sign off.

If your conversation hits a snag somewhere, it's essential to smooth it out before ending the call. Follow the customer service commandment of "taking the blame," and offer an immediate apology. You wouldn't, of course, adopt the "I'm Sorry" strategy as a way of life in your sales career, but it is a gracious response to use in a difficult moment.

Further Considerations

Every cold call you make should bring you closer to a sale, even if it's only by inches. Each time you have an encounter that ends on a positive note, you've enhanced your own image, as well as that of your company, and you've thereby moved closer to a potential sale. If your cold call ends on a positive note, you can label that call a success. And we all know what success breeds.

Ask Yourself

- Did my voice convey warmth and enthusiasm?

- Was I courteous?

- Did I aim to keep the conversation short?

- Did I avoid making negative statements about others, including my competition?

- Was I flexible in responding to the prospect's needs?

- If the call happened to turn somewhat negative, did I take the lead in offering an apology?

- Did I follow up on any promises made in the conversation?

- As an exercise, think back to any transactions you've had as a customer in which you thought the salesperson handled a difficult situation particularly well. Why was that so?

Dialog 8

You Must Leave a Message

Scenario

You've tried numerous times to reach a particular person, but you've been unsuccessful in making contact. You know this person is a good prospect and you don't want to give up on her, so you decide to leave a message.

Strategies

Incorporate strategies from those explained earlier in this chapter, including the following, when appropriate: gathering good information; creating compelling solutions; making reference to personal and professional connections; making reference to others who use your products (and are well known to your prospect); and delivering your message with warmth, confidence, flexibility, and—most importantly—brevity.

Two specific strategies you can employ when leaving a message are the Partial-Invitation strategy and the Customized-Creation strategy. The Partial-Invitation strategy is, as its name suggests, one in which you leave a partial invitation in hopes of enticing a return call for additional information.

In the Customized-Creation strategy you'd take one of your prospect's products and customize it with the products or services that you offer. Then when you leave your message, you'll try to tantalize your prospect with seeing your creation. It's hard to resist getting a free look at a possible improvement to one's product. Plus, the prospect will likely be impressed with the fact that you've done your homework and are offering a custom presentation—not just a canned one.

> **EXPERIENCE SHOWS**
>
> Consider leaving a voicemail message rather than giving that message to a receptionist. In voicemail, you can actually accomplish quite a lot: You can give a short commercial for your product or yourself; you can convey a certain warmth and enthusiasm; and you can control the content. Even if you gave the same message verbatim to a receptionist, you would never know what kind of translation it got (if any!).

> **EXPERIENCE SHOWS**
>
> Be especially conscious of the way you sound. If you tend to speak very rapidly or very slowly, be sure to regulate your rate of speech.

You Must Leave a Message

> **You:** Hello, Mrs. Jankowicz. This is Peter Taylor of Itech. I noticed on your Web site that you're moving into educational software. My company has worked with the number-one educational software maker in Australia for years now, and we've had lots of experience from which I'm sure you could benefit. I'd like to share it with you over lunch. I'm free Tuesday and Wednesday this week. You can reach me at 309-555-1234. I'll look forward to your call. Again, that's …

Notes: You left your message and included the most meaningful information that you had to inspire a call back. When you're really anxious to "wow" your prospects, and if you're willing to go the extra mile in order to impress them, consider using the Customized-Creation strategy to hook them.

Customized-Creation Strategy

> **You:** Good morning, Ms. Wilson. This is Sam Berne from Outside the Box. We make packaging for products like yours, and I've designed some samples for a few of your products. I think you'll be thrilled to see what I've come up with using our exclusive new technology that produces a superior package at a lower cost. I could come by Thursday morning or Friday afternoon. Thank you, in advance, for calling me back at 555-1276. Again, that's 555-1276.

Note: Use this practice judiciously. You may spend valuable time customizing a product and still reach a dead end. Also, avoid giving away an idea that could simply be copied by your prospect's current supplier.

Partial-Invitation Strategy

> **You:** … and we're having a company cocktail party I'd like to invite you to. Please call me back at 555-8889 for details.
>
> *Or* … and I have some tickets to an upcoming Lakers game that I thought you might like to attend. You can reach me at …
>
> *Or* I'm holding a virtual sales presentation next week that I'd like to invite you to. We're demonstrating our latest software, and all you need to join in our live two-way meetings is a computer, a phone, and 15 minutes. Those participating will be the first to see this cutting-edge product and how it boosts productivity and sales. Please call me at 555-6134 for details.

Note: See Chapter 10, "Employing Atypical Methods," for more information on virtual meetings.

Further Considerations

If you're not always in the area, consider mentioning that in your message. It might lend some momentum to your efforts. For example, "I make it to Rockville only about once a month. I'll be coming to your area Friday and would like to stop by then."

If you're still getting no response after a few voicemail messages, consider switching to a different medium. You may have more success with an e-mail or a fax.

Some salespeople include an amusing cartoon with their faxes. (Be careful not to violate any copyright issues, though.) Some reps fax a page from their appointment calendars with circles drawn around available meeting times. They make a point of leaving visible the appointments they've booked with others along with those people's names and the companies. However, this practice is a bit risky because some clients want exclusivity. If they know you're working with their competition, it may hurt rather than help your cause.

Consider this twist on faxing a page from your calendar: Reference recent events with well-known people. Cross out a "Thursday 1:00 P.M. lunch with President Bush" and write to your contact: "Now that the president's been called to the Middle East peace talks, I'm free for lunch tomorrow. How about 12:30 at Hamilton's?"

If you are determined to get through to this prospect and are willing to bear the expense, consider having something relevant delivered to help make your point. For example, send a box of chocolate "coins," each covered in gold foil. Add a note such as, "The taste of success is sweet! Please let me show you how I can help your company succeed in saving a fortune!"

EXPERIENCE SHOWS

State your return phone number and then restate it when leaving a voicemail message. This practice helps ensure that your number will be heard correctly. It also makes writing down your number a little easier for your contact.

BE CAREFUL

Decide when enough is enough so that you don't end up harassing a contact. Move on to another source when you hit a complete dead end. You can always return sometime in the future.

WHAT THE EXPERTS SAY

"Having intention" means having a positive mindset with a genuine expectation of success. Experts say that if you're able to convey intention in your voicemail messages, you'll be more successful with them. Briefly meditating before making a call may help put you in the right frame of mind. Using phrases such as, "Thank you, in advance, for ...," also helps convey your intention.

WHAT THE EXEMPLARS DO

Bill Cates, sales pro and writer, suggests in an article at www.selling.com that in certain cases salespeople should seek telephone appointments. If you've established a good rapport with the gatekeeper and have been put through to a prospect's voicemail but haven't yet caught him in, then ask for a specific time to have a telephone appointment.

Ask Yourself

- Did I do my homework so that my message contains unique and compelling components?

- Did I write out key points (or even the entire message) before placing the call? (Remember, you get one shot at leaving a message. You can't erase and re-record it!)

- Do I keep accurate records so that I'll know exactly how long ago I left a message?

- Do I follow up with whatever action I state in the message (for example, "In the meantime, I'll send you …," or "I'll try you again at the end of the week")? Even though you may not have made contact yet with a prospect, you're still in a position to start building credibility by following through.

- Do I analyze my own received messages in order to determine what makes them effective or not?

Chapter 3

Overcoming Objections

Overcoming objections is probably the hardest part of a salesperson's job. And the most important step in overcoming objections is preventing them from happening in the first place! The need to overcome objections will never disappear altogether, but it can be diminished with three little words: qualify, qualify, qualify.

Qualifying the company is your first action in overcoming objections. Before you make that first sales contact, gather good information to help answer the following questions: Is this company part of an industry that typically uses your products or services? Is the company likely to have the funds to purchase your products or services? Is there a general industrywide problem you could help them address? Could your products or services provide a solution to a problem that's unique to this particular company? Craft some compelling solutions to present: Paint a picture for your prospects that illustrates what's in it for them if they use your products or services.

Your next action is to gather additional information to determine who at this company makes the buying decisions for this type of product. Are there any other people who need to give consent? Is this a companywide policy, or do different locations and different departments make their own choices? If so, who in particular makes those decisions? Draw an organizational chart for each company and fill in the blanks as you find the answers to these questions. Of course, qualifying the contact also means listening to what each person has to say about specific wants and needs so that you can respond accordingly.

Objections can be legitimate and straightforward, or they can be artificial and misleading. You must work to qualify the prospect's objections—the "can't"—and determine whether the objection is a legitimate one or not. Ideally, your initial sales presentation would address any legitimate objection, never to arise again! But in reality, a salesperson will likely hear no some seven times before hearing a yes. Typically you can expect a variety of objections to surface throughout a sales cycle.

When you hear an objection, you must keep the dialog going long enough to determine what the prospect is really saying and really seeking. Is this a genuine objection or a brush-off? If it's the former, see how you can solve the issue for your prospect. Be creative and work out compelling solutions to your client's problems.

On the other hand, if the stated objection is actually just a way to prematurely dismiss what you're offering, you've got to dig deeper to isolate the distinct issues that cause concern in your prospect and then work to overcome them. If objections can be boiled down to specific issues, they can often be used to help you set up the close to your sale.

When dealing with objections, keep this in mind:

> "Problems are not stop signs, they are guidelines."

> —Robert Schuller

Dialog 1

"The Price Is Too High"

Scenario

You've given your sales presentation and you hear, "Sorry, I can't. The price is too high." Your prospect might be saying any number of things with this statement. For example, "I like the product, but I think I can find a better deal somewhere else." Or "Based on what you've presented as the benefits, this cost isn't justified," or "It's not really too high, I'm just testing to see if you'll come down any." Or "I honestly don't have that much money available."

Strategies

You'll try to determine what the real objections are for your prospect and let that information guide the rest of your dialog. You'll try to identify concerns he may be feeling but not articulating by using a Perhaps-You-Feel strategy, and you'll express understanding of any objections that are raised by applying a Yes-But strategy. You'll refer to other situations where customers initially had similar objections with a Feel-Felt-Found strategy. And you'll talk about ways in which any remaining concerns could be addressed satisfactorily by way of an Eliminate strategy.

> ### INSIGHTS
>
> "The American car buyer wants economy so badly he'll pay almost anything to get it!"
>
> —Lee Iacocca

> ### EXPERIENCE SHOWS
>
> Don't use up all your supporting sales materials in your initial pitch. You may overwhelm your prospect and have nothing left to present in response to the specific objections you get from him later in the meeting.

Further Considerations

Make sure you know your company's pricing policy in advance. Do you have any latitude for first-time customers, big orders, or other special cases?

Have information available on any financing plans your company offers.

"The Price Is Too High"

Prospect: Sorry, I can't. The price is too high.

You: So you like the product and think it could be of use to you, but you feel it costs too much?

Prospect: Yep!

Perhaps-You-Feel Strategy

You: Perhaps you're even feeling you might be able to get the same product for less elsewhere?

Prospect: Well, as a matter of fact, yes!

You: *(As you pull out a chart showing what the competition charges.)* Fortunately, I've done your homework for you. This chart shows what the other suppliers charge. You see? Our prices are competitive.

Prospect: Okay. So all of you charge about the same. It's still an awful lot of money to pay.

Notes: You ascertained the genuine objection by utilizing the Perhaps-You-Feel strategy. In your dialog, you articulated an objection the prospect might be feeling but not voicing. You then addressed any of the prospect's specific objections by using dialog and support materials.

Yes-But Strategy

You: *(As you pull out another chart showing the cumulative costs associated with not using the product or of using an inferior product.)* Yes, at first the price does seem high, but when you consider the savings you'll accumulate over the years, I think you'll agree it's not high at all. Here's what the figures show.

Prospect: I see what you mean. But it's still a big chunk of change to put out.

Notes: Even if you don't agree with the prospect's opinions, you need to agree with his words so that you don't alienate him. The Yes-But strategy helps achieve that goal.

Feel-Felt-Found Strategy

You: I know how you feel. My best customer felt that way initially, too. But she actually found that this product boosted her bottom line in the first year of use. Here's a letter she sent me about her experience and the savings she accrued.

Prospect: That's encouraging! But I just don't know if we can come up with the funds.

You: Look, we have all sorts of financing plans available. I'm sure we can work out something for you. Let's write up the order, and I'll take it to the finance department.

Notes: In this classic Feel-Felt-Found strategy, you acknowledged your prospect's feelings and described how others felt the same way initially but then found their actual experience was different from what they had expected.

continues

"The Price Is Too High" (continued)

Eliminate Strategy

You: Which part of the package I just presented would you have us eliminate to reduce the price?

Notes: A question like this might make the prospect realize that if he wants all the features you're offering, it's impossible for you to lower the price. However, this question might also help the prospect identify a feature or two he could do without. By using the Eliminate strategy, you are initiating a constructive conversation that may lead to a creative solution for your prospect: a smaller package at a smaller price.

In order to help advance the sale, consider preparing sales tools such as the following, which can be handed out at a presentation or sent as follow-up:

> **BE CAREFUL**
>
> Make sure the facts and figures on your materials are accurate, and put a date on the data. What may be an innocent error on your part may be perceived by your prospect as deliberate dishonesty. Also, don't overstate your case. Doing so will compromise your credibility.

- A chart that shows price comparisons of competitors

- A table that measures price versus cost for the short term and the long term, including factors such as shipping, guarantees, service by you and others in your company, cost and availability of parts and/or supplies, training, storage, and other issues

- A list of product benefits, including any dollar amount you can attach to them (for example, absenteeism, turnover, morale, downtime, injury protection, peace of mind)

- Testimonial letters that address various issues (for example, service, results, and length of relationship)

- Corporate literature

- Relevant articles, reports, or other information

WHAT THE EXEMPLARS DO

Zig Ziglar, master motivator and sales maven, recommends in his book *Secrets of Closing the Sale* this response to a price objection: "I don't think there's any question about the price being high, Mr. Prospect, but when you add the benefits of quality, subtract the disappointments of cheapness, multiply the pleasure of buying something good, and divide the cost over a period of time, the arithmetic comes out in your favor. ... If it costs you a hundred dollars but does you a thousand dollars' worth of good, then by any yardstick you've bought a bargain haven't you? "

Ask Yourself

- When have I paid a lot of money for a particular product or service? What were the circumstances surrounding the purchase that helped convey its value to me? Can I apply those principles to my selling practices?

- Have I made a list of every response I can think of to overcome price objections to my products?

- Have I rehearsed those responses so often that they no longer sound rehearsed?

- Are my sales tools compelling in their content and their appearance?

- When I do a presentation, do I always bring lots of extra copies of sales tools?

Dialog 2

"We're Happy with Our Current Supplier"

Scenario

You're making cold calls and your prospect cuts off your conversation by saying, "We're happy with our current supplier." That response might mean, "I have a supplier; that issue has been dealt with and I have ten other issues on my desk that haven't been dealt with yet." It might also mean that the prospect is 110 percent satisfied with the present supplier (highly unlikely) or that the prospect is 51 percent satisfied with the supplier (more likely).

Strategies

You'll try to determine how satisfied your prospect is with the current supplier and why, using a Satisfactions strategy. When you ascertain what he values most, you'll reference those issues in your dialog.

"We're Happy with Our Current Supplier"

Prospect: We're happy with our current supplier.

You: That's always nice to hear. What pleases you the most about your current supplier?

Prospect: (Speaking rapidly.) They know my needs, they save me time, and they've got quick delivery.

Satisfactions Strategy

You: It's clear you really value time. In just 10 minutes, I can show you how our products will save you more time and more money than those of your current supplier.

Notes: You've isolated what your prospect values by using a Satisfactions strategy. This prospect was clearly rushed. But if time permitted, you could follow up with a strategy that queried, "What would you change if you could?" You'd then utilize all of this information to customize a dialog that reflects a Larger-Loyalty strategy and a Backup strategy.

Larger-Loyalty Strategy

Prospect: No, we're staying with our supplier.

You: That sort of personal loyalty reflects well on you. But I need to ask if your company would also want you to be loyal to things such as the highest-possible levels of productivity and profits?

Prospect: Of course. But we feel we get that with our current supplier.

You: Well, if you did, that would be great. But experience has proven that we consistently outdo our competition on both those measures. In a 10-minute meeting, I can show you what I mean and then you can make an informed decision about where you would do best. A 10-minute investment is a small price to pay for the peace of mind you'll have from knowing you've made the best choice. Don't you agree?

Backup Strategy

Prospect: You're sure it wouldn't take more than 10 minutes?

You: Absolutely. And it will not be a wasted 10 minutes because even if you decide to stick with your current supplier, I can still set up an account for you that would be ready for you to use as a backup at a moment's notice! That could save you a lot of time when you're in a pinch. How does Wednesday look for you?

BE CAREFUL

Never say anything offensive about your competition. It will certainly make you look bad, and it might insult your prospect if it is perceived as a criticism of his buying decisions.

INSIGHTS

"Progress is impossible without change, and those who cannot change their minds cannot change anything."

—George Bernard Shaw

WHAT THE EXPERTS SAY

Research shows that if a frog is dropped into a pot of hot water, it will automatically jump out. However, if the same frog is placed in cool water that is then heated slowly, the frog will not notice the change in temperature and ultimately the heat will kill it. Some business people are slow to perceive the changes developing in their environments and fail to make a switch when they should.

You'll also recognize the difficulty in pulling a client away from a current supplier. One way to address that issue is with a technique called the Larger-Loyalty strategy. You'll recognize that building a relationship often requires many small steps taken over a long period of time. When necessary, you'll employ techniques such as the Backup strategy to help build a long-term relationship as you court this prospect.

Further Considerations

Oftentimes, change takes place slowly. You may have to court prospects over a long period of time before they will make a switch. Be sure that a given account is worth the effort and that your energies would not be better spent elsewhere.

Consider keeping in touch with prospects you're pursuing by sending different sales tools every now and then. For example, a relevant article, promotional premiums, or even an attractive postcard with a message such as "I'm still seeking your business!" are all ways to let the prospect know that you'd like his business.

Consider e-mail cards, too. Visit www.bluemountain. com, www.awards.com, or www.ivillage.com (at the iVillage home page, look for "favorites"; click on "postcards"; then go to the "work" category).

Try to identify any of your customers who used to do business with a competitor. Prepare a list of them to give to prospects that you're courting. Or, see if any of them will give you a letter about why they're glad they made the switch. Such third-party testimonials make compelling sales tools.

Inertia is powerful and change is scary. What can you do to make your prospects feel safe about making a change? What practices could you employ to help them limit their risk? Start small? Offer guarantees? Do a free trial? All of the above?

Ask Yourself

- Have I ever been persuaded to switch to another product or service after being brand-loyal for a long time? How and why did that happen? Can I apply any of those principles to my own sales presentations?

- What are my personal competitive advantages? What unique qualities do I bring to my profession? How can I best convey that information to my prospects and customers?

- Do I need to prepare some materials that will make my prospect feel more comfortable about making a change? Perhaps an explicit money-back letter of guarantee signed by the president of the company? Perhaps a simple one-page short-term contract to be used for an introductory offer?

- Technology is causing rapid changes in the world of business and in the behavior and expectations of customers. How do those realities apply to my business? How can I incorporate this information into my sales presentation to make it more compelling?

Dialog 3

"I Need to Think About It"

Scenario

You've made your sales presentation, and all seems to have gone well. Then you are hit with the dreaded, "I need to think about it." The statement could mean any number of things, including "I'm not yet convinced that the benefits you've presented are worth the costs," or "I want to check around to see if I can get a better deal some other place."

"I Need to Think About It"

You: So let's write up this order.

Prospect: I need to think about all this.

Why-Hesitate Strategy

You: That surprises me! I'm wondering why you would hesitate to order at this point.

Prospect: That's just the way I am.

Act-Now Strategy

You: Well, you'll be further ahead if you act now. *(Here you supply any relevant and truthful particulars for taking immediate action.)* This introductory offer ends on Monday.

Prospect: Hmmmm.

Ben Franklin Strategy

You: Why don't we just think it over together? Let's list all the reasons for acting now and all the reasons for waiting and see what we've got. I think the biggest benefit is that, besides the savings you'll get from the introductory offer, you'll see additional savings the minute you plug in this equipment. Do you agree?

Prospect: Yes.

You: What do you see as the other major benefits?

Notes: You'll continue with the list until you've covered all the pros and cons. You'll pull out any additional sales tools you have if you need to back up a position (for example, "This chart shows how we can provide this product for less than other suppliers"). The final list should give you a very clear picture of where your prospect stands and where you need to focus your dialog in order to close the sale.

Strategies

You'll probe to determine the true nature of your prospect's objection and direct your dialog accordingly. If you sense the problem is that your prospect is a habitual procrastinator, you'll use strategies that aim to expedite the decision-making process, specifically the Why-Hesitate and Act-Now strategies. If the true objection centers around your product or your presentation, you'll readdress those issues through the Ben Franklin strategy, so that your product's benefits and values are clearly conveyed. In this practice, attributed to Ben Franklin himself, you'll invite your prospect to join you in listing on one half of a sheet of paper the advantages of buying and on the other half the reasons for waiting.

Further Considerations

Engage the power of the senses to help persuade prospects. What can you include in your presentations to help people see the vision you have of how your product can help them succeed? How can you illustrate its impact or results? In addition to charts and graphs, perhaps you can include photos of your product being used by satisfied customers? Can you show samples of the solutions you've crafted for other clients? Is there any relevant way to utilize sound to help sell your product? Perhaps a recording that features audio elements of your product? Or a recorded endorsement from a loyal client? Is there something for your prospect to touch, or taste, or smell?

If you're so inclined, prepare a customized sample of your product as it applies to your prospect's business. The more easily a prospect can see how your products benefit him, the more persuasive your presentation will be. Such samples also help sell an initial meeting (for

INSIGHTS

"If you want to make decisions, then eliminate all the alternatives with the power of factual data. If you do not want to make decisions, then do us all a favor by staying out of the way."
—John Mott

INSIGHTS

Thomas J. Watson Jr., when he was chairman of IBM, asked an employee how he had come to a certain decision. The employee said he'd just listened to his gut and made a "visceral decision." Watson responded, "Well, if there are going to be any visceral decisions around here, I'd like to use my own viscera."

EXPERIENCE SHOWS

Deadlines are among the most effective tools for getting people to take immediate action. If you have no particular deadline to work with, then focus on the costs of waiting (for example, "There may be a rise in price"; "This item may be gone next time"; "You'll miss out on the immediate increases in profits and productivity this product provides"; and so on).

WHAT THE EXPERTS SAY

Experts in the field of communications say that men and women often have different styles of communication. In a "typically male" style, a person thinks through an issue in his head in order to reach a conclusion and then makes a statement about the conclusion he's reached. In a "typically female" style, a person will converse with others in order to help sort through her thoughts and feelings on an issue. She examines pros and cons by thinking out loud in order to help her come to a conclusion. Be aware of different communication styles when selling.

BE CAREFUL

Don't be too quick to fill a conversational void. When you've asked a question, remain silent until you get a response. Sometimes a little silence can be golden in more ways than one!

WHAT THE EXEMPLARS DO

Peter Drucker, author, academic, and all-around business expert, says this about taking time: "Everything requires time. It is the only truly universal condition. All work takes place in time and uses up time. Yet most people take for granted this unique, irreplaceable, and necessary resource. Nothing else, perhaps, distinguishes effective executives as much as their tender loving care of time."

example, "I'm really excited about how this mock-up turned out, and I can't wait to show you!"). However, be careful not to invest too much time in preparing a sample for what may turn out to be a dead end. Also, avoid giving away an idea that could simply be copied by a current supplier.

Ask Yourself

- If I'm hearing a lot of "I need to think about it," do I need to improve my sales presentations so that they're more persuasive or convey more urgency?

- Have I prepared a list of all the reasons why it's important to "act now" in regard to my products or services? Do I have the whole list memorized?

- Do I have some examples to share about times when a customer of mine was glad he didn't wait?

- Have I prepared a Ben Franklin–type form, and do I carry plenty of blank copies with me to sales presentations?

- In my own life, do I notice what motivates me to act rather than delay? Do I try to incorporate such motivations into my sales presentations?

- Do I analyze how much time and energy I'm willing to invest in a particular prospect and compare it with the potential gains I might see if this prospect became a life-long customer?

Dialog 4

"We Have Everything We Need Right Now"

Scenario

You're making a round of cold calls and the dialog turns to the classic "We have everything we need right now." This response could mean several different things, including "I don't see the importance of this product," or "I don't see how my company will profit from using it." Or "I don't want to waste money." Or "I'm not in a position to buy right now."

Strategies

At the start of your call, you will of course try to hook your prospect's interest with a novel pitch. You'll follow up by citing your product's best benefits and the needs it fulfills. Sometimes with a newer product, consumers have to be educated about its benefits before they can really understand how it will address their needs. Accordingly, you'll try to find the most compelling ways to convey that information through a By-Product-Benefits strategy. If you reach a dead end in all your efforts because a prospect truly does have everything he needs, your call can still be fruitful: Use it to generate new leads with the "Okay But Refer Me" strategy.

Further Considerations

Consider all the possible by-product benefits that your products supply. See if you can find some current research studies or general articles that relate to those benefits. Get copies of the articles or list the study highlights, and have these materials available to give or send to your prospects.

INSIGHTS
"In the factory we make cosmetics, but in my stores we sell hope."
—Charles Revson of Revlon Cosmetics

EXPERIENCE SHOWS
If you're looking for materials to document issues that relate to, and support, your product's benefits, check out these Internet sources: www.webmd.com, www.healthfinder.gov, www.wsj.com, www.cnn.com, and www.newshub.com.

EXPERIENCE SHOWS
Customers often have to be educated about the "need" for certain products. For example, no one "needed" a cell phone or personal computer 20 years ago, but as people came to understand their benefits and accept their costs as reasonable, demand grew.

"We Have Everything We Need Right Now"

You: Hello, Mr. LuTrec. I'm calling today because I want to send you on vacation.

Prospect: Pardon me?

You: I'm with Ukon Office Furnishings, and we have a new executive office massage chair. After getting even a five-minute massage, you'll feel like you've just had a holiday. I can bring the chair to your office so you can try it. Would you like to book your vacation for Thursday afternoon or Friday?

Prospect: Neither. My old reliable leather chair works fine. It's been with me my whole 13 years at this company.

Notes: You've identified your product's best features, but you clearly need to elaborate. You deflect the "don't need" response by addressing the less obvious (but perhaps more important) needs the product fills. These are often "by-product benefits": It's not the chair but the state of mind it produces; it's not the copier but the productivity it allows; it's not the phone equipment but the efficiency and profits it creates.

By-Product–Benefits Strategy

You: Wow! Well, Mr. LuTrec, I can understand not wanting to part with a chair like that! But you wouldn't have to give it up if you got ours. Many of my customers put our chair in their employee lounges so that everyone in the company can "go on vacation" during breaks.

Prospect: All our employees get two weeks off every year. I don't need to send them on vacation while they're at work!

You: Actually, Mr. LuTrec, maybe you do! You know, stress is more and more of an issue in the workplace. Sometimes it becomes a matter of life and death! My company's concerned about that, so we've actually conducted studies that measure the effect that our chairs have on reducing stress levels and improving productivity and employee morale, all of which are so important in keeping turnover low and profits high. Our chair impacts all of these needs, which must concern someone in your position.

Prospect: No, I'm certain we don't need any kind of chair like that at this time.

"Okay But Refer Me" Strategy

You: Okay. Well, perhaps I'll check back with you in six months to see if things have changed. For now, though, I'd appreciate it if you would tell me who else in this office complex might need some office furniture products like mine?

Prospect: Maybe the temp agency across the hallway.

You: Great! What others are there?

Notes: If you use every tool at your disposal but are completely convinced that this contact isn't going to budge, seize the opportunity to at least get a referral—the "Okay But Refer Me" strategy.

Also consider what it might cost your prospects to be without your product (for example, stress, absenteeism, morale, productivity). See if you can attach a dollar figure to any of these costs.

Consider future trends. How will your product or service benefit customers whose current lifestyle or business environment is changing? How will it continue to benefit them in the future? As technology impacts our lives to a greater extent, will it address any new needs that are developing?

Think about purchases you've made that fulfilled a less obvious need. How were you convinced of that? Can you apply anything from that experience to your own selling practices?

Ask Yourself

- Do I have a list of my product's benefits on paper or in my head?

- Do I have a comparable list of costs; that is, what kinds of burdens or inefficiencies might a buyer incur if he went without my product? Such a list is handy to have, along with supporting articles or documents.

- Do I spend time with the end users of my products so I can get a better idea of what their problems are and what solutions I might provide?

- Problems reveal needs. Am I attuned to the problems, difficulties, snags, and inefficiencies that occur while taking care of my own personal business? Do I analyze any business transactions I have that are particularly difficult or particularly smooth in order to determine what makes them so?

WHAT THE EXPERTS SAY

Abraham Maslow, one of the founders of humanistic psychology, devised a hierarchy of needs based on the notion that as one level of needs is satisfied in the individual, another level of needs emerges. Starting at the bottom of the hierarchy, needs consist of: physiological needs (food, water, shelter); safety needs (security, stability, order); belongingness and love needs (to give and receive affection); esteem needs (competence, self-confidence, respect, recognition); and self-actualization needs (following one's talents, gifts, interests).

WHAT THE EXEMPLARS DO

3M Corporation's experience with Post-it Notes provides an inspiring example of perseverance in establishing a need. The initial reaction to this product was not promising because people could not see much of a need for the little restickable papers. 3M had presented the idea to office-supply distributors and received an unfavorable response. It then conducted market surveys that also produced negative results. Finally, it sent sample Post-it Note pads directly to the secretaries of Fortune 500 CEOs. It was only then that the product began to be viewed favorably. Post-it Notes have gone on to become one of the most successful products in the company's history.

Dialog 5

"I Have to Talk It Over With …"

Scenario

You sell training seminars and have made your presentation to the human resources director at R-Wonderful Company. He tells you, "I have to talk it over with management." You realize this statement has many possible meanings, including "It's hard for me to weigh pros and cons in order to arrive at a decision, so I'll get some other opinions," or "It sounds good to me but I don't want to be responsible for making a mistake, so I'm going to get someone else in on this." Or "I'm truly not the sole decision-maker; I'm actually required to get the approval of so-and-so." Or "I'm trying to brush you off."

BE CAREFUL

If your prospect absolutely refuses to allow you to meet with the decision-makers, make sure the materials you leave behind for them are clear, compelling, creative, and clean! They'll have to speak for you in your absence. Always carry extras since you never know how many different decision-makers you may have to provide for.

WHAT THE EXPERTS SAY

"Committees of twenty deliberate plenty. Committees of ten act now and then. But most jobs are done by committees of one."

—C. Northcote Parkinson

Strategies

Perhaps in qualifying this prospect you wrongly concluded he was the sole decision-maker. Sometimes it's impossible to ascertain all such details in advance of a meeting. So, you'll now seek explicit information about exactly who holds the decision-making power. You'll also try to isolate any other objections this statement may be conveying through an Isolation strategy, in which you ask, "What, exactly, do you need to discuss?" and "What other concerns do you have?" Based on the responses you receive to those questions, you'll address any remaining objections by using strategies in which you get conditional agreement to the sale, including the If … Then strategy and the Just-You strategy. You'll then try to get a meeting with all the decision-makers through an "It's My Job" strategy.

"I Have to Talk It Over With ..."

Prospect: I'll have to talk it over with management.

↓

You: What, exactly, do you need to discuss with them?

↓

Prospect: Well, this is a really big package, and I'd have to make sure I have their approval.

You: I'm delighted you're ready to do business with us.

↓

Prospect: Well, maybe that's the case, but not without their approval.

Isolation Strategy

You: It sounds like you may have some other concerns. What are they?

Notes: At this point you'll revisit relevant issues surrounding product, price, service, and so on to address any objections your prospect may still have. You'll reiterate the highlights of your sales presentation, pointing out the benefits and value of your product.

↓

If ... Then Strategy

Prospect: This training program seems great, but it's a really big package with a really big price tag attached.

↓

You: We could certainly reconfigure the package to give you a shorter training period at a reduced price. (You pull out some related material.) If we reduced the package that way, would you be ready to proceed then?

↓

Prospect: I'd feel more comfortable starting out with a smaller package, but as I said before, I need management approval.

Notes: At this point you can proceed toward closing with another strategy. You'll use the Just-You strategy.

↓

Just-You Strategy

You: So if this decision were up to just you at this point, we could proceed with the training program?

Prospect: Yes. But it's not up to just me.

↓

You: Who else do we need to meet with to get this approved?

Notes: Having obtained your prospect's commitment, you start emphasizing "we" in your dialog. Your prospect may resist your meeting with the other decision makers, in which case you can pull out the "It's My Job" strategy.

↓

"It's My Job" Strategy

Prospect: Two senior managers are the ones who decide such things.

↓

You: I'll call them so we can set up a meeting.

↓

Prospect: That's okay. I can meet with them.

↓

You: Let me take that job off your hands. I'm sure they'll have questions that I'll have the answers to, and that's what I'm paid for. It's my job.

↓

Prospect: No. It's important that I meet with them.

↓

You: Then at the very least, let's meet with them together!

Further Considerations

Rehearse a complete list of relevant "If … then" statements that could resolve any objections to your particular product or service. For example, "So, you're saying that if I could get billing postponed for this computer system until after the first of the year, then you'd be willing to place your order today?" Or "If you were certain that this was the best price you could get anywhere for these microprocessors, then you'd be ready to order?" Or "If you were convinced this training actually made a difference in profits, then you'd be willing to go for it?"

Consider trying to get an initial contract signed by your prospect along with your promise to make it null and void if the necessary approvals don't come through. Any steps you can take to make the sale more real or tangible will help advance the transaction.

Every time you get additional information on the structure, dynamics, and relationships in a particular company, enter that information for future reference on the organizational chart you're keeping for that company.

Ask Yourself

- In order to get all the decision-makers in the room at the same time, do I do everything possible to accurately qualify a prospect in advance?

- Do I work hard at getting included in any subsequent meetings with other decision-makers, knowing that I will make my case better than anyone else could?

- If I'm explicitly excluded from such meetings, do I consider offering alternatives, such as a virtual sales presentation on the Internet?

See Chapter 10, "Employing Atypical Methods," for more information on virtual meetings.

Dialog 6

"We Haven't Budgeted for This"

Scenario

You've just made a presentation for your corporate valet service. Your prospect seems intrigued but says, "We haven't budgeted for this." This statement could mean, "This concept/product/service is too new. Of course it isn't in the budget—we've never even heard of it before!" Or "I don't want to spend money on something risky." Or "I like this product, but I truly don't have the money." Or "I don't want your product and I'm trying to get rid of you politely."

Strategies

INSIGHTS
"If money talks, I need a hearing aid."
—Joe L. Whitley

You'll use probing questions to try to ascertain the true nature of this objection. If you sense this objection is legitimate, you'll offer creative solutions to make your offer workable with, for example, the Exception strategy. If that strategy leaves you at a dead end, you can try a Reduction strategy. In this strategy you do not reduce the price; you reduce other features in order to limit cost. For example, you offer to sell one product instead of the entire product line, or you offer to sell two weeks of a service instead of the standard one-year contract. Alternatively, you can employ a Bundling strategy in which you find an item that has been budgeted and tie a new item to it.

INSIGHTS
"Show me a millionaire, and I will show you almost invariably a heavy borrower."
—William Nickerson

"We Haven't Budgeted for This"

Prospect: I'm sorry. We don't have the money in the budget.

↓

You: In other words, you'd be willing to buy this service if all your money weren't already tied up?

↓

Prospect: But all our money *is* tied up.

↓

You: We have favorable credit terms and may even be able to delay billing until your next budget cycle. When would that be?

Prospect: Not for another 10 months.

↓

You: Well, we're not talking about huge sums here. It could probably come out of a discretionary budget.

↓

Prospect: No, I'm afraid we have no such thing.

Notes: You've pointed out possible financing options yet you're still being met with resistance, so you'll try a different tack. You know for a fact that most every company has one or more people empowered to override a budget. You'll try to determine who that might be through a dialog utilizing the Exception strategy.

Exception Strategy

You: Someone must have the authority to make an exception and exceed or reconfigure the budget.

↓

Prospect: No. We run a very tight ship here.

Reduction Strategy

You: Well, Ms. Pollack, our usual minimum on this service is a one-year contract. But I'll tell you what I can do. I'll let you go ahead and take a one-month contract so you can give your employees a taste of it. I know they'll love it, and you'll see the benefits in terms of increased productivity and improved morale. You can turn it into a one-month promotional perk for your employees! If you don't want to carry on after that time, you're out of your contract, no questions asked.

↓

Prospect: No, we don't have it in the budget.

Bundling Strategy

You: Okay, this service is a new concept, and I'd be surprised if there were an explicit spot for it in the budget. But I know that other office expenses and perks are standard budget items, such as office birthday parties, holiday celebrations, and so on. Perhaps you could use some of those funds to give your employees a bit of Christmas in July with a one-month contract for our valet service. They'll love it.

↓

Prospect: Well, that might actually work.

Further Considerations

If the best you can get from a prospect is an RFP (request for proposal) to submit for the next round of budgeting, be sure to find out exactly what that process consists of and follow all necessary steps. Check and double-check that you have all the proper forms and required paperwork, that you distribute the materials to all the right parties, and that you do so on time. In addition, confirm a callback date so you can meet with your contact before the budgeting process begins.

Consider yourself and your contact as a team. Reference your efforts with "we" and "ours." Enlist her support in all possible ways. You may want to prepare a short letter of endorsement and see if she'd be willing to sign it. Then send the signed letter to the other decision-makers and include it with any written proposals you're presenting. Also, see if she can introduce you to some of the key players in advance of any required budget meeting. Also see if she could get you in to make a presentation during the budget meeting.

Ask Yourself

- Do I keep notes about the annual budgeting date for a particular company so that my timing will be right the next time around?

- Do I put a reminder on my calendar to call before that date and say to my contact something like, "I know your company will be doing its annual budget soon, and I'd like to meet with you in advance"?

- Do I continuously add facts to the organizational chart I keep for each of the companies I deal with? Do I show who teams with whom on purchasing decisions and other relevant issues?

BE CAREFUL

Avoid the appearance of telling a prospect how he should run his business. Offering a suggestion as a creative solution is one thing ("Perhaps this could be covered under some other budget category"). But dictating or presuming to know the internal workings of a company could be very off-putting ("Take it out of your office products budget" or "We both know budgets are made to be broken").

WHAT THE EXPERTS SAY

Some businesses operate under strict budgets; others are looser. Some budgets are prepared annually with a review at the six-month mark; others may be done quarterly. Some businesses follow a calendar year for budgeting; others conform to a fiscal year. A fiscal year frequently begins after a business's "busy season" and is set up at the beginning or end of that quarter (but not in the middle of it). You might be able to glean some information about a company's fiscal patterns from its annual report.

EXPERIENCE SHOWS

You can find annual reports at Web sites such as www.wsj.com, www.reportgallery.com, and www.prars.com.

81

- Do I know explicitly what my company will allow me to offer a customer in terms of delayed billing, credit, and financing plans? Do I have support materials that explain those plans in detail?

Dialog 7

"Could You Send Something in the Mail?"

Scenario

You sell software and you're working your way down your call list, trying to reach some prospects. You're hit with "Could you send something in the mail?" It's likely that this statement is made either because the prospect is somewhat interested and wants to review the material in detail at his leisure without a salesperson present or because he's giving you a total brush-off.

INSIGHTS

"A man's success in business today depends upon his power of getting people to believe he has something they want."

—Gerald Stanley Lee, circa 1900

EXPERIENCE SHOWS

To improve your success rate, remember to reference meaningful people, products, and places when making cold calls. For example, "Hello Mr. Brown. I recently installed the audio system for ABC Company, right down the hall from you. They suggested I contact you to show you what I did for them." (See Chapter 2, "Cold Calling," for more tips.)

Strategies

You'll do everything you can to try to get a face-to-face meeting by focusing on the fact that literature fails to present the whole picture. This is the essence of the Time-It-Takes strategy. But if necessary, you'll go ahead and mail the information—with a twist by utilizing the Tap-into-Technology strategy. This strategy utilizes the power of e-mail to help advance the sales process. If you have the e-mail addresses of prospects, you can communicate with them directly rather than through a gatekeeper. You can also communicate with them in a way that is less intrusive than a telephone call might be. And you can leave your message at any hour of the day or night, which makes it more convenient for you! Finally, if you're still met with resistance and you sense that the request for material is just a brush-off, you can address that resistance head-on with a strategy that attempts to identify and overcome unspoken objections: the "I'm Curious" strategy.

"Could You Send Something in the Mail?"

You: So, Soren, I could come by any morning this week.

Prospect: I think it would be better if you sent some information in the mail first.

Time-It-Takes Strategy

You: Well, I could certainly do that. But I've found that for a product like this software, the literature is too general and it usually raises more questions than it answers. In the time it would take you to digest it all, I could give you a live demonstration that would really show what our software could do for your company specifically. And it would take only 10 minutes max! How's Monday morning?

Prospect: No, Monday's not good, and I really would like to see some material first.

Notes: You've attempted to get a face-to-face meeting by employing the Time-It-Takes strategy in your dialog. But your prospect is still not biting. As your conversation with this prospect continues, you conclude that he is somewhat interested, so you decide to comply with his request—but you give it a twist with the Tap-into-Technology strategy.

Tap-into-Technology Strategy

You: Okay, Soren. The material that best shows our product comes in the form of a two-page e-mail document. I'll send it right off to you. What's your e-mail address and that of others who would be involved in this decision?

Note: While it's true that your e-mail messages may not get read, the potential benefits of this direct access to your prospect make it worth trying. E-mail addresses are gold: Always try to dig for them.

If you sense that your prospect says "Send literature" because he wants to end the call without hearing about your product, try addressing the issue head-on with the "I'm Curious" strategy.

"I'm Curious" Strategy

You: Well, Soren, I've found that when people ask for literature, sometimes it's because they've already decided they don't want what's being offered and are just looking for a graceful exit. If that's the case with you, I'm sure you have a good reason for feeling that you don't want this product. I'm curious about what it is.

Notes: At this point your prospect will probably state his objection(s) and you'll address them accordingly.

BE CAREFUL

When you hear a message such as "Send something in the mail" and you've determined it to be a brush-off, you must decide how much time and effort you should spend on following up and whether your energy would be better spent elsewhere.

WHAT THE EXEMPLARS DO

You should not necessarily disdain the notion of "putting something in the mail." The concept can be utilized as an effective sales tool when that something is unique and compelling. A well-known public relations firm did just that when it saw a local company getting a bad rap in the press. The PR firm felt the company wasn't defending itself effectively and really needed help. It took the initiative to "put something in the mail" and sent a pair of boxing gloves to the president of the beleaguered company, along with a short note. He immediately signed on as a client.

Further Considerations

If you do send something via e-mail, consider sending it as an attractive, full-color attachment instead of just an e-mail message. The more visually appealing your material is, the more interesting it will be to your prospect and the better it will reflect on you.

When you send out information, consider how and when you'll follow up. Also, remember to include your company's Web site address in your e-mail so your prospect can visit.

Always seek a face-to-face meeting to explain or demonstrate what the literature doesn't. Also, if you ever hold a virtual sales presentation to demonstrate your product, you can send your contact an e-mail invitation to attend. (See Chapter 10 for more information on virtual meetings.)

Ask Yourself

- Have I tried to get the personal e-mail address of every individual involved in a decision-making process?

- Do I always follow up on material I send out?

- Do I know how to utilize the current technology in order to make virtual sales presentations?

- Do I sometimes mail an ad specialty or some other item along with my material to make it stand out and create an impression?

- Have I ever ordered something based only on materials that were mailed to me? How and why was that so? Can I apply any of those factors to material that I send out?

Dialog 8

"I'll Get Back to You"

Scenario

You've finished giving the sales presentation for your computer system and are ready to write the order. Instead you hear, "I'll get back to you." You ponder the possible interpretations of this response, including "I'm not convinced of the benefits and see no urgent need to act," or "I've got more pressing problems than this that I need to handle." Or "I want to check out some other sources." Or "I don't want this product now, but I do want you to leave now!"

Strategies

You'll try to ascertain what it is your prospect wants to do between now and when she gets back to you. This will help you determine why she is hesitating and what her genuine objections might be. You'll design your dialog accordingly in order to address any concerns she might have and to try to urge more-immediate action by focusing on the present by using a technique such as the At-This-Point strategy. You'll also employ strategies that aim to bring you nearer to closing the sale including the Tie-Down strategy and the Subordinate-Question strategy. Tie-downs are closed-ended questions that end with phrases such as "isn't it," "won't you," "can't you," and "don't you agree." They are used to try to elicit a positive response from a prospect and to secure a measure of agreement. Subordinate questions seek commitment on smaller issues rather than the big one.

EXPERIENCE SHOWS

Don't be discouraged by a delay in a purchasing decision. Remember that most sales reps usually stop their sales calls after the third try, but that most sales transactions actually occur after the seventh call. Think of the first six calls as steps that are bringing you closer to "Yes." Think of "No" as being short for "Not yet!"

INSIGHTS

When asked how many times he would contact a prospect before quitting, salesman Harry Collins said, "It depends on which one of us dies first."

"I'll Get Back to You"

Prospect: Thanks for all this information. I'll get back to you on it.

↓

You: Sarah, what will you be doing in the time until you contact me again?

↓

Prospect: I'll be reviewing this material.

You: Perhaps there are some things I didn't make clear. What questions do you still have?

↓

Prospect: I have no other questions. I just want to digest all of this.

At-This-Point Strategy

You: Let me just ask this: At this point, what do you like best about this computer system? What do you see as the major benefit it will provide for you?

↓

Prospect: Well, I think it could really streamline operations.

↓

You: I'm certain it could. I, too, see that as the major benefit. Do you also agree that it could produce significant savings and increase productivity?

↓

Prospect: Yes, I do.

↓

You: Given that, what concerns you about acting now?

↓

Prospect: It's a really big purchase.

Notes: You've determined what your prospect likes best about your product in an effort to help move the sales process forward. You've isolated any remaining objections and will attempt to address them. In your dialog, you'll utilize the Tie-Down strategy to ask about basic areas of agreement and the Subordinate-Question strategy to get agreement on smaller issues. These strategies will help you move forward toward closing the sale.

Tie-Down Strategy

You: You're right. It is a big purchase. But we agree that you could start producing significant savings the minute you install the system, right?

↓

Prospect: Yes.

↓

You: And that it could really streamline your operations, right?

↓

Prospect: Yes, I think so.

Subordinate-Question Strategy

You: How do you think your superiors will feel when you immediately start improving operations and cutting costs with this system?

↓

Prospect: Great, of course.

↓

You: Then we should start right away. When would you like to have delivery?

Notes: Other examples include the following: Which one would work better for you? Which color do you prefer? How many could you use?

Further Considerations

Other useful questions to ask in this type of scenario are these: "Do you ultimately see yourself buying this product?" "When will you be ready to make a decision?" "What would have to happen in order for you to make a buying decision right now?" "When will you be getting back to me?"

Consider asking your prospects if they will be looking at other suppliers for your product. Have sales tools prepared that show how and why you're better than the competition.

Always have your prospect give you a date by which you will hear back from her. Make a note of it, and call if you don't hear from her by then, referring to the fact that this was the date she gave you.

Ask Yourself

- If I have to wait quite a while before the prospect can get back to me by phone, do I consider using other forms of communication (fax, e-mail, regular mail, deliveries) to stay in touch and remain on the prospect's "radar screens"?

- Do I actually ask for the sale, or do I accept statements such as "I'll get back to you," without employing closing practices?

- Do I collect useful "narratives" and add more as I find them?

- Do I emphasize reasons for acting now rather than waiting? Do I point out applicable deadlines, offers, discounts, and so on, to try to urge more immediate action?

- Am I prepared to make at least seven contacts with a prospect before giving up? If not, what is my callback limit?

BE CAREFUL

True to form, this same Harry Collins is said to have made 130 calls on a single prospect during the course of one year before closing a sale. Determine whether the potential return over the life of a given account is worth a big investment of your time and energy.

WHAT THE EXEMPLARS DO

Richard Gallagher is an author, academic, consultant, and counselor and was twice a representative to the White House Conference on Small Business. He recommends the use of narratives in response to objections. Narratives are true stories that educate the customer. For example, "I met with a prospect who hesitated to place an order for a certain product line. She wanted to wait for a sale, but instead our supplier actually increased prices! She ultimately purchased from us, but she found she lost money by waiting. You wouldn't want something like that to happen, would you?"

Chapter 4

Questioning

As far back as Socrates, the world's greatest thinkers have acknowledged the value of questions in shaping thought. Smart salespeople take advantage of this fact and know the value of questions in making a sale. The successful salesperson uses questions to …

- Determine the extent of potential clients' knowledge of product/services.

- Develop rapport.

- Learn clients' needs.

- Involve prospects.

- Arouse interest.

- Gauge the likelihood of a closing.

Asking questions can be a fine art, and the most successful salespeople are artists in this regard. For example, questions can be categorized far beyond the basic open-ended and closed-ended types. The skilled salesperson uses questions to accomplish a variety of functions, as the preceding list shows, and knows that different questions can create different results. As a salesperson, the more aware you are of the power that questions possess, the more likely you are to tap into that power.

Benjamin Bloom of the University of Chicago is one of many outstanding thought-shapers who've explored this power. Bloom established the taxonomy that is well-known in academic circles. It has direct relevance for sales circles as well. The six types of questions, illustrated in the first six dialogs in this chapter, involve different thought processes. From the lowest level to the highest, those processes involve the following:

- **Knowledge.** These questions are the most basic, asking your customer to simply recognize or recall specific facts. For example, a knowledge question might be, "Remember when we had to use carbon paper in order to make copies of documents?"

- **Comprehension.** If you're asking questions on this level, you're expecting clients to possess enough understanding to handle mental calculations, comparisons, or interpretations. A comprehension question might be, "From what you know of other hotels, how does your own compare?"

- **Application.** It's not enough to know and to interpret. There are times when you'll want your prospects to actually apply some of the concepts or products you give them. To illustrate, you might ask, "Based on the needs of your office, which of these features would be most valuable to you?"

- **Analysis.** On this level, you ask prospects to delve into a topic. You might ask the prospect to probe a cause/effect issue or come to a conclusion; you might ask for evidence to support a commonly held belief. An example of an analysis question might be, "What factors influence your decision to purchase one car or another?"

- **Synthesis.** Even more challenging than an analysis question, a synthesis question requires your client to produce original thoughts or to project or to engage in some problem solving. A common question in this category asks for a familiar speculation: "If price were no object, what would your dream house be like?"

- **Evaluation.** The answers to evaluation questions are typically neither right nor wrong. Instead, the client is asked to make judgments or offer opinions. For example, you might ask, "What do you think is the biggest barrier to productivity in your workplace?"

The seventh dialog will help you (and sometimes your prospect, too) uncover both blatant and latent attitudes toward your product, company, or industry. The final dialog explains the use of divergent questions. Those are questions that are atypical, unexpected, unusual, and often not literal. Such questions help bring fresh perspectives to the selling process. They cause users to re-examine assumptions and attitudes, policies and procedures. They challenge established thought.

Whether you're using convergent or divergent questions, though, you're bound to benefit. Questions not only help us to qualify prospects, they help us to qualify the needs of customers. Without them, we're likely to go off on tangents that matter little to us or those we serve.

Dialog 1

Ask Knowledge Questions

Scenario

In this situation, you're meeting with the owner of a local gift store for the very first time. Although she's a stranger to you, she's no stranger to the product you're selling—handmade aprons. You'll use knowledge questions to ascertain what she already knows so that you won't waste her time or yours.

Strategies

The first letters of the four strategies introduced here spell "LEAD." And, in a very real sense, you will be leading your prospect in the direction you feel will benefit both of you. We recommend following the dialog in the order presented here. However, there will be some circumstances that call for you to place one step or another ahead of those suggested here. With the **Listen** strategy, you'll try to get at root causes for the client's decision not to carry such a product line. In the **Educate** strategy, you'll try to overcome the objections she's just starting to formulate. Then, using the **Ask** strategy, you'll ask her another knowledge question— you'll ask her to define what she means by "a lot." Finally, in the **Drive** strategy, you'll drive toward a close by offering her a guarantee.

Further Considerations

One hundred years ago, Samuel Butler observed, "Every man's work is always a portrait of himself." Think about what your customers see when they look at the way you work.

EXPERIENCE SHOWS

To develop your ability to make segues from an irrelevancy to your product, gain practice with exercises like the following. Get 100 three-inch-by-five-inch index cards or other suitable paper. Write one word on each card. The words should have no relevance whatsoever to one another. Include words like "peacock," "sailboat," "cheese," and "debit," for example. Mix the cards up. Once a day, select two and prepare a smooth verbal transition from one to the other. If you really want to challenge yourself, connect the two words to your product.

INSIGHTS

"Ask tough, thought-provoking questions. Get to the meaningful issues quickly."

—Bill Bachrach, writing about ways to establish trust with customers and prospects ("Trust Me," *Personal Selling Power*, April 1995)

BE CAREFUL

Don't condescend. Your questions must appear to be motivated by enthusiasm; they must not convey a sense of superiority.

Ask Knowledge Questions

You: Do you currently carry any handmade aprons?

Client: No.

Notes: This basic knowledge question has elicited exactly what you need to know. It tells you that you have an opportunity to introduce a new line to your client's existing stock. Had she said "Yes," you would have had to take an entirely different tack. You would either demonstrate the superiority of your product over her existing stock or else show how your product complement-ed what she was already carrying. As you read through the rest of the script, notice the other knowledge questions that the salesperson asks.

Listen Strategy

You: Have you ever carried handmades, Mrs. Cross?

Client: No. I guess no one's ever asked us to, but I don't think they'd look as professional as the machine-made ones.

Notes: One sentence, two possible points for you to turn in your favor—if you were listening well. First, because she hasn't had much exposure to this product, she's probably not dead set against it. Second, the professional-look objection is a fairly easy one to overcome.

Educate Strategy

You: Let's think about it now. I can show you a line that's hand-stitched by senior citizens. The aprons look as professional as any you'll find from the major manufacturers, but they have the advantage of being personalized. A little bio of the senior seamstress appears on the tag attached to each.

Client: They must cost a lot.

Ask Strategy

You: What do you mean by "a lot"?

Client: Well, the most expensive apron we carry now costs $30. Anything in that range is what I consider costly.

Drive Strategy

You: You're going to like what I have to tell you, Mrs. Cross. These aprons cost only $21.50.

Client: Twenty-one fifty! They're probably wrap-arounds, not the over-the-head kind.

You: They go over the head. Honestly. The cost is low because the seniors make these as part of their arts-and-crafts projects at the senior center. Here's what I'd like to offer. Try carrying these aprons for a month. Put this little announcement in the window to let people know that the Senior-Seams are here. Whatever stock you have left at the end of the month, I'll take back. If you're not pleased with the number of sales, I promise not to contact you again for six months!

Client: Fair enough.

If you'll be making a client presentation soon, ask these knowledge questions beforehand:

- Have I customized the presentation for this customer?

- Is my presentation both informative and entertaining (at least in part)?

- Am I planning to involve the customer in some way?

- Do I need a hard-sell or soft-sell approach with this particular group?

- What worked best in my last presentation?

- Have I incorporated it in this one?

Your client may ask some knowledge questions of her own. If they relate to the sales dialog, explore them at length. If they're irrelevant, get the dialog back on track by answering quickly and then make a segue like this, "Let me show you how your question relates to the product features we've been talking about." You'll have to do some quick thinking, but salespeople are nothing if not quick thinkers.

Ask Yourself

- Do I know enough about my product/service?

- What excited me when I first learned about the product/service that my company provides?

- If my knowledge of my product/service were an overlay, would it fit perfectly on top of my boss's knowledge?

- How would it fit over the knowledge my best customer has?

- How can I fill in the gaps that might exist?

Dialog 2

Ask Comprehension Questions

Scenario

Successful selling is a two-way street. You, of course, are trying to influence the prospect to buy. But the prospect is trying to explain her needs. If you're too intent on getting your message across, you won't even hear those needs expressed. In this scenario, you're meeting for the first time with your prospect, following a successful initial cold-call overture. You'll ask comprehension questions to learn more about your prospect's needs.

Strategies

As you ask those questions, you'll be following the CUE strategies: Clarify, Uncover, and Enclose. You'll *clarify* your understanding to ensure that the prospect is a qualified prospect—it's a waste of your time and hers if there's no need for the product/service you're offering. Next, you'll *uncover* what the prospect really needs, wants, or deserves. (In the process, you'll also learn what she doesn't need, want, or deserve.) The final step involves *enclosing* the whole exhange with an overarching verbal umbrella derived from the information you've acquired.

Further Considerations

Realize the value of questions that are not really questions. And recognize that when the prospect asks you such questions, she may be simply voicing her opinion. For example, if you hear "Don't you think all these directories contain the same information?" you'll know you're hearing an objection, not a question.

EXPERIENCE SHOWS

Too many salespeople begin the selling process hesitant to mention cost. Don't beat around the price-bush. If your product costs more than your competitor's, use the price as an advantage. Everyone's familiar with the maxim "You get what you pay for." You can use the dollar figure as a selling advantage by pointing out your product's superiority.

WHAT THE EXEMPLARS DO

Bob Kimball, writing in the *AMA* (*American Management Association*) *Handbook for Successful Selling*, advises, "The purpose of the telephone call is to get the appointment. Nothing more." As tempting as it might be to try selling over the phone, resist the temptation. You can't make personal connections over the phone. Better to have face-to-face, eyeball-to-eyeball contact than to try making a sale via teleselling.

Ask Comprehension Questions

You: Thank you for taking the time to learn more about the sample directory I sent. Before we begin, let me ask how you plan to use the directory.

Prospect: My hope is to identify all the manufacturers of corrugated paper in California, Washington, Oregon, and Utah whose sales volume is between $15 and $30 million a year.

Notes: This comprehension question tells you what you need to know: Does the prospect have a sufficient understanding of your product to know whether it's what she needs? Her answer reflects that she does, indeed.

Clarify Strategy

You: This directory will definitely do that for you, Elaine. It'll also give you the names of the companies' officers and the companies' sizes. Would it be helpful to you to know the name and location of the accounting firm or law firm used by a given company?

Prospect: I don't see how it would.

You: Well, how about the professional associations and background of the senior executives in these companies? Would that information be useful?

Prospect: Again, I don't see how it would be.

Uncover Strategy

You: Let's think about what you'll do once you find the names of the corrugated paper companies you're looking for. Will you try to sell to them or merge with them, or will you try to find a Pacific Rim partner? It'll help me to help you if I have some sense of how you plan to use the directory.

Prospect: I don't want to divulge any company secrets here. Let me just say we may be looking for a regional firm with whom we can partner.

You: I don't need to know anything more than that, Elaine. You'll definitely find regional firms here. And, by knowing who their law firms are, you can avoid potential conflicts of interest. On the other hand, knowing who their accountants are could save you quite a bit of time.

Prospect: How so?

You: If a given accounting firm is already familiar with your potential partner, they can structure a deal based on what they already know. They wouldn't have to invest a lot of time learning about your partner.

Prospect: That makes sense.

You: I think you'll find our directory more useful than you now realize. It lists more than 100,000 corporations, both publicly and privately held. You can learn a company's sales volume, its number of employees, a complete description of the business, its SIC codes, profiles of the top executives, and much more.

continues

Ask Comprehension Questions (continued)

Enclose Strategy

> **You:** If you need to make a decision about a possible partner, you'll find everything you need for your initial inquiries. Once you've explored the avenues the directory gives you, you'll be in a much better position to make your decision about partners.

> **Prospect:** What haven't you told me?

> **You:** I haven't told you that you can learn other things, like whether a given company is listed on the exchanges, what its ticker symbol is, what year it got started, and so on. I also haven't told you that you can choose to get all of this either online, on CD-ROM, or in the standard print version. What more do you need?

> **Prospect:** Just whether you need payment today or if you'll take a purchase order.

On occasion, repeat your question, using different words. A slightly different phrasing may yield nuances that were not apparent in the initial question.

Be attuned to hostile questions. They may signal a need to terminate or postpone the meeting. Judge the situation and decide whether a question is a better "answer" than an actual response, for example, "Have I said something that bothered you?"

EXPERIENCE SHOWS

Try reversing positions once in a while. For example, after a prospect has defined her current problem, ask her what she thinks some possible solutions might be. Not only will the question demonstrate your willingness to listen, but also it will probably lead to an opening or opportunity you might not have uncovered.

Ask Yourself

- With what type of client should I use comprehension questions?

- What's the possible downside to asking these questions?

- Have I learned what I need to know about this prospect's buying power?

- Have I assessed the potential value of this account?

BE CAREFUL

The way you ask a question often shapes the answer you get. If you control your emotions at all times, your voice won't betray you; it won't convey the impatience or frustration or desperation you may be feeling. Not only should your vocal traits convey professionalism, but also the questions themselves should be free from any phrases that smack of negatives, such as sarcasm, overeagerness, anger, and so on.

Dialog 3

Ask Application Questions

Scenario

It's been said that salesmanship starts when the customer says "No." In this scenario, your customer has just said that very word, and now you're off to either a good or a bad start, depending on your perspective. Your goal in this sales exchange is to persuade a midsized firm to hold its next off-site meeting in your hotel. The vice president's secretary has just told you they're about to sign a contract with another hotel. You still have time, though, to convince her that your hotel can offer a special value.

Ask Application Questions

You: I understand that you've nearly finalized your decision and you don't want to start all over again. But let me ask you something, Sue. What's the biggest problem with conferences, from the attendees' point of view?

Secretary: When you've been doing this as long as I have, you know there's no one problem. Some attendees complain that the sessions are boring; others complain there's no exercise facility. Some don't like the meals, and others don't like noise coming through the walls from the other sessions. Some attendees complain the hotel isn't near the airport, and others complain because it is. Organizing a conference isn't easy, you know.

You: I know. I used to make conference plans myself before I opened this bed and breakfast. Taking the boring sessions out of the equation, I can show you how to overcome all those complaints with a two-second gesture. Interested?

Secretary: *(Laughing.)* Does this gesture fall within the realm of ladylike behavior?

Notes: You've learned that this prospect has a sense of humor and that she's experienced. She's probably heard it all before, so you've done well to suggest something she's probably not heard before. When you ask her whether she's interested, it'll probably be hard for her to say no, especially because you've built some rapport by revealing that you've "been there" in terms of organizing conferences. You've hooked her with this question. Now let her answer lead both of you to a sale.

Verify Strategy

You: It does. We have a simple brochure that addresses each of those concerns. It would take you about two seconds to share it with the attendees. We can send you enough to include with the other information you'll be distributing to them. Then, no matter what complaint they voice to you—and we both know there will always be complaints—you'll have a guaranteed response ready.

Secretary: What do you mean by "guaranteed"?

You: If there's a single complaint during the course of the conference, we'll either fix it within the hour or else refund the room charge for that person.

Nullify Strategy

Secretary: What if they ask about a gym? Notice I'm avoiding the word "complain."

You: I noticed! I like people who think positively, Sue. For the people who want to work out, we have a state-of-the-art equipment room. If they remind you that the meals were bad at the last conference, you tell them that our chef is a Frenchman with a flair and a big appetite—he gives generous portions. If they worry it's going to be noisy, you tell them not to worry. We have only one ballroom, and it'll be reserved in your company's name. If they complain that the hotel isn't near the airport, tell them it is. Our van will have you here five minutes after you've collected your luggage. And if they start to complain that it is near the airport, you tell them that it'll seem as if they're in the countryside. Ours is a bed and breakfast situated on two acres of land in a residential area. We're not like the other hotels that surround the airport.

continues

99

Ask Application Questions (continued)

Secretary: What complaints have you heard about your hotel?

Edify Strategy

You: You probably won't believe me, but we have very few complaints. That's because we try harder, Sue. It's difficult for us to compete with the big hotels around here, so we try to offer something different—the kind of personalized service you can find only in a bed-and-breakfast location.

Secretary: Such as?

You: Such as a maid who does your laundry and turns down your bed at night. Such as chocolate-chip cookies she'll bring you in the evening at 8:30, along with a cold glass of milk. Such as a work desk and dataport in each room. Such as voice mail. Such as free membership in our B'n'B Club.

Secretary: I don't think we'll be coming back. We never have the convention in the same city twice.

You: Life has a lot of tricks up its sleeve. You just might. But the attendees can give their membership card to any other family member. It entitles them to a 10 percent discount off the room price.

Simplify Strategy

You: Assuming we can offer you a competitive room rate, what would prevent you from holding your conference here?

Secretary: Just the fact that we don't know you. At least with the big hotels, there's a sense of familiarity.

You: If I have our last three conference organizers call you, would that make us seem more familiar?

Secretary: It would. Then I'd be prepared to sign a contract.

You: We believe in the honor system here. There's no contract for you to sign. Just show up, Sue. We'll bill you afterward. It's as simple as that.

Strategies

In the script that follows, you'll see how an application question can lead your prospect to the single "correct" answer, that is, the selection of your hotel for its conference. (You ask her to apply her experience.) Then you'll begin the four-step process that follows this lead. In the Verify strategy, you'll *verify* the prospect's assertions (positive or negative), demonstrating your understanding of her concerns. Next, with the Nullify strategy, you'll *nullify* them by showing that your establishment can offer everything she's seeking, and more. In the third leg of this exchange, the Edify strategy, you'll *edify* your client; that is, you'll explain the special value to her. Finally, using the Simplify strategy, you'll stress the fact that you can *simplify* both her life and the lives of conference attendees.

Further Considerations

Disneyland opened a half century ago. Naturally, management was eager to learn what visitors found most impressive. Exit interviews revealed it wasn't the amusement rides, nor the fantastic decor, nor the theme that was carried through in every conceivable appeal to the senses. Instead, it was the cleanliness of the place. Spend some time thinking about the attributes associated with the promotion and delivery of your product or service. Learn what assumptions you may be incorrectly making about why people are buying it.

As a continuous learner, you're constantly picking up new techniques: about the use of questions, the use of guarantees, and the ways to turn a negative into a positive (for example, making a bed-and-breakfast seem

INSIGHTS

"There are objections to every proposition, no matter how attractive; good salespeople set up situations where the customer sells himself, regardless of the objections." With these words, Harvey Mackay, CEO-turned-author, applauds the old Huck Finn trick of making someone want what you have to offer. Mackay asserts that selling is not the act of convincing someone to buy what you have. Rather, it's the act of "creating conditions by which the buyer convinces himself." You've done that in the Ask Application Questions Script by using your hook, your questions, your guarantees, your empathy, your specifics such as cookies and milk, and your promise of simplicity.

EXPERIENCE SHOWS

No matter what you sell, you're selling more than the product. As Charles Revson so succinctly stated, Revlon sells "hope in a bottle," not just cosmetic products. If you've not yet pinpointed what you're selling besides your product, make that analysis right now.

WHAT THE RESEARCH SHOWS

According to the American Telemarketing Association, if you call your prospects between 9 and 10 in the morning, you are five times more likely to reach them than at any other time during the day. You might even try to call earlier, at 7:30. You just might reach a senior executive who knows the value of quiet time and has arrived early to take advantage of it.

homey compared with the large hotel chains). But don't let your success make you overconfident. Overconfidence breeds complacency—the archenemy of successful sellers.

It's important to use the other person's name from time to time. Doing so makes your conversation more personal. It also suggests you cared enough to remember the person's name.

Ask Yourself

- What do our customers believe they're getting when they buy our product/service?

- What do we believe we're selling?

- If our best customer could spend a day with me, how might her opinion of our company change?

- On what assumptions do I base my sales efforts?

- What calculated risks have I taken recently to verify my assumptions?

Dialog 4

Ask Analysis Questions

Scenario

A salesperson who's lost her enthusiasm can turn into a simple paper pusher. Fortunately, you'd rather sell than do paperwork, and you've kept your level of enthusiasm for your product high. Following a mailing for your incentive product, you've had a call from a potential buyer. You're going to try to set up an appointment, and you're hoping to get the sale at the same time.

Ask Analysis Questions

You: I'm glad you liked what you saw, Carla. What factors influenced your call today?

↓

Buyer: I guess it was the customized logo that I liked best.

↓

You: Why is that?

Buyer: We need to get our name out there more, to be recognized for quality service but also to be remembered for it. I think the customized key ring will do that for us.

Notes: These analysis questions give you an immediate sense of the buyer's priorities. She is satisfied with the reputation her company has achieved but apparently feels that the company needs to acquire more brand recognition. You know your product can help her do this.

Sample Strategy

You: It certainly will. Every time your customers open their car doors or open the front doors of their homes, they'll think of your company.

↓

Buyer: I was thinking of giving them out to our employees, too, in the hope that other people would see the key ring and ask about it.

↓

You: *(Laughing.)* I'm the salesperson here. I should have thought of that myself. I'll use it for sure in my next call. Carla, let's set up an appointment. I'll need only five minutes to show you two samples: one with a company logo and the other with a message. Then you can choose which one will work best for your company.

↓

Elicit Strategy

You: Once you've made your selection, Carla, will you be able to place the order then and there to save us both some time?

↓

Buyer: Well, actually, no I won't. The order would be above $5,000 if we give them out to both employees and customers, and I'm not authorized to issue a purchase order above that amount.

You: Who would be authorized?

↓

Buyer: That would be my boss, Su-Lee.

↓

You: Could you ask her to stop by when we meet? Again, I promise I'll be in and out in five minutes, and I'll even bring doughnuts!

Lead Strategy

You: If you like, I'll send you testimonials we've received—unsolicited—from satisfied customers. But one in particular may be of interest to you. It's from a new firm, one that was as eager as you are to get their name out into the community. They gave the key rings to the purchasing agents of all the local hospitals and clinics. One recipient called for more information, and the call led to a very large order for the firm.

↓

Buyer: So you're saying a small investment in a promotional product can lead to a large sale?

continues

103

Ask Analysis Questions (continued)

You: That's exactly what I'm saying! You'll be saying it, too, in the very near future, I hope.

Leave Strategy

You: I won't take up any more of your time. But I'll plan on seeing you and Su-Lee one week from today for five minutes, tops. I'll have doughnuts and, equally important, a number of samples—color or black-and-white, logo or message, butterscotch or black leather. Make your choice, give me a purchase order, and you'll have your key rings within the week.

WHAT THE EXEMPLARS DO

Mark Goldstein, chief marketing officer at Fallon Worldwide, an advertising agency, reaffirms the many-stages view of selling. If you're hoping for the "final pitch" to clinch the deal, it probably means, "You haven't done a good job to the point of establishing a relationship of trust and respect, of making the client feel as though you'd be a worthy partner."

Strategies

You'll use the SELL strategies, the letters of which stand for Sample, Elicit, Lead, and Leave. You'll offer to send a *sample*. But, to ensure it's not a waste of your time, you'll *elicit* information regarding who the real buyer is. Then you'll *lead* by citing successes from other satisfied buyers. Finally, you'll *leave* the buyer wanting more—just as the best entertainers do.

BE CAREFUL

Analysis questions usually call for critical and in-depth thinking; they call for answers that cover a wide range of possibilities. When prospective buyers respond to analysis questions, they have to analyze information in order to make an inference, specify a reason, or substantiate a belief. Therefore, you need to allow more time than you would with a knowledge or a comprehension question. If there's a pause, resist the urge to jump in and fill the verbal vacuum. Allow your buyer time to think.

Further Considerations

Realize that the selling process is just that—it's a process. Don't expect to achieve success with a one-time effort. Let your product speak for itself in the mailing stage, and then you speak for it in subsequent telephone or in-person stages.

Keep yourself from getting discouraged by reminding yourself that the superstars in your profession were not born that way. They acquired their talents by honing their skills. You can certainly do the same.

You immediately evinced concern for the customer: You got her talking about her needs rather than focusing on yourself and your product. With this customer-centered approach, you can more readily meet those needs.

Ask Yourself

- What analysis questions should I be asking of other salespeople? of my manager? of my clients?

- Does my impatience interfere with my listening?

- How good am I at learning what customers' priorities are?

- How do the best salespeople I know maintain their enthusiasm?

Dialog 5

Ask Synthesis Questions

Scenario

Here's a mental challenge for you. It's prompted by the industrial giant W. Alton Jones, who said, "If you were to list the one hundred most successful business organizations in America, I am sure you would find that the great majority of them are successful because they have employed unique or intensive sales methods." Think about the most successful companies you know. (You don't have to list a hundred—three or four will do.) Try to pinpoint their innovative techniques.

Ask Synthesis Questions

You: Ms. Slekiak, my name is Jennifer and I'm calling about the Executive business card.

↓

Prospect: I'm not an executive. Good-bye.

↓

You: Wait! Wait! Please don't hang up. Just give me one minute of your time. You don't have to be an executive to sign up for our card.

↓

Prospect: Why should I spend any more time with you? I already have a credit card.

You: I bet you don't have a disaster plan. Tell me: What do you think is the worst-case scenario that could happen to your company?

Notes: You're forcing the prospect to think now, instead of simply to listen. Unlike the application question, which asked the prospect to apply her past experience to the present, the synthesis question asks her to project, to predict, and to speculate about the future. Although you won't dwell on doom-and-gloom, you will ask her to recognize that disasters could happen to anyone, to any firm, at any time. Once you have the prediction you need, you can segue into the fact that this card offers an easily accessible $75,000 for emergency situations.

Clear Strategy

Prospect: I tend to think about the present, not the future, but I suppose we could be sued, we could have a virus wipe out our files, we could have a natural disaster, we could have a strike.

↓

You: Just to name a few, right? Which would be the worst?

↓

Prospect: In terms of cost, I suppose if we lost all our files, that would be the worst.

↓

You: How long would it take you and how much would it cost to get you up and running again, Ms. Slekiak?

↓

Prospect: At least $50,000, I would guess.

You: Well, our credit card allows $75,000 for working capital. You can get the money by check, card, or even at your local ATM. And the interest rate is remarkably low. Further, you pay no annual fee. You can obtain additional cards for your employees, with still no annual fee. And, if you wish, you can establish limits on those extra cards. Not only that, you can download a report from our Web site so that you have constant and immediate access to the data you need for tax deductions. There's more, but let me see if you have any questions first.

↓

Revere Strategy

Prospect: If something did happen, how long would it take to get the money?

→

continues

Ask Synthesis Questions (continued)

You: It would take just _____ minutes! As long as it takes to get to the bank for an advance or to cash the convenience check we offer. For a small business like yours, it's important to have a financial safety net in case something goes wrong. Our card is that safety net. It's your insurance against disaster.

Prospect: You're sure we could get money the same day?

You: Absolutely. Time is important to all of us, but it's especially important when an emergency occurs. Our card allows you to respond quickly, no matter what the situation.

Steer Strategy

You: I can sign you up right now. It'll take only three minutes. You have nothing to lose.

Prospect: Are you sure there's no annual fee?

You: I'm sure.

Extend this kind of thinking to your own sales approach and to this scenario in which you're attempting to sell a business credit card over the phone. You pride yourself on your ability to deviate from a script and, because your sales record is impressive, your manager allows you this flexibility. You're going to use a synthesis question as part of your Clear, Revere, and Steer technique.

WHAT THE EXEMPLARS DO

In the October 1994 issue of *Personal Selling Power* ("The I-Power Action Plan"), Martin Edelston lists 20 questions that provoke productive ideas. Among them is this: "What can our company do to increase sales?" This simple synthesis question might lead to some interesting questions if asked of both salespeople and nonsalespeople.

Strategies

Beginning with the Clear strategy, you're going to be very *clear* about the features you can offer. One, two, three—bam, bam, bam. You don't have to talk faster than usual, but you do have to have your thoughts

---

BE CAREFUL

While "salesperson" and "curmudgeon" are mutually exclusive terms, there is a danger in being too friendly, especially at the very beginning of your relationship with a new customer. If the person doesn't know you, she may interpret your good nature as "slick" or "insincere." Avoid the jokes and concentrate instead on helping your prospect find what she needs—whether or not your company provides it.

EXPERIENCE SHOWS

Don't dwell on the negative. Trying to get a sale by scaring the buyer is unethical and manipulative. Once both of you have established that disasters can occur, emphasize the fact that you're offering protection against an event that probably will never occur.

EXPERIENCE SHOWS

Maintain your professionalism at all times. Never denigrate the competition. Instead, acknowledge their good points and remain close-mouthed about their bad ones.

---

and your product-ducks in order. Then, in the Revere strategy, you'll emphasize the values that most businesspeople *revere*. Finally, the Steer strategy will assist you to *steer* your prospect toward a close by offering to complete the transaction then and there.

Further Considerations

Too many buyers and sellers view the sales encounter as an adversarial one. If you tend to think of your prospects as people whose minds you want to change so that they'll do something you want them to do, it may be time for some mind-shifts away from the mind-sets. Walk into meetings confident that you can provide the buyer with something she really needs and doesn't yet have. Thoughts, as you've probably already learned, can create the reality.

General Colin Powell maintains that "perpetual optimism is a force-multiplier." Ask veteran salespeople how they keep their optimism perpetual.

Remind yourself that rude people are not attacking you personally. They don't even know you! They're probably chronically unhappy folk, or perhaps they're having bad hair days, or they've had 12 calls in a row from people trying to sell them things. View their abrasiveness as "anonymous anger" so you don't take it personally. Always remind yourself that such people may turn out to be lucrative accounts because other salespeople have been scared off. The competition for their business may in fact be nonexistent.

Ask Yourself

- What percentage of my sales exchanges do I actually have fun with?

- What percentage of my customers/prospects would say they find meeting with me enjoyable?

Dialog 6

Ask Evaluation Questions

Scenario

It's been said that buyers should never ask a tire sales-man if they need new tires. In this scenario, you're ask-ing and answering high-level questions. You're dealing with evaluation questions, ones that call for judgments, opinions, and perhaps even arguments. You're meeting with a school principal, hoping to sign up her staff for membership in your Eco-Club.

> **WHAT THE RESEARCH SHOWS**
>
> The average salesperson is using only a third of her workday on actual selling. How can you reduce the time you spend on the remaining activities—the two thirds that are less productive?

Strategies

The strategy you'll employ is one advocated by super salesman Mark McCormack, the founder of the world's leading organization for marketing sports and managing athletes (International Management Group). According to McCormack, your customers assess you on three bases: *communication, service,* and *added value.* Clarity is the operative word in the Communication strategy. When you think Service strategy, you'll offer an ongoing stream of attention to client needs. And in the Added-Value strategy, you'll separate your organization from the competition by emphasizing the added values you alone are providing.

> **EXPERIENCE SHOWS**
>
> Questions have an unassailable place in the salesperson's toolkit. But they must be asked judiciously. If you have a question that's especially penetrating, you can soften it a bit by asking another question first, "Is it okay for me to ask about your budget authority?"

> **WHAT THE EXEMPLARS DO**
>
> Mark McCormack maintains that if you want to be a better salesperson, you have to find better customers. Or, to quote an old maxim, "If you always do what you've always done, you'll always have what you've already got." It's not enough to maintain. It's not enough to find new clients. You have to find new clients better than the ones you already have.

Ask Evaluation Questions

You: What do you think your teachers want more than anything else in the world?

Principal: It certainly isn't money. They don't come into the profession hoping to earn huge salaries. I'd have to say the one thing they most desire is more time.

Notes: You were hoping she'd say that. (In case she didn't, though, you would have been prepared to stress a different feature.) And you're ready to show how the Eco-Club will save the teaching staff time with its off-the-shelf lessons.

Communication Strategy

You: My sister-in-law is a teacher, and I'm always surprised by how much time she puts into planning her lessons. By joining as an institutional member, you can get reproducible unit plans for each month of the school year. The themes are related to holidays and seasons, and focus on topics such as recycling, trees, plants, birds, mammals, reptiles, and amphibians. These unit plans have been endorsed by the American Association of Elementary Schools.

Principal: What's the cost?

You: It's included in the annual membership of $150. If you have a staff of 30 teachers, that's only $7.50 a year per person for unit plans that span a three- or four-week period.

Principal: But it wouldn't work for my whole staff to be teaching the same unit. We have different grade levels here. What works for sixth-graders will probably not work for first-graders.

You: We've already figured that out. The plans are adaptable for primary- and middle-school levels. Furthermore, you can access our archives for the last 10 years. A given student would be well into high school by the time any one unit were repeated. Let me put this another way: For $150 a year, you get reproducible lesson plans for a three- or four-week environmental unit. You also get downloads of unit plans for the last 10 years. And all our curricula are approved by a national education organization.

Service Strategy

Principal: It sounds wonderful, but, as you probably know, public education is limited in the size of its budget.

You: We have some schools that have purchased memberships with everyone contributing money out of their own pockets. They still come out ahead. And don't forget that a representative returns to your school once a year to either present a full-school assembly or to Build-a-Tradition.

Principal: Tell me more about that.

You: A good example is what happens in Nome, Alaska. On December 26 each year, residents plant leftover Christmas trees on frozen bodies of water. When the ice melts in the spring, the trees are swept into the water. But until that time, residents have a chance to see green in an otherwise all-white landscape. We've taken that concept of recycling for beauty and have created new traditions—many of which attract the attention of the local media.

Principal: What are some of those?

You: I'm not at liberty to tell you, but if you become a member, you can choose the assembly or this special tradition builder every year.

continues

Ask Evaluation Questions (continued)

Added-Value Strategy

You: Our organization actually realizes very little profit from our school accounts. Nevertheless, we continue to develop them for three very good reasons. One, we feel teachers deserve all the breaks they can get. Two, the publicity from the assemblies and tradition builders often benefits Eco-Club. And three, we know that children who care about the environment grow up wanting to protect the environment. And that's our corporate mission: to provide goods and services designed to protect this fragile world we live in.

Principal: So your values embrace several generations?

You: They do. And to help spread those values, we send an e-mail tip each month.

Principal: Relevant to the lessons?

You: Relevant to the environment. For example, this month the tip concerns fruit-bearing trees. If you have a pear tree that's bearing only flowers, not fruit, you probably have a problem with cross-pollination. These tips can be used by the staff—many of whom are probably gardeners—or incorporated into the lessons.

EXPERIENCE SHOWS

An intellectual, one anonymous wit observed, is a person who can listen to the William Tell overture and not think of the Lone Ranger. By extension, an intellectual salesperson is one who can meet with a prospect and not think sales—or, at least, not think only of sales. The next time you're out on a sales call, concentrate on ways to help your prospect solve the problem she's having.

Further Considerations

"I think that American salesmanship can be a weapon more powerful than the atomic bomb," Henry J. Kaiser, world-renowned entrepreneur, once observed. Hyperbole aside, assess your own sales skills. Ask acquaintances and associates to do the same. If the ratings fall below 9 on a 10-point scale, commit to spending a day with a mega-salesperson, inside or outside your field. Watch for techniques that work like dynamite to ignite a prospect's interest and inclination.

Life is truly a question of choices. Say you've done everything you can think of doing to win an account. At some point, you have to choose: Do you continue to expend time and energy, or do you lose all the time and energy you've already invested and simply stop trying to sway this particular prospect? It's a difficult choice, knowing when dogged persistence crosses the line and becomes foolish perseverance. Talk to those more experienced than you are. Chances are that most will recommend that you continue your efforts, if only in a more limited fashion.

At least twice a year, evaluate your accounts on two bases: gains and growth potential. List your current profit per customer and honestly assess the likelihood of expanded sales, assigning a dollar figure for each. Assign a "1" to the most promising and "2" and "3" to less promising customers. Study the figures, including the total, and determine what percentage of accounts falls into each of these three categories. You'll probably discover that the Pareto Principle applies to you: A few of your existing customers comprise most of your sales. (Vilfredo Pareto was an eighteenth-century Italian economist who formulated the 80/20 rule: a fraction of the things we do account for the majority of the results we achieve.) Are you spending time and effort accordingly?

Ask Yourself

- When was the last time I took a class or read a book to improve my communication style?

- When was the last time I defined the meaning of "service"?

- When was the last time I asked my best customers how I could assist them in making the best use of the product or service they've purchased?

- How often do I ask evaluation questions of my prospects and/or buyers?

Dialog 7

Ask Attitude Questions

Scenario

Humorist Jane Wagner wryly observes, "When we talk to God, we're praying. When God talks to us, we're schizophrenic." It's often a question of perspective, isn't it? And perspective is shaped by attitude. While awareness of your own attitude is critical to successful selling, so is awareness of your prospect's attitude. With the right questions, you can uncover just what those attitudes are.

WHAT THE EXEMPLARS DO
Xerox's former number-one salesperson in the United States, Hal Becker, asserts there are three qualities that make an ordinary salesperson extraordinary. Top salespeople, he maintains, are organized, persistent, and incredibly honest.

Strategies

There's a right way and a wrong way to do virtually anything and everything in life—including making a sale. The more readily we perceive a given effort is not working, the more readily we can find one that will work. After asking a question to learn about the prospect's attitude, you'll proceed to learn more about her needs.

BE CAREFUL
What words, phrases, or mannerisms turn you off when you're listening to or watching someone speak? Are you guilty of manifesting such turn-off behaviors yourself? Tape-record a cold call or have a trusted colleague shadow you for an hour to learn what you may be doing wrong.

But when you realize your initial overture is getting you nowhere fast, you switch your tactic to a revised approach. (If you're a fast learner, you may not need to switch at all; just read the following and mend the error of your intended ways.) You're attempting to sell greeting cards for the upcoming holiday season to the head of a large dental clinic.

Ask Attitude Questions

You: Well, the holidays are right around the corner, aren't they?

Prospect: Yes, indeed. It's my favorite time of year. Peace may not be on all of the earth, but our patients definitely come in with better spirits.

Notes: This question is really a declarative statement with a little tag at the end, "aren't they?" The question seems innocuous enough, but it's enough to tell you what you need to know: The prospect is inclined toward the sentimental side of the season.

Initial Strategy

You: I know you send out cards every year because my neighbor gets one from you. If you order just $100 worth of cards from us, I'm prepared to give you a radio/cassette recorder. Let me show you what it looks like. I have that picture somewhere in this briefcase.

Prospect: I don't really need that. I'm more concerned about our professional image.

You: But this is a $35 value. You can have music playing all day long while your patients are being drilled. Or you can stay tuned for late-breaking news of the world. Or, if you want to tape-record your staff meetings, this is the perfect way to do that. And all you have to order is $100 worth of these beautiful cards.

Notes: You've completely overlooked the cue that the prospect offered—the reference to peace on earth. Instead of showing her a line of traditional favorites, you've moved to an enticement that doesn't seem to interest her at all. It's better to save that gift to help sway her if she seems undecided rather than to push it on her before she even knows what your product is like. Plus, you're creating the impression of being disorganized.

Revised Strategy

You: We actually have some traditional cards that talk about peace. Look at this one with the manger scene on the cover. Inside it says, "May you have the joys of the season, the peace of the holidays, and the very best of health in the new year." That line is perfect for a dental clinic.

Prospect: I like that. Do you have anything else like it?

You: We have about two dozen. Why don't you look through them. I need to run out to my car for something. *(Five minutes later.)* See anything you like?

Prospect: Several actually. I'm having a hard time making up my mind.

You: You don't have to right now. Think about your choice and, if it reaches $100, we'd like to show our appreciation with this radio/cassette recorder. You'll get a lot of use out of it, I'm sure.

Notes: You've made a number of right moves here. You picked up on the earlier indication that she likes a more traditional tone, and you responded with a related product sample. Then, you allowed her time to review the selection. Finally, you offered a premium at a point when the question was not "Will I get the sale?" but rather "How much of a sale will I get?"

Further Considerations

America's first psychologist, William James, observed, "The greatest revolution of our generation is the discovery that human beings, by changing the inner attitudes of their minds, can change the outer aspects of their lives." What are some inner attitudes you need to change?

Be sure to pay attention to body language and *paralanguage*— the messages sent by vocal traits such as volume, rapidity, pause, and tone. For example, if a prospect's voice conveys excitement, you know you've found a feature that especially interests her. If she hesitates or becomes more subdued, you may need to discuss her hesitation before starting to close the sale.

Don't be put off by a statement that seems to spell rejection. For example, if a prospect tells you she already has several insurance policies, suggest meeting with her to give her a free review that will ensure she truly has what she needs.

Ask Yourself

- How would my worst critic describe my attitude?

- Why have I chosen to center my work life around being a salesperson?

- Who or what works best to adjust my attitude?

- How patient am I?

WHAT THE EXPERTS SAY

David Hall, president of D.C. Hall Sales, Inc., in Honeoye Falls, New York, cautions against the hope of closing a sale in a single call. Says he, "It can take a year or more in engineering-related sales to get from the conceptual to the drawing stage, and from management to purchasing approval."

EXPERIENCE SHOWS

Instead of win-win outcomes, think of win-win-win possibilities that could benefit your customer, yourself, and a third entity as well. For example, if you sold a sophisticated day-planner, you'd benefit from having made a sale. Your customer would benefit because her life will be better organized. And your client's secretary would benefit by having a boss who's where she's supposed to be. Get your creative juices going and incorporate the third beneficiary as part of your next sales pitch.

WHAT THE RESEARCH SHOWS

A report by the McGraw-Hill Research/Laboratory of Advertising Performance, #8013.8, shows that an industrial sales call can cost up to $230. In light of that surprising fact, it may be time to reevaluate the need for face-to-face meetings. The obvious advantage of such meetings may be offset by their cost and by some customers' dislike of face-to-face meetings that take up more time than simply speaking on the phone.

Dialog 8

Ask Divergent Questions

Scenario

Students of the mind know that most of us think convergently (focusing on a single, correct answer), while the more creative among us think divergently (realizing an uncommon or atypical response to a common situation). A relatively few people are lateralized—they can find an appropriate strategy, no matter what the situation calls for. Lateralized thinkers can put on a convergent thinking cap as easily as a divergent cap. They're mentally ambidextrous. Let's use the definition of the word "gentleman" as an example. A convergent definition would allude to a courteous, gracious, honorable man. The divergent definition of a gentleman, as an anonymous wit once said, is "a man who can play the accordion but doesn't."

Strategies

You're going to begin with a divergent question, one designed to yield an unusual perspective on the sales situation you're dealing with. From there, you'll move on to the animal kingdom and see how three different sales types would handle the same situation. In the Lamb strategy, the *lamb* takes a low-key approach. She sells so softly, the sales pitch can barely be heard. And, in some situations, no more than this is needed, especially if the prospect is soft-spoken or reserved herself. In the Gazelle strategy, the *gazelle* moves swiftly, but only because the client has indicated a need for speed. The *chimpanzee* can swing from tree to tree, from topic to topic, as easily as the prospect is doing, without losing sight of the sales goal in the Chimpanzee strategy.

Ask Divergent Questions

You: Good morning, Ms. Johnson. I'm calling on behalf of Managers for the Millennium and our upcoming conference.

Prospect: I don't think we'd be interested.

You: Does Tom Peters interest you?

Prospect: Is he speaking at the conference?

You: No, but we're offering a number of sessions that reflect some of his core beliefs.

Prospect: Could you explain that?

You: Like the creativity session, for example. It's based on one of his favorite sayings, "Every organization needs at least one weirdo onboard."

Prospect: Our organization goes well beyond the requisite number of those!

Notes: You're off to a good start here. You've asked a question about a management guru—not a typical opening at all—and you've used it as a lead into a funny statement. You've built some rapport here. Depending on your assessment of the prospect's personality, you can use any one of the following three strategies quite successfully.

Lamb Strategy

You: The creativity session is one of four that run concurrently in the morning. We believe sessions should be in-depth, not just scattered chunks of knowledge. We also believe it's difficult to derive value if participants have to spend their morning running from hour-long session to hour-long session. Our keynote is a really motivational topic, Superman don't need no airplane, followed by the sessions.

Prospect: I'd really like to go, but I don't know if my manager would approve it.

You: Would cost be her objection?

Prospect: That and the fact that we're so far behind on everything.

You: Well, in our morning session on the networked society, you'll learn tips that can save as many as 50 hours a year. That alone makes it worthwhile for you to come. As far as cost is concerned, here's a sheet of testimonials noting that the cost was worth every penny. We're having a special now: Buy one and get one free. Perhaps you should take your boss along with you!

You can also tell her that conference attendees receive a copy of all session handouts. In a sense then, you'll be gaining knowledge about eight different sessions, even though you can attend only one in the morning and one in the afternoon. Let me leave the brochure with you and an extra one for your boss. I'll stop back in a few days; if there's interest, I'll have a copy of last year's session handouts as a gift for signing up.

continues

Ask Divergent Questions (continued)

Gazelle Strategy

Prospect: What have you got besides creativity?

↓

You: What are you looking for?

↓

Prospect: Transformation.

↓

You: Perfect. We have an executive vice president for a major hotel chain discussing "Inventing the Future, Transforming Vision to Reality, Driving Out Fear, and Building Support."

↓

Prospect: What does it cost?

↓

You: One session? One person?

↓

Prospect: Right.

↓

You: $425

↓

Prospect: It's a done deal.

Note: If you're attuned to paralanguage—the messages conveyed by vocal traits as opposed to words alone—you'd have picked up very quickly the staccato, monosyllabic nature of the gazelle's communication, and you'll respond in kind.

↓

Chimpanzee Strategy

Prospect: Wasn't it Tom Peters who said imagination is the only source of real value in the new economy?

↓

You: I believe it was, and at this session you'll learn to optimize real value.

Prospect: How would you define "value"?

↓

You: In simple terms, getting the most for your money, and that's exactly what will happen if you sign up for this seminar.

↓

Prospect: Are you rushing me to sign on the dotted line?

↓

You: Not at all. It's just that I want to "optimize the value" of your time by telling you what we can offer, letting you decide, and then getting out of your way.

↓

Prospect: You know, I've thought about going into sales. How much time do you spend on the phone?

↓

You: It varies. But I like the variety of it. Speaking of variety, you know we have several other important topics—not just creativity.

↓

Prospect: Like what?

↓

You: Like "E-speed for E-business," or "Change Before You Have To," or "Forming Strategic Alliances."

Further Considerations

Plato commented, "You can discover more about a person in an hour of play than in a year of conversation." Depending on how well you know your customer or how accurately you judge your prospects, you can engage in playful conversation from time to time. Not only will you learn about the person, but you'll also develop and sustain a good rapport.

"Vision," said Jonathan Swift, "is the art of seeing the invisible." Help your prospects envision themselves enjoying or benefiting from your product or service.

Anticipate the many directions in which the exchange might go. Have a response ready for any side road the prospect may want to travel down, away from the main road of your intended pitch.

You needn't go to the extremes advocated by some psychologists, extremes that have you mirroring the prospect's vocal and body traits, but you should be able to adapt your style, as shown in these dialogs, to the prospect's personality: reserved, harried, or spontaneous.

EXPERIENCE SHOWS

They say the only thing worse than learning from experience is not learning from experience. Periodically review the mistakes you've made, the decisions you wish you had made differently, the words you wish you hadn't used, or perhaps the words you wish you had. Keep a log of lessons learned and review them before especially important sales calls.

WHAT THE EXPERTS SAY

Harvard psychologist Dr. George Miller asserts the average person can hold only seven separate units of information in mind at a given time. Just think of the sevens you see or hear each day: seven digits in a phone number, the Seven Dwarfs, the seven habits of successful people, the seven wonders of the world, and so on. Try reducing your sales philosophy to a set of seven principles.

Ask Yourself

- Am I tapping into my creative potential?

- Does surprise continue to delight me?

- How do I show my customers I value them?

- Am I viewing the sales situation from a wide-angle lens, or do I tend to regard price as a single selling point?

Chapter 5

Listening

Selling is a transformable landscape that is always, yet never, the same. As you work in your field, you are in a position to capitalize on the trial-and-error results others have achieved before you. These results include things like the Puppy Dog close that have worked since televisions were given away for weekend loans. Once the customer had tried the television in his home for a weekend, he almost always returned Monday morning, ready to buy. Giveaways that are irresistible to consumers have been labeled Puppy-Dogs, because of their irresistibility. Using them at the end of your dialog helps cement the close. Even so, you can still play a pioneering role, trying new ideas. The techniques that succeed will become new landmarks in the sales terrain.

No matter how often you make triumphant forays into the land of sales, though, there will always be some trips that are less than memorable. You may find that:

- The prospect forgot the appointment.

- You're having a bad day and your mental faculties are not as sharp as usual.

- Despite qualifying the lead, you find out, once you're there, that the call is futile.

- The standard techniques backfire.

- The scheduled one-on-one appointment suddenly becomes a group thing, calling for you to speak and listen to five times as many people as you'd planned on.

- You have to toss aside your carefully prepared plan because the prospect has an agenda of his own.

- You've trapped yourself in a corner from which there's no escape, unless you're willing to pay dearly.

In these and dozens of other situations, you may find that better listening is the answer to your problem. That's what this chapter is all about: listening better than you already do.

We begin with a one-person dialog, an extremely effective way of pumping yourself up by listening to yourself. Then comes a dialog about awareness building: Without challenges you simply would not be as good as you are nor as good as you can become. If you can hear the embedded opportunities without having your mind go blank, you can deal with them more effectively. In the third dialog, you'll contact a top salesperson, someone whose words, if you listen carefully, will inspire you to fight the good fight. Learn from the experiences of such individuals. Play back their words in your mind from time to time.

In dialog four, you'll be encouraged to hear what the prospect is trying to tell you and then to use rejection as a spur to greater accomplishment. You'll hear "possible" when the prospect says "never." In the next dialog, you'll be asked to identify what motivates you and to listen to your inner voice.

Dialog six focuses on guiding the sales exchange by asking the prospect to talk about what's important to him. The success of these interactions depends on both listening and being heard. In dialog seven, the importance of definitions is illustrated—provided, of course, that you're listening to the prospect's needs, sometimes disguised in the form of small talk. In the final dialog, you'll see how critical it is to listen to the customer in the role of boss.

Dialog 1

Listen to Yourself

Scenario

This has been one of the worst days so far in your career. Apart from factors you can't control (stormy weather, snarled traffic, and family misunderstandings), you're finding that everything else is going awry, including those things you thought you could control. It's time for a one-person dialog. You'll actually play two roles—yourself and your alter ego; you raise objections and your alter ego fights against them.

Strategies

The Positive-Viewpoint strategy essentially requires you to look at every negative from a *positive point of view*. The Stop Whining, the Quit-Feeling-Sorry-for-Yourself, and the Get-On-with-It strategies require you, respectively, to *stop whining*, to *quit feeling sorry for yourself*, and to *get on with your life*. Although the three examples are shown as separate strategies, in truth they're usually combined as one ongoing self-dialog. Listen to yourself complaining. Then listen to your alter ego urging you to replace complaints with confidence.

Further Considerations

It works for Olympic athletes. It'll also work for you. Visualize your success long before it happens. You have nothing to lose by imagining the person on the other end of the line being receptive to your call. With your inner ear, listen to him telling you what a great product you have. Or, in the middle of your pitch, visualize your prospect signing the dotted line.

> **INSIGHTS**
>
> Your parents or grandparents may have thought landing a man on the moon was a physical impossibility at one point. But wondrous things are happening every day of the week. Listen to the words of scientist Wernher Von Braun, one of the masterminds behind the moon landing: "I have learned to use the word 'impossible' with the greatest caution."

> **BE CAREFUL**
>
> Is your work environment/briefcase/car conducive to positive self-speaking and self-listening? If you're surrounding yourself with a large number of emotional toxins, you may be engaged in self-defeating action without even realizing it. Periodically, go through and make your surroundings more user-friendly. You might even consider the benefits of feng shui, the Asian art of creating an environment that emphasizes harmony.

Listen to Yourself

> **You:** Another rejection. That's the 10th call I've made today, and no one will give me the time of day.

> **Alter Ego:** Maybe the next one will be the one you've been waiting for.

Notes: Those who deal well with feelings of rage, rejection, and revenge know the power of self-talk. So do those who successfully face critical or fearful situations. These individuals have learned to self-talk and self-listen in order to remain centered and focused. The technique is incredibly simple: You simply counter every self-damaging thought with a self-boosting one. You have to take a hard line with yourself from time to time to get through the slumps.

Positive-Viewpoint Strategy

> **You:** I've been waiting a very long time. I'm tired.

> **Alter Ego:** The god of sales has determined there's a requisite number of nos you have to hear before you hear a yes. With each rejection, you're getting closer and closer to the word you want to hear.

Quit-Feeling-Sorry-for-Yourself Strategy

> **You:** But Joe Citron only pampers two large accounts and pulls in 50 percent more than I do each year.

> **Alter Ego:** Yes, and he also has a child who was born visually impaired. As green as the grass may seem to you on the other side of the fence, it's the same grass. It's just cut at different times.

Stop Whining Strategy

> **You:** I work so hard. I really deserve to be making more money.

> **Alter Ego:** Look around you. There are hospital orderlies and coal miners and garbage collectors who work much harder than you do and make much less.

Get-On-with-It Strategy

> **You:** I'm so tired and so discouraged. Maybe I should give up for the day and go see a movie.

> **Alter Ego:** Maybe you're right, but try just one more call. Then you can go pamper yourself, you big baby.

Stanford professor and author Jim Collins speaks often of BHAGs (Big, Hairy, Audacious Goals). Don't limit your potential with SHAGs (Small, Hole-infested, Apologetic Goals). Think big. Act bigger.

Try thinking of "objections" as "challenges." You "meet" challenges, fully confident of your capacity to do so, whereas you have to "overcome" objections. And "overcome" suggests a lot more effort than "meet" does.

EXPERIENCE SHOWS

Although it's tempting to do so, try to avoid the trap of blaming others when things don't go your way. It's a coward's way out. It's better to assume some responsibility for whatever failures you experience and then resolve to make your next gesture more successful.

Ask Yourself

- Do I listen more to myself or to others when things go wrong?

- How well and how often am I able to "laugh myself out of myself"?

- What voices do I most respect?

- To what extent do they guide my thinking?

WHAT THE EXPERTS SAY

Five hundred years ago, William Shakespeare had one character urging another, "Laugh me out of myself." It's possible to self-talk ourselves out of bad moods, but you have to work at it.

Dialog 2

Listen for Opportunities Embedded in Challenges

Scenario

Author Marcelene Cox insists, "No man knows his true character until he has run out of gas, purchased something on the installment plan, and raised an adolescent." If challenges like these reveal a man's character, then sales setbacks reveal a salesperson's character. Do you rise to the inevitable challenges that life places before you, or do you allow yourself to become discouraged? The dialog that follows is filled with challenges. You'll meet them head on, determined to find the opportunities in disguise.

Listen for Opportunities Embedded in Challenges

You: Good morning, Mr. Edwards. I'm Blanton Garety with the Neighborhood Savings Bank. I'd like to have a minute of your time.

Prospect: What for?

Notes: The prospect sounds cantankerous, but at least he didn't hang up on you. Be prepared for more challenges, find the silver lining in each as you reflect upon them, and then deflect the criticism or nastiness with a comment that will motivate you and, ideally, win you the sale.

Reflect Strategy

You: When you opened your account with us, you also filled out a reply form for information about our renewable and convertible term life insurance.

Prospect: If I did, it was a mistake. I'm not interested in insurance.

You (internal dialog): He may be confused about this, but the fact remains that he did fill out the reply card. I have it right here in my hand. I'll have to tread carefully, because I don't want to sound as if I don't believe him. Worse still, I don't want to imply that he's confused.

Deflect Strategy

You: Mr. Edwards, if I could have just a moment of your time. *(Pause.)* You probably already have life insurance for your family. Is that correct?

Prospect: I don't think it's any of your business how I spend my money.

Reflect Strategy

You (internal dialog): This one guards his privacy. I don't want to seem intrusive, but he's probably not spending enough on life insurance. I need to assure him that I only want to help him make the right choices for his family.

Deflect Strategy

You: You're right. It's none of my business how you spend your money, but protection is my business, and we want to make sure all our clients are well protected. That's why we've come up with a 15-year insurance plan. It provides up to a half-million dollars worth of protection at a very low cost.

Prospect: Right. A low cost for the first year. Then I'm sure your premiums rise astronomically.

You: Actually, the premium remains the same for the whole 15 years. And, speaking of protection, this plan is backed 100 percent by the federal government.

Strategies

In this scenario, you are going to alternate using the Reflect and Deflect strategies. Your basic response to the challenges set before you is to *reflect* (listen to an internal dialog). Next you *deflect* (refuse to let the objection, rudeness, stall, or whatever discourage you). You're attempting to sell life insurance over the phone to a lead you believe is qualified: someone who already does business with your bank and who has asked for more information.

Further Considerations

Resist being pushed in a direction you're not ready to go. Postponing the answer to an ill-timed question from your client may not win you the sale, but it probably won't cost you the sale either. Acknowledge that you've heard what he asked and reply with firm but diplomatic words, such as "I'll be coming to that in just a moment. "

Many salespeople are guilty of shooting themselves in the foot that's been successfully placed in the prospect's door. Ideally, you're not one of those who get to the point of closing the sale and then fail to do so because you leave the client hanging. "I'll leave these materials for you, and then I'll call you in a week or so after you've had a chance to read them" is not a closing. It's self-destruction. Listen for the signals that say, "I'm ready to buy," and then act on them.

On the other hand, asking for a close too early in your presentation can put undue pressure on the prospect. Don't be surprised if he recoils from it. If you think you heard a closing signal, respond to it tentatively at first and then more strongly once you've determined you heard it correctly.

EXPERIENCE SHOWS

Know that the customer has both implicit and explicit needs. The former are based in the ideal world and the latter in the real world. It's possible to satisfy both, but not without some unobtrusive probing and keen listening on your part. Sometimes, a plea will help you overcome your own desperation and the prospect's reluctance. "Can you help me here?" or a similar line often works quite well to build rapport and elicit information.

INSIGHTS

"The best way to persuade people is with your ears—by listening to them." The words of statesman Dean Rusk lend further credence to the need to remain nondefensive. Often in our rush to diminish the effect of a criticism, we cut off the customer and begin rapidly explaining our own position without giving him a change to finish explaining his own.

EXPERIENCE SHOWS

Visit the Web site of the International Listening Association, www.listen.org, to obtain additional information on this all-important topic.

Ask Yourself

- Do I give up too easily?

- Am I training myself to listen beneath the surface of an objection?

- Whom do I admire as an outstanding listener?

- What errors have I made because of information I heard incorrectly?

Dialog 3

Let Those at the Top Hear from You

Scenario

Comedian Jackie Mason once bemoaned his lack of monetary rewards. "I have enough money to last me the rest of my life," he revealed, "unless I buy something." Is that plaint only too familiar? Maybe you'd like to do better. You probably know some selling exemplars who've done remarkably well in their chosen field. In this scenario, you've decided to approach an exemplar and learn from him. You've chosen one with a reputation as an outstanding listener.

Strategies

Quite simply, you're going to ask for the help you need. You'll employ the acronym ASK as your overall strategy. Beginning with the Assistance strategy, you'll acknowledge you need *assistance* for getting out of your current slump. Then you'll use the Seriousness strategy in which you demonstrate *seriousness* by letting your exemplar know you've done your homework and intend to keep on doing it. Finally, in the Knowledge strategy, you'll share the insights and *knowledge* you've acquired as a result of your contact with him. This final strategy will take place after you've had a chance to put his suggestions to work.

Let Those at the Top Hear from You

You: Mr. McCarthy? This is David Green. I've recently joined MegaMoments, and so far 12 people have mentioned you as the best salesperson this company has ever seen.

Exemplar: I fooled them all, didn't I?

You: I don't think so, Mr. McCarthy. The sales records you established still haven't been beaten, even though it's been four years since you retired. Over and over, I hear people say you knew how to really listen to what the customer was telling you.

Notes: You're taking just the right approach here. Your flattery is sincere but not effusive. And you clearly have your facts straight. Now you're ready to come out and ask for help from the exemplar.

Assistance Strategy

You: I'm trying to learn all I can about the field. Before you ask, the answer is yes, I'm doing my homework. I read two books a month, I go to training at least once a quarter, I listen to audio tapes, and I revise my script, but there's no-thing like going directly to the source of excellence. Would you accept my invitation for a long lunch, during which I plan to ask you numerous questions and listen avidly to your answers?

Exemplar: I wouldn't mind having lunch with you, but I don't think I could help you very much. You see, excellence is developed incrementally. You won't see any dramatic change in your sales record after having lunch with me for an hour or so.

Seriousness Strategy

You: I appreciate your honesty. Those incremental steps you mentioned have to be taken from a foundation of knowledge. And you have knowledge I need. In fact, if you have time, I'd like to have lunch with you once a month for a very long time. This way, I could update you on the incremental steps I've been taking. And we can both assess excellence as it develops.

Exemplar: You're pretty persistent.

You: Well, as you probably know, that's one of the marks of successful salespeople.

Knowledge Strategy

You: *(Three weeks after your lunch meeting.)* Mr. McCarthy? It's David Green. I have some exciting news to share with you. I know we've been expecting incremental improvements in my questioning-based-on-listening techniques, but one of your suggestions just led me to an order worth $100,000!

Exemplar: Which one was it?

You: I'll tell you, but you'll have to have lunch with me to get all the details. Agreed?

WHAT THE EXEMPLARS DO

According to *Issues and Answers in Sales*, if you are a sales manager, you should be making one call a day: to a satisfied customer, to a dissatisfied customer, to an executive whose business you want, to your own company (in order to hear how inbound calls are handled), and to a geographically distant sales rep. What five calls could you make in the week ahead to learn more about improvement?

WHAT THE EXPERTS SAY

Psychiatrist John H. Reitmann notes, "It takes an average person almost twice as long to understand a sentence that uses a negative approach than it does to understand a positive sentence." Try speaking of your setbacks in positive terms—this is easier to do than you may think. Listen to yourself to learn whether you're using more negatives than positives.

Further Considerations

The words of author F. Scott Fitzgerald offer good advice for the salesman in a slump: "Never confuse a single defeat with a final defeat. "

It may be that you're missing sales because you're not attuned to the promise heard in questions like these: "Could you show me how that works once more?" or "What would we do if this widget suddenly stopped working?" or "Do you have one of these yourself?"

Consider compiling an arsenal of weapons for fighting back against discouragement. You might use inspiring words, restorative actions, or meditation. Perhaps talking to those who inspire you simply by their presence will give you the boost you need.

Think twice about the small talk you make. Are you using it as an effective sales tool or as a time-waster for your clients? Are you truly listening to the small talk they make or are you dismissing it as ice-breaking fluff?

Ask Yourself

- Do I hesitate to ask for assistance when I need it?

- Whom do I regard as exemplars in this field?

- What can I do to repay an exemplar for the time he has taken with me?

- Might I serve as an exemplar for someone else?

- Do I have an established pattern or routine for pulling myself out of slumps, including listening to the words of people I admire?

Dialog 4

Hear "Possible" When Others Say "Never"

Scenario

You've no doubt heard true stories like these:

- Outfielder Tris Speaker declared ruefully in 1921 that Babe Ruth had "made a big mistake when he gave up pitching."

- In Wayne Gretzky's own words: "I was told that I wasn't big enough, maybe not fast enough, and not strong enough [to play hockey]."

- In 1837 British surgeon Sir John Ericksen firmly asserted, "The abdomen, the chest, and the brain will be forever shut from the intrusion of the wise and humane surgeon."

- When television was first becoming popular, the head of Twentieth Century Fox made this prediction: "People will soon get tired of staring at a plywood box every night."

- As a child, Albert Einstein was called to the headmaster's office and told, "Your mere presence offends me."

- A sports expert once defined Vince Lombardi's coaching skills this way: "He possesses minimal football knowledge. Lacks motivation."

It's important for you to remind yourself periodically that others have heard defeating words but have refused to listen to them. Instead, they worked to overcome hurdles much more daunting than the ones you face. They heard "possible" when others said "never." Rejection spurred them on. It can spur you on as well.

> **INSIGHTS**
>
> "One of the things I learned the hard way was it does not pay to get discouraged. Keeping busy and making optimism a way of life can restore your faith in yourself." Although these are Hollywood words from the Lucy everyone loved, they apply nonetheless to salespeople as well. Remind yourself of them once a week at least.

Hear Possible When Others Say Never

You: Morris? It's Cass Mahoney. We met in your office about two weeks ago. I left our heavy-duty flat clinch stapler for you to try out. How'd you like it?

Prospect: I didn't. You can come by and pick it up anytime. It'll be at the receptionist's desk. Don't bother trying to get in to see me.

Notes: It's clear something is going on in your prospect's life that has little to do with you or your product. There's no other explanation for the treatment you're receiving. It sounds rude, and it is rude. You can make a last-ditch effort to understand what's going on—but make it fast! It's clear he's not in a listening mode.

Summarize Strategy

You: You've decided not to order them for the secretarial staff then?

Prospect: Don't you listen? That's what I've just said.

Positive Strategy

You: You're the first person I've ever met who didn't like it. But certainly, I'll do what you asked. I'll stop by today to pick it up.

Prospect: Thank you.

Understand Strategy

You: And thank you for trying it out. Could you tell me what you didn't like?

Prospect: It jammed whenever we tried to staple our internal directory.

You: How many pages in that directory?

Prospect: I don't know. About 80, I guess.

You: That's the problem, Morris. The model you have is designed for only 50 sheets at the most.

Prospect: Look, Cass. Just pick it up. We've already ordered one from another company.

Resolve Strategy

You: Morris, I'm going to "eat" the cost on this one because I apparently wasn't listening when you told me how big your documents are. Please, just keep it, with my compliments. And have your secretary cancel the order with the other company because I'm going to leave off the model that takes up to 250 sheets.

Prospect: Are you sure?

You: I'm sure. *(Realizing the prospect may have heard "free" in the words "leave off" and not intending to give away a second stapler.)* But I would like to call your secretary in a week or so to see how she likes the heavy-duty model. I hope by then you'll be ready to order them for the whole staff. If not, I'll just pick it up from her. In either case, you can keep the 50-page one you have now with my compliments.

Strategies

In the scenario that follows, you're recalling the rejecting words and then using them to SPUR yourself to action with the Summarize, Positive, Understand, and Resolve strategies. You'll *summarize* what happened, put a *positive* spin on it, seek to *understand* what constitutes appropriate action or reaction, and then *resolve* to move forward.

Further Considerations

At the famous Pike Place fish market in Seattle, employees know they have choices regarding how they'll react to everyday occurrences in the workplace. You have the same choices, especially the choice of the attitude you'll adopt toward what you hear.

Before becoming discouraged about what you perceive as an unshakeable objection, acknowledge that some people are born negotiators—they're the ones who always try to get a lower price on hotel rooms instead of just checking in the way "normal" people do. Try to separate the natural bargainers from the objectors who really are worried about cost.

At the other end of the spectrum are those who fear low prices mean inferior quality. If you have low prices but high quality, do all you can to assure your prospect that the low price does not negate the other.

Ask Yourself

- If not rejection, what does spur me to action?
- What could I do to get the most motivated salespeople to share their secrets with me?
- What causes the figurative death of a salesman?
- What "sins" do the worst salespeople commit?

Dialog 5

Listen to What Moves You and Your Prospect

Scenario

It's time to energize yourself. You're already energetic, you say? Perhaps, but some things are zapping your energy without your even being aware of them. Things that hide in the back of your mind and nag you are known as "tolerators." You know you should take action on them, one way or another, but you keep putting it off because there's no urgent need to do so. You tolerate the nudge, telling yourself that you'll get around to it one of these days. With this dialog, we're asking you to make a commitment, to restore some lost psychic energy. How? By listening to what moves you and what moves your prospect.

EXPERIENCE SHOWS
It's only natural for prospects to enclose themselves in a protective shield, at least at first. The sales process has long been viewed as adversarial: Prospects may fear you're trying to take something they have (their money) and leave them with something they don't want (your product). To get prospects to lay aside that shield, you need to hear their fear and then offer assurances that it's ill-founded. You might give them a list of satisfied customers or give them a guarantee of some sort. Think of other assurances.

Strategies

In this script, you're going to explore typical motivators with a prospect. (Later, when you engage in further considerations, you'll explore which of these motivates you yourself.) Begin by using the Motivate strategy to ask a prospect which *motivator* moves him the most. Then in the Relate strategy, establish rapport by *relating* that motivator to your product (and sometimes even to yourself). Finally, with the Integrate strategy, *integrate* the motivator, the benefit, and the close.

Listen to What Moves You and Your Prospect

> **You:** Good morning, Vito. This is Tom Jankens from CPD Securities. I sent you some information recently about long-term care.

> **Prospect:** Yes, I read it, but I'm not ready to make a commitment.

Notes: Listen to what he's telling you here: He doesn't want you to use high-pressure tactics on him. Assure the prospect that you won't push him to do something he's not ready to do. But don't let him go without doing a little more prodding and making a promise to contact him again.

Motivate Strategy

> **You:** That's fine. We can discus the pros and cons of this kind of insurance whenever you're ready. I would like to ask you a question, though, before you hang up.

> **Prospect:** Go ahead.

> **You:** This is really for my own benefit. I've been doing some reading about what moves people to buy. Could you tell me which of these desires is most important to you? Do you desire pleasure, more money, a feeling of importance, fame, protection of your family, a good bargain, an attractive appearance to others, or good health?

> **Prospect:** It depends on what I'm buying, naturally, but the most important thing of all for me is the desire to remain healthy. If you don't have good health, none of the other things matter.

> **You:** What's second?

> **Prospect:** For me, the desire to protect my family.

Relate Strategy

> **You:** One last favor. Will you think about these two facts this week? Twenty percent of Americans over age fifty will need long-term care in the next year. And 60 percent of Americans over 65 will need long-term care in their lifetime.

> **Prospect:** Are you trying to scare me, Tom?

> **You:** I'm trying to protect you and your family, Vito. Ideally, your health will remain perfect for a very long time to come. But, to be on the safe side, you may want some insurance in case it doesn't. I've taken it out myself now that I'm nearly 50.

Integrate Strategy

> **You:** I'll call you in a week or so, and we can talk about the peace of mind that insurance buys.

> **Prospect:** Same time next week?

> **You:** If it's convenient. If not, maybe we can meet for breakfast.

Further Considerations

Look at the list of common motivators you gave the prospect. Isolate the one that is most important to you. Speak to other sales professionals to get some ideas on how to better listen to the message your selection is trying to tell you.

There are some salespeople who refuse to establish quotas, which they feel can set limits on their potential. Does this argument hold any merit as far as you're concerned?

Don't rely solely on your company for listening-skills training. There's a great deal you can do on your own to enhance your current skills and to add to the tools on your sales toolbelt.

Consider serving as a mentor for a newly hired salesperson. Listen to his doubts and let the voice of your experience assuage them. You'll learn a great deal about yourself in the process.

Ask Yourself

- What assurances do I typically offer my clients?

- What connection is there between good speaking and good listening?

- How much reading have I done on the topic of listening?

- What do good listening skills say about the listener?

- How can I develop my concentration abilities?

Dialog 6

Guide the Sales Exchange

Scenario

In this scenario, you'll be capitalizing on ancient wisdom: "Every living creature loves itself." That assertion by Cicero is as true today as when he made it more than 2,000 years ago. Translated for the modern salesperson, the maxim could read, "Every living prospect loves to talk about himself." The trick, of course, is asking the question and listening to the answer so you can guide the sales exchange to a logical and mutually beneficial outcome: the sale. To do this, you'll focus on the other person's needs. Listening equals concern for his problems.

Strategies

You'll employ a 3-D approach in this script. First, in the Direct strategy, you'll *direct* the conversation, setting the tone for the meeting. Then, the Deal strategy will enable you to *deal* with the objections that arise. Finally, you'll *decide* together what's the best solution to the prospect's problem by using the Decide strategy.

Further Considerations

It's been said there have been no new sales discoveries in the last hundred years. The principles that work today are refinements of principles first laid down by the early pioneers of the profession. Which of these principles works best for you?

INSIGHTS

"Selling, to be a great art, must involve a genuine interest in the other person's needs. Otherwise it is only a subtle, civilized way of pointing a gun and forcing one into a temporary surrender." H. A. Overstreet has captured the essence of consultative selling. When you show how your product best meets the prospect's needs, you're practicing the art of selling. First, of course, you must listen to understand exactly what that need is.

WHAT THE EXEMPLARS DO

Alfred C. Fuller, the original Fuller brush man, is the undisputed champion in terms of getting the salesperson's foot in the door. He did it by giving away a small gift. And if the housewife seemed inclined to refuse the gift, he told a small lie: "I get credit for giving them out." Is a gift of some sort included in your calls? If not, define and redefine what that gift might be. Don't overlook the gift of being a good listener.

Assume you were asked to give advice to a son or daughter about to enter the selling field. What has your experience taught you that you would most want to share?

Guide the Sales Exchange

You: I appreciate the appointment, José. I know you're busy and I won't take much of your time. For this meeting, I have just two goals.

↓

Prospect: What are they?

Notes: With this opening, you've demonstrated courtesy and an understanding of what his schedule is like. Equally important, you've articulated the fact that you have two specific goals. You've virtually invited him to ask what those goals are.

Direct Strategy

You: I'd like to show you the types of potted plants we have available for office beautification, and I'd like to have you select one that we can leave with you today. If people tell you they like having it here, then I hope you'll call and place an order with us.

↓

Prospect: I'm not really concerned about beautification.

↓

You: Tell me what you are concerned about.

Deal Strategy

Prospect: Our staff is starting to talk about Sick Building Syndrome, SBS, and it's worrying me. That's why I asked you to stop by today. I know plants can help filter ventilation and remove some of the organic compounds that are found in stale office air. I've noticed my employees are tired and irritable for no good reason. I'm afraid the culprit is SBS, and I want it taken care of. These kids are like family to me. I need to restore their good health.

↓

You: So, you're hoping that potted plants will be the solution for Sick Building Syndrome?

↓

Prospect: Short of replacing all the foam insulation, it's the only solution, from what I've heard.

↓

You: It would be deceitful of me, José, to let you continue thinking that.

Prospect: If you're about to tell me plants cannot get rid of these organic compounds, then you're about to lose the sale.

↓

Decide Strategy

You: The problem is actually more important than the sale, José. Let me tell you what I've recommended to some other clients who had been given wrong information about the power of plants to rid the air of pollutants. First, you may want to hold an open forum to see if this irritability you've mentioned has a source other than the air. If so, you may want to call in an environmental scientist to see if there is a link between your employees' health and the quality of the air in your building.

↓

Prospect: And what if there is a link?

↓

You: Then I can give you the names of three contractors who remove formaldehyde and insulation with a minimum of disruption to the offices.

↓

Prospect: What else?

↓

You: Choose one of the plants in this brochure. I'll leave it with you as I had planned to do. Then, if we find you don't really have an air-pollution problem and if your staff likes the look of the plant, I hope you'll get back to thinking about beautification.

↓

Prospect: Sounds like a plan to me.

You've been told repeatedly how necessary it is to know your product well. That advice is thousands of years old: "Better be ignorant about a matter," Publilius Syrus, a Roman slave-turned-philosopher, said, "than half know it." If you haven't already turned to some of the "elders" within your organization to learn more about your product, now is the time to do so. Listen to the wisdom of the aged.

Ask Yourself

- Could I be called a consultative seller?

- Do I tend to spell out every step, or do I leave some things to the prospect's imagination and/or intelligence?

- Do I begin my pitches with an overview that indicates the general direction I want the exchange to take?

- Do I typically encourage the prospect to talk about himself?

> ### WHAT THE EXPERTS SAY
>
> Tony Alessandra speaks often of the triangle of selling skills: management, interpersonal, and selling skills. The most important selling skill, he says, is the ability to translate a feature into a benefit. You've heard it before. You'll hear it again. But many salespeople fail to make that translation. (Ideally, you're not among that number.) You need to ask questions and then listen to answers before you make the translation. Otherwise, you may be translating the wrong benefit.

Dialog 7

Get and Give Definitions

Scenario

Introspection leads to some interesting definitions of one's self and one's career. To illustrate, Edgar Jones, former San Antonio Spurs player, brought self-definition to a whole new level when he observed, "I didn't develop as a basketball player. I evolved. First, I was a defensive specialist. Then, I incorporated the shot blocking, and then I threw the dunking and jump shooting into the mix. I came up with a dominating, exterminating, germinating, postulating machine." With somewhat less fanfare, you'll be asked in this scenario to think about definitions, including the traits and behaviors that constitute your selling persona. Ideally, being a good listener is among them.

Get and Give Definitions

You: I know you can spare me only 10 or 15 minutes this morning, Bob, so let me tell you what I'd like to do.

Prospect: Fire away.

Notes: It's clear you're planning to use your time well. The prospect will appreciate it. You've obtained tacit permission in just a few seconds to determine the flow of the conversation. Don't lose the edge you've acquired. From this point on, work your plan, which includes both giving and getting definitions, both asking questions and listening for answers.

Give-Definition Strategy

You: I'd like to tell you what our company regards as a successful sale: one that meets or possibly exceeds the client's need.

Prospect: That's admirable. I guess you'll need to know what we need. Right?

You: Right! First, though, let me ask you this: How would you define a successful meeting?

Get-Definition Strategy

Prospect: One that ends on time! Around here, we spend hours agreeing on a single sentence and then someone moves to delete the whole darn paragraph! We file out angry, frustrated, and stressed out.

You: Any other element you'd include in your definition of a successful meeting?

Prospect: I suppose it's one where people understand and agree to do some things before the next meeting.

Give-Definition Strategy

You: At Meetings'R'Us, we provide an audiotape that guarantees successful meetings, provided people listen to the tape and then commit to do five things: distribute an agenda in advance, with time allocations beside each agenda item; appoint a topic monitor; appoint a time monitor; summarize; and assign action items for the next meeting. These are the elements that constitute success.

Prospect: Are you saying we'd actually get things done if we did these five things?

You: You heard me right. You have a need to stop wasting time with unsuccessful meetings. We can satisfy that need with our set of five half-hour audiotapes.

Strategies

The strategies in this scenario are simple ones: the Give-Definition and the Get-Definition strategies. You'll both *give* and *get definitions* of three elements: your intent, your product, and the prospect's need. Although these particular elements are illustrated here, there are many other possible elements for which you can both give and get definition(s) in the selling you do. Don't limit yourself. Rather, be on a continual quest for greater clarity with each of your prospects.

Further Considerations

Top salespeople know how many barriers can stand in the way of getting the message the prospect is trying to send you. Those barriers include physical, emotional, physiological, intellectual, lexical, and psychological factors, among many others. You have to work hard to keep these distractions at bay in order to let the words sent your way actually get into your ears and then into your mind.

Keep a list of words that are emotionally charged for you. Then work to lessen their impact on you. If you can't maintain some neutrality, you're going to miss some of what people are saying to you.

Certain visual aids can supplement the words you're using so that your prospect can both see and hear what you're talking about. Use them, but use them sparingly and only after you've supplied your prospect with a general definition of what your product or service can do for him.

WHAT THE RESEARCH SHOWS

Research conducted by Herbert Greenberg, president and CEO of Caliper, shows that the best salespeople have the ability to understand the viewpoint of other people. Definitions will help you achieve such understanding.

EXPERIENCE SHOWS

It's been said that the planting and cultivating—not the harvesting—are what brings the crop to fruition. For salespeople, it's the time spent in the preliminary work— not the minutes needed for the close—that determines successful sales calls. The careful definition of needs is an integral part of the preliminary work.

INSIGHTS

Author Charles Roth has harsh words for nonclosers: "Salespeople who cannot close sales are not salespeople; they are merely conversationalists." Certainly, definitions make a significant contribution to the sales exchange, but they should always play a secondary role to the overall goal of closing the sale. Use them not to converse but to close.

Ask Yourself

- How would I define what I do?

- What are some definitions related to work or life or selling that I believe in?

- Am I comfortable asking a prospect to define his problem?

- Once I have a definition, do I usually try to deepen it by asking myself, "How would my boss define this? my biggest prospect? my major competitor?"

- How would I define good listening?

- When I hear a prospect make critical remarks about my product or my company, do I immediately become defensive? Or, do I listen for root causes?

Dialog 8

When the Customer Speaks, the Employee Listens

Scenario

Ever since H. Gordon Selfridge announced that "the customer is always right" with a sign displayed in his newly opened store, salespeople and customer servers have had a high standard to live up to. His philosophy has led us to regard the customer as both boss and king. In this scenario, you'll be encouraged to treat the customer with the same deference you'd extend to your boss. (Ideally, that same deference is what you extend to everyone with whom you come in contact.) And, just as you wouldn't hesitate to respectfully contradict something you heard a boss or co-worker or family member say, you shouldn't hesitate to correct or contradict a customer who's laboring under erroneous information. In terms of information, the customer is not always right.

When the Customer Speaks, the Employee Listens

You: Do you have any questions about what I've presented so far, Mr. Jackson?

Prospect: No, I understand that men don't really have a choice when it comes to formal wear. It's either wear the tuxedo or stay home.

Notes: It's good that you've paused in your presentation to find out if you and the customer are accurately hearing each other. However, in doing so, you've opened the door, and he's walked through it, spouting an opinion that could actually cost you your sale. Because you're unwilling to make a sale based on deceit, you're going to correct him at this point.

Object Strategy

You: Actually, I may have given you the wrong impression. And, at the risk of losing a sale, I must tell you that the tuxedo is certainly the most popular option, but there are other ways to achieve that formal look.

Prospect: Something that would make me look like less of a fool?

You: Actually, if everyone else is wearing a tuxedo, you'd probably want to do the same thing. Otherwise, even though other attire is appropriate, you'd stand out, I'm afraid. We sell only tuxedos, but I could give you the names of stores that deal in other formal wear.

Correct Strategy

Prospect: Ruffled shirts and powder-blue chiffon are just not part of my persona.

You: Actually, we recommend the classic look, with a single-breasted notched label and a simple bow tie.

Prospect: Do I have to wear a shawl like that blond-haired movie star does?

You: It's an option, but, again, we prefer the simple classic look in a lightweight wool.

Prospect: Why lightweight? The wind chill factor is 20 below zero out there.

Connect Strategy

You: Buying a tuxedo may strike you as a waste of money when you could rent one at a third of the cost. But if you wear the tux three times in your lifetime, you'll spend less money than you would on rentals. And, if it's lightweight wool, you could wear it whenever a formal occasion arises—no matter what the season.

Prospect: What if the one I choose goes out of style?

You: We recommend the classic look for a reason—it never goes out of style. Try this on. If it fits, you can take it today. If it needs alteration, we can get it to you by Wednesday, well in advance of your daughter's wedding.

Strategies

Here, the customer has expressed a belief that is clearly inaccurate. In the Object strategy, you'll *object* in the most diplomatic of terms. Then you'll use the Correct strategy to *correct* the inaccuracy by providing the correct information. Avoid excesses and a preachy tone when you do this. Finally, you'll use the record you've just set straight as a selling point, and with the Connect strategy you'll *connect* it to the reason why the customer should buy from you at this time.

Further Considerations

Acknowledge the incorrect assumption before setting out to correct it. You can use a phrase such as "Many people believe that" or "If I heard you correctly, you're saying ..." or "It's easy to see why you would think that."

Just because you've been granted an appointment, don't make the mistake of assuming your client is interested in your product and your product alone. Obviously, his statement (correct or incorrect) regarding your product is one measure of interest, but you'll want to work hard at widening, heightening, and deepening that interest.

Think about a specific step you could include in your sales presentations to help ensure that you not take for granted the client's interest in your product. Write that improvement in the form of a pledge and then recite that pledge to yourself just before calling or calling upon a customer.

Ask Yourself

- Has my discomfort at correcting a customer lessened over the years?

- Have I ever had a customer correct me regarding information about my product?

- What do I do to restrain myself when the customer has pushed the limits of propriety?

- How often do I turn a deaf ear to customer complaints?

- Do I typically filter what the prospect is saying?

Chapter 6

Moving Past the Stall

According to Dr. Maxwell Maltz, stalls should never happen—not if you've qualified the prospect, framed your product in the conditions most conducive to a sale, and carefully prepared your pitch. Unfortunately, like the bride or bridegroom with last-minute reservations, the prospect sometimes gets the same jitters—no matter how carefully you've planned your techniques. When this happens, you're facing a "stall": a sudden hesitation on your prospect's part, a fear (articulated or not) that she may be making the wrong decision. This fear causes her to pull back and proceed no further with the potential sale.

What causes the jitters? Let us count the possibilities:

- Fear of commitment

- Doubts about value of the product or service

- Suspicion that the salesperson cannot be trusted

- Memory of earlier purchasing mistake

- Concern that purchase may not be needed after all

By understanding the nature of the stall, you can often anticipate the objections and overcome them before they turn into concrete refusals. That's one general thing you can do. Another is to talk to those who have given you concrete refusals in the past. Try to learn why your approach didn't succeed. You can also talk to those master salespersons whose prospects never get to the concrete-refusal stage, those consummate professionals for whom prospects are like putty in their hands.

In specific terms, you can study the eight scripts in this chapter and apply the lessons in them to your own techniques for changing the prospect's objection to your objective—namely, closing the sale. In the first dialog, you'll learn to forestall the objection or take the offensive so that you can avoid getting defensive. Next, you'll learn some techniques for directing the sales exchange toward your goal. In the third dialog, you'll engage in some fancy verbal footwork as you circumvent the objections your prospect may be proposing. Sometimes, as in the fourth dialog, empathy can lead to a close, especially if your overtures are sincere.

On occasion, you can turn around a prospect's objections and have her actually agree with your answers to the objections. We'll show you how that's done in the fifth dialog. Another strategy that works is to engage your prospect in a leadership move, using your product or service as leverage. In the seventh dialog, you'll learn ways to offset some common stalls. In the final one, you'll learn strategies for substantiating both your claims and the prospect's jitters.

Dialog 1

Forestalling Objections

Scenario

Good lawyers, debaters, lobbyists, and arguers know that by introducing a "negative" before your opponent does, you can often lessen its impact. You might even be able to convert that negative to a positive. In this scenario, you anticipate that your prospect might object not to price or to the value on which the price is based, but to the time required to take full advantage of the product—a publication devoted to good health in general and good heart health in particular.

Strategies

You'll employ the Three-A technique as you forestall the objection. In the Anticipate strategy, you *anticipate* the objection in advance of the telephone or in-person pitch. Then, using the Admit strategy, you'll *admit* the objection has some merit. Finally, with the Assure strategy, you'll *assure* the prospect that her good health is more important than anything else and that your product can enhance it.

Further Considerations

Experiment with a number of different hooks. Ask other salespeople what works for them. Pay attention to the hooks that telemarketers use on you. Then narrow your list to a dozen that you think will work best for you. Try them out to learn which work most effectively. Use those for several months and then replace the least successful of the three with a new one you'd like to try out. Do this four times a year.

INSIGHTS

"Successful salesmanship is 90 percent preparation and 10 percent presentation" (*Salemanship: Practices and Problems*, McGraw-Hill, 1958). The proof of author Bertrand Canfield's words will be found in the "pudding" of your successful closes. Once you've honed your basic approach through preparation and empirical feedback, you'll be able to use that successful combination of words and actions over and over again.

WHAT THE EXPERTS SAY

Author and self-proclaimed super-salesman Jay Abraham encourages salespeople to dangle the freebie carrot in front of inactive accounts. With a metaphorical carrot such as a welcome-back certificate, you can make passive customers become active again. Accompany the freebie offer with a sincere letter that asks for their business.

Forestalling Objections

You: Good morning, Mrs. Heathcote. I'm Sue Williams with LifeLabs. I'd like to ask you a question.

↓

Prospect: I'm sorry, I don't have time for this.

↓

You: Just one question, and you don't even have to give me an answer.

Notes: In this very brief exchange, you've learned the prospect is busy. She's made it clear you won't even get to the stall stage. She's ready to end the conversation right now. You replied with a hook. While the prospect is wondering why you'd ask a question if you don't want an answer, you're busy getting the question out.

Anticipate Strategy

Prospect: Why ask if you don't want an answer?

↓

You: Because I want you to answer yourself, not me. Here's the question: Do you suffer from excess stress, low energy, shortness of breath, varicose veins, anxiety, poor circulation, or high cholesterol?

↓

Prospect: I don't think that's any of your business.

↓

Admit Strategy

You: Exactly. That's why I don't want the answer. I want you to give yourself the answer.

↓

Prospect: What if the answer is yes?

↓

You: If it is, I'd like to offer you a free trial subscription to *LifeLong*, a new publication dedicated to helping people live healthier and longer lives. We focus on natural health, but not exclusively. We have articles from leading doctors and scientists explaining the latest medical discoveries.

↓

Prospect: I'm very busy, too busy to read.

Assure Strategy

You: Mrs. Heathcote, nothing's more important than your health. Every 34 seconds, someone in this country dies of a heart attack. You don't want to be one of the statistics.

Reading a magazine like *LifeLong* could prevent you from becoming one of the 70 percent of Americans who will be affected by this grim disease.

↓

Prospect: What if I find I don't have time for it or that it's not very useful?

↓

You: I hope you will make time for it. But if you can't, you've lost nothing. It's a trial subscription, so all you have to do is let us know after three months that you don't want to continue.

Study television and print ads to learn which hooks are most effective. Transfer the concepts to your opening lines.

Look at worst-case scenarios in order to turn your sales exchanges into best-case outcomes.

Ask Yourself

- When was the last time I tweaked my opening?

- Do I typically use a hook?

- What words hook me?

- On those occasions when a salesperson has succeeded in effecting a mind change, what did she say that moved me from no to yes?

Dialog 2

Directing the Sales Interaction

Scenario

Researchers like Hans Selye have found there's only one thing that causes stress—the feeling that we are no longer in control. People who go through life feeling more victim than victor have essentially succumbed to the belief that things are no longer in their control. The stress associated with believing that you no longer control your own destiny is overwhelming. You can apply this research to the dynamics between yourself and a prospect by controlling the direction of the interaction. Not only do you save time, but you also save your sales effort.

In this scenario, the prospect is a garrulous catalog enthusiast. If you're not careful, she'll emote for an hour without making a purchase. It's a different kind of stall, but it's still a stall.

Strategies

Try using the Relate, Inflate, and Update strategies for keeping the conversation on target. First, express your feelings, paralleling her own. *Relate* to her, using the product's quality as the common denominator. Then *inflate* her ego a bit by connecting what she's told you to the product's place in her life. Finally, at a later time, *update* her by letting her know about specials she might be interested in.

BE CAREFUL

There's a difference between being in control and being a control freak. If you feel a need to control every conversation, you're closer to the latter category than the former. Control only those conversations that veer from your intended goal (no matter who's doing the veering).

EXPERIENCE SHOWS

Spend some time doing research into economic trends and buying patterns. Study demographics, for example, to learn who's likely to be your next customer. It needn't be extensive or expensive, but, combined with your experience and your intuition, you can find potentially lucrative opportunities. This is the advice of *Issues and Answers in Sales Management* ("That Vision Thing," September 11, 2000, page 5).

Directing the Sales Interaction

You: Mrs. Pike? This is Mary Ellen with the *Family Facts* magazine. You received our catalog?

Prospect: I not only received it, I loved it. Every day I go back and look through it again, cover to cover. I just can't make up my mind. Of course, I've always been known as an indecisive person. Maybe that's because I'm a Gemini, but then my sister's just as indecisive as I am and she's a Leo, so you really can never tell.

Notes: The good news is that the prospect likes the product. The bad news is that she's both talkative and indecisive, so you'll have to take charge of the conversation before it eats up time as well as profit for you.

Relate Strategy

You: I know exactly what you mean. So many great gifts, so little money. I wish I could buy them all. Which one, though, did you like best?

Prospect: Well now, I don't like to think of myself as a selfish person, but there were five things I'd really like to have. Of course, I saw many things I could get for my husband, but he usually gets his own things and doesn't even wonder if there's anything I'd like. I'm not saying he's self-centered, of course, just that he's typically unaware of any need but his own.

You: Well, there's nothing wrong with being self-indulgent once in a while. Which were the five things you liked best?

Prospect: That browning plate for the microwave is terrific. I'm so tired of taking out bland food every time I open that little white door. And all my life, I've wanted an electric pencil sharpener. It's not that I'm a writer or anything, but I like things that are crisp and clear. Can't stand a dull pencil any more than I can stand a dull man. Now you may be picking up that I'm a neat and tidy person. And you'd be right.

That's why I just loved the Clip/Collect nail cutter. Don't you just hate it when your toenail clippings fall all over the floor? Here's my next one. Up here in

Montana, we face winters that make Siberia look like paradise. And I just hate having to get up early every morning to scrape the ice off my car windshield. That snow shield cover you have on page 42 is just fantastic for snow bunnies like me.

You: That's four so far, Mrs. Pike. What else?

Prospect: Well, that cherub blanket on page 84 would be great on a cold night. I can just see myself snuggling under it with a cup of hot cocoa and a good book.

You: What about Mr. Pike?

Prospect: No way I'd let him under that blanket with me!

You: No, I meant what about any items you'd like to order for him?

Prospect: Not today. He's in the doghouse.

continues

Directing the Sales Interaction (continued)

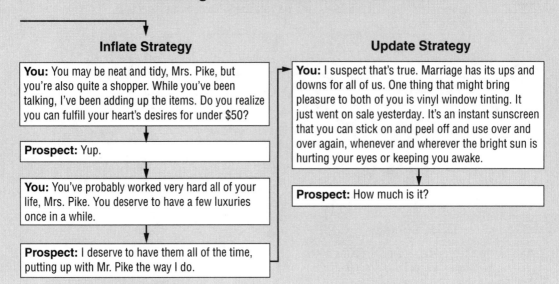

Inflate Strategy

You: You may be neat and tidy, Mrs. Pike, but you're also quite a shopper. While you've been talking, I've been adding up the items. Do you realize you can fulfill your heart's desires for under $50?

Prospect: Yup.

You: You've probably worked very hard all of your life, Mrs. Pike. You deserve to have a few luxuries once in a while.

Prospect: I deserve to have them all of the time, putting up with Mr. Pike the way I do.

Update Strategy

You: I suspect that's true. Marriage has its ups and downs for all of us. One thing that might bring pleasure to both of you is vinyl window tinting. It just went on sale yesterday. It's an instant sunscreen that you can stick on and peel off and use over and over again, whenever and wherever the bright sun is hurting your eyes or keeping you awake.

Prospect: How much is it?

WHAT THE EXPERTS SAY

According to author Allan Boress (*The "I Hate Selling" Book*, AMACOM, 1995), the "sales saints" avoid cardinal sins. First, they know when a sale's been closed. (The sinners do not.) Second, they ask questions instead of making assumptions. Finally, they avoid giving away too much. You have to listen closely to determine when the sale has been closed and when the prospect, like the one in the "Directing the Sales Interaction" scenario, is merely waxing effusively with no intention of buying.

Further Considerations

Just as there are window-shoppers with no desire to buy, there are product-line lovers content to "ooh" and "ahh." Qualify your lead before investing too much time with her, as gratifying as it may be to hear your product extolled.

Prepare an outline of where you'd like the dialog to go so that you can refer to it throughout the conversation and ensure you're on target.

When prospects purchase personal items (as opposed to business-related items), they're more likely to respond to emotional probes on your part. Consider familiar words like *comfort, pleasure, attractiveness, fun, pride,* and so on. Relate these terms to the product under consideration.

Ask Yourself

- At what point does good listening become a waste of time?

- How can I control the conversation without being rude or manipulative?

- Do I use words and gestures that are friendly and encouraging to offset the appearance of needing to control the flow of the dialog?

- Do I know my product line so well that I can quickly suggest items related to or complementary to those in which the prospect has indicated an interest?

Dialog 3

Circumventing Obstacles

Scenario

"Circumvent" literally means to "come around." When you move a prospect from mild interest to enough-interest-to-consider-the-purchase and then to the actual close, you've persuaded her to come around to your point of view. You've convinced her that the item in question will improve her life or her job.

In this situation, you've made the appointment: You're meeting a busy client for lunch in hopes of persuading her to use your travel agency for a cruise she's planning. You're determined that it's time to move along the interest continuum without getting stalled at the midway point.

> **WHAT THE RESEARCH SHOWS**
>
> Advertisements that contain the word "you" pull in more responses than those that don't. Take this information and run with it. Use the word "you" repeatedly in your telephone, written, and face-to-face communications with your prospects.

> **BE CAREFUL**
>
> Don't be too effusive when you congratulate your prospect. Few things are more off-putting than excessive praise, especially if it seems exaggerated or insincere.

Circumventing Obstacles

You: What is it about a cruise that appeals to you, Chynna?

↓

Prospect: Oh, I don't know. It's partially the romance of it all, partially the intrigue of foreign cities, and maybe even the chance to be unreachable for a whole week.

Notes: You haven't heard any objection yet that you need to circumvent, but you have heard enough to know that you could use any one of the CIRC strategies. Your prospect's longing is very apparent. Capitalize on it.

Congratulate Strategy

You: You've made a decision that reflects a lot of thought. But it also reflects a lot of emotion and that's the perfect combination when selecting a vacation. There's nothing like a cruise for getting away from it all, and if you're fortunate enough to be taking it with a loved one, you'll find not only romance but also a partner with whom you can share that intrigue you mentioned.

↓

Prospect: I don't have a significant other in my life right now.

↓

You: Not to worry. You've heard of shipboard romances, haven't you? I can't promise you'll meet Mr. Wonderful, but I can promise you'll have a wonderful time meeting new people.

Inquiry Strategy

You: Which part of the world intrigues you most—the Mediterranean, the Far East, the South Sea Islands?

↓

Prospect: My family is from the Far East, but I've always wanted to see the Greek Isles. That's going to be pretty expensive, though, isn't it?

Relegate Strategy

You: Here's my advice, Chynna. A lot of people wait until they have the time and the money to take a cruise. You see them being wheeled on to the ship because they're elderly and are often confined to a wheelchair. True, they have time now and they have money. But they don't have youth. Don't wait until you're too old to enjoy the cruise fully. There are many shipboard sports available; and when the ship docks, you'll certainly want to go ashore and discover new treasures, new intrigues. Now's the time to enjoy yourself.

↓

Prospect: What's the bargain-basement price?

↓

You: If you don't mind a cabin without a view, you can get a rate that's about a third less than the regular rate. And, if you can go at the last minute, you can get a rate that's a fraction of the regular rate.

Cement Strategy

You: None of us knows what the future has in store, Chynna. Why not take pleasure now, when you can? After all, you work hard for your money. Why not let it work for you?

continues

Circumventing Obstacles (continued)

> **Prospect:** What you're saying makes a lot of sense. I suppose I should.

> **You:** Chynna, I don't want to appear to be twisting your arm. Why don't you make a deposit today? It's totally refundable if you change your mind in the next two weeks. Then, in the meantime, I'd like you to call a few of our clients who've recently taken a cruise. Ask them if they're glad they did.

Strategies

You'll use the "CIRC" set of persuasion tools to circumvent the stall prompted by indecision. Any one of the four elements of this set is effective enough to get the sale for you. Depending on the various prospects you meet in a given week, though, you may want to combine one or two or even use all four as a complete set. With the **C**ongratulate strategy, you're actually appealing to the pride factor. You're complimenting the individual for some success she's achieved on her own terms. An alternative is to use the **I**nquiry strategy. You'll learn as much as you can about the prospect's hopes and wishes. Another possibility is the **R**elegate strategy in which you relegate concerns to a secondary or tertiary position. Finally, you could cement the sale with the **C**ement strategy by assuring your prospect she deserves to have what she wants. (Don't we all?)

> **INSIGHTS**
>
> Jim Dickie, managing partner for Boulder, Colorado–based Insight Technology Group maintains that you have to be prepared, you have to know not only your prospect but also your prospect's needs and product and operations. (*Objections*, "Sales No Longer Just a Game of Lowest Price," The Dartnell Corporation, Sample Issue, page 1) That's why it's so important to have a strategy such as the CIRC plan in place before you meet your prospect. If you do, you can direct the flow of the dialog directly toward a win-win outcome.

Further Considerations

Make continuous improvements in your listening skills. Ask others to critique you for a full week. Don't become defensive when they offer feedback. Instead, duly note it and vow to use it.

When you're ready for the Cement strategy, remember to use the information you obtained at the beginning of the dialog. Doing so reinforces the prospect's inclination and gently pushes her closer to the close.

In using the Relegate strategy, be sensitive. You don't want to seem as if you're dismissing concerns. Rather, you want to show the prospect how those concerns should, if only occasionally, take a backseat to the prospect's well-being.

Ask Yourself

- How much do I know about our customers?

- Can I typify them?

- What do they regard as our product's weakness? Its strength?

- Would our internal assessments match the customers' assessments?

Dialog 4

Empathize

Scenario

"Differentiate or die!" This admonition from marketing expert Jack Trout requires the salesperson to get her creative juices flowing in order to set herself and her product apart from the competition. That's exactly what you'll do in this scenario, as you work to tele-sell your company's training programs to a corporate client.

Strategies

You'll find two pairs of examples here in which you differentiate yourself and your product by using first the Manipulative strategy and then the Nonmanipulative strategy. As we've noted before, today's prospects are increasingly more savvy. They won't be pushed, prodded, or propelled forward unless they wish to be. In the examples shown in this dialog, you'll deviate from the traditional opening or closing methods in order to deal more openly with the prospect. In each nonmanipulative example, you'll see how *empathy*—a sincere understanding of the prospect's situation—is extended. It replaces the use of fear and competitor denigration found in the manipulative examples.

Further Considerations

Spend some time researching current users of your product and users of products similar to yours. Ask them what they consider to be the most satisfying and the most dissatisfying aspects of their experience with the product. Use that knowledge to prepare a pitch for a new prospect.

WHAT THE EXPERTS SAY
According to David Ringlein, president of HealthFirst Services in Lansing, Michigan, you should maintain a positive attitude toward negative responses. When he hears an objection, Ringlein replies positively with a phrase like, "I'm glad you said that." He then acknowledges the concern by saying something like, "I felt that way myself when I first heard about this service. But, since subscribing, I realize the savings far outweigh the cost."

EXPERIENCE SHOWS
Yes, you should empathize. But make certain your product is speaking for itself and that your personality is not overwhelming the sales interaction. That's the advice of CEO and author Harvey Mackay (*Swim with the Sharks*, William Morrow and Company, 1988, page 57).

Empathize

You: If you have a moment, I'd like to tell you about a new program we've developed: "Quick Wits."

Prospect: We have a similar program we're already using.

Notes: It sounds like an objection, doesn't it? But it tells you that the prospect's company has an interest in this topic, and it gives you the opportunity to distinguish yourself from your competitor.

Manipulative Strategy #1

You: I suspect it can't compare to ours. Does it, for example, address the legal ramifications of casual references to age?

Prospect: *(Fearfully.)* No, it doesn't.

Nonmanipulative Strategy #1

You: How satisfied are you with the program you're using now?

Prospect: We like it, but it's more theory than practice.

You: It sounds like you're familiar with the statistic that only 15 percent of what people learn in training programs, apart from computer training, is ever applied back at the worksite.

Prospect: Actually, I wasn't familiar with that statistic, but I know if people don't practice, they don't retain knowledge.

Manipulative Strategy #2

You: I'll bet it's the one put out by XYZoom, isn't it? Did you know there are rumors that they're going bankrupt?

Prospect: Oh, no. We've just signed a two-year contract with them.

Nonmanipulative Strategy #2

You: The other products we've seen are actually very good. What do you like best about the program you're currently using?

Prospect: Well, it's not just classroom lecture, but there's a concerted effort to make the learning ongoing.

You: May I ask how they do that?

Prospect: Apparently, there are team leaders appointed during the session who are asked to meet with small groups of participants on a regular basis to discuss what was learned.

You: That's excellent. We do something similar but, in addition, we encourage immediacy.

Prospect: Meaning what?

You: We send two second reminder e-mails to all participants for 30 days following the class. There's no additional charge for this.

Ask Yourself

- How carefully have I studied the competition?

- Have I found the best words for touting our product without denigrating competing products?

- What examples of manipulative selling have I encountered this week?

- How did I feel once I realized what was being done?

WHAT THE RESEARCH SHOWS

Robert Montgomery, author of *Get High on Yourself*, maintains that every product has a story, and if it doesn't, it has no right to exist. "Salesmanship," he explains, "is telling that story." If you're not intimately familiar with your product's story, learn as much as you can, as soon as you can.

Dialog 5

Turn Around the Objection

Scenario

Recent presidential candidates have provided us with a good example of turning things around. One candidate assured voters that considerable progress had been made on several counts. But he promised even more. "You ain't seen nothing yet!" he declared enthusiastically.

His opponent managed to take the phrase and turn it around. He reminded voters that in terms of certain reforms in Washington, "You ain't seen nothing yet," implying that no progress had been made in all this time.

EXPERIENCE SHOWS

It's important to have product knowledge, of course, but you can have too much of a good thing. Avoid relying excessively on features and not enough on people. Instead of spending too much time singing the praises of your product, concentrate on the needs of your client.

The Turn Around the Objection Script moves you and your prospect past the stall by taking an objection and turning it around until it becomes a selling point in the buyer's eyes. Rather than ignore the objection or moving around it, you'll use the objection itself as leverage for selling the buyer.

Turn Around the Objection

You: Good morning, Mrs. Santiago. I'm Marcia from Cut'n'Carve.

Prospect: Pardon me?

You: I'm Marcia from Cut'n'Carve. We sell kitchen knives.

Prospect: We have all we need!

Notes: The phrase "Pardon me?" can be used if someone has not heard or understood an earlier comment. But, it can also be used to suggest superiority or an absolute lack of interest. You've done well to get immediately to the point: telling the prospect exactly what your company does. Unfortunately, the description has led her to conclude that she doesn't need what you have to offer. You'll capitalize on the word need now.

Word Strategy

You: Do you need to carve the turkey for the upcoming holidays?

Prospect: Of course, but we have a carving knife.

You: Is it fully tanged?

Herd Strategy

Prospect: What do you mean?

You: Does the blade run the full length of the handle, or does it go only a little way into the handle?

Prospect: Now how would I know that?

You: How does the knife feel in your hand? Does it feel solid? Does it stay firm and not slip? How sharp is your knife? If turkey carving isn't an art, it's at least an important part of your family's get-together. You need a good knife to have a good carve.

Gird Strategy

Prospect: You're making it sound as if the knife is more important than the turkey.

You: At Cut'n'Carve, we think it's just as important. You wouldn't serve your Thanksgiving meal on chipped china. You wouldn't serve beverages in fruit jars. And, ideally, you won't carve the turkey with anything less than the finest instrument.

Prospect: And just how much does this fine instrument cost?

You: When you consider it has a lifetime guarantee, you realize that the cost of $29.99 is very reasonable. And, we're offering a holiday special. If you order today, we'll send you a five-year supply of sharpening stones and directions for sharpening the blade. We also provide directions for carving. It can be done incorrectly, you know. In fact, every year, about 800 Americans wind up in emergency rooms as a result of poor carving techniques.

Prospect: Is that a scare tactic?

You: Not at all. It's a precaution we like to share with our customers by showing them the best way to carve and the best way to serve. For example, did you know you should allow the turkey to cool for about a half hour before carving?

continues

Turn Around the Objection (continued)

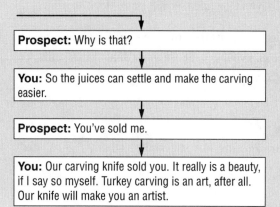

Prospect: Why is that?

You: So the juices can settle and make the carving easier.

Prospect: You've sold me.

You: Our carving knife sold you. It really is a beauty, if I say so myself. Turkey carving is an art, after all. Our knife will make you an artist.

Strategies

You'll use the Word, Herd, and Gird strategies, in this order. First, isolate the *word(s)* that contains the essence of the objection—it's the word "need" in the following. Once you've identified it, you'll *herd* it and related thoughts into a compelling argument. You'll bring a close to the meeting or telephone pitch by *girding,* or enclosing, the argument with some incontrovertible or hard-to-resist points.

Further Considerations

Time yourself with each call you make, especially the successful ones. The more quickly you can close a sale, the better it is for both you and your prospect—assuming, of course, that you're not forcing them into a direction that does not benefit them.

If you work from a script, force yourself to deviate from it to keep it sounding fresh. Few things are more distasteful than a rehearsed or canned speech. And, if

WHAT THE EXPERTS SAY

Master salesman Tom Hopkins advises immediately creating a "Positive Expectancy." That is, you get to the point immediately with a question or statement that hints of benefits to come.

BE CAREFUL

Don't waste time with inanities like, "How are you today?" It's obvious you don't really care how the person is—she's a stranger, after all. The false sincerity turns prospects off. Plus, it wastes precious time. "Do you have a few minutes?" is equally inane. Further, you run the risk of having the prospect say "No" and hang up. Instead, try a more direct declarative statement ("I'd like a few minutes of your time to tell you about a special we're running") or a question related to the purpose of your call ("Are you satisfied with the quality of the copies your copier produces?").

your prospect asks you to stop reading or asks a question you haven't covered, you'll be in deep trouble.

Try using references to family and holidays as a way to engage your prospect, or tie your sales pitch into seasonal events.

Ask Yourself

- How attuned am I to the words people use?

- How well do I think on my feet?

- Do I practice moving past the stall by having colleagues offer objections in simulated sales exchanges?

- Do I pay attention to turnarounds used by others, whether or not they're salespeople?

- What percentage of the meeting time do I spend talking?

Dialog 6

Leading the Way to a Successful Sale

Scenario

Author John R. Graham (*The New Magnet Marketing*, Chandle House, Worcheser, MA, 1998) believes there's a danger associated with assuming you know more than your customers do. He also believes we can be overconfident about the trust customers may have in us.

You hold these beliefs to be self-evident. Consequently, in this scenario, you're eager to emphasize the relationship aspect of your beliefs as you introduce your product, wedding rings, to recently engaged couples. You read the social columns faithfully and use them as a source of qualified leads.

Leading the Way to a Successful Sale

You: Good morning, Wanda. I'm Felicia from Bluell's Jewels. I saw your engagement notice in the paper this weekend, and I'm hoping you'll stop by so we can show you our wedding rings.

Prospect: No, thanks. We're getting them from the same place we got our engagement rings.

Notes: You still have about 15 seconds to interest your prospect. Since you've anticipated this reply, you have your next questions ready. Fire away.

Educate Strategy

You: When you purchased your engagement ring, did the salesperson tell you about the four C's?

Prospect: Yes, I know all about that. Cut, color, clarity, and ….

You: Carat. Were you thinking of a round diamond or an oval one, a pear or a princess, a trillion or a heart-shaped, an emerald or a marquise cut?

Prospect: To tell you the truth, I wasn't thinking. I was just planning to buy one that "spoke" to me, if you know what I mean.

You: I know exactly what you mean. And it's important that you buy what you like. But it's also important that you know what you're buying.

Prospect: Well, which one gives off the most light?

Notes: The prospect's reply, "I was just planning to …," suggests that she is willing to change her mind. Be alert to such clues. Ask questions that will lead you to the prospect's needs or desires, in this case, a diamond that rivals the gleam on the chrome bumper of a '61 Cadillac.

Induct Strategy

You: We have some very beautiful wedding rings here, but the ones that sparkle most are the round diamonds. That's because they have 58 facets to them, which act like tiny prisms. They reflect the light, but only if the cut is an ideal one, neither too shallow, nor too deep. All our diamond cutters learned their cutting techniques in South Africa.

Why don't you stop by soon? If you decide to purchase a round diamond and if you mention that you spoke to Felicia on October 2, we'll give you a 10 percent discount. In addition, you'll have certification from the GIA—that's the Gemological Institute of America—telling what the diamond's grade and evaluation are. Sparkle, savings, and certification—you'll get all three when you buy your wedding ring at Bluell's Jewels.

Prospect: How long have you been in business?

You: That's another reason to come here: security. My great-grandfather started the business 113 years ago. We've been serving our community ever since, and we have a triple A rating from the Chamber of Commerce.

Strategies

You make calls inviting couples whose engagement notices you have read to visit your store. Your strategy requires considerable creativity and persuasion because most of them are inclined to purchase the wedding ring from the same place where they bought the engagement ring. To win them over, you'll use the Educate strategy to lead them via a literal definition of *educate:* to lead out (out of ignorance). Then you'll wrap up the commitment using the Induct strategy. You'll use an inductive approach to lead the prospect into the sale.

Further Considerations

Continuous improvement became the mission of quality-dominated organizations in the 1990s. Fortunately, it's a mantra that continues to be heard into the new millennium. Periodically, ask yourself (and others) how you can distinguish yourself from the competition. How can you treat prospects better, faster, more intelligently, in order to gain a competitive advantage?

Consider holding a meeting modeled in the format of a focus group. Have a moderator ask questions about the company, the product, the methods used to sell it. An observer will take notes. (If possible, the session should also be videotaped.) Afterwards, analyze the replies to uncover successful techniques, assess motivation levels, and determine whether any problems have been brought up.

In a reversal of prevalent wisdom, some of the most successful salespeople know that they simply have to work harder, not necessarily smarter, to come out ahead. How hard do you work at being the best? Working smarter may simplify certain processes, may streamline certain practices, may separate efficient work from effective work. But, the fact remains, that nothing replaces good, old-fashioned hard work.

Ask Yourself

- Have I ever met a customer or potential customer who knew more about my product than I did?

- When was the last time a customer called to tell me my product/service had made a difference in her life?

- On a scale of 1 to 10, how innovative are my lead-generating techniques?

- Do I appeal to emotions, rely on facts, or use a combination of the two?

> ### WHAT THE EXEMPLARS DO
>
> Several years ago, Hal Becker was named Xerox's number-one salesperson—at the age of 22! He reminds us of the importance of paraphrasing customers' objections or concerns. By restating their point, you show you understand it. Having understood it, you can move the dialog to the next level, at which you overcome the concern.

Dialog 7

Offset Negatives in the Selling Equation

Scenario

Master salespeople distinguish between objections and conditions. According to Nancy Stephens, author of *Streetwise Selling,* objections are "temporary reasons for not buying, often because the prospective customer is either skeptical or unclear about your product or service." Conditions, she says, are things that are real and over which you have no control.

For example, if a respected colleague leaves your company and takes her big account with her, there's little hope for you to claim that account as your own now. The best you can do is prime the prospect-pump so that when conditions change, you'll be in a good position to win the client over.

- Maintain good, if casual, relationships with the prospect.

- Let the prospect know you'd like to have her business if and when the opportunity presents itself.

Offset Negatives in the Selling Equation

You: Hi, Sally. This is Tina Williams with Pro-Line Products. How are you today?

Prospect: Too busy to talk to you.

Notes: Lawyers know you never ask a question to which you don't know the answer. Good salespeople know you don't ask a question that can be answered with a rude response and a hang-up. (We've already cautioned against the insincere inquiry.) Let's chalk up this icebreaker to a bad experience and have you start again, moving from the icebreaker to the Realize strategy.

Realize Strategy

You: Hi, Sally. This is Tina Williams with Pro-Line Products. I'm sitting here thinking about the Christmas presents I have to buy and wondering if your company gives business gifts to its best accounts.

Prospect: We do, but we buy handcrafted items from the Association for the Visually Impaired.

You: All your gifts?

Prospect: Yes, all our gifts.

You: It sounds as if you have an unshakeable commitment to the less fortunate.

Prospect: You're correct. It's unshakeable.

Recognize Strategy

You: I'd like to ask just two questions. First, have you ever asked your clients if they'd prefer a choice? Second, is there a possibility that the association might have its members offer something other than handcrafted gifts?

Prospect: No, and I don't know.

Request Strategy

You: Should either condition change—for example, should a client indicate that she'd prefer something other than a handcrafted gift this year or should the visually impaired move to a new line of products— we would certainly like to have your business. I'd like to call upon you once or twice a year to find out if things have changed.

Prospect: Fine with me.

- Send an occasional e-mail if your company is having a special offer in which the prospect might be interested.

- Establish a tickler file and call every three months or so to learn whether conditions have changed.

In this scenario, you're working to offset a condition that seems unalterable, but you're going to give it your best shot nonetheless.

Strategies

You'll use the 3-R approach, which consists of three strategies: Realize, Recognize, and Request. To begin, you'll explain that you *realize* the condition exists. Then, you'll *recognize* that the current condition is not necessarily a permanent condition. Finally, you'll make your *request* to be considered when conditions change.

Further Considerations

If you read the secrets of successful salespeople, they all discourage the adversarial approach to selling. Instead, they regard the sales process as the solving of a problem, with you and the potential buyer working as a team to find the most appropriate solution. Remind yourself of this basic strategy each time you pick up the phone or begin a meeting.

Weave in a little bit of information about your company in the first few minutes of the exchange. Not too much information, but enough to establish your credentials and those of your firm.

INSIGHTS

Jack Welch, widely known as the "manager of the century," once observed that if the rate of change outside an organization is greater than the rate of change inside that organization, it's the beginning of the end. You can use this warning to ensure that people in your own organization are aware of external forces and their potential impact on internal operations. You can also use the observation to make prospects more aware of outside changes and the ways your product can help them avoid facing the "beginning of the end."

EXPERIENCE SHOWS

Use an icebreaker, but don't waste your time or the prospect's with false pleasantries in the opening moments of a telephone prospecting call. Sharing a personal insight that helps the prospect envision you is an excellent strategy but one that should be done with a minimum of setup time.

BE CAREFUL

A good sales pitch can be used over and over. However, it must never sound trite or rehearsed. To avoid sounding stale, take a tried-and-true line and express it in 10 different ways without losing the original meaning. Do this once a week to avoid scripts that sound canned.

Force yourself to view objections as simple requests. When a prospect raises an objection, she is either misinformed about what your product offers or correctly informed but hoping to negotiate.

Ask Yourself

- Do I optimize the information sent via body language?

- Do I look for things I might have in common with the prospect or her company?

- Do I typically ask for referrals?

- Do I typically give them?

WHAT THE EXPERTS SAY

Telling a prospect to imagine her company newsletter on steroids is a visually gripping approach for a salesperson trying to sell clip-art that will make such in-house communications more appealing. You can and should think of a "sound bite" that might appeal to some of your customers. In the "Substantiate Your Product-Claims" scenario, for example, you might have said that massages are "stress eradicators in our fingertips."

EXPERIENCE SHOWS

Let your enthusiasm shine through your questions. For example, rather than ask, "Would you be interested in something like this?" instead ask, "This program would really make a difference in your productivity, wouldn't it?" Make certain your voice reflects the excitement you feel and want others to feel about your product or service.

Dialog 8

Substantiate Your Product-Claims

Scenario

Enthusiasm transforms. Girl Scouts know this and use it to their advantage as they persuade the already full-figured to buy even more fattening food. It's hard to resist someone who truly believes her product will enrich your life. (And so it will, if only in the caloric sense!) In this scenario, you're trying to sell your massage services to the director of a corporate wellness program.

Strategies

You'll employ the Fun, Stun, and Done strategies. Share your excitement first of all and let the *fun* aspect of your service captivate your prospective client. Next, *stun* her with statistics—in this case, statistics regarding the effects of stress on the workforce. Finally, close by citing what will happen once the deal is *done*.

Substantiate Your Product-Claims

You: Thank you for seeing me, Ms. Marshall. This won't take long at all. My company, R'n'R, is currently providing antistress services to 35 companies much like your own. Would you like a list of our clients?

Prospect: Not right now. I'd like to know more about what you do.

Notes: This is the dream scenario: A prospect wants to know more. Don't ruin your opportunity by talking too much about your service. Instead, cite the benefits, but also try to learn more about the client's needs. Do some consultative selling.

Fun Strategy

You: We set aside a quiet corner of the office and have employees come one at a time for 10-minute massages. If people want their arms massaged, we use hypoallergenic, perfume-free massage oils. If they just want an ordinary back rub, of course, we don't use any oils. Jazz plays very softly in the background to help drive away all stressful thoughts. The client sits in a comfortable chair and our masseuse stands behind him, using fluid, continuous movements.

These massages are such great tension relievers that people sometimes fall asleep in their chairs. That's why we serve them coffee before we let them go back to work!

Prospect: Wow! Can you give me a free demonstration right now?

Stun Strategy

You: I will, but let me ask you this first. As the director of your company's wellness program, you're familiar with the statistics related to stress. Estimates run as high as $17 billion a year, owing to mistakes, bad decisions, lost time, lower productivity, litigation costs, and other factors.

Prospect: I hadn't realized it was that high.

You: I've actually read some estimates that are even higher, but I've also read that reduction in stress translates to improvements in quality, service, and productivity—sometimes with gains as high as 50 percent.

Done Strategy

You: If we can begin next week and spend 10 minutes a week with each person on your staff, we guarantee stress levels will be reduced within a month.

Prospect: How could you possibly make that guarantee?

You: We do a pre-intervention strategy in which we ask all participants to assess their stress levels before the massage treatments begin. Then, a month later, we ask them to assess their stress levels once again. All of our accounts report improvement. Are you willing to try our program for one month? You have nothing to lose. If there is no improvement, you don't have to pay.

Further Considerations

American industrialist Henry Ford once noted, "Whether you believe you can do a thing or not, you are right." Positive thinking doesn't always equate with success, but it happens often enough for the wise salesperson to take heed. The product virtually sells itself when it has an enthusiast as an advocate, an enthusiast who believes she can sell it and that others will benefit from the sale. If you're comfortable and if your prospect is comfortable, tape-record one or two of your appointments. Analyze them afterward to determine whether your enthusiasm comes through.

Good advice is good advice, no matter how old it is. Nearly 100 years ago, Walter Dill Scott wrote about the psychology of advertising. His words have relevance for today's salesperson. He advised using habit, recentness, and vividness to make a product stand out in the mind of a potential buyer. If your product or service can be habitually associated with an experience the prospect has, the connection will work in your favor. It will work even harder if the association is recent and vivid.

Ask Yourself

- How good am I at building rapport?

- How readily do I establish trust with a new client?

- Am I flexible enough to revise my sales pitch midstream if asked an unanticipated question or if the conversation veers into areas I'd not planned for?

- Do I typically leave a sample or some reminder of my contact with the prospect?

- Are my values/my company's values clear to the prospective buyer?

"Nonverbal communications are crucial in selling because they play such an important part in determining the prospect's reaction to you and consequently to your product."
—Ken Delmar, Winning Moves: The Body Language of Selling, *Warner Books, 1984*

Chapter 7

Recognizing Signals

Don't assume you know what your customer's needs are. As long as you've been in sales, as many as you've made, you still cannot assume you know what a given prospect wants, needs, deserves, and/or desires. You have to be sensitive to the signals and be ready to change horses midstream if and when you find that your logical assumptions have an erroneous (and sometimes illogical) foundation.

Many emotions surround the buying decision—fear, insecurity, and the desire to impress, among others. By reviewing lists like the following before meeting a prospect for the first time, you'll be better positioned to recognize the signals being sent and to take advantage of their meaning. (We encourage you to add to this list as you learn from experience.)

Emotion	Signals	Your Approach
Fear	"I'm worried about …."	References: "Other clients had that same concern—but not for long!"
	"I don't think Accounting would approve this …."	"Let me show you how the widget can pay for itself in six months."

Emotion	Signals	Your Approach
Insecurity	"We've never done anything like this before."	"You've no doubt heard it said that if you always do what you've always done, you'll always get what you've always got."
	"My boss would have my head."	"If you like, I could prepare a cost justification for her."
Desire to impress	"This ties into something the boss said last week."	Benchmarks: "We've found a number of executives who endorse the theory behind this practice."

Of course, verbal signals aren't the only ones you have to listen for. You also need to watch for nonverbal signals that you're moving in the wrong direction. If you observe such signals, be prepared to switch vehicles or directions quickly.

The more common nonverbal signals are listed in the following table. Beside them are the possible interpretations. We say "possible" because there's always room for error. (Arms crossed on the chest, for example, usually means disapproval or rejection. However, it may also simply mean that the person finds the room too cold.)

Signal	Possible Interpretation
Crossing arms	Person disapproves or rejects your idea.
Rubbing face	Person is not interested.
Looking up and to the left	Person is visualizing uses for your product or service.
Looking up and to the right	Person is analyzing what you've just said.
Folding hands on stomach	Person feels threatened by you or your style.
Leaning forward in chair	Person likes what he hears.

Signal	Possible Interpretation
Touching nose	Person has decided against your proposal.
Tapping foot	Person is impatient.
Doodling	Person is bored.
Touching fingertips	Person is developing a concept, building an idea.
Removing glasses	Person is stalling.
Placing hands flat	Person is ready to do business, to make a deal.

All these signals point up the need for the successful salesperson to be a many-splendored thing; in other words, someone who has good observation skills, excellent persuasion skills, the ability to think quickly on his feet, and more.

Dialog 1

"This Is Taking Too Long"

Scenario

In this scenario, you are observing and interpreting the prospect's verbal and nonverbal signals. A signal may come from actual words: "I know all of that," for example. The signal may come from a gesture—the prospect looks at his watch. It may come from a facial expression—the prospect repeatedly opens his mouth as if to interrupt you, as if to say it's time for you to stop talking.

In such circumstances, you have to attune yourself to the signals. Once you've received them, you have to deviate from your plan. To ignore the signals, to fail to adapt to them, is to doom your chances of closing the sale.

INSIGHTS

"Keep everything simple ... but not simpler [than it has to be]." These words of wisdom from Albert Einstein apply to the salesperson who suspects his prospect is growing impatient. Have two presentations ready. Begin with the full presentation of your product/service/company, but be ready to switch to the shorter version if need be.

Strategies

You'll depend on words to respond to the prospect's signals; and you'll employ the Late, Bait, and Narrate strategies to do so. First, you'll allude to time via the Late strategy. Then you'll use the Bait strategy to entice the prospect by offering a choice. Finally, in the Narrate strategy, you'll employ your raconteur abilities to tell a story pertinent to the situation.

WHAT THE EXEMPLARS DO

Best-selling speaker and sales-author Tony Alessandra writes about the importance of determining customer needs. "The more detailed your analysis is, the better prepared your sales force will be to sell the account." He encourages questions that help you learn about the company's dreams, nightmares, goals, problems, needs, and decision-making process.

Further Considerations

Magazines and books are filled with information on body language. At least once a year, read an article or book on body language in order to keep abreast of nonverbal clues and what they may be telling you.

"This Is Taking Too Long"

You: I know you have quite a bit of responsibility on your shoulders, Phil, having to order supplies for the entire organization. We can make it easy for you. As a Dividend Customer, you'll receive electronic updates on a monthly basis—news about specials we're running, new products, and coupons for discounts.

Prospect: I don't know whether that would make my life more or less complicated.

Notes: You have your first signal right here. The prospect sounds overworked and is looking for ways to streamline his work life. Sending more e-mail may not appeal. If you're sensitive to his signals, you'll pick up on the clues and adapt accordingly.

Late Strategy

You: Oh, can we ever uncomplicate your life! For one thing, we can customize your account so that you'll receive notices only about the products or services you've ordered in the past. For example, our records show that you or someone from your company visits our Shipping Center on an average of twice a month. As you know, this is a timesaver, because while you're getting the supplies you need in the aisles, our well-trained staff is getting your packages ready to go out in same-day mail. It doesn't matter how bulky or how small the package is. We pack it in the right size box with a guarantee of no breakage. Then we ship it. You can stop by when you're through filling your shopping cart, and we'll give you a receipt and another guarantee: on-time delivery.

(Noticing a signal of impatience.) Well, enough about our Shipping Center. What help would you like us to give you?

Prospect: Well, since it's the last quarter of the year, I'd like to give the whole staff a gift that will increase their productivity. Do you carry day planners that will keep us all organized?

Bait Strategy

You: We carry a wide range, including the well-known brand, priced at $29.95, and our store brand, on sale this month for $19.95. For every 10 of ours that you order, you'll receive a coupon for $10 off your order in the Shipping Center.

Prospect: How good is the generic brand?

You: Personally, I think it's better than the nationally recognized one. Ours has zip code and area code information listed in the back and weekly motivational quotes. The other doesn't. Feature for feature, we have everything they have and then some. I use it myself.

Narrate Strategy

You: *(Noticing the prospect is starting to straighten papers on his desk, as if he needs to get back to work.)* Phil, I think the day planner is a great gift. Do you know about Ivy Lee? *(You see that his head is down, and he's shaking it as if to say, "I don't know and I don't care.")* Mr. Lee increased productivity by 30 percent at Bethlehem Steel with a mere four words: "Things to do today." We use those four words on each page of our day planner. Now, how big is your staff?

Periodically, try to typify the customers you serve and would like to serve. Ask questions such as, "What general needs do specific customer types have?" "What specific needs do these groups have?" "What specific needs do specific individuals within these groups have?" "Might some of these needs apply to others as well?"

Your product or service and the features and benefits associated with it are already well-defined. But definitions need revision from time to time. Brainstorm alone or with others to find additional reasons why customers should buy from you instead of your competitors.

Ask Yourself

- Am I explaining my sales presentation in the simplest possible terms?

- How sensitive am I to signals expressed both directly and indirectly?

- What's the value of offering choices to prospective clients?

- What recent time-savers have others sold or offered to me?

- What can I learn from these overtures?

WHAT THE EXPERTS SAY

Michael Angelo Caruso is an account executive with Supply Technology. He has strong words to say about the value of voice mail in establishing contact. "Never, ever leave a voice-mail message on an initial call." Cautioning about the habits of prospects (if they don't return your first call, they won't return the second or third, either), he advises continuing to call until you reach your prospect directly.

Dialog 2

"You're Talking Too Much"

Scenario

It's often been observed that no matter what we do for a living, we all sell. That observation is echoed in the advice of author Anne Miller (*Presentation Jazz*, AMACOM, 1998), who encourages creative approaches when your closing efforts seem to be failing. Additionally, she encourages developing your dramatic qualities to make a point on occasion. One quality she does not encourage in salespeople is talkativeness.

Fortunately, in this scenario, you've picked up the signals warning you that you're talking too much. You're calling local residents, hoping to open new accounts for the florist shop you've recently opened.

Strategies

During your phone call, you'll employ the Interest, Inexpensive, and Invade strategies. First, you'll share a point of *interest*. Then you'll stress the *inexpensive* new-account specials available during the opening month. Finally, you'll *invade* the prospect's space in the most pleasant way possible, suggesting that flower purchases become a habitual part of his life and the lives of those he cares about.

EXPERIENCE SHOWS

Proxemics is the study of space and how we use it. Be aware of how people place their bodies in the space between you and them. Don't intrude on the space of people who shy away from physical contact, and don't hesitate to make contact with those who seem to like it. Similarly, in telephone selling, don't be overly friendly with those who are naturally reserved. And don't tone down an ebullient personality if you're dealing with an extrovert.

EXPERIENCE SHOWS

Experts say you should smile when you're on the phone; it will cause your voice and your words to be warmer. In fact, many experts encourage imagining that the other person is facing you. Respond as you would if he were actually in your presence.

WHAT THE EXPERTS SAY

When you're asked a question you can't answer, it's tempting to beat around the product bush. Avoid the temptation. Don't talk for the sake of talking. Instead, do what author (Joan Guiducci (*Power Calling*, Tonino Publishers, 1992) recommends: Pass the ball to someone else, someone whose expertise far exceeds your own. Don't be afraid to admit you don't have all the answers.

"You're Talking Too Much"

You: Good morning, Charles. I'm Max with the Flower Shop just a few blocks away. We've just opened and we're offering some specials this month. I think you'd be interested.

Prospect: I'm not.

Notes: Your first temptation is probably to add this call to the large percentage of unsuccessful cold calls most salespeople have to make. Try harder. Have a reply ready to interest him before he can hang up.

Interest Strategy

You: You know, Van Gogh painted irises so magnificent that someone was willing to pay $53 million for them. I'm sure you have employees who are celebrating special events in their lives or secretaries on staff who are expecting something special for Secretary's Week. In fact, you probably have clients to whom you want to express appreciation from time to time. What better way than irises—or any other flower of your choice?

Prospect: We typically don't send flowers.

You: Could I ask why not?

Prospect: They're too impractical. They don't last.

Inexpensive Strategy

You: But the impression they make lasts forever. Why don't you try just one order today? We have irises on sale for $19.95.

Prospect: Does that include delivery?

You: *(It doesn't, but you're going to "eat" the delivery cost because you recognize a closing signal.)* When a new account is opened, there's no delivery charge for the first month.

Invade Strategy

You: And, if you open a bouquet-a-month account—for your mother, perhaps—then there's never a shipping charge if the person lives anywhere in this state.

Prospect: My mother lives in Boca Raton.

You: Well, perhaps there's someone else whom you can delight every month—your secretary perhaps, your wife, your daughter in a college dormitory.

Prospect: Hmmm. My daughter's up in Boston. What's the delivery charge for out-of-state?

Further Considerations

Traditional sales strategies encouraged using the telephone as a means to an end—the appointment during which the sale would be made. But, as author (*Streetwise Selling*, Adams Media, 1998) Nancy Stephens notes, "With the information explosion, buyers have more and more information at their fingertips." Because they can know so much, so fast, many prospects prefer to be sold over the phone, and it's certainly quicker for you and them than a face-to-face meeting. Consider revamping your traditional approaches and at least offering potential buyers the chance to select one medium or the other.

> **WHAT THE EXEMPLARS DO**
>
> In his book *Non-Manipulative Selling*, Anthony Alessandra advises that you reduce and circumvent "noise." Noise is composed of environmental distractions. Of course, when you're in the client's environment, there's little you can do to reduce external noise, for example, ringing telephones that get in the way of the message being sent and received. It's important, says Alessandra, that you force yourself to concentrate on the words being used and that you develop figurative earplugs and eye blinders for the things obstructing the oral connection.

It's been said that two great talkers will not go very far together. If you're dominating the conversation, you're losing the sale. Mentally assess the time you spend listening. It should constitute at least half of the sales exchange.

When you receive a rude response to your opening inquiry, consider this alternative. Thank the person (if he hasn't already hung up), make a note of his tendency to be curt, and have a good line ready for next time. Then call again in several months and use the prepared line. Try this with all your hang-ups and keep a record of how often the second call works.

Ask Yourself

- Is "talkative" one of the qualities people generally associate with me?

- If so, is this quality a positive or a negative in my interactions with prospects?

- How much ego gratification do I need?

- How much talking did I do in the last situation where I was a buyer instead of a seller?

BE CAREFUL

It's a delicate balance, asking if you're boring without tainting yourself via word association. You'll find the words you need. To hasten your actions, remember the story of the secretary involved in a terrible scandal with an evangelist. A reporter once suggested that she had been hired, not for her secretarial skills but for other, more libidinous ones. "How do you reply to the charges that you're not very intelligent?" he asked. "Well, I'm not a bimbo!" she declared. Alas, the very selection of the word suggests bimbo-ism.

WHAT THE EXPERTS SAY

Author Milo Frank (*How To Get Your Point Across in 30 Seconds,* Simon & Schuster, 1986) maintains we have only about 30 seconds to grab a listener's attention and keep it. When you hear yourself rambling, force yourself to stop.

Dialog 3

"I'm Bored"

Scenario

Pundits are always dividing the world into two types of people: Prospects who are bored can be divided as well: those who will politely conceal their boredom and those who won't. Either way, you have to notice the signals and calibrate accordingly. Otherwise, you're just continuing along a path of destruction.

Here you're meeting with a prospect who's expressed an interest in motivational materials that your company publishes. Soon after the meeting starts, though, you sense he's bored. Without labeling yourself a dullard, you'll try to verify the signals you're getting. Then, based on the response you get, you'll either continue with your planned remarks or toss them and proceed with plan B.

Strategies

The three rhyming strategies you'll use are Clarify, Verify, and Gratify. Begin with background information that *clarifies* what you, your company, and your product are all about. But don't spend too much time here, because you also need to clarify the customer's needs. Then, when you sense the prospect is no longer attending, *verify* that what you sense is correct or not. Finally, *gratify* the prospect by offering him what he indicates he wants and by confirming the wisdom of his decision.

"I'm Bored"

You: I know you're busy, Jim, and this presentation should take about 15 minutes. As you can see *(pointing to products on display)*, we have a wide range of inspirational materials.

Prospect: So I see.

Notes: At this point, it's time to stop talking and start listening. What exactly is the prospect's problem? Why does he think he needs to motivate his staff? What is he hoping your materials will do for him?

Clarify Strategy

You: Is there a specific problem, such as low morale, that you're hoping the inspirational materials will overcome?

Prospect: Times are uncertain for everyone, but in our case, there's been some talk of a merger. The rumors have been neither confirmed nor denied, but people are beginning to feel unsettled. I think we need reminders that, one, we're in this together; two, no matter what happens, the company will help us as much as they can; and, three, even in a worst-case scenario, we're capable of finding other jobs.

You: I think we have just what you need. The challenge you're facing is one that numerous other companies in this country have faced. Apart from that, each of us has challenges every day of our lives—challenges from family, from faith, from neighbors, from the political situation. But it's not enough to spout good intentions; we have to do things that prove we really care about others ....
(You notice the prospect stifling a yawn.)

Verify Strategy

You: I may be giving you more information than you need here. So let me ask you: Were you thinking about videos, motivational booklets, posters, or a program of motivational quotations sent weekly?

Prospect: I think the booklet would work best for us. That way, employees can talk to each other about what they've read. They can also take the booklets home and share them with their families.

Notes: In the first sentence, "I may be giving you more information ...," you are attempting to verify your feeling that the prospect is getting bored. If you've mistakenly interpreted his yawn as a sign of boredom, then he'll protest that he really does want to hear all the information. Otherwise, you'll move on to the Gratify strategy.

Gratify Strategy

You: It's apparent that you're concerned about the effects of the merger possibility on your staff. Our booklets will help express that concern. And if you like, we can have them personally autographed by the author. For some people, that's a special bonus.

Prospect: I just thought of another. Maybe I could write a letter to be included with each booklet, assuring our people that we know they're wondering about the future and telling them that the books are designed to motivate them to think positively.

Further Considerations

Unless you've chosen your words carefully, a Verify strategy can be tricky because the prospect can easily interpret it as a criticism or an insult. Because the English language contains over a million words, with a little thinking you can find the right words to say what you need to say in the most diplomatic way possible. Experiment with several versions of a Verify strategy, and then choose the one that you (and others) feel will make the inquiry without casting aspersions.

Consider the use of a letter of introduction—even if you have to write it yourself—advises sales psychologist Donald Moine of Rolling Hills Estates, California ("Cold Calling in the 90s," *Selling,* September 1996, page 39). Send the letter by snail mail or fax to the prospect before you place the cold call. A friendly introductory letter may help you get the appointment—or the sale.

As you plan what you'll say for either the phone or the in-person contact, remind yourself that your script shouldn't sound like a script. If you do choose to read from it over the phone, underline key words for a more natural intonation. If you're meeting with the prospect in person, write the key words on a three-inch-by-five-inch card and review it just prior to entering the person's office.

As you move on to the Gratify strategy, listen to yourself. Words such as "I think [we have just what you need]" suggest you're really not certain. It's much better to make a declarative statement: "We have just what you need."

Ask Yourself

- Whom would I trust to tell me the truth if I asked whether I was boring?

- Who or what bores me?

- Do I exhibit any of the traits or negative aspects of boring people or things?

- What specific aspects of my product or service arouse true enthusiasm in me?

- Has anyone ever told me I seem passionate about my product or service?

Dialog 4

"I'm Scared"

Scenario

Buyer's remorse is a real-world phenomenon. Faced with a life-altering decision, people often begin to pull back, to wonder if they should go ahead with the wedding, finalize the purchase of the house, or sign the adoption papers. These concerns are understandable. Unfortunately, a simple sale, while not a life-altering event, often produces the very same symptoms. Prospects reach the brink of the sale and then become fearful, frequently drawing back from closing the sale.

Your goal in this tele-sell call is to convince the prospect (already qualified) that your financial services firm is the best one for him.

WHAT THE EXPERTS SAY

According to management guru Tom Peters, if you've gone a whole week without being disobedient, you're doing yourself and your organization a disservice. "Disobedient" doesn't mean you're free to break the laws of the land. Rather, you're free to challenge the existing order, to make continual improvements, to break the molds that have been shaping opinion and action for far too long. Sit down with your manager from time to time and challenge some of the practices that have been done for so long that no one remembers why they started in the first place.

"I'm Scared"

You: You're doing the right thing, Ranier, thinking about retirement long before you have to.

↓

Prospect: "Thinking" is the operative word here. I don't know if I'm ready to invest.

Notes: Even though this is a qualified lead, he won't be an easy sell. He's already pulling back, and you haven't even begun to make your pitch. If you're sensitive to responses, though, you'll realize immediately that you can't take a steamroller approach with this person. Give him time and give him space.

Sell Strategy

You: Of course. Let's just consider this an exploratory meeting. You know, Ranier, there are a lot of negatives associated with retirement, the most scary of which is the thought that we might not have enough to live on. No one likes to think about the bad things that can happen, but thinking about and then acting on those fears usually changes negative possibilities to positive outcomes.

Rebel Strategy

Prospect: I'm probably too young to think about retirement.

↓

You: On the contrary. There are 30-somethings who have invested, then retired, and are now working to make a difference for one cause or another. As a nation, we've shattered the stereotypes about retirement.

↓

Prospect: What about the government? Didn't Congress just vote to raise the IRA contribution limits from $2,000 to $5,000?

↓

You: They did. And the limit for 401(k) contributions has been raised from $10,000 to $15,000. But there's a problem with depending solely on the government.

Prospect: There is?

↓

You: There is. We're living longer and healthier lives, which means we'll need more money than ever to continue our active and fulfilling lifestyles. Ironically, because we're living longer, health-care problems will eventually catch up with us and will place additional financial burdens on us.

↓

Prospect: So I should start retirement planning

Excel Strategy

You: In my opinion and the opinion of every financial planner I've ever met or heard about, yes!

↓

Prospect: What does your company offer that the others don't?

↓

You: In addition to a 100-year old tradition of excellence and the highest ratings on Wall Street, we have an automated investment plan that takes the emotions out of the equation. You can invest as little as $50 a month with deductions from your bank account. This can even be set up for your IRA, if you wish. We also offer free retirement planning to answer all your questions and provide you with peace of mind. Most other firms charge for this service.

Strategies

Sell, Rebel, and Excel are the three strategies you'll use, although not necessarily in that order. When you *sell*, you convert features to benefits that the prospect cannot do without. Sometime during the dialog, you'll want to *rebel*; in other words, you'll politely contradict something he's said or you'll set yourself apart from the way competitors handle a problem, for example. *Excelling* means emphasizing the uniqueness of your product or service, convincing the buyer that it will provide solutions no other product or service can.

Further Considerations

When the word "charge" comes up in your conversation with a prospect, you have a natural lead-in to a discussion of pricing. Even if the natural transition doesn't occur, you can move on to the topic with or without a question from the customer. In the discussion, you could give the price, ask how many the prospect needs, or give further information about different prices for different models. If you recognize the closing signal, you'll find out about quantity, quote the price, and close the sale—even if you had other information to share.

> **WHAT THE RESEARCH SHOWS**
>
> Cahners Advertising Research in Boston found that only 16 percent of the sales representatives surveyed called on their entire customer base. If you belong to the other 84 percent, the ones who don't call on all their customers, you're not reaching all your prospects and you're not making all the sales of which you're capable.

> **INSIGHTS**
>
> "The sale merely consummates the courtship; then the marriage begins." These words from Theodore Levitt, former editor of the *Harvard Business Review,* suggest the need for ongoing attention to your customers. In one way or another, you need to provide ongoing service. It need not be often and it need not be expensive, but it must occur, if only in the form of a thank you expressed in a Christmas card.

Suppose that a prospect asks you whether your product ever melted in the sun. If you merely assure the prospect that you've never heard a complaint, you may be costing yourself the sale. You need to be more convincing. Know your product well enough that you can speak with conviction, or else promise to find out and perhaps obtain a no-melt guarantee.

You never expect to close every single sale you ever attempt. You are aware that there will be some nos and some yeses, some peaks and some valleys, some acceptances and some rejections. Every no you hear just means you're closer to the yes you're seeking. Don't take rejection personally.

Ask Yourself

- How often do I contact those to whom I've made a sale?

- How common are post-purchase contacts in our company or industry?

- Am I keeping a log of all the objections I've heard about our product?

- When I'm asked about terms, am I likely to spell them out or turn it around and ask the prospect what kind of terms he wants. (Of the two, the second is more likely to lead to a close.)

Dialog 5

"I Don't Believe This"

Scenario

Nolan Bushnell, founder of Atari, once commented, "Business is a good game—lots of competition and a minimum of rules. You keep score with money." It's the money part that usually causes poor winners and sore losers. In the game of sales, you can circumvent bad outcomes by recognizing signals early in the game and then modifying your game strategy.

You've picked up a signal of incredulity during a sales presentation and have quite logically interpreted it to mean the person is having a difficult time accepting the price. In addition, your prospect has clearly expressed his doubt in words. Your challenge is daunting: You're attempting to persuade a local grocer to carry a new product your pharmaceutical firm believes is as good as the current market dominator. In spite of the signal you're getting from the prospect, you'll press on because the opportunity is so good.

EXPERIENCE SHOWS

When faced with a multipart objection from your prospect, break it down into its component parts. In the "I Don't Believe This" scenario, you've dealt with quality, effectiveness, and cost separately and effectively.

"I Don't Believe This"

You: Mr. Wegstaff, I know you're busy these days. I hear you're opening a new store in Pennsylvania now.

↓

Prospect: That's right. But we like to give local vendors and local salespeople the opportunity to put their products on our shelves whenever we can. So tell me what you've got.

You: I appreciate that. Let me get right to the point. We're introducing a new product that rivals the current over-the-shelf product in terms of quality, effectiveness, and cost.

↓

Prospect: I find that hard to believe.

Notes: You don't have to interpret this signal—it couldn't be clearer. But you do have to determine what exactly the prospect is finding hard to believe. You'll do this with a series of questions.

Test Strategy

You: Is it the quality you're wondering about, the effectiveness, or the fact that we can produce it at around the same cost as our competitor?

↓

Prospect: All three, but primarily quality. You know, our reputation is built on it.

↓

You: I'm going to ask you to read the ingredients in our competitor's nasal decongestant *(handing him the bottle).*

↓

Prospect: Just three: camphor, eucalyptus oil, and menthol.

↓

You: That's right. Now read what we have in TLC, our newest product.

↓

Prospect: Well, how about that? They're exactly the same.

↓

You: You see, there's no magic formula for topical cough suppressants like this. It's a pretty standard formula, but certainly an effective one.

Best Strategy

You: We're working very hard to gain entry into the market. To introduce consumers to the product, we're providing a booklet of a 101 ways that parents can provide children with TLC while they're administering our "TLC" cough suppressant. There's nothing like this booklet on the market. And, even if it were available, it wouldn't be free.

↓

Prospect: Do you have a copy of that?

↓

You: I do. Notice who the author is.

↓

Prospect: No. You're in partnership with Sister Enunciata?

↓

You: That's right! This best-selling children's author has signed a partnership agreement with us. In return, a portion of all sales go to UNICEF.

Notes: This bonus is bound to entice your potential customer: it's a giveaway that accompanies your product; it's created by a well-recognized figure; it helps create sales and a portion of the sales will go to UNICEF. While your price is not compromised, the prospect will no doubt feel he is getting the better end of this deal.

continues

"I Don't Believe This" (continued)

Suggest Strategy

You: I know how valuable shelf space is, Mr. Wegstaff, and we certainly wouldn't want you to lose money by replacing the famous brand with our lesser-known product. I also know that money isn't everything with your company, because I've read about the scholarships you provide and the generous donations you make every year to a number of worthwhile causes.

Let me suggest this: Would you be willing to carry just a dozen and have your cashiers give the free booklet to anyone who buys our product? The last page of the book is a quick survey that is perforated. It asks consumers to return the form to the store where they bought the decongestant. If the results are less than either of us hope for, we won't ask you to continue carrying the product.

Prospect: And if they're better than we hope for?

You: Well, I'm known as someone who thinks big. If the results are as good as I think they will be, then I'll ask you to take the famous brand off your shelves and replace it with TLC!

BE CAREFUL

The danger of asking, "Which part are you wondering about?" is that the prospect might glibly say, "All of it," when he is actually wondering about only one part of it. To prevent this from happening, consider saying, "Well, if it's quality you're concerned with, here are ...."

Strategies

First, you'll have to *test* your assumption by using the Test strategy. Verify that you're correctly interpreting the signals you're getting. If the person truly is having a hard time accepting some point or price you've quoted, you'll move to the Best strategy, making your *best* offer, without compromising your goal. You make an offer that could win over the decision-maker. Finally, with the Suggest strategy, you'll *suggest* an outcome that provides a win for each of you.

Further Considerations

You won't always be able to depend on words for clarification of a signal. Sometimes, to express doubt, a prospect might shake his head as if to say, "This is incredible." Or, he could click his tongue against the roof of his mouth, making a sound that suggests, "How dare you?" Use your natural and honed ability to read body language. Rely on your instincts, but also carefully test your impression.

When the sales dialog is not going the way you want it to, consider putting aside all pretense and politeness. Sometimes simply coming out and asking, "What did I do wrong?" or "Have I said something that concerns you?" is better than trying to delicately decipher the situation. Your choice will often depend on the kind of person you're dealing with.

> **WHAT THE EXPERTS SAY**
>
> Sales expert Art Sobczak has some two-word phrases he encourages salespeople to use. "Sell soft" and "Talk straight" are two of them. As you look back over your sales career, determine which two- or three-word exhortations have worked best for you. Prepare a list of 10, and review it just prior to your most important sales efforts.

> **EXPERIENCE SHOWS**
>
> A **lagniappe** is a boon, a gift, given to a customer. A lagniappe can also take the form of an offer that you don't have to make but that you do make in order to create goodwill between you and a current or future customer. If you don't typically offer such gratuities to new customers, think of novel ways that you can.

Ask Yourself

- Do I automatically assume my interpretation of a signal is correct, or do I try to find out if I'm correct?

- To what extent do I rely on my intuition?

- Do I appreciate how great some opportunities are?

Dialog 6

"I'm Lost"

Scenario

Humorist Tom Lehrer once announced, "I wish people who have trouble communicating would just shut up!" The myth that all salespeople are good communicators is shattered every day of the year. Even if you count yourself among those who do communicate well, you still have probably confused your prospect occasionally.

"I'm Lost"

You: As some of you know, I'm Brett Wong from AptApts.com. We are an online company that provides temporary corporate housing, and today I'd like to show you just how that works.

Prospect #1: Hold on. From your company name, I'm assuming you provide just apartments. Is that correct?

Notes: You can either answer the question, postpone it by saying you'll get to it soon, or backtrack and start all over. If you decide to return to the beginning, you have another choice: Do you admit you've jumped the gun, so to speak, or do you gloss over the omission of information the client wants or needs? There are pros and cons with both choices, but of the two, minimizing the error (of not having provided information) is the more professional way to do it.

Back Strategy

You: Apartments and much more. AptApts.com is a temporary housing provider for businesspeople who prefer the amenities of home over the sterility of hotels. It's designed for stays of one week or longer. We have a range of accommodations, from apartments to condominiums to bed and breakfasts to actual houses.

Prospect #2: Houses?

Track Strategy

You: Houses! But before I proceed, let me ask each of you what is the primary complaint you've heard from executives who travel on extended stays?

Prospect #1: I hear complaints about the boring hotel menu.

You: Let me jot this down *(writing on the flip chart)*. Okay, Chad, what complaints do you hear repeatedly?

Prospect #2: That there's no refrigerator or stove for people who'd prefer to fix their own meals once in a while. Vegetarians especially bring this up.

You: *(Calling on the last person.)* Jacques, it's finally your turn. If you had your druthers, what would you like corporate housing to provide?

Piggyback Strategy

You: Well, gentlemen, I think you'll be pleased to know that AptApts.com can solve each of these problems, including the seemingly impossible one.

Prospect #3: You mean not having a fireplace for lonely winter nights?

You: Actually, I was thinking about being away from the family for so long, but we have the answer to both problems. We actually have some listings that have real fireplaces for those who prefer them, and the guest doesn't even have to chop his own wood.

Prospect #3: This is fantastic. Do you provide marshmallows, too?

You: You're on your own with those. But let me get back to the family issue. One of our locations is next door to a copy center that has videoconferencing capability for just $50 an hour. You only have to go next door and set up a conference. It's the next best thing to being there.

You'll know that your prospect is confused when you see him scratching his head or raising his eyebrows quizzically. If the prospect wears glasses, he's probably peering over them. He may have his eyes closed and be rubbing them with one hand or rubbing his forehead. You've probably been on enough sales calls in your career to recognize these signals.

In this scenario, you're making a presentation to a group. Moments into it, you spot confusion. You quickly backpedal and decide to learn more about the group before proceeding with your plan. You also decide they need to learn more about you and your company.

Strategies

You'll be employing the Back, Track, and Piggyback strategies. You'll go *back* to the beginning and spend some time clarifying what your firm actually does. Then you'll *track* their concerns or needs by asking each person around the table exactly what he hopes to learn in your presentation. Make note of these as each person speaks. Then proceed with your presentation, making certain to *piggyback* as appropriate on their input.

Further Considerations

If possible, use a flip chart to record any concerns that are expressed during the Tracking stage. Then check them off as you address them. Make certain you've covered all of them before your presentation ends.

Knowing in advance how much time you have for the presentation will help you structure the elements that you want to include.

EXPERIENCE SHOWS

An anonymous sage has noted that "the infinite capacity of human beings to misunderstand one another makes our jobs and our lives far more difficult than they have to be." To minimize crossed signals, check periodically with your prospects. Ask questions such as, "Do you have any questions at this point?" "Is this clear?" "Have I answered all your questions so far?" "Am I going too fast?" or "Is there anything you'd like repeated?"

EXPERIENCE SHOWS

As you prepare your presentation, imagine that the scene is reversed and that you're seated around the table rather than standing at the head of it. What questions would you have about the presentation? List them so you'll be sure to include answers before the questions are actually asked. Ideally, you can do this in the first few minutes of your presentation.

WHAT THE EXPERTS SAY

Larry Dotson, a sales consultant whose speciality is Web site promotion (*Sales Leader*, "How to Outsell Your Competition," Dartnell Corporation, Sample Issue, 2000), offers tips that apply to conventional and e-selling both. Ask yourself a number of questions, he suggests, that will help you compare your product to your competitors. Then use your answers to make your presentation more convincing.

193

Consider asking current satisfied customers why their levels of satisfaction with your product are so high. Incorporate those insights into your sales presentation—at least one per 15-minute segment.

Ask Yourself

- Do I appear overanxious?

- Do people generally have a hard time following what I'm saying?

- How often have I been accused of talking too fast?

- Do I tend to use big words?

Dialog 7

"I'm Not Getting My Questions Answered"

Scenario

Humorist Oren Arnold has written a prayer for the modern American: "Dear God, I pray for patience and I want it right now!" In this era of lightning-quick decisions, you are more likely to pick up signals of impatience. If prospects are not getting their questions answered, they will let you know by way of verbal and/or nonverbal means. You might see fingers tapping on a desk or you might spot a cupped hand making a semicircular motion that says, "Get on with it." As we've noted, you may have to respond to such messages and abandon the script you had planned.

Strategies

In this scenario you'll rely on three strategies: Switch, Itch, and Hitch. If you suspect you're not hitting the target, you'll have to *switch* to a different approach. Then "scratch the *itch*" by answering the question that the client still has. Finally, *hitch* your proverbial wagon to the client's purchasing-power star. Show how a union of your solution and his problem could be mutually beneficial.

"I'm Not Getting My Questions Answered"

You: Good morning, Sam. This is Joe Faraday with Teletraining. Did you receive the catalog we sent recently, featuring our latest training videos?

Prospect: I might have. We get so much stuff from you that I don't have time to look it all over.

Notes: Not exactly an enthusiastic response. Persevere. Switch from talking about the catalog to what's new in your offerings. Find out what his needs are and keep them uppermost in your mind throughout. The verbal volley in which you engage from this point on has a format, which you'll follow, but it also has room for flexibility, which you'll need if you are to be truly responsive to the prospect's needs. In other words, the exchange will move quickly—like a volley—based on the direction set by the customer. Because you can't follow the plan you'd mapped out, if you want to be responsive to your customer's needs, you'll have to have answers that directly address his concerns and indirectly allow you to address your own.

Switch Strategy

You: We have some new videos in which you might be interested. Our most popular one is "Green Grocer." It illustrates the importance of having fun at work.

Prospect: That's the last thing we need. Most of these young people are having too much fun, and the work's not getting done.

You: In that case, we have an excellent video on productivity. Would you like to preview it?

Prospect: I'm not sure a video can solve our problems.

Itch Strategy

You: Tell me. What exactly is the problem?

Prospect: It's a question of sustainability. As good as a video might be, it's just a bandage. We need emergency surgery around here.

You: Our videos are designed with continuous learning in mind.

Prospect: What does that mean?

You: Well, employees do more than sit in a room and watch a video for a half-hour. They are asked to commit to a program that calls for a team-appointed leader, who is given a "Leader's Manual." This manual contains short modules that reinforce the key concepts of the video. The leader meets with the team for a half-hour each week. We actually recommend lunchtime meetings so that the workflow isn't interrupted by these learning meetings. Also, we've found that when the team eats together once a week, they form some strong bonds.

Prospect: But these so-called leaders have no training in educational theory.

You: They don't need it. All they have to do is be able to read. The manual does everything else. It states the learning objectives, and it contains a synopsis of the video and application of key points through exercises, quizzes, energizers, role-plays, and discussion starters.

continues

"I'm Not Getting My Questions Answered" (continued)

Prospect: You say they meet once a week. For how long?

You: There are 52 half-hour workshops—enough for a whole year—that extend the theme of the video, whether it's the productivity video or any of the others in our product line.

Hitch Strategy

Prospect: The cost must be prohibitive.

You: On the contrary. Think about the cost of low production, and think about the cost of sending each of those persons out for 26 hours worth of training. By comparison, our program is a bargain.

Here's a list of our current customers and their phone numbers. I'll put an *X* next to those who were interested, as you are, in improving productivity. Why not give them a call and find out about the results they've achieved using our program?

You're certainly not alone, Sam, in wanting to increase productivity. Our product shows you how to do that, inexpensively, every week of the year.

EXPERIENCE SHOWS

Avoid technical jargon unless a client is asking for technical information. When most people ask for the time, they don't want to know how the watch is constructed.

Further Considerations

Age of Paradox author Charles Handy, a Harvard professor, says we live in an age of paradox. The effective salesperson has learned to comfortably walk the tightrope between two extremes. In this scenario you had to be very well prepared, and you had to be able to leave the preparation behind and answer certain questions spontaneously.

If you're selling over the telephone, you may find yourself entering information for the customer's order on your computer. If this is the case, keep the customer apprised of what you're doing on the computer. Doing so keeps the customer engaged and keeps him from thinking, during the long pauses, of other things he should be doing.

When you hear a direct or implied complaint, don't avoid dealing with it. In the scenario, the client stated that he gets too much promotional material. Sometime during your exchange, make a note to ask him whether he'd prefer e-mail notifications or perhaps he'd prefer being notified only about new products.

Ask Yourself

- What paradoxes do I have to balance on a daily basis?

- Would I honestly want everything to go as planned?

- What's the upside of having to switch gears?

- Have I learned how to control my frustration when things don't go as planned?

- Do I ever give visible evidence to prospects that I have metaphorical "itches" of my own?

- If so, what might they be?

WHAT THE EXPERTS SAY

Many, but not all, sales experts encourage the use of **NLP** (Neuro-Linguistic Programming) techniques. Basically, these techniques require you to mirror the signals the prospect is emitting. For example, if he primarily uses simple language to express his ideas, you would do the same. If he speaks formally, you'll use a more formal tone. If he uses words like "see" and "look" and "eyeball," you'll make the presentation more visual. If he uses broad, expansive gestures, you'll do the same.

EXPERIENCE SHOWS

Try NLP on a limited basis. If it works for you, continue using it and increase the extent to which you depend on it in each sales exchange. Be mindful, however, that it's not without risks. For one thing, the prospect may realize what you're doing and feel manipulated as a result. Second, you may be concentrating so hard on studying the prospect's behavioral patterns that you pay less attention to the script you've prepared.

Dialog 8

"I'm Ready to Buy"

Scenario

In the best of all possible worlds, you'll get buy signals long before you've had to expend much time, energy, or nervousness. If you get these signals, go directly to "Close." The insensitive or unaware seller plods through his entire script, from *A* to *Z*. The seller who can boast numerous successful closes will pick up on the buy signals no matter when they're emitted.

You're representing a nonprofit organization in this scenario. Your goal is to sell businesspeople on the need to give back to the community by supporting a foundation for physically handicapped children.

Strategies

Use the We-Three strategies: Weave, Weed, Wean. Begin by smoothly *weaving* a response to the closing signal. You'll need a smooth transition here. You can't just stop midstream and overreact to the buy signal. Then you'll *weed* out extraneous discussions—both yours and the prospect's. Finally, you'll *wean* the prospect away from any last-minute jitters and move quickly to finalize the sale.

EXPERIENCE SHOWS

The inexperienced salesperson will often bring in choices when he should be *weeding* them out. For example, if the prospect asks, "Is the aluminum trim available with the siding?" don't reply, "Yes; and storm windows, doors, and insulation are available, too." Too many choices could thrust your prospect into a quandary. In order to emerge from it, he may need to consult others and the sale might never get made.

EXPERIENCE SHOWS

Allow pauses as appropriate. Notice whether or not the prospect is writing down some of the things you're saying. If so, don't keep feeding him information.

Further Considerations

Salespeople are very often called upon to be diplomats. As seen in this scenario, it's possible to avoid an awkward moment by being direct and straightforward, by moving quickly to another point so the other person doesn't have too much time to remain mired in the mud of his faux pas.

"I'm Ready to Buy"

You: Good morning, Mr. DeLucia. I'm Francisco Goya, calling on behalf of Helping Hands, a local nonprofit dedicated to helping exceptional children develop their potential.

Prospect: If they're so exceptional, why do they need help?

Notes: This is tough. The prospect apparently is not familiar with the current meaning of the word "exceptional" as applied to children with handicaps. You need to explain without making him feel embarrassed about a seemingly rude question. If you're fortunate enough that your explanation prompts him to action, immediately weave his interest into your closing remarks.

Weave Strategy

You: These children are exceptional because they're succeeding despite having physical handicaps, such as blindness. But they need more help than children blessed with good health. Our organization gives them the tools they need to achieve both their goals and their dreams.

Prospect: We're corporate sponsors for the Special Olympics.

You: Please consider sponsoring these special children who work not toward physical goals, as the Special Olympians do, but toward intellectual goals, which we feel are just as important.

Prospect: I agree.

You: Could I list you as a corporate sponsor then? Your gift of $10,000 will help youngsters realize their dreams of becoming contributing members of society.

Weed Strategy

Prospect: What are some of those dreams?

You: *(Restraining yourself because you could talk for hours about these children.)* We actually have a yearbook that is sent to all our corporate sponsors, identifying all graduates, both high school and college, and describing what they're doing with their lives. The new one is coming out in four weeks. If you sign up today, I'll make sure you get a copy.

Wean Strategy

Prospect: It certainly sounds worthwhile, but $10,000 is a large commitment, especially since we're already sponsoring the Special Olympics.

You: Why don't we arrange for quarterly install-ments? That way, if you're having a difficult quarter at some point in the future and could not afford to continue, you could stop the corporate sponsorship.

Prospect: I don't think our straits would ever be that dire.

You: I certainly hope not, but we understand the ebb and flow of business cycles. And, if need be, you could donate at a lower level than corporate sponsorship.

When you can, bring the prospect back to times in his own life that he can recall with poignancy. Building an emotional bridge between those times and your product requires artful planning, of course, but the task is far from impossible.

In situations like this, one of the best ways to keep in contact with customers—and thus keep them as customers—is a newsletter. Simple to create, it affirms for the customer the importance of his gift. If you do depend on such postsale connections, ask your readers from time to time how the newsletter could be improved.

Ask Yourself

- Do I talk too much?

- Could my approach be described as "Wham, Bam, Thank You, Ma'am"?

- How often do I think I have the sale only to find myself walking away without it?

Chapter 8

Making Your Pitch

Harry G. Moock, former vice president of Chrysler, once defined the ideal salesperson as having "the curiosity of a cat, the tenacity of a bulldog, the friendship of a little child, the enthusiasm of a Sinatra fan, the assurance of a Harvard grad, the good humor of a comedian, the simplicity of a jackass, and the tireless energy of a bill collector."

With the possible exception of a jackass's simplicity, a good salesperson is all this and more. Everytime you make a sales pitch, you're calling upon internal resources that you may not even realize you possess. The next time your pitch leads to a successful close, play back the dialog in your head. Make a list of the various roles you played. Then try to determine which seemed to "click" with your client. That role(s) should be incorporated into your basic style.

That style should include, in addition to the Moock definitions, the self-confidence of an NFL player, the product knowledge of a manufacturer, the spontaneity of a stand-up performer, and the preparation of a lawyer. At this point, you're wondering how you can simultaneously be both spontaneous and prepared. Indeed, these two words do seem contradictory. Nevertheless, it is possible. Although some sales experts advise never using a script and others always using one, we recommend a middle-of-the-road course: Prepare an outline of your script that allows you to be both prepared and spontaneous at the same time.

As you think about the roles and the traits just mentioned, also think about a role switch; try looking at the situation from the prospect's viewpoint. Use the following table to help orient yourself to the prospect's needs. The "Medium" column describes the mind-set you can take during the pitch; the "Method" column suggests helpful questions that you can ask as you consult with the prospect. As you gain experience in the consultative process, add questions of your own to the list.

Medium	Method
"A mile in prospect's shoes"	Ask: "What would solve this problem?"
	"What's the biggest problem you're having?"
"Creative solutions"	Ask: "What would the ideal widget look like?"
	"If you had your druthers, what would you ask for, as far as this problem is concerned?"
"Alter egos"	Ask: "What solution would your boss like to see?"
	"What does your staff think?"
"Partner"	Ask: "How can I help?"
	"What would you like me to do if I can?"
"World view"	Ask: "How have others solved this problem?"
	"What solutions have you found online?"
"Socratic"	Ask: "What has worked in the past?"
	"What led to the current situation?"

By questioning your prospect, you can isolate her true need and then respond to it accordingly. Of course, you wouldn't ask all of these questions during one sales pitch, and the ones that you do ask should be appropriately spaced. If you sense that the prospect is resisting giving answers, discontinue the questions.

Dialog 1

Hook the Prospect

Scenario

You've been given a list of qualified leads and you're calling them now. You hope to introduce yourself and complete the first step in the process of building a relationship with a prospective customer.

Strategies

The following script illustrates the Multiple-Role strategy in which you play many roles on the stage of introduction. It's a starting point that can be adjusted to the particular needs of your own situation. A good script should reflect some or all of the traits mentioned by Harry Moock:

- Curiosity
- Tenacity
- Friendliness
- Enthusiasm
- Assurance
- Humor

- Simplicity
- Self-confidence
- Product knowledge
- Spontaneity
- Preparation

Once the script reflects your best shot at prospecting, read through it and pick out the key words. Write them in sequential order in large letters on a sheet of paper. Then when you make your next call, follow the key words of the script to their logical conclusion—which may be an appointment or even a sale.

Hook the Prospect

Prospect: *(Picking up the phone.)* Andrea Mucci, Purchasing.

↓

You: Andrea, this is Germaine Andson of Sako Corporation. If you have two minutes, I'd like to tell you about an offer we're making to new clients.

Prospect: I can give you one and a half.

Notes: This two-minute opening line can backfire but probably won't. If the prospect says "No," you can ask, "Well, how about one minute then?" The beauty of it is that almost everyone can afford two minutes. Naturally, you have to keep your promise. Streamline your hook so that it really does take only two minutes.

↓

Multiple-Role Strategy

You: I'll talk faster than normal then. We're offering a desktop notebook to new customers at half the regular price.

↓

Prospect: I already have notebooks on my desk.

↓

You: Not like this one. Can I send it to you on a trial basis?

↓

Prospect: Then if I don't like it, I have to take the time to mail it back, right?

↓

You: Not quite right. If you don't like it, I'll make it a point to stop by and pick it up. You don't even have to talk to me. You can simply leave it with the receptionist.

But I have to tell you, I have one of these myself. I use it every day. When people ask me about it, I don't have to do any selling. Really—the notebook sells itself. If you have a stapler on your desk, pick it up. The notebook weighs less than that.

↓

Prospect: And if I do like it, what is the cost?

↓

You: Only $12.95.

↓

continues

Hook the Prospect (continued)

Prospect: Only $12.95? That's pretty expensive for a notebook.

You: Andrea, you know what your time is worth. This notebook will save you at least an hour a week, because it organizes your time and your information. An hour a week times all the weeks you have left to work—that's worth a lot more than $12.95. And, if you compare it with similar products, you know they're going for four times that amount.

Prospect: How are you making any money if you're giving these away at half-price?

You: The half-price offer is only for new customers. But I'm confident you'll benefit from this notebook so much that you'll want to order several more for your department, maybe even as gifts for your friends or business associates.

Prospect: If I do, do I pay the $12.95?

You: No, that's just for the trial offer. But if you recommend the product to associates, they can order it themselves at the half-price rate. And, if five of them mention your name, you'll get a referral gift as a token of our appreciation. Oh, I just noticed my watch: The minute and a half is up. I'll call you next week.

Prospect: Hold on a minute. What's the referral gift?

You: If you tell five people about the notebook and if they call me, we will show our appreciation with a sleek Montnoir pen that matches the leather look of the notebook.

Prospect: Well, I guess I don't have much to lose. Go ahead and send it to me.

You: Look on the bright side, Andrea. You have a lot to gain. I'll send out your notebook this afternoon. Then I'll call in a week to see how it's working. Remember, if you're not satisfied, you can just leave it at the front desk and I'll pick it up. I promise that if you don't like it—and we've had only two people who have ever returned it out of thousands who have tried it—I'll pick it up, no questions asked.

Further Considerations

Find ways to make it easy for the prospect to be involved. Anticipate her reluctance and be ready to circumvent it.

Many people are touchy about their names. (Using galvanic-skin-response tests, researchers have found that the three words causing the greatest physiological reaction are "home," "mother," and the subject's own name.) Pay attention to the way the prospect refers to herself. If she uses her first name when she picks up the phone, it's safe to repeat it. If she says, "Mrs. Jones," you had best use the same term. If the person strikes you as very formal, you may want to ask if you can use her first name before you do.

Respond to each of the prospect's concerns as they arise. Here, the prospect indicated she could spare only a minute and a half. (Role: Time Manager) You conformed to the time limit, but then she asked further questions, including one about your hook, the referral gift. She was concerned about the bother of returning the trial item. (Role: Concierge) You offered to pick it up. She implied her desk was already cluttered. (Role: Space Organizer) You explained how small the notebook was and you differentiated it from the others. She objected to the cost. (Role: Accountant) You responded with a statement regarding the value of her time.

Ask Yourself

- If the circumstances were reversed and I was the one who had received this prospecting call, would it have led me to buy the product?

- How can I advance the action or get my foot farther in the door? (In the scenario it was done with the promise to call in a week.)

- Do I make it easy for the prospect to eliminate risk? (The offer to have the item picked up with no questions asked is both a guarantee and an assurance.)

Dialog 2

Build Trust

Scenario

Trusting relationships are predicated on several factors, probably the most critical of which is time—time enough to prove that we mean what we say and we say what we mean. Unfortunately, the sales process doesn't often afford that luxury. Therefore, you must rely on other factors to convince prospects that you deserve their trust. What are those other factors that persuade prospects to trust you? Famed journalist Edward R. Murrow identified three: believability, credibility, and truthfulness. "To be persuasive," he observed, "we must be believable; to be believable, we must be credible; to be credible, we must be truthful."

In this scenario, you are dealing with an initially distrustful and even abrasive prospect. You'll need a wide range of tools to establish trust.

> **EXPERIENCE SHOWS**
>
> Locate some humorous quotations related to your field and memorize them. They'll come in handy more often than you can now realize. For example, if you're in the food or services industry, you might reference actor and food entrepreneur Robert Redford: "Health food may be good for the conscience, but Oreos taste a hell of a lot better."

Strategies

You'll try the Ignore, Explore, and Restore strategies. First of all, you'll *ignore* the deliberate slights and swipes from the prospect. If you can get past the insults, then you'll be able to *explore* the prospect's position and position your own product. Finally, you'll work to *restore* the confidence that the prospect has lost from earlier experiences, which left her skeptical about the true motives of salespeople in general.

207

Build Trust

> **You:** Good morning, Angelina. I'm calling on behalf of Tru-West, the nation's leading provider of long-distance telephone services.

> **Prospect:** I've never heard of you and, besides, we already have a long-distance provider. Good-bye.

Notes: You've anticipated this possibility, and you have your reply ready.

Ignore Strategy

> **You:** *(Speaking with authority.)* Just a moment, please. Have you heard of MicroStrong?

> **Prospect:** Yes, of course, and have you heard of being cut off?

> **You:** *(Chuckling as if to acknowledge her cleverness.)* Tru-West has just merged with MicroStrong to provide small businesses like yours with lower long-distance rates.

> **Prospect:** Have you ever thought about going into acting? You'd be perfect for playing a woman of limited brainpower.

> **You:** *(Having decided you'll make one more effort and will end the conversation if there's one more insult.)* It doesn't take much brainpower to realize how six cents a minute can add up to big savings.

Explore Strategy

> **You:** Could I ask what you're currently paying for long-distance service?

> **Prospect:** It's a whole lot more than six cents.

> **You:** How about the monthly fee?

> **Prospect:** How about it? I'm sure yours is twice what we pay now.

> **You:** Actually, we don't have a monthly fee.

> **Prospect:** What's the catch?

> **You:** We don't call it a "catch." We call it a monthly minimum of $25.

> **Prospect:** That's all? We pay over a hundred a month in long-distance fees.

> **You:** Then you'll easily qualify for the no-monthly-fee plan.

Restore Strategy

> **You:** MicroStrong is a name you can trust, even if you're not familiar with Tru-West. We stand behind our service, so much so that we'll even pay the switching fees for you to join us. Then, if you're not satisfied with the service or if it doesn't live up to the promises I've made you, you have three months to cancel, during which we will pay the switching fee, even though you're leaving us.

continues

Build Trust (continued)

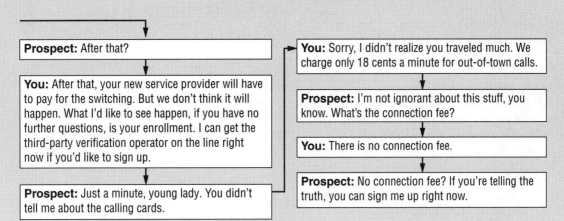

Prospect: After that?

You: After that, your new service provider will have to pay for the switching. But we don't think it will happen. What I'd like to see happen, if you have no further questions, is your enrollment. I can get the third-party verification operator on the line right now if you'd like to sign up.

Prospect: Just a minute, young lady. You didn't tell me about the calling cards.

You: Sorry, I didn't realize you traveled much. We charge only 18 cents a minute for out-of-town calls.

Prospect: I'm not ignorant about this stuff, you know. What's the connection fee?

You: There is no connection fee.

Prospect: No connection fee? If you're telling the truth, you can sign me up right now.

Further Considerations

This prospect in this scenario was a difficult one, curt and sarcastic. Nevertheless, if you find yourself dealing with such a person, fight the temptation to be equally caustic. If you can refrain from responding in kind, you'll likely win her over.

Your voice is capable of a very wide range of projections, including authority. Be aware of your tone of voice and practice conveying different emotions, such as authority, composure, and confidence.

You know yourself. If you're quick to anger, it's better to politely terminate a rude response than to tolerate numerous verbal slams.

WHAT THE EXEMPLARS DO

It's possible to stand up for yourself (or your product or your firm) without alienating the prospect. A good example of the persuasive power of carefully chosen words comes from John Kieran, *The New York Times* sports writer. Dissatisfied with the salary he was earning and determined to quit if he didn't get a raise, Kieran approached his boss and uttered a mere 14 words: "Mr. Ochs, working for the *Times* is a luxury I can no longer afford." Just 14 words, but enough to get him the raise he wanted.

Ask Yourself

- Am I known for my sarcastic wit?

- If so, can I fairly easily rein it in?

- At what point do I decide that making a sale is not worth taking verbal abuse?

- How easy is it for me to laugh at myself? How about when the laugh is at my expense?

Dialog 3

Position Your Product

Scenario

Positioning is a matter of making the connection between the prospect's landscape and your product as a landmark in that territory. In today's highly competitive marketplace, what sets you apart is not product. Chances are that many products out there are as good as, or better than, your own. What sets you apart is the match between your product and the client's hopes, needs, and expectations. In this scenario, you're meeting with members of a restaurateurs' association, hoping it will order your product for its respective restaurants and choose your product as the focus of the association's annual food theme.

Strategies

The strategies are Heed, Need, and Keyed. To begin, you'll *heed* the words of the restaurateurs. (The script that follows has moved past the introductory stage.) Then, using what you've heard, you'll confirm the *need*. In the final step, you'll position your product by *keying* the need to your product's ability to satisfy that need.

Position Your Product

Member #1: We need something new, and oysters may be it this year. Persuade us.

You: Happily. But let me ask you something first. You say you need something new, and then you used the words "this year." Do you have one food a year that serves as the annual theme?

Member #2: We do. Last year it was potatoes. This year we want something a little more exotic, which is why we called your company.

Notes: You've made immediate and important inroads into the heart of the problem. It's hard to offer a solution when you don't know what the problem is.

Heed Strategy

You: So, if you'll allow me to quickly restate what you're looking for, it should be exotic, it should be novel—if not itself novel, then perhaps the way it's prepared or served—and it should have enough variety to last for the whole year's theme.

Member #3: *Mais oui!*

Need Strategy

You: I think we can offer you exactly what you need. You should know that the employees of Oysters by Rocky Fellers consider this little mollusk magical, mythical, and downright mysterious. After all, it's the mother of a pearl. It's associated with one of the wealthiest families in America. It's a delectable hors d'oeuvre, a delicious entrée, or even an unusual dessert! It's the inspiration for much culture—no pun intended—like Botticelli's acclaimed depiction of the birth of Venus. And … *(pausing dramatically)* many believe this tantalizing marine inhabitant is an aphrodisiac.

Member #1: I think this is going to work.

You: We have a collection of recipes that show the versatility of this little bivalve creature. That alone takes care of your need for variety. However, we've also done our research at Oysters by Rocky Fellers.

We know that the goddess of love, according to a myth, emerged from the sea on an oyster shell. And when she bore a son, it was Eros, god of love. This is how the oyster's reputation began. That reputation caused the ancient Romans to trade gold for this little sea treasure. A few hundred years later, Casanova was eating fifty of them each morning. But there's substance behind the myth: Oysters have a high mineral count, including zinc. And you probably remember from high-school chemistry what zinc is responsible for.

Member #4: Well, there's the erotic, I mean, the exotic theme right there. And it sounds as if we have more than enough ideas for the novelty theme as well.

continues

Position Your Product (continued)

Keyed Strategy

You: We've just installed a whole new computer system. The darn thing's so efficient that our accountant finds herself with a little extra time on her hands. She's quite a creative woman, and I suspect she'd be delighted to offer you some ideas for making the pearl concept both novel and exotic. For example, she's always bringing in oyster references from the world of literature or music or even sports. Just yesterday, she was telling me about Earl "The Pearl" Monroe.

Member #2: When can we meet her?

You: Just call her at extension 42. Of course, her services are available only if you decide to go with Oysters by Rocky Fellers as your vendor.

WHAT THE EXEMPLARS DO

Mark McCormack, founder and chairman of the International Management Group, advises that "If you want to be a better salesperson, you should seek out better customers." Discuss with your manager just who those customers might be and where you could find them.

Further Considerations

You have a distinct advantage when you pitch face-to-face as opposed to pitching over the phone. Don't lose the advantage by ignoring body language.

Of course, you yourself are on display when you stand in front of prospects. Be especially careful that your body language does not betray whatever frustration or impatience you may be experiencing.

Think about the things that make you feel good, such as praise. Then consider ways you might incorporate those things into your pitch to make your prospect feel good as well.

Ask Yourself

- What risks have I taken in the last two weeks?

- Do I spend as much time preparing for high-potential accounts as I do for low-potential accounts?

- Should I?

- To what extent do I let past successes help create future ones?

Dialog 4

Develop Rapport

Scenario

"Results," Don Peterson, former head of Ford Motor Company, was fond of saying, "depend on relationships." Salespeople who consistently meet and exceed quotas have learned the art of developing rapport in the most sincere way possible. Here, you're hoping to win over an office secretary responsible for the purchase of paper products.

You've spoken to her before. You've even dropped off a new sample, but so far there's been no interest beyond surface politeness.

Strategies

You'll focus on the Less and More strategies. *Less* talk, *more* listening, for example. *Less* featuring and *more* questioning. *Less* push and *more* pull. The script examples illustrate how you can improve results by improving the relationship with your prospect, by offering fewer gift incentives but more answers to her problem.

Further Considerations

Selling by phone is distinctly different from telemarketing. The former is typically conducted by salespersons who view the phone as just one of their tools, whereas telemarketing is done by people who rely on the telephone as their only medium of connection. Salespersons have a script from which they can comfortably deviate. Telemarketers typically depend totally on the script in front of them for the words they'll use in their presentation.

EXPERIENCE SHOWS

What kind of sales approach do you most dislike? In your own selling approach, don't go so far in the opposite direction that you jeopardize your sales. To illustrate, if you hate a hard-sell, don't overreact by taking too soft an approach. You may find yourself losing sales because a more-aggressive approach is needed.

Develop Rapport

You: Hi, Tamara. This is Aliana with OfficePacks. I stopped by a few weeks ago and dropped off some samples of our new interior file folders.

Secretary: Are you the one who left the big tin of caramel popcorn?

Notes: Not a good beginning. It's hard to tell whether she's genuinely mixing you up with a competitor or whether she's hinting that you left samples but none of the lip-smacking variety. File the food possibility for a later time, and concentrate this time on establishing a relationship that sets you apart.

Less Strategy

You: No, I left a dozen interior file folders in three colors. We leave a premium tin of Mrs. Creole's Cajun Taters when you order five or more boxes.

Secretary: How many folders in a box?

You: A hundred.

Secretary: I don't know if we need 500 right now.

You: Tell me a little about your filing system. Do you use hanging folders, for example, or manila ones? File folders or box-bottom folders? Do you color-code your files? Maybe the staff needs the extra-wide folders with wide expansion pockets? Are you reorganizing your whole filing system or just replacing a few that are worn out, or are you using the folders only as the need arises?

Secretary: Well, I've just started working here, and the files really are a mess. This is the wildest clinic I've ever seen. The dentists and the hygienists are usually too busy with patients to do the filing, so they leave it all up to me. The problem is that the patient records contain everything—x-rays, notes, and billing information. So it's all mixed up.

Then the doctors get impatient when they have to go through the whole file just to locate one thing from the last visit. They're using the regular file folders right now, but maybe they should be using the ones with pockets.

More Strategy

You: I'd like to make a suggestion. It sounds as if they could use the end-tab files. The tabs have letters of the alphabet for quick location, and also the patient's name can be written on the tab. The beauty of these files is that they're wide enough for additional manila files to be inserted. One file could be all the billing information, and the other file could hold the x-rays. How does this sound to you?

continues

Develop Rapport (continued)

Secretary: It sounds great, but I don't know if they'll go for it.	Secretary: Over 600!
You: How about this? I'll drop off six today at no charge. You toss out the old folders for six patients and put everything in these folders, including the smaller manila folder for the billing information and the smaller closed-end manila folder for the x-rays. Then see how the dentists like these six. I'll call you in two weeks. If they find the new system useful, we can go ahead with the order. How many patients do you have altogether?	You: Great. You'll get the free tin of Taters with your order then.

Think of the many important transactions that occur over the phone: notification of hiring, settlement of legal issues, sharing of lab results, decisions to effect change, discussion of proposals—to name but a few. Don't downplay the opportunities a phone can provide to make meaningful connections and extensive sales.

If necessary, acknowledge that your product or service has limitations. It's foolish to try to make it be all things for all clients. If a prospect is seeking economy and yours is an upscale brand, don't waste your time or theirs.

Ask Yourself

- Do I immediately rush to imitate what my competitors are doing?

- Are my overtures of friendliness motivated by the desire for more sales or by the desire to help my customers?

BE CAREFUL

Depersonalization is one negative associated with telephone selling. You can do several things to overcome this association. Use the person's name, for example. Inquire about something she may have told you on a previous occasion. Ask about the spelling of her name, if it's one with several possibilities.

WHAT THE EXEMPLARS DO

Author Tom Hopkins (*How to Master the Art of Selling*, Warner Books, 1982) recommends keeping the client mentally involved. Ask questions that lead her to imagine how she'll use your product. But, he cautions, pay attention. You quickly reveal your disinterest or insincerity by asking a question for which you've already received an answer.

- What is my trademark—the thing by which clients and prospects remember me?

- What were the turning points in my relationships with my biggest accounts? (If they said "No" repeatedly and then one day said "Yes," what was the thing that changed their mind?)

Dialog 5

Tell a Story

Scenario

The importance of storytelling in management has long been recognized. Does it have equal importance for salespeople? It does! It definitely does! Research by J. Martin and M. Powers found that anecdotes had a clear superiority over statistics when it came to the credibility that message recipients associated with the message deliverer.

EXPERIENCE SHOWS
There are few universal experiences, other than being a child, that everyone has had. That's why anecdotes about children have such appeal. All of us were children at some point, some of us still are children, and many of us have children ourselves. Of course, the anecdote must have a direct connection to the point you're making.

Strategies

The raconteur's art provides the strategies for using a story in your pitch. You'll employ the Quarry, Story, and Glory strategies. First, you'll ensnare the *quarry* by establishing the mood, by capturing her interest. Then you'll share the *story*. Finally, and ideally, you'll know the *glory* of transitioning from the anecdote to the sale, a glory in which the quarry can share because of the positioning you've done.

Further Considerations

The anecdote can be used at the beginning, the middle, or the end of a presentation. It can have relevance at any point.

If you sense that your listener is growing impatient, speed up the story. Pace it according to the audience's response, at least in part.

Tell a Story

You: Thanks for taking my call, Mary Jo. I'm calling to learn whether you've made a decision yet about sending your staff to our satellite downlink conference on customer service.

Prospect: Everything's been so crazy here that I haven't really had a chance to think about it.

Notes: Think positively. This stall is better than an outright refusal. You're pursuing this quarry for a reason: You think what you've got is something she truly needs. Press on.

Quarry Strategy

You: Actually, one of the first speakers, J. W. Taneka, deals with the very topic of maintaining sanity in a world that's gone crazy.

Prospect: No doubt about it, our whole division could profit from that.

You: Well, with the satellite download, they can. For one flat fee, the entire group—perhaps in staggered attendance—can hear the entire conference.

Prospect: Some people wouldn't be able to get away.

You: That's not a problem. We provide post-conference videotapes of the entire conference for those who couldn't attend. The video is included in the downlink price.

Prospect: Maybe we should just buy the video. Is that possible?

Story Strategy

You: If you don't mind, I'd like to tell you something that happened to me once. It illustrates the importance of being present for a "live" performance. I was traveling in the first-class section on my way to Los Angeles when, just minutes before the doors closed, there was a sudden flurry of excitement. The world heavyweight champion, Mustafa Allad, strode into the cabin, followed by an entourage that assisted him in removing his coat, stowing his briefcase, and settling into his seat. Then, they put a pillow behind his head and a blanket on his lap.

Prospect: How exciting.

continues

217

Tell a Story (continued)

Glory Strategy

You: It was. There was stunned silence in the cabin as all of this unfolded. But the best part of the whole drama occurred when the flight attendant deferentially walked over and asked him to buckle up. He refused! Then he informed her, in true heavyweight fashion, "Superman don't need no seatbelt!"

The attendant was taken aback—but just for a moment. Then she informed him, "Really. Well, Superman don't need no airplane either. But you do. So buckle up!"

And he did. Now, there was no substitute for actually being there and witnessing that moment. It's an experience I'll treasure for the rest of my life. In the same vein, your staff will find there's no substitute for being part of the audience who can actually feed questions to the speakers. The video, of course, is just a replay, but your people will have an opportunity to tap into the best minds in this field.

You: Very few people have an opportunity to communicate directly with world-famous people in their lifetime. This electronic conference affords your staff the opportunity to ask questions of true gurus.

Prospect: I probably shouldn't even be asking this question, but do they have a chance to identify themselves when they ask the question?

You: Not only can they give their names, they can also tell what company they're from.

Prospect: And that appears in the video of the conference?

You: It does.

Prospect: Our CEO will love this. What are the payment terms?

BE CAREFUL

Refine your story before you present it. That is, make certain that you're a raconteur, not a rambler. The story should be quick and easy to listen to. Strip it of all extraneous details. And time yourself; two minutes is more than enough to make your point.

Stories have been around since long before recorded history. They lend meaning and clarity to our world. Capitalize on their ability to draw an audience, but don't overuse them.

As illustrated in this dialog, you have to know your product very, very well in order to relate it to the prospect's unanticipated remarks.

Ask Yourself

- Am I too set in my ways?

- When I hear speakers, do I actively analyze which elements of their presentations work best?

- Am I constantly on the lookout for anecdotes I can use in my sales pitches?

- Do I ask others for feedback about my stories?

Dialog 6

Keep Their Interest

Scenario

Salesman-turned-author Tom Hopkins urges salespeople to keep their prospects physically involved. Among the many ways you can achieve such involvement are these:

- Ask the prospect to do some calculations.

- Have the customer examine the product you're introducing.

- If your product is a machine, let the customer try operating it after you've demonstrated it in your presentation.

- If product durability is a feature you're touting, invite the prospect to attempt to destroy the item.

- If you've been discussing customer satisfaction, give your client the phone and ask her to dial a recent purchaser of the product under consideration.

WHAT THE EXPERTS SAY

"Personalize your stories when possible," says John Ward, marketing consultant with Branyon-Ward & Ward. You stand a better chance of being believed, he maintains, when the story is based on your own experience.

EXPERIENCE SHOWS

To help dig out personal anecdotes that may be buried in your subconscious, use a time line, divided into 10-year increments. Jot down the most outstanding memories you have from each decade. Then think about each memory and examine it for suitability in your sales presentations.

EXPERIENCE SHOWS

CEO and author Harvey Mackay maintains you can't solve a problem unless you admit you have one. As early in the conversation as possible, help the prospect pinpoint exactly what she needs from you.

EXPERIENCE SHOWS

Don't overlook the power of conceptualizing. As author and lecturer Charlotte Gilman (*Captive Imagination*, Feminist Press, 1992) asserts, "A concept is stronger than a fact." The concept of "wallet share," for example, will strike a more responsive chord with many people than figures relating to current and projected sales.

Keep Their Interest

> **You:** How've you been, Nancy? The last time we spoke, you were going into the hospital for knee surgery.

> **Prospect:** I'm surprised you remember. The surgery went very well and now I feel like a 20-year-old again.

> **You:** That's great. Since you have so much energy, can I divert some of it toward a discussion of e-business?

Notes: This is a classic opening for the consultative salesperson. You've built rapport with your opening question, demonstrating a sincere interest in the individual. Then you've moved smoothly from a client-focused discussion to a product-focused exchange.

Features Strategy

> **You:** Our mission, as I mentioned the last time, is to help our customers help their customers to conduct e-commerce in the easiest way possible. We can redesign your Web site, if necessary, and streamline the order-fulfillment process for you. As you know from last year's Christmas fiasco, e-tailers will lose e-business if they're not quick, accurate, and reliable. Those three words constitute our basic business philosophy.

> **Prospect:** We're doing okay in that regard. We lost only 11 percent of our customer base because of last year's problems, and we fixed those right away.

> **You:** Let's look at this from a different angle. How much difference is there between the largest number of customers you've ever had and the number you have right now?

Involve Strategy

> **Prospect:** I'll have to do some calculating to figure that out.

> **You:** Please, go ahead. I'll just head over to the break room and get a cup of coffee, if you don't mind.

> **Prospect:** *(Five minutes later.)* It seems the number we have now is 75 percent of what we had shortly after our rollout.

> **You:** So your retention rate is three-quarters of what it once was?

> **Prospect:** Yes, but there are some good reasons for that.

> **You:** I understand that. But let's do a little more calculating. If you continue losing 25 percent, or even just 15 percent, a year, how long will it take before you're out of business?

> **Prospect:** I see where you're heading, but what guarantee do we have that you can reverse the trend?

continues

Keep Their Interest (continued)

Zest Strategy

You: If we can't show an increase in numbers one year after taking over your account, you don't pay for our services. However, so far we've been paid by every single one of our customers. You see, our business philosophy is predicated on the need to help our customers manage their customer relationships. If you can keep your current base and if those customers remain yours for life, you'll be in business for a very long time. But if that base continues to erode, then you'll be looking at the beginning of the end.

Prospect: That sounds dire.

You: You have to be realistic and you have to move fast. My company will work not only to make your current customers loyal for life but also to acquire greater "wallet share" among them and future customers.

Prospect: That appeals. Tell me more.

You: We make life easy for your customers, encouraging them to shop online or to shop by phone, by fax, by actual visits to your physical premises, or by snail-mailing their catalog orders. "Multimediums" is the term we use for increasing customer satisfaction and thus customer expenditures.

Strategies

The FIZ acronym is designed to remind you to get "fiz"ical with the client whenever the timing is right. The acronym stands for the Features, Involve, and Zest strategies. First, you'll cite the *features,* translating them into benefits when you can. Then you'll *involve* the prospect via some physical action. Finally, you'll introduce some *zest* to stimulate a successful close.

Further Considerations

According to Joe Kelly, a marketing director at Mall.com, selling is all about "the five C's—content, community, customization, commerce, and customer care." How directly do these C's relate to your core beliefs about selling?

WHAT THE RESEARCH SHOWS

A recent UCLA study found that tone of voice is the most critical element of interpersonal dynamics in 38 percent of one-on-one communications and in 82 percent of telephone communications. From time to time, ask others (but not prospects) what your tone of voice is conveying. If the replies match what you thought you were expressing, you have nothing to worry about. But if you hear responses not aligned with your intention, rethink your basic approach. If emotions or feelings are coming through when you don't want them to, determine not to let your tone betray you.

Consider updating or contributing to the update of your company's Web site. If you're not already featuring a second- or third-generation revision, you're probably not providing the answers your customers need.

The MTV generation demands answers fast. According to General Electric's Jack Welch, if you aren't geared to responding with "speed, simplicity, and self-confidence," then it's time to call in a team of experts to help you revamp your existing site and/or Internet marketing strategy.

Ask Yourself

- Does my voice have a pleasant sound?

- If not, what steps have I taken to alter the sound of my voice?

- Do I know at least one personal fact about each of my existing clients?

- Do I try to obtain at least one personal fact about each prospective client?

Dialog 7

Plan for Spontaneity

Scenario

The word "oxymoron" comes from two Greek words: *oxys* meaning "sharp," and *moros* meaning "foolish"; literally a "sharp fool." An *oxymoron*, therefore, is a combination of two words that seemingly contradict each other—there is nothing more contradictory than a sharp fool. Another oxymoron is the term "planned spontaneity." As confusing as this term might initially sound, it's possible to have flexibility in an otherwise carefully scripted presentation. This dialog shows you how.

Plan for Spontaneity

You: Good morning, Trish. This is Arella from Award/Rewards. We produce achievement awards to help companies recognize outstanding employees.

Prospect: We don't have any outstanding employees.

Notes: You can't be certain whether the person is a curmudgeon who really believes this or simply a leg-puller waiting to see how you'll react. You'll react quickly, that's for sure, because you have less than a unit left for completing the opening. You already have to deviate from your plan, given the nature of this surprising response, but you've left some time and space for the spontaneous reply.

1. Units Strategy (Opening)

You: If that's so, our products will help you develop outstanding employees. Research shows that employees who feel appreciated make much greater contributions than those who don't.

Prospect: What research is that?

You: Fred Herzberg's research into motivation, for one. But it makes sense, doesn't it? If you feel that your opinion matters and that your work is appreciated, you'll try harder than if the opposite is true.

Prospect: I guess.

You: We like to operate on the basis of facts, not guesswork, and we know these awards make a difference. You can customize them, present them as certificates, or give them as wooden plaques; or you can present T-shirts, clocks, desk accessories, or even picture frames. We have awards for every occasion and every corporate pocketbook.

2. Units Strategy (Positioning)

You: What would you like to reward your employees for doing?

Prospect: Ideally, they'd do their job and get paid for doing it. But I know from personal experience that if you're truly turned on by your job, you're willing to give a little more than is expected. That has happened to me—not in my current job, of course, but in the first job I ever had. So, I'd like my employees—some of them at least—to feel that same kind of inspiration. If I see evidence of it, I'd be willing to reward and award.

You: It becomes a self-fulfilling prophecy, I think. The more they're appreciated, the more they do. But the trick is to find them doing it the first time so you can begin the cycle. We actually have some awards that are more generic—simple dual-dimensional frames that say thank you and fit nicely on a corner of a desk. Then, as you note more specific accomplishments, you can identify them by presenting a different kind of award.

continues

Plan for Spontaneity (continued)

3. Units Strategy (Overcoming Objections, Asking for the Order)

Prospect: I don't want to be accused of changing my spots like the leopard with these awards.	**You:** Actually, if you relate them to the upcoming holiday, it'll seem very natural. We have some tied into Thanksgiving that simply say, "We're thankful you're part of our team." Then, if the response is positive, we could supply you with others as employees make contributions in the future.

EXPERIENCE SHOWS

Get in the habit of expressing negatives as positives. If you can't have an order shipped until next Tuesday, don't say it that way. Instead, point out, "We can have it ready for you within a week." Put a positive spin on every negative.

BE CAREFUL

We sometimes forget how many choices we actually have. If the gatekeeper tells you your prospect is out of town, either you can sound disappointed and ask when she'll be back, or you can explain that your own schedule is busy, too. Then say, "I'll be back in town Monday morning and Thursday afternoon. Which is the better time to reach her?"

Strategies

You will be applying the 1-2-3 strategy. No matter how much time you've allotted (or been allotted) for your sales pitch, divide it into six equal parts. So, if you have about 25 minutes to speak, each part or each unit will consist of about 4 minutes. You'll spend one unit (4 minutes) on the introduction, two units (8 minutes) on positioning, and the remaining three units (12 minutes) overcoming objections and asking for the order.

In a tele-selling situation, where you have considerably less time, you may have to take one minute for the opening, two minutes for positioning, and three for handling objections and the close. Situations will vary, of course, but this is a good general guide.

This is your plan. Be prepared to deviate from it if and when spontaneity is called for.

Further Considerations

Don't be too intent on accomplishing your planned spontaneity pitch. Realize that you need to think about what the prospect is saying. Attend to each word and the nuances surrounding it.

You've got a plan. You've built flexibility into it. But now the prospect seems to be going off on a tangent. Listen carefully, because there's something that sparked the digression. However, don't let it go on too long. Find a way to return to the conversational core. A statement like this will help, "I can see why that might concern you, but our current users tell us ...."

While you must speak quickly, especially in tele-selling, speaking too quickly may cause you to slur your words. Tape-record yourself while rehearsing a sales pitch. If you can't hear each word being clearly enunciated, it's time to practice your articulation.

> ### WHAT THE EXEMPLARS DO
>
> Matt Hession, president and owner of Key Medical Supply, Inc., gave himself the formidable task of designing a one-minute pitch to pharmacists. One hundred percent of them agreed to listen to him, and 90 percent of them ended up doing business with him. His pitch, though extremely short, did what it was designed to do. Brevity and a clever marketing ploy did wonders for his sales record. Try something comparable to improve your own.

Ask Yourself

- Do I tend to take things literally?

- Do I tend to "shoot from the hip"?

- Do I tend to interrupt people before they've finished their thoughts?

- Do I jump to conclusions too readily?

Dialog 8

Sell Steak and Sizzle

Scenario

According to the Sales Board, a Minneapolis-based sales training organization, 99 percent of salespeople don't set the right objectives for sales calls. Each situation is different, of course, and is influenced by the prospect, the product, the time factor, the environment, the degree of familiarity, and a host of other possibilities. But no matter what your objectives are, they should always include promoting both the steak (your product) and the sizzle (the psychological elements that make the product more appealing).

Sell Steak and Sizzle

> **You:** Thank you for taking the time to meet with me, Julianna. This must be a great place to work if you take the whole staff on ski holidays every year.

> **Prospect:** Well, we have a very small staff and it's only the second year we've done it. We've had two very good years.

Notes: This is the situation every salesperson dreams about. You've been invited to talk about your corporate incentive programs to a very receptive audience. So far, so good. It'll be fairly easy now to make a pitch that incorporates both features and benefits.

Steak Strategy

> **You:** Let's hope the good years continue. But I must forewarn you: Most people who visit our resort become snow-addicted. They want to return year after year. So, if your good years continue, we'll probably be seeing you on our slopes for many years to come.

> **Prospect:** Perhaps.

> **You:** Our ski weekends are paradise—and not just for snow bunnies. For example, if you have an employee who's an avid skier but she's married to a man who's not, we have all kinds of packages available for family members at half the price you'll pay for your employee.

> **Prospect:** We probably have some people who'd like to include their families.

Sizzle Strategy

> **You:** There's an indulgence for every taste. While your secretary is flying down our crystallized slope, feeling the wind in her hair, the sun in her eyes, and the passion in her heart, her husband might be quietly taking in our magnificent scenery in a horse-drawn sleigh. There are video games in a side room of the lodge, a small casino in another, and a string of exclusive shops on the next side street. Picture yourself relaxing after a hard day of shopping or speeding down our challenging terrain. There you are in the hot tub outside your room, a glass of champagne in your hands. Above you are brilliant stars, dancing for your exclusive pleasure, while in the distance you hear the lonely howl of a coyote. Or think about relaxing with your husband in our lounge. It has a huge, hand-carved fireplace in the center. And if you order wine, it's served with a heated blanket—big enough for you and that special person in your life.

> **Prospect:** Are you referring to my husband?

continues

Sell Steak and Sizzle (continued)

Cake Strategy

You: *(Carefully sidestepping the question.)* Whether you come alone or with someone, I'm certain you'll be captivated by the beauty of our location and the superior skiing on our slopes. And, if you enjoy gastronomic delights, our chefs have all been trained at the Culinary Institute of America. We're told that our nightly fare puts cruise cuisine to shame.

Prospect: Do you have an ice-skating rink?

You: Yes, with instructors and an occasional Olympian. However, we also have snowboarding, jet skiing, and ice fishing. Anything you might associate with winter wonder, we have it here.

Prospect: I don't think we could ask for anything more.

You: Well, there is more, even though you've not asked for it. We close off one room each evening so our corporate guests can mingle before going out for the social hour. So, if you want to hold an informal meeting with your staff before they enter the great room for the evening social, we can accommodate that. And, if you sign up 25 people or more, we'll leave a gift basket in each room, expressing our appreciation for their visit and, indirectly, your appreciation for their contributions.

Chisel Strategy

Prospect: I guess the only problem now will be the cost.

You: You'll find our weekend rates are competitive with any other ski resort's. And, if you add in all these extras, then you'll find our rates are lower than any other major resort's. You've had a good year, Julianna. Let it culminate in a great ski weekend for your staff. They deserve it and so do you.

Prospect: You're right. Just one more thing. You will put Dom Perignon in the gift baskets, won't you?

You: No, but we will put in candy, champagne splits, and fruit.

Strategies

In this scenario, you are practicing the traditional Steak and Sizzle strategies. You cite product features (the *steak*) and then help the prospect envision the tantalizing difference (the *sizzle*) that the product can make in her life. Next you'll use the Cake and Chisel strategies. You'll discover how to add value (to decorate the *cake*) and then how to pare (*chisel*) away at the prospect's objections.

EXPERIENCE SHOWS

Some of the best questions are not questions at all. Rather, they're short, declarative statements used as prompts. "Tell me why" is one example of a prompt that elicits quite a bit of information from prospective clients.

Further Considerations

Master negotiator Roger Dawson advises asking for more than you expect to get. It's a tactic that can often be applied to the sales exchange. Think about exceeding your own goal for your next sales call.

Try this experiment to possibly learn a new or unusual feature, benefit, or advantage of your product: Ask someone who's never seen it or used it before to try it and tell you what she likes most about it. Use that information (especially if it's validated with repeated experiments) when you make your pitch to clients.

When appropriate, find a genuine reason for complimenting the prospect before launching your pitch. At the beginning of the Sell Steak and Sizzle script, the prospect was told, "This must be a great place to work …."

Ask Yourself

- If I had to, could I chisel my pitch down to one minute?

- What simple gesture could I make to add drama to my pitch?

- How much passion do I feel for my product?

- Do I help my prospects visualize what my product can do for them?

*"The sales manager should recognize that each sales repre-
sentative is a unique being."*
—*Stan Kossen*, Creative Selling Today, *Harper & Row, 1982*

Chapter 9

Motivating Yourself and Others

Fortunately or unfortunately, different things motivate different people. Whether we're motivated by love, money, or something else entirely, we are nonetheless inspired to act.

Look at what gives you a sense of satisfaction, pride, longing, enthusiasm, or energy, and you're likely to find a motivator. Notice those same responses in others, and you'll be looking at some of their "hot buttons." Motivators can be used to keep us moving in the direction of our dreams, especially when we're confronted by the occasional nightmare.

You can style a motivation program for yourself or for your staff. The plan can be simple or elaborate, and the goals can be large or small, but motivation programs will generally include three elements: a goal that is clearly articulated, perhaps including interim steps or subordinate goals; a means for measuring and reinforcing progress; and a system of rewards.

The more focused your approach to motivation, the more benefits you'll likely derive. Motivational practices that are used regularly can help strengthen relationships among co-workers and improve morale. Motivational techniques can also help ease the difficulties that are bound to occur in the life of every individual and every business.

Time-honored techniques such as contests, deadlines, and prizes continue to have a role in motivating consumers to act. However, plans and programs aren't the only techniques that can serve to motivate.

Even your choice of individual words can heighten motivation. Sales presentations that are infused with certain words are more likely to motivate customers, so it's wise to be conscious of word choices. Humor, too, has its place as a useful motivational tool.

The following dialogs illustrate all these techniques and more, as they apply to the area of motivation.

Dialog 1

Goal Setting Through One-Person Dialogs

Scenario

You're stepping back for a moment, thinking about your sales career. You're looking at where you've been, where you are now, and where you'd like to go. You're considering the best ways to keep yourself motivated and achieve greater success, in whatever way you define it.

Strategies

You'll determine your daily, short-term, and long-term goals and utilize a variety of techniques to help you reach them while keeping your motivation high in the process. You'll start with the Dreams strategy, in which you'll consider questions such as these: "What are my dreams? If I could imagine a different life for myself and wave a magic wand to make it so, what would I change?" This strategy is important because it opens up a world of possibilities and helps us to "think outside the box."

The Brainstorm strategy helps define ways in which we could turn some of those dreams, in part or in whole, into reality: If it's not possible to live your dream full-time, is there a way to experience it part of the time? If you don't have the means to accomplish your entire dream, could you get just a taste of it? Practices such as these help keep our spirits lifted and our motivation high.

Finally, the Timetable strategy allows us to plot the steps necessary to reach concrete goals within a certain timetable. You'll consider where you'd like to be, career-wise, in a given period of time. You'll include specific figures for income, sales volume, job title, awards, and potential clients. You'll then break down the steps necessary to reach those goals.

> "All achievers experience their goals in vivid detail."
>
> —Joe L. Whitley

Goal Setting Through One-Person Dialogs

You: I feel like I'm floundering. I know I could improve my performance and my satisfaction levels in my career, but I feel overwhelmed at the thought of doing that sort of examination. Where do I want to end up? Where should I even start?

Dreams Strategy

You: If I could wave a magic wand, these are the changes I would make in my life.

(Another side of) You: But that's impossible or impractical.

You: Okay. Just for the moment I'm going to consider fantasies here. If my life were a blank check, here's how I would fill it in for my personal life … and for my professional life …

Note: It's common to react with resistance to this foray into imagination. The rational side of us wants to intervene with practical considerations, but do your best to ignore reality here. Delve into the realm of fantasy and entertain notions of the impossible. We'll get realistic in later exercises.

Brainstorm Strategy

You: How could I turn these dreams into reality, at least in part?

(Another side of) You: But that seems silly. Dreams are, by definition, far-fetched.

You: Okay, if I were forced to consider ways to break down my dreams to incorporate at least a part of them into reality, here's what I'd do. I'd attend fantasy baseball camp for one week each summer. I'd rent a classic car for the weekend every now and then and fantasize that I own it while I'm driving around! And I'd write at least the first chapter of my best-selling, Pulitzer-prize–winning book.

Note: It's not silly at all to focus on dreams. If anything, it's important to stay in touch with dreams and to try to incorporate them into your everyday life in some way. Doing so feeds the soul and helps keep enthusiasm and energy high. Putting a dose of your dream into your everyday existence is part of the recipe for success.

Timetable Strategy

You: Where would I like to be in five years?

You: What specific steps do I need to take *(and by when)* in order to reach those goals?

Notes: Break your goals down into small steps, using specific numbers and deadline dates. For example: make five more cold calls per day, increase sales by 2 percent per month, attend 12 networking events by December.

Create a "goal map" showing what steps you need to take yearly, monthly, weekly, and daily to reach your goals. Transfer your list of steps into your calendar or organizer so that you can stay on top of them. Make a point of recognizing and rewarding yourself for the small and larger goals you reach. That will keep your motivation strong. Also, write out your big goals and post them where you'll see them—in your briefcase or car, on your desk or bathroom mirror. Doing so will help you keep yourself focused and motivated.

Further Considerations

Another approach to goal setting is to create "Priority Statements." A Priority Statement is formulated from an exercise in oversimplification. First, identify the single most important asset in your life. (There are many possible answers here, but most people, if forced to choose one asset, would probably say "health.") Next, isolate the single most important thing you could do on a daily basis to enhance that asset. (Again, many answers are possible, but most individuals and experts would probably say "exercise.") For an individual giving these typical responses, the Priority Statement would be something like this: "The single most important thing I could do today is exercise for 20 minutes."

Your Priority Statement may change from time to time, but remember that only one simple activity is allowed on a given Priority Statement, and it probably shouldn't require more than 20 minutes to accomplish. The statement makes your priority clear and helps cut through the clutter of competing demands. It also gives you a benchmark to look at as the day begins to dwindle. You can say to yourself, "I know that, above all else, the single most important thing for me to do today is _____. Am I going to let the day go by without doing my single most important task so that I can do _____ instead?" Some days the answer will be "Yes" and other days it will be "No," but the statement will help make the choice clear.

Now, try to apply this exercise in oversimplification to your sales career. Ask yourself, "What is the single most important asset for me to have in terms of creating sales success?" (For example, would it be prodigious product knowledge? a huge network? compelling closing skills? long-term business relationships?) "What is the single most important thing I could do to enhance that asset?"

INSIGHTS

"If you don't know where you're going, you could wind up someplace else."

—Yogi Berra

BE CAREFUL

Some of us are more realistic than others in determining what it will take to reach a goal. Share your "goal map" with a trusted (and highly logical!) friend and ask for feedback. See if your friend thinks that the steps you've outlined will get you to your goals in the time you've allotted.

EXPERIENCE SHOWS

Surround yourself with what motivates you. Is it inspiring quotes? certificates of recognition? a chart tracking your sales success? a growing list of customers posted on your bulletin board? contacts with current customers? a file containing letters from satisfied customers or employers?

(For example, would it be reading books and articles daily? listening to training tapes? employing techniques to build my network of contacts by five people per day? increasing my cold calls by 10 per day? making contact with one current customer daily by sending a note, fax, or e-mail just to say hello and to build our relationship?) Once you've identified your priority, act on it daily.

EXPERIENCE SHOWS

Go on a "10-Minute Mission." Sometimes we spend more time agonizing about a dreaded task than it would take to accomplish it. When facing an unappealing job, make a pledge to spend just 10 minutes on it a day. Often, you'll want to carry on longer once you've started; but if not, quit the task after 10 minutes. In a week, you will have spent an hour on it.

INSIGHTS

"Fantasizing, projecting yourself into a successful situation, is the most powerful means there is of achieving personal goals. That's what an athlete does when he comes onto the field to kick a field goal with 3 seconds on the clock, 80,000 people in the stands, and 30 million watching on TV. The athlete, like the businessman, automatically makes thousands of tiny adjustments necessary to achieve the mental picture he's forming of the successful situation: a winning field goal."

—Leonard Lauder, president, Estée Lauder

Ask Yourself

- Do I give myself credit not just for what I did but for how I did it? Even if I didn't make a sale today, can I give myself a pat on the back for the way I conducted myself? for making good efforts? for following through on something I promised? for doing "the right thing" in a difficult situation?

- How do I acknowledge such behavior? Even though virtue is supposed to be its own reward, it doesn't hurt to keep some kind of record of it to look at. Doing so might provide comfort and inspiration during low periods.

- Do I break down goals into manageable steps that I can achieve on a daily basis?

- Do I chart my progress regularly in a visible way?

- Do I give myself a big reward for the goals I meet, and smaller rewards for the interim steps I achieve?

Dialog 2

Embrace Challenges

Scenario

You've been presented with a challenge. Perhaps it's a sales quota, or maybe the challenge takes the form of an especially oppositional prospect. The challenge could be self-imposed, such as a decision to revive a former account. Whatever the realm, you've taken on something outside the ordinary.

> "Challenges are what make life interesting; overcoming them is what makes life meaningful."
>
> —Joshua J. Marine

Strategies

> "It is not the mountain we conquer, but ourselves."
>
> —Edmund Hillary

Challenges are, by definition, difficult endeavors. They require a special mind-set and special behaviors to be overcome successfully. Useful strategies for dealing with challenges are the Find, Bind, and Remind strategies.

You must first identify the challenges you're willing to take on. This is the basis of the Find strategy. While you certainly don't want to take on every challenge you see, neither do you automatically want to run from every challenge, either. Seeking challenges helps you grow in capabilities and in character. But personally selecting your challenges, when possible, helps ensure your success with them.

Once you find a challenge you're willing to accept, bind yourself to it. The Bind strategy encourages you to write out a contract with yourself or announce to others your commitment to this goal. The more tangible your "binding agreement," the more likely you'll stick to it. You'll need to be specific about the behaviors you're undertaking, the

235

time frame in which the job is to be done, and the rewards attached to meeting your goals.

Taking on challenges is not easy. The Remind strategy recognizes that the more supports you build into the process, the more likely you'll stick with it until you succeed. Such supports might include records of your progress toward this goal, a written statement of why you took on this challenge, inspiring quotes to keep you motivated during low periods or cool in heated moments, and appropriate rewards for achieving interim steps.

Remember, too, that your choice of words can convey your comfort level with challenge; your words can show others that you're not afraid of a difficult situation and that you're not one to avoid the hard work (and the rewards!) of a tough task. Keep in mind that your customers face their own challenges. When you come across as someone who's comfortable with challenges, customers may see that as a real asset. If you appear to thrive on challenges, they may come to regard you as someone who can help them with their own difficulties. Tap into the subject of challenges with questions such as the following and then seek solutions based on the responses you receive.

- What are the biggest challenges facing your industry today?
- How about your particular company?
- How is your company attempting to address those issues?
- How are your competitors addressing them?
- What kinds of challenges does your particular department (division, location, office) face currently?
- What do you see as possible solutions to those problems?

Further Considerations

Try to incorporate fun into your challenges as much as possible. If you can depersonalize the challenge and see it more as a game, you may be able to inject some fun into it, and that element of fun may improve your chances of success.

Embrace Challenges

You: So, Mrs. Chen, I'd like to stop by and show you what I'm talking about.

Prospect: No. We're satisfied with our current supplier.

You: Then I'll have to work especially hard to get your business. Would you give me just a five-minute meeting? I can come by tomorrow morning at 10:00. If I haven't sparked your interest by 10:05, I want you to throw me out. Fair enough?

Notes: Your words here convey that you feel undaunted by the prospect's initial resistance. They reflect the fact that you're willing to take on (and perhaps you even welcome) challenges! Using the Find, Bind, and Remind strategies gives you a way to examine challenges, both your own and those of others. Perhaps the next challenge that you'll find is an even more difficult one, such as re-establishing a relationship with a former customer.

Find Strategy

You: I want you to know that I've taken on the personal challenge of working to re-establish your relationship with our company. I know there've been some difficulties in the past. But we've made some changes that I think you'll be pleased with. May I come by to share this information with you?

Former Client: I don't think so. We had a really bad experience with your company.

Bind Strategy

You: I know there is some repair work to be done between us and it's going to be a challenge to regain your trust, but I want to take on that challenge. We're under new management now, and I've made a commitment to them to do whatever I can to re-establish our relationship. I'm making that commitment to you as well now.

As a first step, may I take you out to lunch so that you can tell me everything that went wrong in the past? I really want to understand this situation thoroughly.

Former Client: Well, okay.

Remind Strategy

You (to yourself): Hurray! I've succeeded in this first step of my challenge. I'm going to make note of this step in my client records. I'm also going to post some memento of it at my desk. Also, I'll call my boss to tell him of my progress. I'm one step closer to my reward of a weekend away when I actually win back this customer.

237

Notice which elements are included in formal incentive programs and see if you can apply them to any goal setting that you're doing on your own.

The tone for any endeavor is often set at the top. Be aware of your own participation, level of involvement, and enthusiasm if you're the one setting up an incentive program.

Ask Yourself

- What strategies or techniques are the most effective for me in terms of embracing challenges?

- What people do I admire for the way they handled challenges? Do I keep reminders of them around me for inspiration?

- When were the times in my personal life when I acknowledged a challenging situation, accepted the challenge, and then met or exceeded it? What principles from that experience can I apply to my professional life?

- Do I keep a list of the challenges I've embraced throughout my life, knowing that such a list can be a source of encouragement and strength?

- How do I help others facing personal and/or professional challenges?

- If someone came to me with the very same problem I'm facing myself, how would I advise them to handle it?

Dialog 3

Let Exemplars Inspire You

Scenario

You're looking at the practices of others in order to give yourself a fresh perspective on your own selling techniques. You make a point of keeping your eyes open for successful practices that you could incorporate into your own repertoire.

Strategies

Throughout your sales career, you'll make a point of observing successful selling practices and applying those that are most appealing to you. The strategies of some successful salespeople are presented here, including the "Sell Myself First" strategy that features the practices of salesman Joe McGuire.

The Make-It-Memorable strategy is illustrated with exemplars such as salesman John Henry James, described in a book by Victor Kiam called *Going for It!* James was a large man who made his presence felt. He was impeccably dressed, and made his sales calls in a chauffeur-driven limo. He certainly knew how to make a memorable presentation.

But exemplars are everywhere from the corner lemonade stand to the White House. Find those that inspire you the most and study them. Then try to incorporate their best features into your own selling techniques.

Further Considerations

All of us are selling all the time, whether in our personal or our professional lives. Some of the people considered to be the world's best salespeople aren't technically in the profession of selling at all. Even though these people achieved their success in other fields, it was their use of sales techniques that helped them attain their success. Study effective selling techniques wherever you find them.

Let Exemplars Inspire You

> **You:** *(Concluding your sales presentation.)* So that's how our computer system works, complete with an array of software pre-installed. It's an all-inclusive package with everything you might need.

↓

> **Prospect:** Well, all that computer equipment sure takes up a lot of space.

"Sell Myself First" Strategy

> **You:** That's because we connected every possible function so that you could have it all at your fingertips. Isn't that great? No running down the hall for copies. Just use the scanner here and print out anything you need on the printer.

↓

> **Prospect:** Yes, that's true, but I imagine all this equipment adds up to a pretty big price tag.

↓

> **You:** Actually, the price is the best feature. This entire package is only $6,395.

↓

> **Prospect:** Holy cow!

↓

> **You:** I knew you'd be impressed! You probably thought that the whole setup would cost much more!

Notes: The preceding script, based on the "Sell Myself First" strategy, is inspired by the practices of a salesman named Joe McGuire. Joe always worked to persuade himself that his product was the absolute best on the market, and whenever someone remarked about the product, he naturally took the comment to be a compliment.

He didn't feign this attitude; he truly believed in his product because he sold it to himself before he tried to sell it to anyone else. Once he became convinced of the quality and value of his product, it was easy to convince others.

Make-It-Memorable Strategy

> **Limo chauffeur:** *(Having literally rolled out a red carpet.)* Mr. John Henry James has arrived!

↓

> **John Henry James:** *(Stating his intention as he saunters into the store.)* I do believe we're going to do some business today.

Notes: Supersalesman Bob Englud made-it-memorable with a practice of wearing a raccoon fur coat throughout the entire year. The coat was his trademark and his conversation piece. It was a way to get around the sometimes awkward start of a sales conversation, and it was something that made him stand out, be talked about, and definitely be remembered.

On the assumption that it's more important to work smart than it is to work hard, ask yourself what your "prime-time endeavors" should be. Think about how your exemplars might answer that question. Then figure out which practices generate the best return on your investment of time and which activities bring you closer to your goals.

Have you developed a mentor relationship with someone you admire? According to Jean Paul Lyet, former CEO of Sperry, "Very few people get to the top without being taken under the wing of an older person somewhere along the way." If you don't have a mentor, see if there's a colleague with whom you could share each other's motivation when necessary.

Assume, for the sake of this exercise, that deep inside you is your own personal "exemplar"—a wise being who already knows all the secrets for creating a successful sales career. Consult your inner exemplar and write a list of those secrets.

Ask Yourself

- Do I really believe in my product? Do I consistently convey that to my customers?

- If not, how can I better illustrate my belief?

- Do I note the effective techniques I observe and try to include them in my own repertoire?

- Do I keep reminders of my favorite exemplars around me for inspiration? Do these reminders include quotes, pictures, books they've written, and so on?

- When facing difficulties, do I try to envision how my exemplars would handle them?

INSIGHTS

"I have had a lot of success with failure."

—Thomas Edison

"The real secret of success is enthusiasm. Yes, more than enthusiasm I would say excitement. I like to see men get excited. When they get excited, they make a success of their lives."

—Walter Chrysler

"The formula for success is to double your failure rate."

—Thomas J. Watson Jr., former president of IBM

EXPERIENCE SHOWS

If you're not the flamboyant type and you're looking for a more subtle way to stand out from the crowd, consider doing something unique with your business cards. What could you do that would give them a different slant and enhance your image? What would give people a reason to talk about them? Some salespeople have done things as simple as attaching candy to their cards. Others have handed out cards that proclaim an outrageous title. If you sell books, perhaps your business card is a long, narrow laminated bookmark. If you sell pet food, create a business card for a dog that happens to include information on how to contact you. The possibilities are endless.

- What do I do to make myself stand out from the crowd and make people remember me?

- Have I established any mentor-type relationships? Do I call on my personal mentors for advice? Do I make use of resources such as SCORE (Service Corps of Retired Executives)?

- Is there someone I'd like to shadow by spending a day observing him or her at work?

Dialog 4

Use Rejection as a Spur

Scenario

You've experienced some form of rejection. It might be as simple as someone hanging up on you in the middle of a cold call or something as significant as losing a major account. It's a given that unwelcome events will occur in the career of every successful salesperson, and it's natural to feel somewhat depressed or defeated when they do. Your first instinct may be to run from such rejection and all the negative feelings it stirs up. But rejection can actually be used as a tool that strengthens you and makes you more committed to your goals.

Strategies

As a sales professional, you know that you can expect to hear an average of seven nos before you hear a yes. You'll acknowledge this reality every time you hear a no by translating it to mean "not yet," rather than interpreting it as a complete dead end. You'll look forward to a different outcome at some other time, and will use an Open-Door strategy that allows for future developments to take place.

Use Rejection as a Spur

You: *(Finishing up a sales presentation.)* … and so that's our product and all it can do for you.

Prospect: *(Pulling out every conceivable objection in the book.)* Very nice. But we couldn't possibly use a product like this at this time. Even if we did, I don't have the budget for it at this point.

Open-Door Strategy

Prospect: *(After citing her complete list of genuine objections.)* So I'll just have to say no!

You: *(Having already addressed all her objections individually.)* Well, Samantha, perhaps I'll check back with you in a few months to see if your needs have changed.

Notes: In this simple example, you make it clear from your dialog that you are not one to simply take "no" for an answer and that you are wise enough to know that things (and people) *change, so you always try to leave doors open. Such an attitude helps reveal your character to others and helps you reaffirm your commitment to your own beliefs.*

Customer-Success Strategy

Prospect: Okay. Feel free to check back with me.

You: I definitely will. In fact, I'm marking it into my calendar right now. I'm certain my wireless communicator would be of enormous value to you, and I'd like to see you reap the benefits of it. I admire what you're doing with your company. I'd really like to see it succeed and to be part of its success.

Notes: This is another way to convey your tenacity. You state your intention to keep pursuing your prospect's business because of your conviction that what you have to offer will be of solid benefit to her and to the success of her company.

Accept-Project-Protect Strategy

You: *(Taking out a piece of paper and quickly writing out the following, right off the top of your head.)* I accept that my *(product, proposal, services)* have been rejected. This makes me feel *(insecure, depressed, unconfident, nervous, incompetent).*

You: When I project from this point forward, my worst fears are that *(I'll be fired; I will never make another sale in my life; no one will respect me).*

You: *(Considering the worst possible consequences of this event and quantifying them)* The worst that could happen is that (I'll be out $5,000; I'll be embarrassed the next time I pick up the phone to make a cold call; I'll never get another job in this industry).

You: *(Considering whether there would be any way to handle the horrible outcome—if it were to actually occur—to protect what you hold dear or whether this would truly be the end of the world.)* Well, even if that were to occur I could do …. I'd get help from …. I could even ….

Note: Each time you do this exercise, you can come up with new perspectives and new solutions. Repeat it until you have a reasonable handle on the situation and feel more comfortable about it. Then crumple the paper, along with your fears and worries, and throw them all in the trash—literally and figuratively.

BE CAREFUL

Make sure that the company you work for doesn't object to its salespeople having individual Web sites. The sites may conflict with company policy for a number of reasons.

WHAT THE EXPERTS SAY

Dr. Martin Seligman of the University of Pennsylvania says that each of us has an "explanatory style" that influences our interpretation of events. For example, if your explanatory style tends to be optimistic, you will be inclined to put a positive spin on how you explain events to yourself. If your explanatory style is typically pessimistic, you're likely to assign negative or self-critical reasons to your understanding of given events. Studies show that your style can have a big impact on your sales performance. Seligman says that explanatory style is learned and can be modified.

It's clear that tenacity is an essential trait for the successful salesperson, so you'll employ a variety of strategies to keep yourself going after a rejection. The Customer-Success strategy encourages you to keep pursuing your prospect's business when you're convinced your products or services will be of benefit to her. The Accept-Project-Protect strategy involves the use of a "self-talk" dialog to help you get through an upsetting rejection. This strategy provides a useful technique for neutralizing negative thoughts and discarding self-doubt. It emphasizes the fact that, short of death, we always have options and that our fears and worries, while real, often diminish in importance when articulated, quantified, and faced squarely.

Further Consideration

As demonstrated previously, difficulties can be used to restore your perspective and self-esteem, and to help strengthen and protect them. They can also be used to strengthen and protect your commitment to your career. Remind yourself of why you chose this work, what you're particularly good at, and where you're going. You can then start out again with a clean slate and a renewed commitment to your goals. Remember that peace of mind doesn't come from the absence of difficulties, but rather from an ability to handle them.

Think back to a rejection or other difficult event from your past, something that felt truly devastating at the time. How did it turn out? What did you do to help make it okay? If you're like most people looking back, you can't find many situations that you didn't somehow overcome.

Keeping a journal of difficult events can help in working through them at the moment. Journals also provide a useful reference to look back upon when you need to regain perspective.

Consider creating your own Web page that touts your achievements and abilities. Include any honors, awards, degrees, customer lists, letters of reference, and so on, and ask prospects to visit it, particularly if you find it difficult to toot your own horn. Visit it yourself, too, if you're feeling low or in a slump!

Ask Yourself

- How do I typically react to rejection? How do I tend to handle such feelings? What techniques are most effective in helping me get past such feelings?

- How would I advise someone who was having trouble coping with a recent rejection?

- Do I use difficult periods as a time to recommit myself to my purpose?

- Do I recognize how difficult times add to my range of experience and depth of character?

- Does my "explanatory style" tend to be optimistic or pessimistic? What could I do to put a more positive spin on my interpretation of events?

> **WHAT THE EXEMPLARS DO**
>
> Aristotle Onassis said, "You don't fail until you give up." Successful people are usually those who refuse to quit, such as R. H. Macy who failed in his first 7 attempts to create a successful department store; author John Creasy who received over 700 rejections before having more than 60 million copies of his books in print; and Thomas Edison who failed 10,000 times before perfecting the incandescent light. Edison's view was that he didn't fail at all: "I didn't fail 10,000 times. I successfully eliminated, 10,000 times, materials and combinations which wouldn't work."

Dialog 5

Know the Motivators

Scenario

You are trying to become more attuned to motivation—your own as well as that of others. While there are some things that people are universally motivated to do (eat and sleep, for example), other motivators are unique only to certain individuals and not others. Becoming more aware of motivators in general, as well as those that are idiosyncratic, will make your professional relationships smoother.

Know the Motivators

Salesperson: It seems silly for me to be traveling out west so much to cover territories when I'm based in the east.

↓

You: I know what you mean.

Identify/Rectify Strategy

You: But you've been with those accounts a long time, and I know they don't want to lose you. Let me make sure I understand what you're saying. You don't object to serving those accounts, just all the travel it takes to do so.

↓

Salesperson: That's it exactly.

↓

You: Let me see whether it's possible for you to hold some virtual meetings with these customers to cut down on the travel. That's one possible solution; let's both brainstorm for others.

Notes: Remember, problems are a tool that help you identify what the motivators are for different people. Encourage your staff to use this strategy as a way to help keep customers happy. Ask the staff to report any customer "grumblings" or other dissatisfactions to you, even if there seems to be no solution.

Save Strategy

You: These product display racks automatically reload, saving you time and money!

Notes: Saving is a big motivator. Do you know anyone who doesn't want to save time, trouble, or money? Who doesn't want to protect their health and other assets? Think about what your product saves for customers. Emphasize that feature in your dialogs and, whenever possible, include the word "save" in them.

More Strategy

You: I know that you really like to make good use of your time, and I've got the perfect tool for capitalizing on it.

Notes: Having more is, of course, another big motivator. Pepper your sales presentations with words such as boost, advance, expand, increase, strengthen, multiply, and capitalize; then attach those words to whatever the relevant hot button is.

Compliments Strategy

Prospect: Yes, I know Jim Orville. He makes that company run as smooth as silk.

↓

You: *(At an appropriate time—not necessarily right after the above comment.)* I know you really value efficiency and things that are "done right." This new intranet tool of ours will streamline your operations so that your business operates at the peak of efficiency.

Notes: You identified that this prospect values efficiency based upon his compliment. Therefore, you'll reference efficiency when making your sales pitch, knowing that it's a likely motivator for this prospect.

Strategies

Motivation begins with your belief that you can accomplish something. As Henry Ford said, "Whether you believe you can do a thing or believe you can't, you are right." Dare to believe in your dreams, and listen to yourself regularly to see if your dreams have changed. (Use techniques such as the "Goal Setting Through One-Person Dialogs" found at the beginning of this chapter for that purpose.)

If you listen well to yourself, you'll always know where your heart lies and what the direction of your dreams is.

If you listen well to your staff, you'll be better able to work out problems with them, as is shown in the Identify/Rectify strategy. With this strategy you'll first try to identify a problem as accurately as possible. Then you'll brainstorm and use other creative problem-solving techniques to come up with solutions that satisfy and thereby lend momentum to motivation.

If you listen well to your customers, you'll be equipped to help them identify and satisfy needs and wishes. When people compliment someone or something, they are identifying something they value and, hence, a likely motivator. This is illustrated in the Compliments strategy, which helps identify the different "hot buttons" that serve as motivators for different people.

Use of some more general motivators is explored in both the Save strategy and the More strategy in the following script.

Further Considerations

Is there anything about your products that will help your customers motivate their own employees in some way? Do you emphasize that in your sales presentations?

INSIGHTS

"If you aren't fired with enthusiasm— you will be fired with enthusiasm.

—Vince Lombardi

EXPERIENCE SHOWS

Try this tactic to motivate yourself to do an unpleasant task. Set up a scenario in which you use a highly desirable reward and assume that someone has just come up to you and said something like, "If you can finish this (whatever the unwelcome task is) in (15 minutes, one hour, etc.), you'll get (a million dollars, a trip to Hawaii, etc.)." Of course, this is just an exercise, but it reveals the fact that if the event were to occur in real life, you'd jump at the chance to try to achieve it. Clearly, the motivation is there within us. Sometimes the power of the imagination can help us tap into it.

WHAT THE EXPERTS SAY

Studies show that when teachers expect children to perform well in school, they do. Such studies illustrate the principle of a self-fulfilling prophecy, wherein preexisting expectations are met. The expectations can come from any source, including instructions in a research experiment, prejudice, myths, labels, or one's personal convictions. But regardless of the source, results conform to expectations when a self-fulfilling prophecy is operating.

When problems are addressed early, before they have a chance to become messy and complicated, people are more motivated to see them through. If you're working with a staff, try to identify problems early by listening well. The problems might be those of the staff members themselves or those of your customers, as revealed through your staff. Regardless of the source, welcome them all.

Keep in mind that success itself is a great motivator because it usually begets more success. Some people may get lucky with an initial success, but usually success comes from sheer hard work:

> "I'm a great believer in luck, and the harder I work the luckier I get."
>
> —Stephen Leacock

> "Luck means the hardships and privations which you have not hesitated to endure; the long nights you have devoted to work. Luck means the appointments you have never failed to keep, the airplanes you never failed to catch."
>
> —Margaret L. Clement

> "Luck seems to have a peculiar attachment to work."
>
> —Anonymous

Ask Yourself

- What tends to motivate me? How can I utilize that motivator in explicit ways to move me toward my goals?

- Knowing that it's easy to ignore motivators that aren't personally meaningful, do I make note of the kinds of things that motivate others but have no impact on me, especially if I'm responsible for managing a staff?

EXPERIENCE SHOWS

The subconscious can be your ally in developing motivation. Visualizations, affirmations, and sometimes even hypnosis are tools used by athletes and others concerned with purpose, performance, and power. Visualizations are a sort of meditation that features the creation of a detailed mental image of a desired outcome. Affirmations are positive statements about the present and/or future, and are often repeated in writing on a daily basis.

WHAT THE EXEMPLARS DO

Consultant Jeanie Marshall provides information on affirmations and related topics at her Web site, www.mhmail.com, where you can listen to online meditations, read relevant articles, and even register to receive daily or weekly e-mail affirmations. Dr. M. J. Bovo offers a section on affirmations at www.mjbovo.com/Affirmations. htm. The site lists a variety of affirmations, grouped by topic, that appear onscreen with musical accompaniment.

- Do I note what is important to my customers or what motivates them—their "hot buttons"?

- What expectations am I predisposed to? What self-fulfilling prophecies do I experience?

- Do I use visualizations and affirmations to help myself achieve my goals?

Dialog 6

Empower Employees

Scenario

As a sales manager, you are regularly responsible for making sure your team meets deadlines, sales targets, and other goals. You require reports, meetings, and more! You want them to perform as a cohesive unit, and even have some fun while they're doing it! You want to be a good manager and an effective motivator.

Strategies

You'll take every opportunity to have a dialog with your employees and make them active participants in the process of reaching goals, accomplishing missions, solving problems, and reaching solutions. You'll welcome their feedback and allow them latitude in the "how" of getting things done, as is seen in the Direction strategy. You do all this because it is an effective way to manage and because it spurs motivation.

You'll also aim to inject humor into your work environment because of the power it possesses to diffuse tense situations and to put fun in the workplace. The Humor strategy is a technique that serves this purpose. A variation on the Humor strategy is to keep a (growing) arsenal of clever comebacks to ease you out of an awkward situation and keep everyone's feelings intact.

> **INSIGHTS**
>
> "Motivate employees, train them, care about them, and make winners of them. At Marriott we know that if we treat our employees correctly, they'll treat the customers right. And if the customers are treated right, they'll come back."
>
> —Bill Marriott Jr., chairman, Marriott
>
> "The job of the manager is enabling, not a directive job ..., coaching and not direction is the first quality of leadership now. Get the barriers out of the way to let people do the things they do well."
>
> —Robert Noyce, founder, Intel

249

Empower Employees

You: *(At a staff meeting.)* We've got many things to review today. We've got to review our preparations for that big sales presentation next week. I'd also like to review our new sales reporting procedures.

Direction Strategy

You: *(Later in the meeting.)* So here are the targets we need to reach this month. I want you all to think about how we can best reach and even exceed them, and report back to me at next Monday's meeting.

Notes: You were following a Direction strategy. George Patton is quoted as saying "Give direction, not directions." By using a strategy in which you outline broad goals and leave the details up to individuals, you are involving your staff in the process. Studies show that the more they are involved, the more likely you'll see success.

Clever-Comeback Strategy

Co-worker: So, in a year, how much do you pull in?

You: *(Feeling that this question crosses the line and is a little too personal, you smile, squint your eyes, and maybe even scratch your head a little.)* Um, do I have to answer that?

Or Oh, I'll never tell!

Humor Strategy

Salesperson: *(In a staff meeting, feeling overworked and rather disgruntled.)* I just don't see how we're going to cover all these territories by the deadline.

You: *(If the moment is right for a joke.)* You remember that salesman who came into our office the other day with a computer program that he claimed would cut our workload by 50 percent. We should just call him up and tell him we'll take two! That would eliminate our workload entirely!

Further Considerations

Use humor whenever it's appropriate to do so in the workplace. In addition to making work more enjoyable, humor cements bonds among co-workers. Even if you feel that humor is not your strength in conversation, you can use humor in nonspeaking ways. For example, send humorous cards or e-mail greetings. Give humorous books as gifts. If you want to e-mail someone a joke every now and then, visit sites such as www. jokingaround.com, www. humorshack.com, and www.oracle. com. Or, if you find a humorous article in a magazine, pass it along. Always exercise good judgment when using humor, though. Never be the source of any questionable material. Remember that what is humorous to you may be highly offensive to someone else, so always err on the side of propriety.

In order to strengthen your team, consider ways in which you can visually track their success as a team, perhaps through charts posted in the office, in newsletters, or on the company Web site.

Some companies conduct anonymous internal surveys in order to gather information from employees on a variety of issues. When the surveys are done regularly, the results can be compared to determine trends from year to year. Employees often like the fact that their ideas are being sought, if not instituted, and surveys thereby tend to boost morale and motivation. If your company does not do so already, perhaps you should consider using surveys.

Most businesses take customer service seriously. A few, though, go the extra mile by empowering their employees with this customer service policy: "Each employee is required to satisfy the customer and do whatever it takes to make the customer happy on the spot. Any employee planning to make an exception to this rule has to first seek permission from management to do so." How does your company compare in terms of empowering employees to give great customer service?

BE CAREFUL

In order to help ensure success, make interim checks to confirm that progress toward goals is being made in a favorable way. Don't wait until a big job is nearly finished before checking in. This applies to everything from annual sales goals, to preparing for a major sales presentation.

EXPERIENCE SHOWS

Keep a collection of clever quips in a file folder. Add to it regularly and use it as a resource for your conversations and correspondence.

WHAT THE EXPERTS SAY

Studies show that, in general, the way that employees treat customers is similar to the way their employers treat them. The tone is set at the top, from where it permeates the entire company and beyond.

Ask Yourself

- Do I empower my employees? How and why?

- Do I delegate as much as possible, or do I tend to be a control freak? If so, how could I curb that tendency?

- What tone do I tend to set?

- How do I reward employees for their achievements?

- What steps do I take outside of the office to strengthen my team and allow them to get to know one another more?

- Do I try to use humor as a tool at every appropriate opportunity?

- How could I make our workplace more fun?

WHAT THE EXEMPLARS DO

President and CEO Mike Snyder heads the Red Robin restaurant chain, which boasts over 140 locations in the United States and Canada. He charges his employees with delivering "unbridled service" to customers. Snyder's "unbridled" philosophy is defined by him this way: "At Red Robin, Unbridled is an attitude, a style, a passion. To run free without restraint. Unbridled is what sets Red Robin apart from all other restaurant companies in the world."

The company empowers employees to perform "Unbridled Acts," spontaneous good deeds (or planned events) that help customers, co-workers, and charitable causes. The company emphasizes what it calls the "Red Robin 'WOW' factor" by publicizing such acts (and the employees responsible for them) in print, on its Web site (www.redrobin.com), and even on its menus.

The company considers its employees its most valuable asset. It refers to them as "team members" and acknowledges that "what really keeps Guests coming back are the people. A positive experience with an unbridled team member can turn a first-time Guest into a regular." Red Robin aims for a low employee turnover by offering generous incentive and reward programs and by celebrating staff successes with special events.

Dialog 7

Perk Up Your Sales Staff

Scenario

You're a sales manager concerned with how to keep your staff's motivation and morale high. Even if you're part of the staff and not a manager, the following principles still apply. Consider yourself the manager of your own sales career; set goals; use perks to stoke your motivation; hire yourself, supervise yourself, and if necessary fire an old self and rehire a new self.

Strategies

"Perquisite," the word from which "perk" comes, is defined by Webster's as "something additional to regular profit or pay, resulting from one's position." Take the time to learn what motivates the different people on your staff and you'll improve their performance. With some employees, money will be the motivator, though usually not for its own sake but rather as a means of measuring and keeping score (for example, "I earned more this year than last year; my sales are up 15 percent for the quarter"). Other people like to be the sole winner in a competition. Some respond to praise and recognition.

EXPERIENCE SHOWS

Remember the importance of humor in the workplace. People who have more fun at work have higher levels of productivity. Humor is said to nurture creative thinking and to prevent burnout. Consider hiring a "humor consultant" who offers services such as keynote speeches, seminars for employees on how to use humor in the workplace, and even advice on how to put humor into company newsletters. Find humor consultants at sites such as www.humorsearch.com, www.humorconsultants.com, or www. uconsultus. com/humor.

Perk Up Your Sales Staff

You: *(In a staff meeting.)* I wanted to take a moment at the start of this meeting to say that we are delighted to have Mary back with us now that her mother is well on the road to recovery. As you know, Mary, our thoughts and prayers were with you during that time.

↓

Mary: Thank you all for your support.

↓

You: You're welcome Mary. Now, turning our attention to our agenda, James has the results of the internal employee survey. He'll distribute them for your review and we'll discuss at our next meeting, along with some information about how we're restructuring the Human Resources department.

Best-Efforts Strategy

You: *(Continuing.)* I wanted to inform all of you that, unfortunately, I just learned that we didn't get the S&O account. I'm sure you're all as disappointed as I am about that. However, something more important came out of this endeavor. We really pulled together as a team for the first time. I was so impressed with that! The way we worked together is a model for us to aspire to when we make pitches in the future.

Notes: When results are not what you hoped for, it's important to focus on what was right about the endeavor. Doing so will help to boost morale.

↓

Perk-Up Strategy

You: *(Making statements like these every chance you get.)* I appreciate all your hard work.

Or Thanks for staying late (coming in early) to finish this.

Or I knew I could count on you to finish before the deadline.

Or Thanks for thinking of that.

Or Good question. Good thinking.

Or This really makes my job easier.

Or Thanks for being so organized (for being on top of things).

Or Thanks for bringing that to my attention.

Or Your rapport with customers is a real asset to our company.

Or I'm so glad you're on our team.

Or Thanks for your dedication.

Or You outdid yourself.

Or Great job!

Or You're number one.

Notes: Seize every opportunity to give messages such as the preceding to your team, keeping in mind which statements would be meaningful for (and therefore motivational for) which people. Some people pride themselves on their loyalty, others on their ability to follow through. Still others pride themselves on their ability to compete and win.

Still others strive for membership in elite groups such as the "President's Club"—a circle of top sales performers who are often treated to an exotic, all-expenses-paid holiday. As a manager, you'll be called upon to shore up motivation after major disappointments (try the Best-Efforts strategy) as well as on an everyday basis (with a Perk-Up strategy). The Perk-Up strategy encourages you to:

- **P**ay attention to what your staff tells you, and respond appropriately.

- **E**mpathize with their difficulties, personal and professional.

- **R**emember birthdays, employment anniversaries, and other appropriate occasions.

- **K**eep them informed about changes in the company, the industry, and other areas affecting their jobs.

- **U**se every opportunity to reward their efforts and accomplishments.

- **P**ut humor in the workplace.

Further Considerations

If your company doesn't offer a program such as a President's Club for top performers, create one just for yourself if that's the kind of thing that would motivate you! Say to yourself, "If I sell ..., I'll treat myself to ...." Send yourself teasers for the interim milestones you reach, just as any employer would.

Some companies have come up with motivators that are creative and unusual in an effort to get employees to sign on or to stay on. Consider which of the following might be meaningful to you or your

---

EXPERIENCE SHOWS

When you "catch them doing something right," acknowledge your staff immediately. Compliments are most meaningful and most effective at that time. Also, in order to maximize the impact of praise, give it in the presence of others rather than privately, whenever possible. Or, give it privately first and then repeat it in front of others as opportunities arise. Also, think about ways to "accentuate the positive." Was an employee mentioned in the newspaper? Blow up the article to poster size and hang it in a prominent place. Did an employee work very long hours for a stretch of time? Send a thank you note to his family.

EXPERIENCE SHOWS

E-mail can also be used as an effective motivator. Send your staff notes of congratulations or encouragement through sites that offer e-cards, such as www.bluemountain.com, www.awards.com, or www.ivillage.com. (At the iVillage home page, look for "favorites," click "postcards," and then go to the "work" category.)

INSIGHTS

"I can live for two months on a good compliment."

—Mark Twain

BE CAREFUL

Although it's true that you'll need to use different things to motivate different people, try to keep an overall level of fairness in terms of the worth of what you give out as incentives.

WHAT THE EXPERTS SAY

The "1999 Employee Relationship Report Benchmark," conducted by Walker Information and Hudson Institute, states the following: "More than money, employees cite intangible or 'soft' aspects of corporate culture as having a strong influence on their commitment. These include low- or no-cost items like 'My manager pays attention,' 'Asks how I'm doing,' and the confidence that their organization would help in time of need." For more information, visit the site of the nonprofit National Association for Employee Recognition at www.recognition.org.

WHAT THE EXEMPLARS DO

Master motivator Bob Nelson says that employees need to be rewarded almost daily and that practices such as the following tend to be extremely meaningful: recognizing and appreciating employees' work; keeping them updated on changes that will impact them; and being the kind of manager who really listens to them. Visit Bob Nelson's Web site at www.nelson-motivation.com.

staff: a corporate valet service that runs errands for employees, such as picking up dry cleaning, walking the dog, or watering plants for employees who are away on business trips; an on-site ATM machine; a "meals-to-go" service; tickets to sporting events and concerts; take-your-pet-to-work day; free lease and insurance on a high-end car; moving expenses for unusual items such as sailboats or antique cars; day-care services; college tuition programs; gift certificates on each one-year anniversary with the company; on-site gym and diet services; home computer equipment; quit-smoking programs; days off for community service; on-site blood drives; discounts for local stores and services; use of employees in company commercials and literature; mentions in the company newsletter or on the Web site.

Ask Yourself

- Do I make a conscious effort to practice good listening skills?

- Do I make a point of keeping humor present in my personal and my professional life?

- How could I enhance its presence?

- Knowing that enthusiasm is contagious, do I regularly focus on boosting my own enthusiasm as well as that of my staff?

- Do I take note of the different things that motivate different people?

- Do I keep goals specific, measurable, and reachable in order to keep myself and others moving toward them?

Dialog 8

Motivate Your Customers

Scenario

You're dealing with prospects and customers. You want to motivate them to consider you as a vendor; to develop a relationship with you; and to buy from you, now and in the future. In short, you want your customers and yourself to be in business together, with all that this entails.

Strategies

Different things will motivate different customers, depending on their company's needs and their personal needs. Although you will always try to streamline your presentations for the audience receiving them, don't eliminate the qualities that help to motivate customers. These qualities include your own confidence, competence, and credibility, which you'll demonstrate by the way you present yourself and by how knowledgeable you are; and your ability to convey how you can benefit your customers, which you'll demonstrate through your dialogs.

> **INSIGHTS**
>
> "Don't oversell. If you do, it's like knocking on a turtle shell trying to get him to stick his head out."
>
> —David Crawley

> **EXPERIENCE SHOWS**
>
> Shared humor goes a long way in developing bonds. Include appropriate humor in your presentations whenever you can.

In the following dialog, you're about to start your sales presentation and you want to get agreement between yourself and the customer right from the beginning, so you are using a Get-Agreement strategy. This will set up a pattern of getting agreement that you'll try to continue throughout the presentation in order to build toward a successful close. The process will also help your prospects feel in sync with you. In addition, you will employ the Hot-Button strategy to emphasize product features based on what motivates this particular prospect. You will also enhance the power of motivation by referencing others who've had success with your product in an Endorsement strategy.

257

Motivate Your Customers

You: Thanks for taking the time to meet with me, Linda. I'm delighted to be able to show you this cutting edge material and what it can do for your company. I believe it really has the potential for enhancing your success.

Prospect: Tell me more!

Get-Agreement Strategy

You: Well, Linda, first I'd like to show you what our new fabric is all about and give you samples of our complete line. Then we can discuss how the benefits of this material could apply specifically to your company. Does that sound reasonable?

Prospect: Yes. Very reasonable.

Hot-Button Strategy

You: *(Coming to the close of the sales presentation.)* So you see, Linda, these newly formulated fabrics would work perfectly for the kinds of products your company makes. Just looking at your office environment, I can see that you use cutting-edge technology in its many forms. And no material is more cutting edge than this. Even though we've taken it to other industries, you'd be the first to market it in your field. That would be great PR mileage, wouldn't it?

Prospect: No doubt. Look, the fabrics are awfully appealing, but I always use my own designs.

Endorsement Strategy

You: We just finished a project for A-Really-Big Company and I'd like to show you how we worked with them, incorporating their own designs.

Prospect: I'd like to see that.

Get-Agreement Strategy (continued)

You: *(After taking her through the steps.)* Can you see what this material did for their bottom line and their reputation in the industry?

Prospect: It's pretty clear.

You: Would you like to enjoy those benefits, too?

Prospect: If this is an accurate reflection, who wouldn't?

You: Well then, we should get started.

Lighten-Load Strategy

Prospect: I don't know. It appeals to me because it's all so new. But it also scares me for that same reason. I love the cutting-edge part, but I don't love huge risks.

You: I can understand your apprehension. Look, let me pull together some additional information and get it to you later today. It's our research studies that would be over the heads of most of our customers, but not you with your background in chemistry. And if you like, I'll arrange for the president of A-Really-Big Company to give you a call so you can speak to him directly about his experience.

Prospect: That'd be great!

When applicable, use the Lighten-Load strategy to put yourself in the role of a consultant to your customers. Offer advice and solutions to their problems, and lighten their load whenever you can if it will also benefit you.

Further Considerations

Try to learn as much as possible about your prospects before you meet with them. Doing so may help you identify their personal hot buttons. Sites such as www.google.com or other search engines may be useful in obtaining information.

Remember to be observant about the persons themselves and their environment. Jewelry, class rings, lapel pins from different organizations, and even the ribbons that support various causes give you information about your prospects and their values.

Try to make yourself well-informed about your customers' wants and needs, both within the context of their specific company and their industry in general.

Ask Yourself

- Do I make use of ad specialties?

- Do I seize opportunities to garner other sorts of visibility and credibility by making public speaking appearances and attending networking events?

- How should I try to stand out and be remembered at trade shows?

- Do I make a point of building my relationships with current customers by staying in touch through faxes, mail, the phone, and e-mail?

EXPERIENCE SHOWS

Something as simple as seeing the name of your company can remind customers of your products and thereby serve as a motivator. Check your ad specialties to make sure they carry your name, phone, and Web address in a clearly visible spot. Is the specialty something that will likely be used regularly and/or displayed for easy reference? Is your phone number one that can be remembered? (The value of this should not be underestimated—just ask the people at 1-800-FLOWERS!)

EXPERIENCE SHOWS

Many businesses are starting to put company information on compact discs that can be played in the computer. Everything from an annual report to a complete purchasing catalog or a movie promotion can be put on these CDs. The CDs themselves now come in interesting shapes (including stars, squares, and hearts), with photos and other compelling graphics printed on the top side of the CD. See some samples at www.condes.com.

WHAT THE EXPERTS SAY

Promotional Products Association International released the results of a research study that showed that the promotional products industry had sales of nearly $15 billion in 1999. The study cited wearable items as the single most popular promotional product. A distant second was writing instruments, followed by accessories, calendars, and bags.

WHAT THE EXEMPLARS DO

Letitia Baldrige, "America's Leading Arbiter of Manners," the former social secretary to such luminaries as Jacqueline Kennedy, and an expert on business protocol, is a fan of personal-business letters. She states, "The writing of a good letter that is personal in nature but that is business related is not only the right thing to do and the nice thing to do, it is the *smart* thing to do." Visit her Web site at www.letitia.com.

- Are my presentations polished and rich in motivating language?

- Are my sales tools fresh and full of compelling examples of what I've done for other customers?

- Does the company Web site convey polish and professionalism in addition to providing information that is clear and compelling?

- Do I follow through on my promises so that customers know they can count on me?

Chapter 10

Employing Atypical Methods

The history of a wildly successful business often fits the above description. Take amazon.com, for example. It was daring. It was first. It was different, and it changed the way in which people bought things.

As a sales professional, you don't need to be as revolutionary as amazon.com to be considered successful. Nevertheless, you can try certain things in order to give a different slant to what you do. A change in the normal way you proceed may enliven your routines or produce a change in the outcomes you typically experience.

The dialogs in this chapter examine a variety of atypical methods, from different ways of thinking about things to different practices to employ and different tools to use. If you were perfectly satisfied with every facet of your sales career, you probably would not be reading this book. But if you're someone who's willing to consider something different, read on; you may find your interest sparked by what is offered here. Or, this chapter may inspire you to come up with your own ideas on how you might do things different.

Life is exciting because the "You Never Know" principle always applies. It's fun to try new approaches because you never know what might succeed. Even though you may feel more comfortable relying on the tried-and-true for the bulk of your sales transactions, you might benefit by adding the "innovative and new" here and there, to see where it takes you.

The dialogs in this chapter investigate ways in which you can try to employ new methods for everything from prospecting to making presentations. They explore elements such as humor and drama and examine how you might utilize them. They also discuss ways to approach standard problems, such as dealing with the gatekeeper and getting your foot in the door. In the chapter, we look at the subject of "doing well by doing good." Then we examine some selling methods that employ cutting-edge tools, so that you can consider how to use the technology of today to boost your sales figures of tomorrow.

> "A man with a new idea is a crank … until the idea succeeds."

> —Mark Twain

Dialog 1

Prospect for Prospects

Scenario

You're in the habit of using the typical techniques for generating leads. Now you want to try something atypical. You've decided that you'll make a game of tapping into chance encounters for signs of prospects. You'll go about your everyday business with this in mind and therefore strike up conversations with people on planes, in cabs, in restaurants, and even on elevators to see if serendipity strikes.

Strategies

To make it easy to strike up a conversation with strangers you'll use the techniques suggested in the Offer-Info-First strategy.

To carry such conversations even further, you'll consider using the Six Degrees of Separation strategy: Playwright John Guare coined the phrase "six degrees of separation" and used it as the title of one of his plays, which became a feature film. The idea is that any two people in the world can trace a link to each other through a string of just six acquaintances. With that concept in mind, you'll aim to establish rapport with the strangers that fate has placed near you. You'll try to ascertain whether those you meet through chance encounters are connected to someone you already know or should get to know. You'll look with interest at all your serendipitous encounters and consider where they might lead. And even if those encounters lead nowhere beyond a pleasant exchange of dialog, you'll take pleasure in that, too.

> **INSIGHTS**
>
> "Behold the turtle. He makes progress only when he sticks his neck out."
>
> —James B. Conant

> **EXPERIENCE SHOWS**
>
> Consider the following cyber sources for an atypical way of generating leads: www.harrisinfo.com, www.imarketinc.com, www.infousa.com, and www.americanmanufacturers.com.

Prospect for Prospects

You: *(In courtesy van to the ABC Hotel.)* Have you stayed at ABC before?

Or Great weather here in Atlanta *(or simply Hi).*

↓

Passenger: No, it's my first trip.

Notes: The point is to make a quick connection. The least-awkward time to connect with a stranger is after any transition point, such as walking through a door, sitting down, arriving at your place in line. The longer you wait after the transition, the more awkward it may be to get a dialog started. Transitions provide the opportunity for comment, and they allow you to set a tone. Even if you say no more than "Hello," you've established that you are a friendly, approachable person who would be open to further conversation, even if it doesn't occur until later.

Offer-Info-First Strategy

You: Oh, I come here all the time. *(Then offer some personal information.)* I work as a sales consultant for DEF Corporation.

↓

You: *(Allow a moment of silence to see whether the person responds. If not, follow up with something that is friendly but not too personal.)* Are you here on business, too? *(If the answer is "Yes," explore that answer. If it's "No," you can talk about more general things, such as where she flew in from, where her hometown is, or people you might know from there.)*

Notes: You established a connection with this stranger by quickly initiating a conversation. You nurtured the conversation by offering some personal information about yourself before asking personal questions of the other person. If there's a lull in the conversation but you'd like to keep talking, consider mentioning the Six Degrees of Separation theory.

Six Degrees of Separation Strategy

You: You know, they say that any two people in the world can route a connection to each other through a series of only six acquaintances. When I meet someone new, I'm always trying to figure out who those six people might be. I'm originally from Sacramento. How about you?

Notes: You carry on your conversation until you hit a natural close and perhaps at that time offer to exchange business cards.

↓

E-mail Strategy

You: *(In an e-mail.)* Susan, given that you're familiar with my work as a sales consultant for DEF Corporation, I'm wondering who on your e-mail list might be able to use my services. I'd be grateful if you could take a moment to scan your list and forward the addresses of anyone you think I could help. If you prefer to remain anonymous as a source, that's fine. Or I'd be happy to mention you when I contact these individuals. You know me well enough to know that I would never hound anyone by e-mail or in any other way. In fact, that's why I like using e-mail; it's less intrusive than a sales call. You can rest assured that if your contacts aren't interested in my services, I'll just move on.

Finally, you'll tap into the wonders of technology as a means of prospecting for prospects. Using the E-mail strategy, you'll seek contacts from the e-mail address lists of friends, co-workers, acquaintances, and others.

Further Considerations

Public speaking is another great way to connect with strangers and make yourself stand out. Toastmasters is an organization devoted to helping individuals improve their public speaking skills. Contact your local chapter or visit its Web site at www.toastmasters.org.

If you read an article about a stranger whom you think might be able to use your products, consider contacting that person.

Depending on what you're selling, consider the possibility of developing a formal or informal agent-type relationship that could help sell what you have to offer.

Ask Yourself

- Do I seize opportunities to make connections, even those that appear to be long shots?

- Do I offer to do public speaking for my company and for my community?

- Do I use the Internet as a tool for prospecting?

- What novel approaches for generating leads have I observed in others?

- Could I apply those practices, or some variation of them, to my own repertoire?

- What could I do at a trade show to make myself stand out (in a positive way, of course!).

BE CAREFUL

Employing atypical methods and operating in an unconventional manner can certainly yield rewards, but it can also yield risks. People may misinterpret your deeds and words, so be prepared to be misunderstood. Also, be careful of your conduct, so that anyone you approach in conversation doesn't take your overtures to be anything other than friendly business gestures. And be sure to read the cues: If someone doesn't want to carry on a conversation, don't push.

WHAT THE EXEMPLARS DO

Joe Girard is listed in *The Guinness Book of World Records* as "The World's Greatest Salesman." He is credited with creating a novel way of getting referrals. He gives one of his business cards to each of his current customers, with that person's name handwritten on the back. Each time a new customer comes in to his place of business and hands Joe a business card with a current customer's name on the back, Joe sends the current customer $25 as a thank-you.

Dialog 2

Adore the Gatekeeper

Scenario

Boss to secretary: "Why is it that you never pick up the telephone when it's ringing?"

Secretary: "Why should I do that? The call is usually for you!"

If only this scenario were true, it would make the life of the salesperson so much easier! Unfortunately, the reality is that it's often difficult to reach prospects because gatekeepers are screening all the calls—and the typical contact with a gatekeeper can be more like hand-to-hand combat! Gatekeepers usually have a great deal of experience in fending off unwelcome calls, even the worthy ones! They hold the power and can put an end to overtures with the click of a button on the telephone. The challenge is to get them on your side.

Strategies

The fact is that everyone has some degree of self-interest. It's part of how we're wired for survival. You'll try to appeal to that inherent self-interest by getting the gatekeeper to see that what you're offering can benefit him. The typical line of thinking in sales is to get past the gatekeeper. While that may work well in many circumstances, this chapter is not about typical methods but about atypical methods of dealing with typical problems.

Adore the Gatekeeper

You: Good morning. Susan Sloan calling for Sam Wang.

Gatekeeper: *(Rather surprised that you're asking for him and not his boss.)* This is he.

Direct-Benefits Strategy

You: Hi, Sam. I'm calling from XYZ Technologies. We're introducing a new line of Personal Digital Assistants that are being gobbled up by people in your position. They are a huge help in getting your job done quickly and efficiently, and they make you look like the world's greatest assistant in the process.

Gatekeeper: But I already am the world's greatest assistant.

You: I have no doubt about that. That's why I know you'll be thrilled when you see what this tool can do. I'd like to give you a demonstration. I could come by tomorrow afternoon or Friday. Which looks better for you?

Notes: Since your goal is to befriend this person, you'll want to start with a correct name. If you're calling a high-level executive in a company, the assistant's name may be posted on the Web site. Or maybe a general receptionist would be able to provide such information for you.

Indirect-Benefits Strategy

You: *(Calling the assistant to the CEO.)* Hi, Sam. I'm calling today because I'd like to introduce you to a product that has proven to have enormous benefits for companies like the one you're working for.

Gatekeeper: You'll really have to talk to Sharon Kincaid in purchasing.

You: I'll give Sharon a call. But I also wanted to introduce this product to you. It's an electronic pen that works like a highlighter to transfer written material onto your computer screen. It's a valuable time-saving tool that would be useful not only for entire departments, but for high-level executives, such as your boss. I'd love to give you a five-minute demonstration.

Gatekeeper: Well, I'm really busy these days.

You: I promise it will not take more than five minutes. Once you see how this pen works, you'll want to introduce it to your boss. And if it goes companywide, she'll thank you for the money it saves the company.

Gatekeeper: Well, maybe you should show it to me before calling Sharon Kincaid.

You: I'd be happy to. How's tomorrow at 2:00?

Notes: This product didn't directly benefit the gatekeeper, so you emphasized the indirect benefits.

267

Your overall strategy will be to stay with the gatekeeper, befriend him, and make him an ally. That's easy if you're selling a product that will directly impact him by making his work life easier. In those cases you'll use the Direct-Benefits strategy, an approach that focuses on how this product is going to be of help to the gatekeeper. But even when what you're selling won't impact him at all, you can appeal to him with an Indirect-Benefits strategy in which you point out benefits that will accrue to the gatekeeper from his association with you.

Gatekeepers of high-level executives have "shadow power." They may not be powerful on their own, but they do possess enormous clout because they have the ear of their superiors and often speak for them. And remember, many a CEO has risen through the ranks from an entry-level position, straight to the top of the company. Relationships with gatekeepers can be among the most potent you'll develop in your sales career. It's wise to nurture them, not only because treating people well is the right thing to do, but also because doing so can boost your own career.

Further Considerations

After you've made initial contact with a gatekeeper to introduce yourself, consider setting up a meeting simply to get to know him, without making a sales pitch. If there aren't many layers between him and the higher-ups, he could become someone who champions your product with those on the inside and ends up acting in the role of a coach for you.

If you've established good rapport with this gatekeeper, ask for referrals of people in similar positions, both inside the company and out. Fill out your organizational charts accordingly.

If you start at the top and are told by the office of the president, the CEO, or the COO to speak to someone else about your product, be sure to reference that fact in your call: "Hi. This is Sue Sloan. Mr. President's office asked that I call you …."

Ask Yourself

- Do I seek out the names of gatekeepers at the top, along with any other information I can garner about them?

- Do I try to wear my best demeanor at all times and with all kinds of people?

- Do I make a point of staying in touch with the gatekeepers I've gotten to know?

- For the people I deal with, do I try to find out what their work life is like and how my products or services might help them?

- When someone has helped me, do I try to reciprocate by finding out how I might help that person?

- Have there been times when I was in a gatekeeper position myself? What was persuasive to me when I was in that position?

Dialog 3

Get Your Foot in the Door

Scenario

You're trying to get new customers and are meeting with resistance. Some are refusing you on the telephone. Others are refusing you when you appear in person. You're trying to come up with ways to reach them, especially for the accounts that you've determined to be of particularly high value.

> **WHAT THE EXPERTS SAY**
>
> The Carnegie Foundation did a study on what contributes to success for a businessperson. Specific knowledge and technical skills contributed a small portion, but the overwhelming portions were the person's overall outlook and human relationship skills.

> **WHAT THE EXEMPLARS DO**
>
> Mary Kay Ash, the founder of Mary Kay Cosmetics, gives this advice on dealing with others: "No matter how busy you are, you must take the time to make the other person feel important."

Get Your Foot in the Door

Send-Something Strategy

You: Hello, James. Carol Parker here. Did you receive the saucepan cover I sent you in the mail?

↓

Prospect: Yes, although I don't know where it is at the moment.

↓

You: Well, you might want to try to find it because it could be worth dinner for a year at Chez Best Restaurant.

↓

Prospect: What do you mean?

↓

You: I'm visiting prospects to show off our line of cookware—the same line that Chez Best uses. You'll get to draw a number from a hat—or maybe a pot in this case! If it matches the model number of the saucepan that fits your cover, you'll win the saucepan and a chance at the "dinner for a year" drawing!

↓

Prospect: What's the catch?

↓

You: No catch, really. Not everyone will win, but everyone will have a fair chance of winning. I'll show you before the drawing that your winning number is included. I'll do a product demonstration that lasts six minutes, and then we'll do the drawing. As simple as that! I could come by tomorrow afternoon.

↓

Prospect: I'm not so sure I want to do this.

You: Look, I'm going to be in the neighborhood anyway. I promise you that the demonstration won't take more than six minutes. It's worth it to you and to your store. We want to give you the opportunity to carry this line of cookware. It's got great profit potential.

Notes: You've devised an unusual promotion that gives your prospect partial contact with your product (the saucepan cover). You've also made that very item a piece of the promotion itself (if the cover matches the chosen saucepan, the prospect wins the pan and the dinner prize).

Cinderella Strategy

You: Hello, Frank. Raphael Dominguez here, of World's Greatest Company. We're doing a promotion to introduce our newest product line.

↓

Prospect: What's involved?

↓

You: I'll come by to show you what we've got. It'll take about 10 minutes. Then you get to choose a key to a lockbox. When this promotion ends in eight weeks, I'll be back with the lockbox. If your key opens it, you get to keep the contents—worth $2,500 in cash and prizes. We'll be posting winners on our Web site.

↓

Prospect: And I don't have to buy anything to be included?

↓

You: That's absolutely right. I'm available Thursday afternoon or Friday morning.

Strategies

You'll try to use novel approaches to make yourself, your products, and your company stand out so that you are allowed in. You'll try to hook prospects with an approach that sparks their interest but is incomplete. Such techniques can help you "get your foot in the door."

You'll use the Send-Something strategy to entice prospects to agree to a sales presentation. When using this strategy, think of something that is typically paired with something else and then send just a portion of it. Consider things with pieces, such as puzzles, footwear, earrings, gloves, locks and keys, and anything that comes as multiples in a set.

The Cinderella strategy is a variation of the Send-Something strategy. With this technique, you take a desirable item and bring it around to various prospects. If the prospect turns out to be "Cinderella," that person can keep the prize.

BE CAREFUL
Make sure that your promotional tactics don't violate any legal or ethical issues.

WHAT THE EXPERTS SAY
You don't have to be a marketing pro to come up with creative ways for getting your foot in the door. Great ideas often come from people who have no background in a particular field. A study that tracked down the source of 61 inventions found that just 16 of them came from big companies. The idea for the dial telephone is attributed to an undertaker. The first ballpoint pen was designed by a sculptor. What atypical ideas can you generate?

Further Considerations

Any element of mystery or chance generally helps stimulate interest. Consider how you might include those elements in your sales presentations.

When sending out sales letters, consider attaching something of value to them. For example, you might attach a $1 lottery ticket along with a note that reads something like this, "Just wanted to let you know that we'd love to be your consultants and help you make money. We hope you'll choose to use our services. Best of luck! "

Look at the promotional practices you see around you that "get a foot in the door." Examine what you like or dislike about them. Think about how they might be made more effective and about how you might apply any of them to your own repertoire.

WHAT THE EXEMPLARS DO

Sales consultant Steve Miller recounts how he had been trying to get in to see a particular prospect, to no avail. He happened to be at the airport one day and was inspired when he spotted a flight insurance machine. He walked over to it and took out a policy, naming the prospect as his beneficiary. He mailed it off along with a note. The prospect called him after receiving it— and Steve finally got his appointment.

Present your promotional ideas to your company for approval before you carry them out and before you ask for help with implementation.

Ask Yourself

- What methods could I employ, relevant to my particular products, that would help me gain the attention of my prospects?

- Am I careful to make extra efforts such as these only where there's a good potential upside? Am I selective about which prospects I'll use such promos with?

- How could I use the Internet in helping me get my foot in the door?

- What do other salespeople do about this issue?

- If I were having trouble getting my foot in the door to see someone whom I wanted very much as a customer, and a friend came to me with the very same dilemma, what would I advise my friend to do?

Dialog 4

Deliver Drama

Scenario

You are making your sales presentation, introducing a new form of compact discs to a group of prospects. The room has been fully prepared in advance. Gift-wrapped boxes sit on the table, with a gift card bearing the name of each prospect. Also on the table is a beautiful cake surrounded by other desserts. A separate table has been laid out to serve drinks. Some easels, covered by a drape, stand in the corner holding charts, photos, and other visual sales tools.

Deliver Drama

You: *(To co-presenters.)* I think we have everything ready for our presentation, but let's do a run-through before anyone arrives. I want this all to go without a hitch.

Design-the-Show Strategy

You: We've got our visuals all displayed and our handouts color-coded, and they all tie into our theme. We've got our soft music playing for the audience to enjoy as they arrive. James, you'll slowly fade that out as the presentation begins. Our computer demonstration is all set and ready to go. The food and drinks and utensils are all set up. We've each got our list of selling points for our part of the presentation. We've put one wrapped sample in each person's seat, ready for them to unwrap, hold in their hands, and share with each other. Yes, I think we're all set.

Rouse-the-Senses Strategy

Audience: *(Thinking to themselves or stating to others as they arrive.)* It's midafternoon. I can't wait to dig into that cake. It looks yummy and that coffee smells great! … Hmmm, a present at each seat. I wonder what's in it? … And what's hiding on the easels in the corner?

Notes: You've roused the senses by carefully displaying interesting visuals, playing soothing music, presenting appetizing food and drink, and putting an attractive gift in each person's seat, which they'll pick up and touch before sitting down. You've thereby engaged your audience without saying a word.

Activate-Anticipation Strategy

You: I'm delighted you could all meet with me this afternoon so that I could introduce you to our latest brainchild—the custom-cut CD. If everyone already has a drink, I'll begin. I want to talk for a few minutes to tell you why we're so proud to be the "parents" of this new product. Then I'll show you a short computer demonstration. After that, I'll invite you to share in some cake and desserts to celebrate the birth of this latest "baby" of ours! And no peeking into those presents until the end, okay?

Notes: You then launch into your pitch and, at the appropriate moments, unveil the visuals on the easels, start the computer demonstrations, and so on. Throughout your presentation, you involve your prospects as much as possible by asking questions, seeking opinions, and inviting feedback. Then you're ready to conclude your presentation.

continues

Deliver Drama (continued)

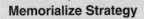

Memorialize Strategy

You: Would anyone else like more cake?

↓

Prospects: No, thank you.

↓

You: Well then, if you would please open the present in front of you. *(Pause.)* Each of these is a custom-cut CD, personalized specifically for your company. If you would all hold up the one you got, everyone can see the different styles we offer.

Afterglow Strategy

You: Please feel free to stay and have some more cake and review our materials here, if you like. And the next time you're at work on your computer, just pop in the CD sample we gave you. Follow the simple instructions, and you'll find a free gift that awaits you.

Notes: You've invited your audience to enjoy the afterglow of a soothing yet stimulating presentation. Even if they don't stay long, you've given them the opportunity to revisit this feeling of afterglow by providing them with your enticing sample. You, too, can bask in the afterglow of a presentation that was well delivered.

All in all, you've made excellent use of the DRAMA strategies.

Strategies

You'll employ drama to illustrate the selling points of your product by using the strategies presented in the acronym DRAMA.

- **D**esign-the-Show strategy. Design your sales pitch in advance by thinking of it as a stage presentation. Give it a beginning, a middle, and an end. Know where the climax will be.

> ### INSIGHTS
>
> "A mediocre salesperson tells. A good salesperson explains. A superior salesperson demonstrates. A great salesperson inspires the buyers to see the benefits as their own."
>
> —Joe Griffiths

- **R**ouse-the-Senses strategy. Think about the senses of seeing, hearing, smelling, touching, and tasting. Consider how you might employ them in demonstrating your product.

- **A**ctivate-Anticipation strategy. Think of your product as being a present that you are unwrapping, layer by layer. Make visual and verbal reference to what's coming up, in order to make their mouths water. Tantalize by giving a hint of what's to be seen; partially expose and partially hide your product to create a sense of mystery and excitement. Consider using props such as menus, wraps, covers, and other appropriate devices.

- **Memorialize strategy.** Provide samples of your product that incorporate your prospect's company name or other signs that would be present if you were already doing business together. Demonstrate your product, or a part of it. Consider video or computer demonstrations of your product. Also demonstrate the *impact* of your product through charts, photos, testimonials, and so on.

- **Afterglow strategy.** Bask in the completed presentation. Let the prospect savor the show. If possible, leave your product (or a sample of it) in the prospect's possession in order to help you move closer to a close.

Further Considerations

Humor is an important element of drama. Include appropriate humor in your sales presentations.

Notice what creates drama in everyday situations and see if you can employ any of those tactics in your sales presentations. For example, you might do one or more of the following: Shut off the lights and light candles when presenting a birthday cake, observe a moment of silence, get dressed up, use fancy china, give flowers, use the element of surprise in various forms, or set the stage with statements such as, "Sit down. You're not going to believe what happened."

BE CAREFUL

Remember that drama should be used to present the facts—never to *overstate* the facts. Doing so may undermine the trust you're trying to build. Always be ready to back up your assertions.

BE CAREFUL

Try thinking of your presentation as a stage show, and always do a dress rehearsal. Whenever possible, prepare the "stage" in advance by setting up equipment and props; checking power sources; and bringing backup batteries, extra copies of software (videos, CDs, computer programs), and extra copies of any "leave-behinds" that you'll be handing out, including your business cards. Remember, too, to shut off your cell phone and/or pager and, if possible, to temporarily disconnect any outside phone in the room. Also, remember that drama is not a license for length. Don't make presentations any longer than they need to be, and make sure that, on the whole, they're appropriate for your particular audience.

WHAT THE EXPERTS SAY

One of the accepted theories about learning styles is that different people learn in different ways: Some prefer to learn by reading, others by listening, and still others by having a demonstration. When making presentations, remember that different prospects will have different learning styles.

EXPERIENCE SHOWS

To find more information on learning styles, visit sites such as www. howtolearn.com and www.mindtools.com.

EXPERIENCE SHOWS

Using metaphors or stories is an effective way to give structure to a presentation. In the earlier example, the birth of a "baby" was the operative theme in the dialog and the props. Other metaphors might come from fairy tales, myths, and the Bible; or from well-known books, plays, and movies. Holidays and customs; traditional games, such as scavenger hunts, or games from current TV game shows; and themes such as school, the seasons, and sports provide still more ideas for themes and stories.

Rehearse your presentations in front of trusted friends and colleagues. Ask them to critique you. For most of us, it takes several rehearsals to create a polished presentation.

Ask Yourself

- Do my sales tools present information in the most compelling format possible?

- Do I examine how I might appeal to all the senses in my sales demonstrations?

- What examples of drama have I seen in sales presentations I've attended?

- Can I adapt those to what I'm selling?

- How can I build more anticipation into my sales presentations? What props might help me achieve this?

- What is my preferred learning style? Do I take into account that others may have a very different style?

Dialog 5

Harness Humor

Scenario

You know that humor is a potent force in communication. You've seen how it can create bonds between people and provide comic relief in tense situations. You regularly make sales presentations to groups of potential customers and want to employ this powerful tool more often.

Harness Humor

> **You:** Good morning. I'd like to start right in with the statistical analysis showing the benefits of our product over the competition's. Research shows that …

Notes: This dialog is devoid of humor. You'll inject some into it, not just by stating a joke, but by providing a set-up for the joke so that the humor stands out more.

Set-Up Strategy

> **You:** *(Beginning a sales presentation at 8:00 on a Monday morning.)* I appreciate the fact that you've all come out here so bright and early. Business makes big demands on all of us. You know, they say "Money is the root of all evil." But I think a variation on that statement is more appropriate today. I think it's more accurate to say "*Monday* is the root of all evil."
>
> *(Attempting to end your sales presentation with a humorous punch.)* I think you've seen how much time, trouble, and effort this equipment will save you and your staff. The guys who designed it confided to me that their motivation for creating it was sheer laziness. They hate to see people doing work that can be done automatically by machines. Their motto is: "Hard work never killed anybody—but why take chances?"

Notes: In the script above, you didn't just launch into the punch line by stating "Monday is the root of all evil." Rather, you set the stage and provided a background so that the contrast (Monday rather than Money) *would be clearer.*

Sales-Tool Strategy

> **You:** Dilbert is one of my favorite cartoons. The humor in that strip is really relevant to the materials we're working with, so I've included several of them in these handouts. I hope you'll enjoy them as much as I do.

Notes: This more passive form of delivering humor works well for those who don't feel they can deliver humor well through speech.

Apology Strategy

> **Customer:** That late shipment of yours really hurt us.

> **You:** I apologize that we failed to deliver our product to you on time. Our supplier couldn't get the parts to us, but that's not your problem. We take full responsibility. We know you recognize that "to err is human, to forgive is divine." But that's not the way we see it. We think that "to err is human but to forgive is against company policy." *(Pause.)* We don't forgive ourselves the mistake we made. Therefore, we want to make it up to you by giving you ….

Props Strategy

> **Professional Humorist, Art Gliner:** My silliest suggestion was to wear something outlandish for a necktie. Why shouldn't silly bureaucrats wear a fish necktie? I made a hole in the tail and threaded some string through it. The result was a dandy prop I hung around my neck at our appearances to show how silly, or humor-impaired, a human could be.

Notes: This example was mentioned on the Web site of the Art Gliner Center for Humor Studies at the University of Maryland (www.otal.umd.edu/amst/ humorcenter), Gliner writes about his use of this prop while making some presentations in the former Soviet Union.

Strategies

You'll consider the advice of humor experts to see how you might inject a little levity into the different parts of your sales presentations—the beginning, the middle, and the end.

According to consultant Ron Culberson, once you've been introduced to a group, you have 90 seconds to capture their attention. He recommends telling a funny story or a joke to start and end your presentation. You'll employ the Set-Up strategy by providing a context for your jokes in order to help the humor stand out.

Culberson often uses amusing activities in the middle of his presentations and also tries to add humor by including catchy phrases on slides, flip charts, and handouts. You'll utilize the Sales-Tool strategy by incorporating (with any necessary copyright permission, of course) cartoons or funny phrases on some of your sales tools, including charts, reports, overheads, etc. This strategy can add a little levity to the dry material that often comes in the middle of sales presentations.

You can harness the power of humor in any situation. It can be an especially valuable tool for handling awkward situations, such as when you've made an error. The Apology strategy suggests taking a well-known quote and altering it in a humorous way to provide a light touch in a heavy situation.

Humorist Art Gliner suggests adopting the occasional accent or funny voice for comic effect. In addition, he utilizes unusual props to harness humor. You'll adopt your own version of the Props strategy by seeking suitable props that might add a dose of laughter to your sales presentations.

Further Considerations

Even if you feel that you're not a naturally funny person, try giving humor a shot. Start small, perhaps by using a single one-liner or a humorous quote. Even if you don't have great delivery, people probably won't hold it against you, given that you were only trying to give them a chuckle. They know that your profession is sales, not stand-up comedy, so don't hold yourself to standards that are too high.

Humorist Art Gliner says that people everywhere laugh at a few basic humor techniques, including wordplay, exaggeration, and surprise. He asserts that one way to surprise people is to lead them in one direction and then change that direction. Another way is to take something that everyone recognizes and then give it a new or unusual interpretation. Consider how you might apply these techniques in your sales presentations.

Ask Yourself

- Do I try to find humorous material and activities to incorporate into my sales presentations?

- If appropriate, do I add a funny quote or other light touch to the (often dry) materials I hand out during a presentation?

- Should I attend a seminar on how to use humor in the workplace?

- Do I make note of what I find entertaining in the sales presentations that I have attended?

- Could I adapt those practices to my own sales presentations?

BE CAREFUL

Use humor sparingly to enhance, rather than overpower, your presentations. Test humorous material in advance with trusted friends or colleagues to make sure it's not offensive or otherwise inappropriate.

WHAT THE EXPERTS SAY

Humor has been defined as the juxtaposition of the incongruous. Others see a ubiquitous element of condescension in all humor. Charles R. Gruner, a professor of speech communication at the University of Georgia, sees humor as a game. Read more about it in his book *The Game of Humor: A Comprehensive Theory of Why We Laugh.*

WHAT THE EXEMPLARS DO

Ron Culberson's mission is to help individuals and organizations balance serious issues with a light touch. He has provided entertaining, informative, and fun programs to over 20,000 people in more than 350 associations, government agencies, nonprofit organizations, and Fortune 500 companies. He gives this advice for honing your humor skills: Look for humor everywhere, look at things from a different perspective, expose yourself to the humor you enjoy, and collect humor. For more tips on putting humor to work, visit his Web site at www.funsulting.com or call 703-742-8812.

Dialog 6

Use Unconventional Wisdom

Scenario

You own a travel agency; besides selling trips around the world, you also sell transportation services for trips around the corner. Your company will drive just about anyone just about anywhere. Your office is set up at the airport, where you handle spontaneous requests as well as prearranged transportation services.

Strategies

You aim to keep clients forever, so you're always seeking ways to serve them better. The conventional wisdom in your business might be to maximize the amount you charge for every single trip, so as to improve your bottom line. But you look beyond mere dollar amounts and try to provide superb customer service because you want to hook customers for life. The successful Service strategy that you employ is an example of unconventional wisdom.

Another selling technique that has been used in a variety of ways is one that operates on questionable ethics. It is mentioned here *not* as a recommendation, but rather as an interesting example of a strategy that employs unconventional wisdom. The strategy relies on the notion of reverse psychology, wherein you deny people the very thing you want them to pursue. The technique has been successfully employed in all kinds of businesses that are trying to create an image of popularity and success, and is called the Sold-Out strategy. The idea is to ultimately generate increased demand by creating an illusion of unavailability—and sometimes it works.

> **INSIGHTS**
>
> "People who don't take risks generally make about two big mistakes a year. People who do take risks generally make about two big mistakes a year."
>
> —Peter Drucker

> **INSIGHTS**
>
> "Everybody is a self-made man, but only the winners are willing to admit it."
>
> —Anonymous

> **BE CAREFUL**
>
> Doing something in an unconventional way obviously involves risk. Traditional methods are safe because they're tried-and-true, but it's the unconventional approaches that usually reap the greatest rewards—or cause the greatest failures. Before taking on a risky endeavor, map out and quantify its potential consequences. Determine where your comfort level on the risk/reward scale lies. Identify the threshold beyond which you'd be unwilling to carry on with a given plan. A little forethought can go a long way.

Use Unconventional Wisdom

Potential customer: *(A very well-dressed woman in a panic at your counter.)* My husband and I just got dropped off here and were going to have a nice, relaxing lunch before boarding our flight at 2:30 P.M. We just went to check our bags first, and the airline clerk says I won't be allowed to board because I don't have a picture ID with me. I think I left my wallet at my sister's last night in Sarasota. That's an hour away! Can you get us there and back before the flight leaves at 2:30?

Conventional response: Well, we can try. *(Meaning: It's going to be tight, but I can charge the premium rate for this two-hour trip, booked on a rush basis. If we don't get back in time, they might be upset, but they won't be able to blame me.)*

Service Strategy

You: Let me see. You need a picture ID to get on the flight. That I understand. But is it absolutely mandatory that you get your wallet back?

Potential customer: Well, actually, no. My husband has his wallet with him. It's really just more important that we make this flight to L.A. I'm not even sure the wallet's at my sister's.

You: *(Thinking very clearly about solving this problem.)* Driving back might make you miss your flight, and the wallet might not even be there. So, the number-one priority is actually just getting you a picture ID.

Potential customer: I guess that's right.

You: I have an idea. Let me make a couple of calls while you help yourself to a drink from our refreshment center. I'll get back to you in just a moment.

You: *(After a couple of calls.)* I just got off the phone with the Department of Motor Vehicles, which is right around the corner. They'll allow you to get a temporary license, complete with photo ID. It should take about 30 minutes, total. We can send you there now with a driver who'll wait or else run to pick up some lunch for you if you prefer.

Potential customer: *(Now a customer for life.)* That's great. What a relief! Thank you so much for finding a solution for us. Please give me your card. I'm going to start using your service from now on—and tell all my friends about it, too.

Notes: You demonstrated unconventional wisdom in this example by thinking clearly to identify the needs of your customer accurately and then finding a creative solution. You resisted the temptation to be shortsighted and simply get a big sale from this customer. Instead, you viewed this transaction as a long-term investment.

Sold-Out Strategy

Potential Customer: I'm calling to book a reservation *(or hire a model for a photo shoot, or make an appointment for a haircut, etc.).*

Receptionist: *(With dishonesty.)* I'm afraid we're all booked up. I have absolutely nothing available until next month.

Further Considerations

The notion of unconventional wisdom needn't be limited to your relationships with customers. Look at other relationships as well. Conventional wisdom says that you compete with competitors (and perhaps even with co-workers). Unconventional wisdom would ask whether you might benefit by cooperating instead.

If the idea of doing something unconventional scares you, consider ways in which you could make it less intimidating. For example, try it on a small scale or in "safe" situations, or limit your exposure in some other way.

Consider keeping a notebook filled with ideas on what you'd do if you knew you couldn't fail. How would your day-to-day dealings be different? How would your big goals change?

WHAT THE EXPERTS SAY

Some studies claim that our orientation toward novelty and risk-taking has a genetic component. Certain individuals score high on a personality trait called "novelty seeking" that includes a tendency toward extroversion, excitement seeking, and quick tempers. Those same individuals are also more likely to possess a genetic variation of DNA on one of their chromosomes. If you tend to avoid taking risks, part of the reason may be in your genes.

WHAT THE EXEMPLARS DO

Jan Carlzon employed unconventional wisdom when he took over as president of Scandinavian Airlines in 1981. In one year, he took the company from near financial ruin to high profitability. How? Instead of leaving the organizational chart in its traditional triangle shape, he turned it on its head. The workers who had the most-immediate contact with customers became the ones who started calling the shots. The remainder of the company was assigned to work for those who had all the customer contact.

Ask Yourself

- What business practices have I observed that utilize unconventional wisdom?

- Could I adapt any of them to the work I do?

- Do I make a point of looking at life through an unconventional perspective now and then?

- When was the last time I did something I considered risky? What was it? Professionally, when was the last time I risked a public failure?

- What's my general orientation toward risk? Do I want to try to change that tendency in any way?

- How far am I willing to go to put the needs of my customers above my own interest in maximizing my immediate bottom-line results?

Dialog 7

Do Well by Doing Good

Scenario

You're a do-gooder by nature. Your perspective on the world goes well beyond your office door. You have causes you're passionate about and would like to see them benefit a bit from the work you do in your career. You look for ways to tie the two together, primarily for the moral satisfaction it brings you, but also because you know that many a solid business relationship has been formed in service to good causes.

You've seen how some corporate giants have affiliated with various causes for their mutual benefit. In this particular scenario, you're a sales rep for dental supplies and the company you work for has no affiliation with a particular charity. However, the company doesn't object to your combining a bit of charity with the work you do. The company knows that "good works" generate "goodwill" among customers, and it's willing to let you try to capitalize on that fact—for the good of the charity and for the good of the company.

INSIGHTS
"Success is measured by the degree that one helps and enriches others, even if he helps himself at the same time."   —John Marks Templeton, Templeton Growth Fund

EXPERIENCE SHOWS
If you're seeking information on volunteer opportunities, visit sites such as www.pointsoflight.org or www.volunteermatch.org, which match your interests and availability with organizations in need. The sites also provide information on volunteer opportunities that exist online, in case you don't want to leave the confines of cyberspace to do volunteer work.

Strategies

You'll determine the degree to which you want to bring your "cause" into your professional life and adjust your approach accordingly—from a Minimal strategy to Moderate strategy to a Maximal strategy. No matter what the level, your dialog will remain essentially the same: You'll inform customers about what you're doing and why, you'll seek their support in some fashion, and you'll show them how they'll benefit from doing so. You'll be discriminating about whom you approach regarding your cause and the degree of involvement you'll seek from them. You understand that those who would be most receptive to such overtures are probably the customers who know you best.

Do Well by Doing Good

You: *(Finishing your meeting with a dental technician.)* Petra, I wonder if I might leave some of these brochures in your waiting room?

Customer: What are they about?

Minimal Strategy

You: There's a nonprofit organization called Smiles Across the Miles that I really believe in. They get dentists from around the country to make one-week trips anywhere in the world to provide dental care to those most in need.

Customer: Sounds like a good cause.

You: It is. And displaying the brochures shows that you're in favor of humanitarian efforts. I think it reflects well on your office and will probably generate some goodwill among your patients.

Customer: You're probably right. I'll go ahead and take a stack.

Notes: You sought support from the customer in a minimal way—you simply asked for permission to display some brochures. If you decide your customers would be receptive to a higher level of involvement, you could consider using either of the following strategies in future dialogs.

Moderate Strategy

You: Yes, that's the price for the fluoride foam treatment. And I want to let you know something. For every order I receive over $1,000, I will personally donate $25 from my own pocket to the Smiles Across the Miles charity.

Customer: *(Already familiar with the charity from your previous exchanges.)* How do you document your contribution?

You: Once I get my cancelled check, I photocopy the front and back to show that the money has been deposited into the account of the charity. Then I send the copy to the customer responsible for that particular order so that we can all feel good about it.

Customer: Well, I was going to finish my order with this fluoride purchase. That brings us to a total of $750. But I think I can come up with $250 worth of additional supplies that I could use in the near future to get that total up past $1,000.

You: That's great! I thank you and Smiles Across the Miles thanks you!

Notes: This strategy is considered moderate because even though you're not asking your customer to donate an out-of-pocket sum or to perform any sort of task, you're still asking the customer to order more than she normally would.

continues

Do Well by Doing Good (continued)

Maximal Strategy

You: So, Petra, Smiles Across the Miles is seeking any used but usable dental equipment or supplies that your office might be ready to get rid of.

Customer: Will they come and pick it up?

You: Yes, I'll take care of that personally. And I'll give you a receipt itemizing the donation. I'm sure your accountants will appreciate that, since everything you donate to a nonprofit such as this is a tax deduction.

Customer: Okay, I'll see what we've got.

Notes: A Maximal strategy asks your customer for direct support of a particular cause, perhaps in the form of a donation or some kind of sponsorship in exchange for advertising exposure. It is not recommended unless you have a particularly solid long-term relationship with a given customer and unless your company has given explicit permission.

Further Considerations

If the efforts of your customers result in any contributions to charitable causes, be sure to send a written thank-you note, along with any paperwork that documents the donation. Ask the charity to send a note, as well. If you have a company newsletter or Web site, you might want to include a mention of thanks there, too. Follow up by sending copies of the newsletter to your customers or by sending a note inviting them to visit the Web site to find the acknowledgment.

BE CAREFUL

Use discretion when raising charity issues with customers. Never make them feel pressured about causes, no matter how strongly you believe in them. Always be prepared to pull back on such a dialog if you sense a customer is uncomfortable with it. Your customers may legitimately feel that your primary obligation is to serve them and their needs, not anyone else's.

If your company isn't up for any sort of active affiliation with a cause, see whether it might consider something more passive. For example, it might put some information about a given charity in the corner of its Web site. Some sites will pay a "click through" fee to a particular charity for every person visiting their sites in a given time period.

If your company is opposed to having you mention anything about a charity in your professional dealings, consider reversing the process. Rather than bringing a charity into your professional world, is there any way you could bring your professional world to the charity? Can

285

you offer a charity your sales skills? Might your company be willing to donate any "leftovers" to them, such as discontinued items or castoffs of any sort?

Ask Yourself

- What do I think are the most pressing problems that I might help address through volunteer work? Hunger? Homelessness? Certain illnesses?

- Do I seek out volunteer opportunities, knowing that they often provide volunteers with a chance to balance their lives and broaden their perspectives?

- Once I'm involved with a charity, do I seek out any professional opportunities that might exist within the group?

- In what ways have other salespeople or other companies tied their work into good causes?

- Could I adapt any of those principles to the work I do?

Dialog 8

Go Virtual

Scenario

You've learned that by simply using a phone and a Web browser, two or more parties can have an interactive exchange of any kind involving visual, voice, or video material and including documents, pictures, text, streaming audio or video, live software demonstrations, Web co-browsing, and more. You've found that these meetings can be conducted live, in real time, or that material can be recorded for playback as a Webcast that's available 24 hours a day.

Go Virtual

Prospect: *(After a long series of objections.)* No, I just don't have time for a meeting right now.

Prospect-Meeting Strategy

You: Okay. I can understand that. Doctors are busy people. But let me offer you an alternative. I'm holding a series of virtual presentations to demonstrate this product. If you've got a phone and a computer at your desk, that's all you need in order to attend. You can stay for as long or as short a time as you'd like, but I promise you'll be intrigued by what this laser equipment can do. If you give me your e-mail address, I'll send you the list of times that I'll be online and a simple set of directions for joining in. This way, you can be involved with our latest development completely at your convenience.

Prospect: Okay. You can reach me at …

Customer-Meeting Strategy

You: That's great, Belinda. I'm glad you're back. Listen, I want to show you a new product that we've rolled out since you've been away. It's a laser tool that has incredible applications. I'm going to be demonstrating it over the Internet through a series of virtual presentations. I'd really like you to attend, especially since it'll be a while before I'm back up in the Anchorage area.

Customer: That sounds complicated. And I won't really be able to tell whether I like the product.

You: No, it's not complicated at all. It just requires a phone and a computer. And I promise, you'll get a full demonstration this way. It's a great introduction to the product and it's fully interactive, so if you have any questions, I'll be able to answer them on the spot. Then if you still feel you need a live demonstration, I'll schedule one for next quarter. But in the meantime, I want you to be up-to-date on what's happening in the field.

Customer: Okay. Send me the details via e-mail.

Silent-Dialog Strategy

You: *(During a virtual presentation, silently asking the audience)* How would you rate the pace of this presentation? (1.) Too slow (2.) Too fast (3.) Just right. How would you rate the level of detail? (1.) Too little (2.) Too much (3.) Just right.

Audience response: *(Majority feels the presentation is …)* Just right.

In light of these technological marvels, you decide to hold a virtual sales presentation to demonstrate your latest medical laser equipment. You're pleased that meetings formerly requiring you to travel can now be conducted in the comfort of cyberspace, and you're also pleased with how virtual tools can significantly shorten the sales cycle. You'll utilize these tools with potential prospects as well as with current customers.

EXPERIENCE SHOWS

To schedule a virtual meeting or simply to learn more about them, visit sites like www.webex.com, www.placeware.com, and www.evoke.com.

BE CAREFUL

Virtual presentations may not work well for certain kinds of products or certain kinds of salespeople, nor will they ever completely replace the need for face-to-face meetings.

Strategies

Even though you might prefer holding face-to-face meetings with your new prospects, you find that some of those prospects are particularly resistant to doing so. Using the Prospect-Meeting strategy, you'll offer a virtual meeting to them as an alternative. You hope that the virtual meeting will prove an effective sales tool in advancing your cold calling a step further.

Among current customers with whom you've already established a relationship, you'll rely upon the benefits of virtual sales tools to service them and, at the same time, cut down on travel and all its associated costs to you and your company. In a Customer-Meeting strategy, you'll contact your current accounts to introduce them to the idea of virtual meetings.

The Silent-Dialog strategy takes advantage of the fact that during virtual presentations, a silent dialog can occur between the presenter and those attending the virtual meeting. In addition to the full audio exchange, the presenter can seek silent feedback from the audience on such parameters as whether the presentation is going too slowly or too quickly. The results can be reported back to the presenter with the click of a button and made silently visible to her immediately on a screen. This feedback provides input that people might not normally feel comfortable stating in a face-to-face encounter. Once the presenter has read the feedback, she can adjust her presentation accordingly.

Another benefit of such feedback is that it is concrete and doesn't require the sort of people-reading skills that might be needed in a face-to-face meeting.

WHAT THE EXPERTS SAY

Salespeople who are used to holding virtual meetings recommend them for several reasons. Some find that offering a virtual meeting improves cold-calling success rates because prospects are more inclined to attend a virtual presentation than to book a meeting. Other reps say that virtual presentations give them more control; their presentation starts at a predetermined time and they're not at the mercy of those who would arrive late or constantly interrupt. It's also reported that prospects seem to show more respect for the virtual presentation, perhaps because it's not being held on the turf of any one individual and perhaps because a given prospect may no longer be an audience of one but rather one of many.

Further Considerations

Virtual presentations offer a whole host of additional benefits, including the following:

- Web conferencing can be used for all kinds of corporate communications, including press conferences, work sessions with collaborators across the country, and marketing research studies. Web conferencing is very effective in reaching a large sales staff that's rarely in one place at one time.

- Virtual presentations clearly help reduce travel for a sales staff. This can be a real asset in attracting and retaining sales personnel and reducing burnout.

- Territories no longer need to be defined solely by geography. A rep in any location can cover a territory in another location with the use of virtual tools.

- Virtual tools can be a boon to top sellers who enjoy the virtual mode. By using virtual tools, such reps can extend their reach and do what they do best in less time. Instead of giving the same sales presentation 50 times, they can give it once to 50 people at the same time.

- Virtual meetings maximize scheduling flexibility. If a particular prospect needs to cancel a virtual meeting, rescheduling it is fairly easy and causes less disruption than the cancellation of a face-to-face meeting would.

- Corporate training can be done virtually, saving time and money and offering greater flexibility to trainees.

Ask Yourself

- Am I fully familiar with virtual presentations? Have I actually participated in any?

- Does my product (or any facet of it) lend itself well to the use of virtuals?

- Have I ascertained how I might apply the benefits of virtual meetings to my repertoire of sales tools?

- Has my company embraced the concept of using virtual tools? If not, how might I get them interested in doing so?

Chapter 11

Closing

If you've been in sales for more than a week, you've no doubt heard that the closing is the most important part of your sales presentation. And by now you know that there are classic closes on which you can depend. In this chapter, we'll ask you to depend on what works for you: classic or contemporary closes or a combination of both. Once you've found your closing stride, stick with it.

But keep experimenting. Keep continuous improvement as your motto and seek to relentlessly pursue perfection—as the manufacturers of Lexus cars tell us they do. Try out new possibilities, align certain closes with certain types of prospects, keep on learning about best practices, and modify them to your own circumstances.

Why the insistence on this oxymoronic flexible rigidity? Because, for every endorsement of a particular close, you'll find an eminent salesperson espousing a better way to do it! Rather than be confused by the contradictions, find your own path among them.

To illustrate, Mark McCormack is a real thorn in the side of conventional sales sages. While acknowledging that selling always has been, and always will be, a three-step process of qualifying the prospect, connecting with him, and then convincing him to buy what you have to sell, McCormack unabashedly cites common sense and people sense as the only two ingredients in the recipe for selling success.

He says you should spend less time on improving yourself and more time on improving your relationships. Among his other maverick views are these:

- You won't get his money if you include him with a crowd of prospects.

- Timing the perfect moment to ask for the sale will not work with him.

- He resists salespeople who ask for the order, who follow up aggressively and call back.

- If you listen well, he'll admit that he does too. In his words, you'll "cancel each other out."

- If you try the time-honored technique of urging a close by mentioning that time is limited, he'll outwait you.

You may be thinking that McCormack is more sales savvy than most. You may be assuming that the average buyer wouldn't recognize the ploy, for example, of trying to urge the close by saying, "We have only two left." Perhaps not. On the other hand, the buying public has become very sophisticated. It may be time to polish—or polish off— some of the closes you've become too dependent on.

Realize that some of the closings we'll examine here work some of the time and none of these closings will work all of the time. However, the more choices of closings that you have, the more options you have available for matching the situation with the client.

In short, we endorse adaptability in closings. Pick and choose the ideas that make sense to you. Keep your balance on your own tightrope, and don't worry about the fact that the poles supporting it may contain conflicting viewpoints. Be steadfast in your resolve to proceed at your own pace and with your own sense of timing and destiny.

Dialog 1

Use Trials, Avoid Tribulations

Scenario

In teaching, a *teachable moment* is that unexpected opportunity that occurs when you have to abandon the lesson plan and teach to the point that has arisen at that moment. In sales, the moment is known as the *psychological moment,* the time when you should abandon your sales script and sell to the prompt you've been given.

The problem is in some ways like the weather, which everyone talks about but no one can do anything about. The psychological moment is the topic of much sales advice. Unfortunately, it doesn't proclaim itself and so, despite all this good advice, you have to rely on both intuition and experience to tell you when that moment has arrived.

In this scenario, you're trying to sell a data collection system to your prospect. The prospect isn't sure whether to buy the system or not, but you see the psychological moment. In an effort to show him the advantages of your system, you set up a *trial close,* or test of your customer's readiness to close the sale.

> **INSIGHTS**
>
> According to author Maxwell Maltz (*Zero-Resistance Selling,* Prentice-Hall, 1998), "The Master Closer understands the prospect has doubts, fears, the temptation to avoid confrontation and decision, too." In other words, basic psychological emotions are at work here. The "Master Closer" acknowledges the prospect's emotions and works to neutralize them in order to close the sale. You can acquire the same knowledge by taking a basic psychology course or reading some books on the subject. Your small investment of time will serve you well in your sales.

Strategies

If the prospect passes the trial test, you should be able to conclude the sale. If he doesn't pass the test, you'll have to give him another trial test at a later time, after you've had a chance to "educate" him a bit more. Your TEST will consist of the Tying-Up, Elicit, Sell, and Terminate strategies. You begin by *tying up* loose ends. Then you *elicit* a choice from the customer. Next, you attempt to *sell.* Finally, you either *terminate* the sales exchange or *try* again (at a later time) if you can't close the sale.

> **EXPERIENCE SHOWS**
>
> If you've taken an active role in the exchange up until the close, don't suddenly go passive at the end. Call for action. Don't postpone your chances for a successful close with a limp good-bye: "Call me if you'd like to place an order."

293

Use Trials, Avoid Tribulations

> **You:** There's no doubt about it, Massimo. The e's are taking over: e-commerce, e-tailing, e-mailing, e-business. You're already e-stablished in the office. Why not have the same e-connections while you're on the road?

> **Prospect:** I just don't know if I want to be e-vailable 24/7.

Notes: The prospect is not denying the assertions you're making, which is good. However, you may have inadvertently turned the selling points into an objection. The very accessibility you're painting as a benefit may be a turnoff for this prospect.

Tying-Up Strategy

> **You:** Our system works the way you want it to work. If you want access to the database on your office lines only, you have that choice. If you want to be able to call it up from a laptop, you can choose that option as well.

> **Prospect:** I pride myself on being a macromanager. When I leave the office, I leave people in charge who know as much as I do, if not more!

Elicit Strategy

> **You:** So the office-only feature works best for you?

> **Prospect:** Assuming I wanted to purchase the system, yes.

> **You:** Let's assume for a moment that you do. Can you tell me whether you'd like your call center to be able to handle more calls, improve cross-sell opportunities, or increase sales volume?

> **Prospect:** Is this a trick question? Of course, we'd like to do all that.

Sell Strategy

> **You:** Our IdentiCall system makes all that happen.

> **Prospect:** How?

> **You:** By giving you access to a database that presents identifying information about millions of businesses and millions of households.

> **Prospect:** What kind of information?

> **You:** For businesses, their name, address, fax, phone, e-mail, and Web site information; plus the number of employees, annual sales volume, date when the company started ....

> **Prospect:** All of that?

> **You:** There's more. Historical trends, credit rating, and SIC codes.

> **Prospect:** That's pretty exhaustive information.

> **You:** You can even see what their offices look like!

continues

Use Trials, Avoid Tribulations (continued)

Sell Strategy

Prospect: The cost is prohibitive, though.

You: Lost sales are prohibitive, too. They prohibit you from achieving a close rate that surpasses all other centers.

Notes: When you say "So the office-only feature works best for you," you've managed to pick up on a half-articulated need. It's a psychological moment that you can use to your advantage and, ultimately, to the client's advantage as well.

Terminate Strategy

You: Can I sign you up for a six-month trial period? You can cancel after that if you haven't seen improvement in your data-collection time and sales volume or if you haven't been able to establish critical caller profiles and make significant marketing decisions based on these profiles.

Prospect: We'll give it a try.

Further Considerations

Part of the selling process is citing the specific benefits of your product as they relate to its specific features. But what about its general benefits? A seller of Christmas trees, for example, could cite both specific and general benefits about his trees. Specifically, he could say that the needles of certain trees don't shed as easily and thus the benefit is less mess in the home. He could also cite a more general benefit: the fact that with the sale of a tree, he's selling tradition, the practices that make families cherish their moments together.

Don't disagree with your prospect, no matter how ill-advised his objections may be. Listen fully to his point of view and then try to reason him away from it.

You can reduce the tribulations associated with closing if you avoid asking leading questions that might directly or indirectly insult the prospect's intelligence.

WHAT THE EXPERTS SAY

Advertising genius Walter Dill Scott maintains, "Ideas which have the greatest suggestive power are those presented to us by the actions of other persons. The second most effective class is probably the ideas suggested by the words of our companions." Make certain some physical action is part of your pitch. Try something new: Ask one of the prospect's colleagues to come in and try out your product if you can do so without disturbing the momentum of the presentation.

Ask Yourself

- Have I taken the time to analyze how many of my trials actually get closed?

- How many trials are too many for a single sales encounter?

- Can I "see through" the trial closes that my family members or co-workers use on me?

- Would I ethically refuse to close if I suspected that my product could not meet the prospect's need as well as a competitor's product could?

WHAT THE EXEMPLARS DO

Exemplars ask "preclosing" questions, scattering them throughout the dialog. Until you know the answer to questions such as the following, you can't really attempt to close:

- What does this prospect need?
- What additional service or ideas can I provide?
- What deadlines or priorities does this prospect face?
- What external pressures is he dealing with?
- Does he have any unusual preferences or emotional ties?

Dialog 2

Think of No as Maybe

Scenario

Benjamin Disraeli, author, statesman, and British prime minister in the late nineteenth century, defined despair as the conclusion of fools. He was correct in reminding us that it's foolish to become downhearted as the result of making an unwarranted conclusion. This happens all too often when salespeople realize that their "close" is actually a door being closed in their face. In fact, it may be the opening of another door—even if the opening is only wide enough for a request to come through.

Think of No as Maybe

You: With the holidays fast approaching, Mr. Fisher, would you be willing to expand the meaning of "family"?

Prospect: Not really.

Notes: It's clear you're in his office only because he was too polite to turn down your mutual acquaintance. He's given you the time of day, so to speak, and now wants to turn his time to matters more important than what you're selling. You shouldn't despair, though. You have two exit strategies in mind.

Maybe Strategy

You: How about your employees? Surely some of them would be willing to take in orphaned animals?

Prospect: I couldn't speak for my staff.

You: Perhaps I could speak *to* them?

Prospect: Look, Ms. Starwood. We're running a business here. Time is money. If I let you speak to my employees, even for 15 minutes, that would be 15 minutes of lost productivity.

You: Could we agree on this, then? What if I came to the employee break room with the animals, in cages, for half a day? Then, employees could see our furry family and decide for themselves if they want to expand their families.

Prospect: I don't want cats and dogs crawling all over the place. This is a factory, as I explained.

You: I can assure you that they'll be in their cages. Then, after selections are made, I'll record the names of the new owners and the times that are convenient for them to pick up their new pets. And each adopter is automatically entered into our "Make Your Day: Adopt a Stray" competition.

Prospect: What does the winner get—five new family members?

You: *(Chuckling at his humor.)* No, he gets a year's worth of dog or cat food, plus an appearance on television and in the newspaper.

Prospect: Are you saying we'd get some free publicity out of this?

You: If the employee decides to tell how he or she came to adopt the animal, yes.

Know Strategy

You: This is a nation of animal lovers, Mr. Fisher. Nearly three quarters of us have pets or had them at some point in our lives. And, of course, medical research is proving the strong causal link between having a pet and having a longer, healthier life.

Prospect: Okay, okay, you've sold me. I just don't want to see any of those animals running around loose.

Your appeal for a 15-minute segment of a manager's staff-meeting time is being firmly denied. The "product" you're selling is a four-legged one: You represent a nonprofit animal shelter in desperate need of animal adoptions. You had the bright idea that, rather than calling community residents one at a time, you could accomplish more by addressing a large gathering of employees in a local factory.

Strategies

You were fortunate enough to get this appointment because your aunt knows the manager to whom you're making an appeal. Unfortunately, though, you've received no buying signals at all during the meeting. In fact, the prospect is now making it clear he'd like you to leave his office. Before you do, though, you'll make one or two final overtures, depending on the degree of impatience your prospect is showing. You'll employ the Maybe and Know strategies in which you'll look at "No" as "Maybe," and you'll hear "No" as "Know."

Further Considerations

If your sales territory is in the same area where you live and work, you may be overlooking a rich source of "ins." You probably know people who know the people you want to know, or at least the people you'd like to get an appointment with. Don't let these valuable contacts go to waste. Prepare a list of their names and, from time to time, ask them if they know anyone in those firms that you've targeted for a sales call.

Make sure your body language doesn't reflect nervousness when you ask for the order, or despair if you don't get it. You can gauge your own reaction—sweaty palms, clearing of your throat, darting eye movements, inappropriate laughter. Fight against these small signs of agitation by using visualization techniques.

Especially when there's been a personal reason for obtaining an appointment, show your appreciation by dropping both parties a small note of thanks.

Ask Yourself

- Do I tend to rush into things?

- How much homework do I typically do before the appointment?

- How do I overcome despair?

- How often do I take "No" to mean "No?"

Dialog 3

Empathize

Scenario

Vash Young was one of the world's premier insurance salespersons. He was persistent. He was persuasive. He knew the power of pathos. He "prospected" a particular individual once a week for a whole year, certain that the account would be a veritable gold mine. After a full year of calling on the prospect, he finally got an appointment. The first words out of the prospect's mouth were, "I'm not interested in insurance."

How would you go about effecting a close from such a closed-off response?

EXPERIENCE SHOWS

Learning what you can about the "internal culture" of key individuals can help direct you to the right person. To illustrate, if you had learned about Sam Hurley before setting up time with Mr. Fisher, you could have saved time and trouble all the way around. You might even have asked your contact in a phone call for the name of someone like Mr. Hurley and then proceeded to springboard to a successful close.

EXPERIENCE SHOWS

The close can be initiated by the prospect as well as by the salesperson. Listen for statements such as, "How do I go about signing up?" Act immediately upon this opportunity that comes all too seldom to hardworking salespeople.

Empathize

You: I think you'll agree, Mr. Harrell, that we associate good food with the holiday season, and Go! Diva! is a name you can trust. Ever since it was founded by a true opera diva, we've earned our reputation for excellence among chocolatiers.

Prospect: I think we'll go for nonfattening gifts this year. It's my personal opinion that this country has enough obesity. I don't believe in contributing to an already severe national problem.

Notes: It's hard to argue with an assessment that's as accurate as this one is. However, if you can land this account, you won't have to work for the next six months. Here's where knowing your product line can help you reach the finish line in a contest that seems to have ended before it started.

Agree Strategy

You: You're absolutely right on that account. That's why we've introduced two new product lines: chocolates for diabetics and nonfat chocolate for chocoholics. We also have pretzels, which are fat-free as you probably know, and nuts, which medical studies show are good for heart health.

Prospect: I'm still not convinced.

Assert Strategy

You: The holidays are a time for realizing the richness in our lives, a time to share that richness with others. For many, Christmas parties and edible gifts represent the last indulgent fling before January comes along with its demand for resolutions. Our chocolate will satisfy the choco-lust of those who are not watching their waistlines. But, for those who are, we can offer our nonfat, fresh-baked crunchies, like popcorn and nuts. And for those who don't want food at all, we have a wonderful array of plants and flowers.

Prospect: Sorry, I'm leaning toward gift certificates.

Act Strategy

You: At the risk of overstepping my boundaries here, Mr. Harrell, I think there's a kind of sterility associated with gift certificates. They almost suggest that the giver couldn't take the time to find a truly special gift for the recipient.

Prospect: I've never looked at it that way.

You: Look at it this way. Go! Diva! has a wide array of gifts, from fruit to nuts—literally. If you place an order for 25 gifts, whatever they are, we'll include a CD of operatic excerpts, recorded by the founder of Go! Diva! with each gift sent to a different address. Given your concern for good health, I think you'll find this a wonderful extra that your clients will appreciate.

Prospect: I was planning to send only 22 gifts.

You: I'll bet there are three others you could think of, perhaps even relatives in another state. Here's the catalog. Shall we select 15 for those not worried about weight and 10 for those who should be?

Strategies

The techniques Young used are known as the 3-A strategies: Agree, Assert, and Act. He actually *agreed* with the prospect, acknowledging that he didn't think insurance was very interesting himself. This took the client back a bit. "But you're in the insurance business," the client pointed out.

That's when Young made his *assertion;* he pointed out that the interesting thing was not insurance but what the insurance could buy: a guaranteed income for life. He then *acted* on the interest he had aroused and sold a policy with an annual premium of several thousand dollars.

In this situation, you'll show your willingness to empathize with the prospect's position but your unwillingness to admit that your product can't meet his needs.

Further Considerations

The more you read, the better you'll be able to handle objections that come out of left field. While no one can be an expert in every regard, you'll be pleasantly surprised to find that a cursory knowledge of current events can help you relate the outside world to the insider's world of selling.

When you encounter objections, probe to learn more about them. If you can find data that prove the objections are more fiction than fact, you stand a better chance of winning the sale.

For at least six months, keep a record of the number of calls you make and compare it with the number of sales you close. If you don't see an improvement in the ratio in six months, consider making a greater number of calls upon a greater number of qualified leads. Include a plan for asking for referrals from 20 percent of your satisfied customers.

WHAT THE EXPERTS SAY

"Don't 'unclose' by reopening points or introducing irrelevant points," cautions author (*Selling by Phone*, McGraw-Hill, 1992) Linda Richardson. Just as some writers hate to edit and excise their own words, some salespeople are reluctant to omit any part of what they'd planned to say. Don't fall into the trap of pride.

WHAT THE EXEMPLARS DO

All too often, the close is botched when the prospect asks an unexpected question. When this occurs, you can use a simple device to formulate your reply without hesitation, says author (*Getting Back to the Basics of Selling*, Crown Publishers, 1981) Matthew Culligan. Just "break your response down into three parts: past, present, and future. Since the past is known and the present is obvious, speaking briefly about them gives you time to consider the real question, which is about the future."

Ask Yourself

- Is my failure to close successfully more a function of inexperience or incompetence?

- Could my fear of failure be interfering with the closing process?

- Do I always thank the prospect for giving me the order?

- Do I thank the prospect even when I don't get the order?

- Am I regarded as a pushy salesperson?

Dialog 4

Make a Promise

Scenario

You're a one-person troubleshooting company. Your knowledge is encyclopedic. Because you're young, you're optimistic and the thought of going up against "the big boys" doesn't daunt you in the least. As part of your close, you're going to make a promise—one that you know you can fulfill.

Strategies

Beginning with the Persuade strategy, you'll meet the challenge by trying *persuasion* first. If that doesn't work, you'll turn to the Plea strategy and move the response up a notch by making a *plea*. If this strategy fails, you'll pull out the metaphorical big guns, the Promise strategy, by making a *promise*.

INSIGHTS

Frank Sena, vice president of district services for individual protection sales and marketing at Mass Mutual Financial Group, recommends that salespeople be visible in their local sphere of operations. "Establish credibility in the community," he advises. Among the ways to do this are joining the boards of charitable organizations, sponsoring a drive, and getting involved with a cause you believe in.

Make a Promise

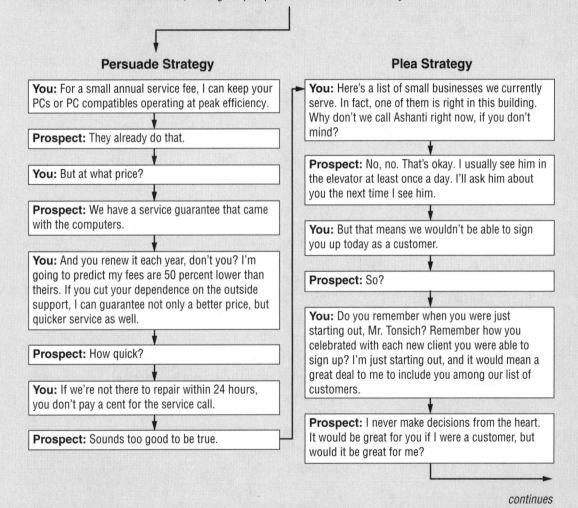

You: Mr. Tonsich, I appreciate your taking my call. I'm Drew Handy with PC Compatibles and I'd like your business.

Prospect: What kind of business?

Notes: Your opening is certainly energetic and, perhaps, deliberately nonspecific. The phrase "I'd like your business" has an allure all its own, inviting the prospect to ask more about what you do.

Persuade Strategy

You: For a small annual service fee, I can keep your PCs or PC compatibles operating at peak efficiency.

Prospect: They already do that.

You: But at what price?

Prospect: We have a service guarantee that came with the computers.

You: And you renew it each year, don't you? I'm going to predict my fees are 50 percent lower than theirs. If you cut your dependence on the outside support, I can guarantee not only a better price, but quicker service as well.

Prospect: How quick?

You: If we're not there to repair within 24 hours, you don't pay a cent for the service call.

Prospect: Sounds too good to be true.

Plea Strategy

You: Here's a list of small businesses we currently serve. In fact, one of them is right in this building. Why don't we call Ashanti right now, if you don't mind?

Prospect: No, no. That's okay. I usually see him in the elevator at least once a day. I'll ask him about you the next time I see him.

You: But that means we wouldn't be able to sign you up today as a customer.

Prospect: So?

You: Do you remember when you were just starting out, Mr. Tonsich? Remember how you celebrated with each new client you were able to sign up? I'm just starting out, and it would mean a great deal to me to include you among our list of customers.

Prospect: I never make decisions from the heart. It would be great for you if I were a customer, but would it be great for me?

continues

303

Make a Promise (continued)

Promise Strategy

You: Mr. Tonsich, if you're not satisfied with the way I recover lost data, if you don't like the way I install software, if you find I'm not knowledgeable about RAM, CPUs, motherboards, and sound cards, you can cancel the contract and receive a full refund for the unused portion of your agreement.

Prospect: But I'll have to pay for the remainder of my current agreement.

You: No, you won't. Your agreement is prorated.

Further Considerations

Serious salespeople usually refuse to take "I don't know" for an answer. To illustrate, if you ask, "Who makes the actual buying decision?" and you hear, "I'm not really sure about that," consider this bold move. Say something like, "Could you make a call right now to find out?" or "Whom could I call to find out?" You have to make such a request with nonthreatening charm. Otherwise, you may be viewed as a too-aggressive toe-stepper.

WHAT THE EXEMPLARS DO

"Of all closing techniques, the one referred to as the positive-assumption close is the most basic and should be incorporated into all your selling activities." These words of author (*Creative Selling Today,* Harper & Row, 1982) Stan Kossen encourage you to have a positive mind-set toward the sales potential that is before you. In other words, assume that the prospect wants to buy what you have to sell. If you've qualified the lead, there's no reason to assume otherwise. State your assumption diplomatically, "Would you like to use a purchase order, or do you prefer to use a credit card?"

The "Help me out here" ploy is often quite successful, though it shouldn't be overused. Prospects typically are sympathetic toward those just starting out; they remember when they were in similar circumstances themselves. Although you don't want to seem pitiable, you can, if the atmosphere seems right, simply come out and explain how much you want the prospect's business.

You may have heard the phrase the "ABCs of closing," which means "Always Be Closing." This simple rule is a valuable one. It'll work to keep you attuned to the opportunity to finalize the sale, no matter when that opportunity arises.

Ask Yourself

- Do I have too much pride?

- Should I think twice about making a plea with certain kinds of prospects?

- How does my age affect my selling attitude?

- How do I distinguish myself from my competitors?

Dialog 5

Respond to a Question with a Question

Scenario

Existentialist Albert Camus once defined charm as "a way of getting the answer 'yes' without having asked any clear question." You'll use your charm to get the yes answer you want, but you'll also use a three-part approach as you try to sell a single computer to a single buyer. If the buyer is sufficiently charmed by your friendliness and the computer's user-friendliness, then you think the buy decision will be expanded in the future.

Strategies

The strategies here are simple. Using the Answer-with-a-Question strategy, you'll answer a promising question with a question that leads to the close. Incorporated within the dialog are two other strategies: the Pause strategy (wait for them to reply instead of continuing to talk) and the Don't-Pause strategy (don't spend a lot of time writing; doing so gives the prospect time to change his mind).

WHAT THE RESEARCH SHOWS

America has more than 25 million small businesses. If you're using the same techniques you use with mega-corporations, you may be turning off your prospects. Typically, they want a no-nonsense, no-frills approach to finding a solution to their problems. And, they do not look kindly upon the highly technical pitch. Keep it basic, make it fast, and relate on a small-is-better level.

BE CAREFUL

Don't overuse the Answer-with-a-Question strategy. If not handled well, it might come across as an interrogation.

WHAT THE EXEMPLARS DO

According to master salesman Tom Hopkins, the 14 most important words in the art of closing are these: "Whenever you ask a closing question, shut up. The first person to speak loses." This advice is harder to follow than you think because your natural tendency will be to fill up the silence. However, try to pause and get used to the discomfort you'll feel at first. The more often you resist the urge to fill in a verbal void, the easier it will become.

Respond to a Question with a Question

> **You:** That's essentially what our product does. Do you have any questions about anything I've said so far?

> **Prospect:** Yes, if I bought it today, could I have it installed in a day?

Notes: This is the question you've been waiting for. You can offer assurances and answer in the affirmative—or you can first reverse the question to deepen the prospect's inclination to buy.

Answer-with-a-Question Strategy

> **You:** Do you want it installed in a day?

> **Prospect:** That would be great.

> **You:** Let's do it then. Just sign here. The sales agreement covers all the terms we've been discussing.

Pause Strategy

> **You:** *(Not saying a word until the client speaks or signs the agreement.)*

> **Prospect:** Uhh. Tell me once more, why is this better than the other models on the market?

> **You:** In truth, all computers are pretty much alike. Where we differ from the competition, though, is in our post-sale service. We have a "Question?" button on our Web site. Just click it, type in your question, and within 10 minutes, a technically savvy representative will get back to you with the answer, any time of the day or night. There's no additional cost for this service.

> **Prospect:** Maybe I should have my lawyer look this over.

Don't-Pause Strategy

> **You:** There's really no need to pay legal fees. The agreement is pretty standard stuff. Is there any part of it you didn't understand or would like me to go over again?

> **Prospect:** No ....

> **You:** *(Filling out the order form.)* How about this? Issue me the purchase order now so I can get the process moving. You wanted it in your office by this time tomorrow, didn't you?

> **Prospect:** Yes.

> **You:** I'll deliver it myself. Then if your attorney finds any problem with the agreement, I'll either take the computer back and rip up the order form or else work out the problem with you. Now, what's that P.O. number so I can finish this form and leave it with you?

Further Considerations

Virtually anything can be used for positive or negative purposes. A car, for example, can be used to transport a child with a broken arm to the emergency ward, or it can be used as a getaway vehicle during a bank robbery. The same is true for pauses: They can help or harm your close, depending on how well you use them.

Consider using questions to wrap up your response to an objection. To illustrate: "Does this make sense to you now?" or "Would you agree that, dollar for dollar, our widget is a better value?"

Have testimonials memorized and use them, as appropriate, to help you close the sale.

Ask Yourself

- What other single and simple things can I use to either help or harm the closing moments?

- Do I tend to give declarative or interrogative responses to questions?

- Do I feel an urge to fill in the blank whenever there's silence in the sales exchange?

- Before I meet with a prospect, do I typically have any calculations done in advance?

WHAT THE EXPERTS SAY

If managers are interfering with your sales strategies, it's one thing. But if they're looking over your shoulder every moment of the day, it's another. Consider this: Joyce Scott, a sales consultant in Round Rock, Texas, tells about a time when she was just about to close a $2 million deal. Suddenly, the prospect's phone rang. It was Joyce's sales manager, checking up on her. Fortunately, the client intervened and advised the manager that Scott was too busy to talk just then.

Colle Davis, CEO of Executive Coaching asserts, "By nature, salespeople are warriors. If you try to control them, they're going to beat it, fast." If you're a sales manager, consider the extent to which you micromanage your staff. If you have a manager who micromanages, are you enough of a warrior to fight against such behavior?

Dialog 6

Use an Example

Scenario

Although the Roman philosopher Seneca wasn't in sales, he knew the power of examples as a sales tool: "Men trust their eyes rather than their ears; the road by precept is long and tedious, by example short and effectual." What kind of example is possible? You're limited only by your innovative spirit. You could use any of the following:

- A statistical example
- A hands-on example
- A satisfied-customer example
- A free-sample example
- A personal example

Actually, you've opted to use more than one in this scenario, which finds you attempting to persuade a local firm to use your orchard for their next off-site meeting.

Strategies

You'll depend on the Some, Soon, and Sign strategies. First, you'll offer examples of how *some* others are using the orchard for business purposes. Then, you'll lightly discuss the need for quick action *soon*. Finally, you'll come right out and ask for a *signed* contract.

Further Considerations

Have enough features-as-benefits in your head so that no matter what reply you get, you can use it as a selling point. That's what the salesperson did here with the reference to "not enough time."

EXPERIENCE SHOWS

Operate on the assumption that businesspeople today have more money than time. Pride yourself on being a salesperson of few words.

This historical example of verbal economy may prove useful to you at one time or another: At a White House dinner, President Calvin Coolidge was once asked by a guest about his reputation for terseness. "I made a bet with a friend," she informed him, "that I could get you to say more than three words this evening."

The President smiled, picked up his fork, and, just before resuming his meal, commented, "You lose."

EXPERIENCE SHOWS

A rose is a rose and a contract is a contract. But the word, for some, carries a weighty legal sound. If your prospect seems skittish, try using the word "agreement" instead.

Use an Example

> **You:** Thank you, Jesse, for finding time for me today.

> **Prospect:** Well, I don't have much.

Notes: You're going to use the fact that no businessperson alive today has enough time as a selling point for the product and service you're offering. Do this whenever you can, no matter what your script calls for next.

Some Strategy

> **You:** That's exactly why I think you'll like what we have to offer at Farnsworth Farms. Once you pick a date, choose your menu, and leave a deposit, your worries are over. There's nothing left for you to do except prepare your after-dinner remarks. We can get all of that done today, except for your remarks, of course.

> **Prospect:** It can't be as easy as that.

> **You:** Actually, it is. Do you know Christine Caulfield?

> **Prospect:** The real estate broker?

> **You:** That's the one. She recently held an Employee Appreciation Day at our orchard. We had vegetarian fare because that's what she wanted, and we arranged all kinds of races for the employees and their families.

> **Prospect:** I appreciate my employees, but our meeting would be a little more serious.

> **You:** Well, then, you may want to do what PayRight did. They held their annual stockholders' meeting in our lodge. We set up 900 chairs and an elevated stage for the board of directors. After business had been conducted, guests were invited to have light refreshments and to stroll among the orchards.

Soon Strategy

> **Prospect:** Our conference wouldn't be until next September. So why don't I give you a call in August?

> **You:** I'm afraid we won't have any dates available by then. Look, here's my calendar for September and October. You can see we have a number of dates already taken.

> **Prospect:** People plan that far in advance?

> **You:** Many do. We have a bride-to-be who's already reserved the orchard for her wedding a year from now.

continues

Use an Example (continued)

Sign Strategy

> **You:** As long as we're looking at the calendar, why don't we pick a date right now? How does the 14th look?

> **Prospect:** That's good. Our fiscal year will already have begun, and we'll all be ready for a change of scenery by then.

> **You:** Do you think you'd like the vegetarian meal? It's really quite hearty.

> **Prospect:** No, they're a bunch of carnivores around here. How about a choice between pasta, roast beef, and fish?

> **You:** Let me mark that down while you're signing the agreement. We'll bill you for the deposit.

EXPERIENCE SHOWS

Attempt to get yeses throughout your presentation, so that when it's time for the final and most critical yes, the prospect will already be in the approval mode.

BE CAREFUL

Flattery is a useful tool, but only if it's used judiciously. Saying something like, "I was told you'd be the best person to talk to about ..." is mildly flattering and less likely to evoke a "who told you that?" question.

Nothing succeeds like success. Whenever you can, cite examples of how others, especially any prominent local businesspeople, have used your product to increase their productivity, improve their staff morale, and so on.

You know you have to overcome objections. But if you take too strong a stance while the customer is in the need-to-think-about-it stage, it may cost you the sale. If the customer, for example, feels the price is too high and you try to persuade him by saying it can be paid for in three easy installments, you really haven't altered the reality to which the prospect is objecting. You also run the risk of alienating him.

Ask Yourself

- Do I consider myself an articulate person?

- Do I ordinarily evaluate my sales presentation, paying special note to what prompted certain responses from the prospect?

- Do I follow up to ensure there's post-sales satisfaction?

- In a situation like this, photos of well-known people (if only in your own community) enjoying your product or service can speak success more loudly than your words. If you can, ask a satisfied client if you can capture on film his use of your product.

Dialog 7

Offer Reassurance

Scenario

It's been said that as far as sales are concerned, there's nothing new under the sun. There's some truth to this, especially if we go back thousands of years and apply the wisdom of Aristotle, who asserted that effective persuasion depends on three things: reputation, audience awareness, and argument. You'll incorporate all three as you work to sell your holiday plants to a manufacturing executive known far and wide for giving generous Christmas gifts to his best clients.

Strategies

The prospect is calling in response to an advertisement. In so doing, he's qualified himself, allowing you to move directly to the Ethos strategy in which you'll emphasize your firm's reputation for quality and its solid standing in the community. (The word "ethos" pertains to the distinguishing characteristics of an individual or group.) With the Pathos strategy, you'll show an appreciation of the constraints within which your prospect must work. (The word "pathos" relates to the arousal of feelings of sympathy.) Finally, you'll deliver a well-rehearsed pitch, the argument phase of your presentation, with the Logos strategy. (The word "logos" signifies reason or logic.)

Offer Reassurance

You: Thank you for calling Fleur Jolie. Are you calling about our special Christmas gifts for your special clients?

Prospect: Yes, I received something in the mail, and I liked what I saw. Tell me more.

Notes: There are numerous gift shops in town and hundreds in cyberspace. To win this account, you'll have to distinguish yourself from the other gift shops that can supply pretty much the same thing you can, if truth be told. Take advantage of the opportunity by adding value with accolades (ones you've received), with appreciation, and with argument.

Ethos Strategy

You: First, let me tell you that Fleur Jolie is a family-owned and family-operated gift shop that's been in business for over a hundred years. We have corporate accounts with four of the five largest industries in the county. In fact, George Allarde, CEO of Bottchers, calls us the Saks Fifth Avenue of the South. We have one full-time employee dedicated exclusively to handling our corporate customers, so we have a good understanding of your needs.

Prospect: *(Gently chiding.)* What are our needs?

Pathos Strategy

You: You probably need a minimal investment of time and effort. Once you make your selection from our eight-page catalog, phone it in with your credit card number, and you're on file with us forever. You probably also need personalized service. For local deliveries, we have a calligrapher who will take the words you want, or suggest some possibilities and write them in a truly beautiful script.

Prospect: You're right on target so far. What else do we need?

Logos Strategy

You: You need a variety of choices. We have fresh flowers: poinsettias in red, pink, white, and marbled in prices ranging from $9.99 to $49.99. In addition, we carry azaleas, cyclamens, cacti, wreaths, and Christmas gardens in the same range. Our centerpieces and bouquets go up to $100, with delivery fees of $5 within the county and $10 out of state. Another area of expertise is our gift baskets, specially designed for businesspeople.

Prospect: It sounds as if there's a sameness to the gifts.

You: The only thing they have in common is their quality. The gift baskets, for example, carry office supplies and copies of the latest business bestsellers. Further, for corporate orders that exceed $400, we make a 10 percent donation to Gilda's Club, a nonresidential home that offers support, lectures, workshops, and social events for people with cancer and their friends and families. So, by placing a Christmas order, you're not only remembering your business associates who make it possible for you to do what you do, but also remembering those in the community who are not blessed with good health. Do you think your order will total $400?

Further Considerations

Consider writing out the dialog that might take place in a sales call, particularly with a potentially lucrative account. Doing so might lead you in directions you wouldn't have thought to take.

If your prospect confirms what you're saying during the Ethos aspect of your presentation, let him take over the conversation. It's quite likely he'll sell himself on the product.

> ### WHAT THE RESEARCH SHOWS
>
> When an 800 number and a coupon are used to attract new customers, 65 percent of those who place orders do so with the 800 number and 35 percent mail in the coupon. Furthermore, Cahner's Advertising Research shows that an 800 number increases orders by up to 23 percent and increases the money spent on each order by 20 to 40 percent.

When you receive an outright rejection, objection, or denial, ask "Why?" or "Why not?" if only to learn more about how to improve your style.

Ask Yourself

- If I asked five people what my reputation is, would they be likely to cite the same elements?

- Are they the same elements I'd like for myself?

- What does the word "salesperson" connote to most people?

- Would I encourage my son or daughter to become a salesperson?

Dialog 8

Ask for the Order

Scenario

You sell in a highly competitive arena: the world of cellular phones. Your job is to sell your services by phone to small businesses. You truly believe yours is a superior service, and this makes the job easier. However, in this scenario, you're dealing with an individual who alternates between indecision and intemperate remarks. You decide to hang in there, for you feel the indecision gives you at least a fighting chance to make a sale.

Ask for the Order

> **You:** Would you prefer the half-price signing bonus or the 200-free-minutes bonus?

> **Prospect:** Hold on. I haven't said I'd buy it yet.

Notes: Back up and off a bit here. You never want to seem as if you're pressuring the prospect. You'll employ some levity now, woven into your apology.

Laugh-Line Strategy

> **You:** My mother always told me that most people become more interesting when they stop talking. I think it's time for me to shut up.

> **Prospect:** Your mother's a smart woman. Now, I don't want to silence you, but I do want to learn a little more about the overseas rentals before I make any decision.

Affirm Strategy

> **You:** You actually rent it here in the States. Then, when you travel overseas, you can reach all your clients, vendors, staff, family, and friends. The cellular phone costs $50 a week.

> **Prospect:** Who pays airtime?

> **You:** You do. Depending on where you're traveling, it's usually about $1 a minute.
>
> You're a road warrior, Mr. Fitzgerald. You know the frustrations involved in communicating when you're abroad. Our service provides local dial-up access to the Internet from practically anywhere in the world. We also have a phone that lets you know when you're reaching your preset limit for calls. And if you visit our Web site before you travel, you'll be able to learn quite a bit about the places you'll be traveling to. We give you all this for one low rate.

Finalize Strategy

> **You:** You know, actress Roseanne Barr once observed that if the kids were alive at the end of the day, she figured she'd done a good job of mothering. In a similar vein, I know that if the prospect hasn't kicked me out of his office by the end of my presentation, then I've done a good job of selling.

> **Prospect:** You haven't sold me yet.

> **You:** Well, I don't have much more to tell you except that if you sign up today, you'll receive one of two bonuses. Do I dare repeat what they are?

> **Prospect:** Sure. As Kissinger once said, "If it's going to come out eventually, better it come out immediately."

Strategies

You'll use a memorized, humorous line to close this deal. Not only will your prospect like you for doing so, but the laughter will serve to propel the action forward as well. To help you remember your three steps, we've chosen the LAF mnemonic, the letters of which stand for Laugh-Line, Affirm, and Finalize. Use your *laugh line*, then *affirm* more seriously what your intent was, and *finalize* by repeating the close once more and simultaneously making a physical movement, such as moving your chair a little closer to the prospect's.

BE CAREFUL

Comedian Henny Youngman once told an acquaintance, "I enjoyed talking to you. My mind needed a rest." For salespeople, there's a serious message hidden between these funny lines. Don't overwhelm your prospect with the burden of a delivery that has too many facts. Let his mind rest once in a while. But, on the other hand, don't have so much fluff that your prospect feels he hasn't learned a thing.

Further Considerations

According to humorist Carl Reiner, "The absolute truth is the thing that makes people laugh." Find such truths in your standard sales exchanges and prepare some funny lines based on them.

Before the sale is closed, you and the prospect are on opposite sides of it. Humor can serve as the bridge that unites you.

Author Janet Elsea (*The Four-Minute Sell*, Simon & Schuster, 1984) maintains that age itself is neither positive nor negative, "but takes on importance in direct proportion to your audience's expectations." Consider what your prospects expect of you. To verify your assumptions, ask them.

WHAT THE EXPERTS SAY

According to author (*Creative Selling Today*, Harper & Row, 1982) Stan Kossen, "When motivational systems are being developed, it's not what the sales manager feels motivates an individual salesperson that's important but what the salesperson feels is a motivating factor." Don't assume you know what will spur yourself and others to ever greater achievement. People are surprisingly different in choosing their motivators. Talk with your manager about what works best for you. Ask for the order, so to speak.

315

WHAT THE EXPERTS SAY

According to author Matthew Culligan (*Getting Back to the Basics of Selling*, Crown Publishers, 1981), you can atone for some of your selling sins: "Some lost sales can be seen, when viewed objectively, to have been the result of an error or miscalculation on your part .... In these cases, the damage may sometimes be undone in a subsequent call or by another salesperson. In any event, you should use the opportunity to analyze your errors, work on correcting them, and prevent them from recurring."

Ask Yourself

- What fears do I have?

- How well do I cope with them?

- Before a potentially uncomfortable encounter, how often do I say to myself, "What's the worst that could happen?"

- Do I act the role of a successful salesperson?

In the minds of stellar salespeople, service begins when the selling ends. To abandon your customer after you have his or her name on the dotted line equates to the loss of both a relationship and future sales.

Chapter 12

Following Through

You've secured a sale and transformed a mere contact into a real live customer. In one sense, you've reached your goal and your job is done. After all, you're in sales to sell. But in another sense, your job has only just begun. Now it's time to deliver, not only the products that were purchased, but the promises your customer bought, as well.

Your first task, of course, is to follow through on any commitments you've made during the sales process—for the small things as well as the large. Did you say you'd follow up with additional information? It's imperative you send it. Did you make guarantees about your product's performance? Be prepared to back them up. Did you sell "personal service" as part of the package? You better deliver. Today's savvy consumers know they can easily turn to all the competition out there if you're not going to follow through for them.

Another facet of following through is good preparation. *Preparation* is the act of following through in advance. The first dialog in this chapter is devoted to the practice of "picturing"—a tool that's useful for doing good preparation work in any sort of undertaking. Preparation through picturing is certain to make any kind of transaction go more smoothly.

However, even with the best preparation in the world, problems will always occur. Dialogs devoted to handling the inevitable difficulties and customer complaints that arise in business are also included in this chapter.

Several other dialogs cover ways to build your relationships with customers and maintain their hard-won loyalty. By most accounts, transforming a prospect into a customer is much harder than simply maintaining a relationship with one. But customer loyalty is certainly not something that can be taken for granted. Every act of follow-through you perform helps create a feeling of trust in your customers that contributes positively to your relationships with them.

The dialog "Sell After the Sale" presents techniques for capitalizing on the accounts you've captured and the relationships you've maintained. It's predicated upon the simple supposition that it's easier to sell to those who are already sold on you and your products.

Finally, this chapter focuses on how to follow through with yourself in terms of professional development. It includes recommendations on what you can do to keep yourself at the top of your game.

Dialog 1

Practice "Picturing"

Scenario

You're a multitalented sales rep. In addition to making routine sales calls to individual customers, you also give formal sales presentations to groups, do public-speaking engagements, participate in trade shows and conventions, and perhaps hold meetings for your staff. The practice of "picturing" is a skill that benefits all such endeavors and any others that require follow-through. Picturing is the act of following through before a given event takes place. In this scenario, the given event is a sales presentation for a large group of prospects.

Strategies

You'll employ your imagination to run through all the steps involved in this event. Your purpose is to detect and correct any problems in advance. You'll see yourself and others arriving at the event and walking through each and every phase of it—from beginning to end—looking for the things you'll need to take care of to make sure everything runs smoothly. When you do your picturing, you'll consider the following factors as part of your Picturing strategy:

> ### INSIGHTS
>
> "People who fail to plan have planned to fail."
>
> —George Hewell

- **Scheduling.** Have the meeting time and place been confirmed? Are directions necessary? Head count? Parking? Are there signs, graphics, or any sales tools that need to be prepared in advance?

- **Setting.** Are signs needed to point the way? Is the room the right size? Is there enough seating? Are coat racks necessary? Consider the senses: Is the lighting right? Is it noisy? Will refreshments be provided along with all necessary accoutrements? Are the chairs comfortable? What about the temperature in the room?

Practice "Picturing"

You: *(To yourself.)* Okay, everything has been taken care of for the scheduling phase. Thirteen people will attend on June 12 at 3:00 P.M., conference room C at F.I.T. Corporation. I better make a note to check with my two associates on transportation from our offices. I want us to arrive an hour early in order to set up. Oh! I better call F.I.T. to make sure we can get into the room at 2:00.

Now let me think about this from the point of view of Tom, my information technology manager. What would he say he'll need?

↓

You as Tom: I'm going to need to do a demo on the computer. We could bring our own computer, but I wonder if the conference room is equipped with an iMac. That would make life easier. If they do have one there, I want to get in the day before to run my software and make sure there are no glitches.

↓

You: Another question to add to my F.I.T. list. I'll call Tom later to confirm any other requests. I'll call Becky, too. As communications manager, I'm sure she'll want us to bring along the most up-to-date corporate literature. Let me think about any other material my prospects might likely request.

↓

You as prospect: You mentioned in your presentation that study about stress-related illnesses. Do you have copies of it?

You: I'd better bring along that study since I've been asked for copies of it before. I'll make a note here to have my secretary prepare it. I know that any other material my prospects are likely to seek can be found on our Web site. Otherwise, I can send them things by mail after the meeting. I don't want to be too encumbered with papers.

Okay, so now I'm visualizing. The meeting begins. We're there to greet people. I'm looking at all the faces in the room and … agghh! I don't know names. I'll definitely need name tags. I'll have my secretary coordinate that with F.I.T., along with the question of refreshments. I wonder if it would be nice to have some classical music playing in the background to set the tone. I'll make a note to see what Peter and Jane think of that idea. I'd also like us to provide paper and our company pens to each participant, with plenty of samples of our product line. Susan can coordinate that. Peter will do the first half of the presentation and Jane the last half. We'll walk through the technical presentations the day before to give ourselves plenty of time to make adjustments.

Now let me think of some special touch …. I know! Those umbrellas we used at the last trade show that were printed with our logo. That ties in perfectly with our pitch to this group—"Let us be your creative umbrella." I know we still have some left, so I'll make a note to get one for each of the scheduled participants, plus a few extra for anyone who shows up at the last minute. As for the next step, I'll need to have my secretary prepare a master list with all the names, numbers, and e-mail addresses of our reps, as well as those of the participants in the presentation. We'll bring it with us to hand out at the end of the presentation to help facilitate follow-up contact.

Notes: You've gone through the various steps of picturing to prepare for your presentation.

- **Technical details.** Can the blinds be closed if it's necessary to show video material? Are there enough electrical outlets and backup batteries? Is other hardware needed? Backup copies of software? Easels or other props needed? Clocks? Provide paper and pens to all participants? Extra copies of "leave-behinds"? Name tags? Business cards? Extra "samples"? Are sales tools (reports, charts, and so on) in proper order? Do you need to record the event in any way?

- **Potential interrupters.** Is there a phone in the room? Should it be turned off? Ask all participants to turn off cell phones and beepers before the meeting begins?

- **Special touches.** After taking care of all the basics, think about how you might go beyond the basics to make the meeting memorable. Is there something that is particularly meaningful to this group of people? (Perhaps visit their Web site to see if something jumps out at you.) Could something be personalized? Could you show a videotaped testimonial from someone who's significant to this group? Is there any other way you could add a special touch?

- **Next step.** What needs to be supplied in order to advance to the next step? List of contact numbers and e-mail addresses? Books or other materials? Any sort of mementos or samples? Photos of the event to be sent to participants shortly after the event? Anything needed for the newsletter or other coverage of the event?

Further Considerations

Although you'll certainly benefit by going through a picturing exercise even once, doing it a few separate times is recommended.

Different things will strike you on different days. It might be useful to carry out the exercise with a group.

After you have gone through a picturing exercise for a particular event, make a list of all the things that must be done. Add to it as you go along. After the event, review the list and include anything that would have improved it. Keep the list for future reference.

WHAT THE EXPERTS SAY

According to the Web site of *Successful Meetings* magazine, any graphics you intend to use at a trade show should be planned at least two months ahead of time. They also suggest preparing a duty roster before the show in order to identify who will cover the booth at what times. In addition, they recommend finding ways to engage trade show attendees through conversation and participation in drawings, demonstrations, and special offers that have been planned in advance. Visit the magazine's site at www.successmtgs.com.

Ask Yourself

- Am I satisfied with the way I prepare for various events?

- When I'm attending the presentations of others, do I make note of what makes them successful or not?

- What can I provide at trade shows to make my products stand out and be remembered?

- After making a public-speaking appearance, do I obtain copies of any articles that were written about the event and use them as potential sales tools?

- What can I do to make staff meetings more pleasant?

Dialog 2

Regard Closings as Openings

Scenario

You've just sold a new customer on a few items from the line of toys you represent. It's not a very big sale, but you're delighted nonetheless.

Strategies

You know that your new customers are hard-won, and every time you get one, you consider it a real victory. To you, it doesn't matter what the size of the initial sale is, because you have a long-range perspective. You see a first sale as the opening page of a long book. You consider all the sales that'll be generated over the entire life of a given account. You know that with each new satisfied customer, your reputation and your sales figures grow. Thus, in the Enthusiasm strategy, you convey your *enthusiasm* for new accounts and let your customers know how much you appreciate them.

You can further reinforce the start of the relationship by focusing on the future. With the Long-Range Plans strategy you'll ask customers where they plan to be in five years or so, and have a discussion surrounding that issue.

Another technique that enhances relationships with customers is the Help-You-Succeed strategy. If you're someone who likes to see others succeed, let your customers know that. They'll appreciate your show of support. In addition, such a practice may contribute to your own success, given that what goes around typically comes around.

Further Considerations

Consider keeping a "routine maintenance schedule" for each of your accounts, the way such schedules are kept for cars (after the first 5,000 miles do this and after the next 5,000 miles do that). You might build in checks, balances, and rewards. For example: Make some kind of contact with this customer at least once a month; if the account becomes inactive for a period, find out why early on; take the client out to lunch at least once a year; celebrate the one hundredth order by personally delivering it along with a bouquet of flowers. Maintaining and nurturing your accounts in this way can help them grow into long-term, profitable relationships.

INSIGHTS

"Flaming enthusiasm, backed up by horse sense and persistence, is the quality that most frequently makes for success."

—Dale Carnegie

WHAT THE EXPERTS SAY

Show your continuing gratitude to customers who remain loyal over time by presenting them with **lagniappes**—small gifts that serve as tokens of your appreciation.

Regard Closings as Openings

You: Thanks very much for your order, Patty. Everything will be shipped out immediately and should arrive by the 7th.

Customer: That's great!

Enthusiasm Strategy

You: I want to tell you that I'm thrilled to have you as a new customer, Patty, and look forward to a long and lasting business relationship with you.

Customer: Me, too! I just love your product line, and wish I had more of a budget! I hope you don't mind that this first order was so small.

You: Not at all. As I told you, I place no minimums on my first order for any customer. To me it's more important that we start doing business together and not to put limits on the amount of the first order.

Customer: I'm glad you feel that way. I sense from some other salespeople that they'd rather not be bothered with a small order.

Notes: You demonstrated your zeal for new customers by employing an Enthusiasm strategy. You helped build reciprocal enthusiasm with the customer by downplaying the small size of her order and instead focusing on the excitement you feel whenever you connect with a new customer. This dynamic sets a positive tone for the opening stages of the relationship you're forming with this person.

Long-Range Plans Strategy

Customer: I hope your line sells well in my shop. I think it will.

You: I do, too! I'll check back with you in a few weeks to see how it's going. I'm curious, though, where would you like to see your business in the next five years or so?

Customer: Well, I've given that a lot of thought. I'm really conservative as a businessperson.

You: There's nothing wrong with starting out small and moving slowly.

Customer: I've always been careful. I want to make sure I'm succeeding on the first level before proceeding to the next. So, in the next five years, I'll see how it goes, but if all my wishes come true, I'll own about five retail stores between here and Washington, D.C. I may act small but I think big.

Notes: By focusing on her future plans, you've conveyed your interest in this customer's future. You've shown that you're someone who's inclined to develop long-term business relationships. This helps instill confidence in customers and enhances your relationships with them.

continues

Regard Closings as Openings (continued)

Help-You-Succeed Strategy

You: I think your five-year plan sounds fabulous! I'd really like to see you succeed. If there's anything I can do to help you build your success, don't hesitate to ask. If I'm able, I'll give it a try.

Customer: I really appreciate that. How about you? Where do you see yourself headed over the next five years?

You: I'd like to become district manager. That way I could utilize my management skills but, at the same time, retain some customer contact.

Customer: Well, here's to our mutual success! It'll be fun to see where we are five years from now.

Notes: By offering your help in making her business a success, you laid the groundwork for your role as consultant (and not just an order-taker) to this person, thereby deepening your relationship. In addition, such offers tend to generate reciprocal offers. If you help her build her business, reach her goals, and realize her dreams, she'll likely want to try to do the same for you at some point.

Consider how you might kill two birds with one stone. Are there ways in which you might reward a customer and at the same time generate more business? For example, perhaps for every year you do business together you could send a card acknowledging the "anniversary" and at the same time offering a discount on her next purchase.

Does your company publish a newsletter for customers? If not, is it possible to do one of your own a couple of times a year? You might include a feature about one of your customers each time, a list of new clients, interesting ways your products are being used, any relevant research, favorite quotes, announcements about your company, contact information and Web site address, and so on.

WHAT THE EXPERTS SAY

Benchmarking is the practice of measuring and studying a certain parameter or parameters over time. Experts recommend that you benchmark customer-satisfaction levels on a routine basis.

WHAT THE EXEMPLARS DO

According to sources at The Business Research Lab, "Customer comments should be taken seriously. They can serve as early warning signs [and] as a pool of useful suggestions." For additional customer satisfaction tips and information on surveys and other research tools, visit the Web site of The Business Research Lab at www.busreslab.com or call them at 1-888-776-6583.

Ask Yourself

- What do I do to commemorate the start of a new business relationship? Do I note the day we start doing business together so I'll have it for future reference?

- Do I ever look at the cumulative total on each of my individual accounts from the time I first started doing business with them?

- Do I rank those accounts and accordingly apportion my time and energy in servicing them?

- Do I keep track of a "routine maintenance schedule" for my customers?

- Do I think of my customers as people with whom I'm having a long-term relationship?

- What do I do to enhance customer loyalty?

- Should any of the practices I rely on in my personal long-term relationships apply to my professional long-term relationships?

- What kind of treatment would please me as a new customer? Can I apply any of those practices to my own new customers?

- Do I attempt to measure customer-satisfaction levels on a routine basis?

EXPERIENCE SHOWS

Commemorate the start of every business relationship in some way. Handwritten notes, e-mail cards, and delivery of a promotional item or some other gift are all possibilities. Web sites offering promotional products include www.gobrightideas.com, www.promotionalproductsrus.com, and www. epromos.com.

Dialog 3

Add a Personal Touch

Scenario

You're a sales rep for cameras and photographic equipment. You believe in building strong relationships with your customers and your co-workers. You employ a variety of "personal touch" practices to strengthen your professional relationships and are always seeking other ways in which to build those bonds.

Strategies

Personal touches need not be elaborate or expensive. They're simply practices that personalize experiences or customize items in ways that are meaningful to the recipient. Whether handwriting someone's name on a place card or sending a personalized e-mail greeting, this sort of personal touch says, "I recognize the individual in you."

You'll make a practice of being more attuned to the interests and concerns of your customers and co-workers by following a Listen-n-List strategy. You'll develop conversation around their interests and make mental note of them while talking. You'll then transfer that mental note onto a written *list* that you keep in this customer's file for future reference. Whenever you find articles or other information about those areas of interest or concern, you'll be sure to pass them along. Keep in mind that this practice need not be limited to a person's hobbies: It can encompass all areas of interest or concern that someone has chosen to share with you—children going off to college, health issues, travel, and so on.

You'll also look for ways to commemorate your shared experiences by implementing a Souvenir strategy. Whenever you share a special moment with a customer or co-worker, you'll consider commemorating it with a simple *souvenir*. Did you share a laugh together because of an unexpected incident that occurred during a meeting? Reference it the next time you talk.

After making verbal reference to the event, consider following up by sending an appropriate remembrance of it along with a humorous note. Employ a similar practice in other instances as well, such as when someone has gone out of her way for you or has been generous in praise or forgiveness.

INSIGHTS

"You can make more friends in two months by becoming interested in other people than you can in two years by trying to get people interested in you."
—Dale Carnegie

EXPERIENCE SHOWS

Include the phrase "As promised ..." when sending a client or co-worker something she's requested. Doing so helps build trust by reinforcing the fact that you're someone who can be counted on to follow through on promises.

INSIGHTS

Send free e-mail cards from Internet sites such as www.hallmark.com.

Add a Personal Touch

Customer: Yeah, it was a great vacation, thanks. We did tours of all these private gardens and they were spectacular. I'm just passionate about gardening.

You: That's nice. Listen, while you were away the new equipment came in. I'd like to bring it by tomorrow.

Listen-n-List Strategy

You: Oh! I didn't know that you had such an interest in gardening! You must have a real green thumb.

Customer: Well, I don't know about that, but I do love the process. By the way, did the new equipment come in while I was gone?

You: Yes, it did. I wanted to stop by with it so I could demonstrate it for you. How's tomorrow afternoon?

Notes: During this dialog, you learned something new about your customer. Rather than ignore this information, you're quick to make verbal reference to it, and then list this information in the customer's file. You'll then keep your eye out for articles or other information about gardening events that might be of interest to him. If you're ever looking for a gift for him, you'll know where to begin. You might even attach a little package of seeds to a future order, along with a note.

Souvenir Strategy

You: I just couldn't stop laughing over that incident. When the poor waiter brought out the box of tea …. Oh, I'll just never forget the expression on his face!

Customer: I know! I've told everybody about it.

Notes: You've made reference to an enjoyable shared experience with your customer. After making verbal reference to the event, you'll consider following up by sending an appropriate remembrance of it, along with a humorous note.

Shutterbug Strategy

You: *(At holiday party thrown by your company for its customers.)* May I take your picture? How about a group shot? Let me have the correct spelling of your name, please. Oh! There's a great candid shot that I just have to capture!

Notes: Send out copies of these photos to your customers in the new year. Photos not only help you get extra mileage from a fun event by memorializing it, but also give you a reason to contact your customers again.

The Shutterbug strategy makes use of photographs and all their potential for making memories and building bonds. Photos are a great way to commemorate shared experiences and thereby enhance relationships. Even if you don't sell cameras and photographic equipment, try to take pictures of your customers whenever possible and appropriate: Ask for permission to take shots of them using your products; take a group photo and include it with your holiday cards; or feature a "Customer of the Month" photo and a write-up in your company newsletter. Just be sure you have all necessary permissions before publicizing photos in any way.

Further Considerations

All sorts of great gifts are available that can be personalized with photos (mugs, mousepads, and more). Consider them if you're in the market for a personalized present.

Think about ways in which you might personalize the things that represent you. For example, you might include your photo on your business card and perhaps put photos of the entire staff on the company Web site. Or, you might want to create your own personal Web page (including your photo and some basic information) so that prospects and others could visit it.

Consider getting a stack of personalized "with my compliments" cards from a stationer. They add a touch of class to articles and other materials you send out. In addition, they save you the time it would take to write a more formal note to attach to such materials.

> **BE CAREFUL**
>
> Be sure that you allow your business relationships to evolve slowly enough that you can't be accused of trying to create instant intimacy.

> **WHAT THE EXEMPLARS DO**
>
> In his book *Twenty-Two Keys to Creating a Meaningful Workplace*, author Tom Terez explores each of the following factors and how they contribute to feelings of satisfaction in the world of work: acknowledgment, balance, challenge, dialogue, direction, equality, fit, flexibility, informality, invention, oneness, ownership, personal development, purpose, relationship building, relevance, respect, self-identity, service, support, validation, and worth. For tips on how to create more meaning at work, visit Terez's site at meaningfulworkplace.com.

If you're making a charitable donation, keep in mind that certain charities are willing to accept a list of names along with a single donation and then send out cards to each person on the list, indicating that you've made a donation in that person's name. It's a great way to do one-stop shopping for personalized gifts and to do a good deed at the same time.

Ask Yourself

- Do I put enough personal touch in my dealings with my customers?

- What personal touches have I noticed as a customer?

- Why were they meaningful to me?

- Could I adapt any such touches into my work environment or with my customers?

- Have I noticed what other sales reps do to add a personal touch?

Dialog 4

Make Unexpected Calls

Scenario

You're a seasoned salesperson who's found that a great way to follow through with customers is to make an unexpected call to visit your clients and observe your products in use. You've held numerous positions throughout your career and have found this technique to be useful in a wide variety of realms, from retail outlets to factories to business offices.

In addition, you've also found that your "nonsales" visits actually end up generating a lot of sales, both immediate and long-term. You currently sell office copiers.

Strategies

Implementing the See strategy, your unexpected calls will sometimes consist simply of a hello or perhaps the delivery of some small token of appreciation. But usually you'll aim to check on your products and their operation during these "nonsales" calls. The primary

INSIGHTS

"I began slowly to discover that progress, whether of the individual or of a business, depends principally upon giving the largest quality of service for the dollar."

—Sebastian S. Kresge

EXPERIENCE SHOWS

Between unexpected visits, make unexpected phone calls or send unexpected notes or e-mails, just to touch base with your customers.

purpose of these calls is to see how things and people are doing. If everything is okay, you'll simply turn around and leave, without making any kind of sales pitch. You'll leave knowing that your appearance has strengthened your bond with your customers—and that alone will yield rewards in time.

Using the Key strategy, you'll check to be sure that all the key elements of your products and services are understood and being used optimally. You'll consider: Do the key players understand the key functions, features, and benefits? Do they utilize them optimally? Do they need further training? Could they do things differently to make better use of your product? Based on what you see, would a different product suit their needs better? What are the biggest problems the users face? What would be the best solutions to those problems?

If you happen to generate some business along the way on your nonsales calls, that's fine, but you make it clear that it's not your primary purpose for such visits. This shows your customers that you care and help create stronger ties with them, thereby exercising the We strategy.

You may find that occasionally your nonsales calls are met with resistance, rather than open arms. If your visit comes at a bad time for your customer, you'll take a Graceful-Exit strategy and leave promptly.

Further Considerations

When you make a "nonsales call," really try to keep it "nonsales" and resist the urge to push any of your products. If you notice some new selling opportunities at this time, wait for another opportunity to discuss them.

After dropping in on a customer, seize any serendipity in the moment to see whether there's anyone present whom you should meet, such as other company employees or neighboring businesses. Even though you may be on a nonsales call with your customer, it may turn into a sales call with someone else in the vicinity.

> **BE CAREFUL**
>
> Unexpected visits can eat up a lot of time. If at all possible, group your spontaneous calls so that you can visit nearby customers at the same time. If one isn't available, it'll be easy to move on to the next. Also, limit the length of your visit by defining your intentions in advance: "I have only 15 minutes, but I wanted to check in and see how our product was working for you."

Make Unexpected Calls

You: Hi, Cathy!

↓

Receptionist: Hi, Nia. Bob isn't in today. Would you like to schedule an appointment for when he returns?

↓

You: Okay.

See Strategy

You: Well, I didn't actually come to visit Bob. I wanted to see you and the other office staffers.

↓

Receptionist: Why is that? You know we can't buy a single thing without Big Bob's approval!

↓

You: I know. But I wanted to see how the new copier machine was working for you.

↓

Receptionist: That's nice! I'm tied up with the phones right now, but Terry can take you down to the copier center so you can see it in action for yourself.

Notes: Touch base with your customers. Put a face to a name. Look at their surroundings. How is your product placed in those surroundings? Do you have suggestions for a better placement? Visit other parts of their operation. Notice how things tie together. After you leave, collect your thoughts. Make note of anything that stands out to you. A fresh pair of eyes may give your customer something to think about.

↓

Key Strategy

Terry: It's been great having this copier, but I do have a couple questions.

You: I'll be happy to answer them for you and the others, and at the same time we can see if you're making optimum use of the machine and all the features it offers.

Notes: During your calls, you'll check to make sure of questions such as the following: Do the users know how to perform the key functions and optimize the key features? Are they aware of related services you offer? Are there things you could show them that would help them save time, money, or effort? Could this operation use any of your other products? Imagine you were hired solely as a consultant to this customer; what would you suggest and why? Depending on the nature of your relationship with your customer, consider what issues might be appropriate to raise in the future.

↓

We Strategy

You: Well, Terry, I think that will take care of everything.

↓

Terry: Thanks a lot. I think we finally got it. I'll tell Bob you came by and how productive this little impromptu session with the office staff was. And I'm going to push for that automatic binder machine. We could really use it!

continues

Make Unexpected Calls (continued)

We Strategy

You: *(Avoiding the temptation to push a product.)* Well, if you think it makes sense for you, fine. You know where to reach me. I'm glad we all had this opportunity to get to know each other better.

Notes: Bask in the afterglow that a great nonsales call creates. People love superb service and will look well upon you for your interest in them. To maximize the impact of such a practice, don't be hesitant about mentioning your visit to your customer, her superiors, and even your own. Talk about it and even document it in a follow-up note.

Graceful-Exit Strategy

You: Hi, Cathy!

Receptionist: Hi, Nia. Bob isn't in today.

You: Well, I didn't actually come to visit Bob. I wanted to see you and the other office staffers.

Receptionist: Why is that? You know we can't buy a single thing without Big Bob's approval!

You: I know. But I wanted to see how the new copier machine was working for you.

Receptionist: That's really nice of you, but the office staff is swamped this week with year-end reports. Could we do this at another time?

You: Sure. That's no problem. I was in the neighborhood anyway and just wanted to check in.

Notes: When you make an unexpected call, it's possible that you'll be met with resistance, rather than open arms. In that case, you'll want to make a graceful exit. Remember the big picture here: Your purpose is to improve relations, not to intrude. You'll still gain points (although not nearly as much information) just for having stopped in.

Ask Yourself

- How often do I make unexpected calls on my customers?

- What would I consider the ideal number of times to make such calls on each customer during a calendar year?

- Have I ever looked at how such calls affect my sales figures?

- Do I ever invite my customers to nonbusiness events?

WHAT THE EXPERTS SAY

Famed clinical psychologist B. F. Skinner asserted, "The way positive reinforcement is carried out is more important than the amount." If you apply his assertion to the practice of making unexpected calls, you could conclude that a good nonsales call, even if done only rarely, has great potential to positively reinforce a customer's relationship with you.

Dialog 5

Dealing with Problems

Scenario

Passengers were traveling from New York to California on a two-engine train. About half way through the trip, one of the engines failed. The engineer carried on at half-power thinking, "This isn't so bad." Shortly thereafter, though, the second engine failed and the train came to a complete stop. The engineer had to give an explanation to the passengers. He took the microphone in hand and stated, "Ladies and gentlemen, I have some good news and some bad news. The bad news is that we're in the middle of nowhere and both of the engines have failed. The good news is that we're not traveling in an airplane."

It's inevitable that, at some time or other and in some form or other, you'll be hit with a problem that's going to make it impossible for you to deliver what you promised to a customer. In this scenario, you succeed in getting a customer to place a first order with you, only to find out later that there is going to be a huge delay in shipping. How do you handle this situation?

INSIGHTS

"An error gracefully acknowledged is a victory won."

—Caroline L. Gascoigne

Strategies

First, you'll be proactive in problem prevention in general by supplying accurate information up front, and not making any promises that you can't deliver on .... This is the Proactive-Problem-Prevention strategy.

When problems do start to develop, however, you'll aim to maintain goodwill with your customers by keeping them apprised of what might occur with the Situation strategy. You'll inform them of the problem situation, once you've had a chance to investigate it and get all your facts straight. Then you'll use a Backup-Plan strategy, by offering alternate plans that can be used if a worst-case scenario develops. You'll also aim to smooth any feathers that get ruffled in the process by using the Smoothing strategy.

Dealing with Problems

Customer: What is your product's history in terms of how quickly the implementation of this system translates into accelerated call-time response ratios and what is the cumulative rate over an entire year?

You: *(Gasping and grasping.)* I'm sure we can guarantee a 50 percent improvement in your overall performance.

Proactive-Problem-Prevention Strategy

You: Those are interesting questions and ones I've never been asked before. I'm sure the record is impressive, but I don't have specifics. So, let me make a note to track down the answer and get back to you on that.

Notes: Perhaps the simplest form of a problem is one in which the customer asks you a question to which you don't know the answer. Naturally, you don't want to appear foolish or uninformed when you're trying to make a good impression, but you must resist the temptation to fake an answer. To do so would be to invite further complications by supplying misinformation and perhaps false expectations. Most customers will accept the fact that there may be a question to which you don't have an answer. When you state that reality plainly, most will understand and even appreciate your candor and give you time to find the answer for them.

Situation Strategy

You: *(Having won this customer's first order and then finding out there will be a two-month delay in shipping and praying that it won't be a problem.)* So that's the situation with our supplier. I apologize for any inconvenience this has caused, but I wanted to let you know in advance what was transpiring.

Customer: I appreciate that. And thanks for having all the facts available for me during this call.

You: Well, it was a call I hated to make. My company and I pride ourselves on delivering what we promise. But, given this is your first order, you've never had a chance to experience that. I assure you this is not at all typical.

Customer: Typical or not, this situation is a real problem for us. We just can't wait two months to install the system.

Backup-Plan Strategy

You: I was afraid that might be the case, so I looked into some backup plans to see what I could offer you as an alternative until the delivery of your order comes through. Now, remember that the supplier said the system might come in earlier and that two months is just the outer limit. But let's operate on the assumption of a worst-case scenario. One alternative is that I could supply you with a floor model of what you ordered. It isn't brand new and doesn't offer all the features of the system you ordered, but it will certainly function satisfactorily. We could install it tomorrow and replace it when your order arrives.

Customer: Hmm. I'm not really thrilled with that option. What other choices do I have?

continues

Dealing with Problems (continued)

Smoothing Strategy

You: Well, here's Plan B. I've checked with some other suppliers and ….

You: Again, I apologize for the inconvenience this delay has caused you. We want to make it up to you, so I'd like to offer a 10 percent discount off your total order.

Customer: Yes, I think that would work out okay.

You: Great. I'll set it up immediately.

Customer: I appreciate that. It more than makes up for this inconvenience. The way you've handled this problem has really impressed me. I think we're going to have a long and fruitful business relationship.

Notes: As part of your preparation for this phone call, you examined possible options for your customer in case this situation was not acceptable to her. You tried to come up with some backup plans that would address any problems caused by this delay. You presented your alternatives for consideration in this phone call.

You: Thank you so much. And if there's anything else you'd like me to address in regard to this situation, please let me know. Otherwise, I'll see you next Monday with the backup system.

Notes: In order to retain the goodwill of your customer, you must somehow make up for the inconvenience she's suffered, in addition to providing a satisfactory solution to the problem itself. Consider what things you might do to go the extra mile in smoothing any ruffled feathers. Then clear those options with your company and offer one or more of them to your customer.

Further Considerations

Even after you first inform your customer that a "situation" is developing, you must continue to check in with the source of the problem for updates. You needn't report every twist and turn to the customer, but you must remain on top of the situation so that you're aware of any significant developments.

INSIGHTS

"There's no problem too big we can't run away from."

—Linus to Charlie Brown

Even though you take full blame for problem situations, consider asking the source of the problem to send a note of explanation and apology to those who were affected by this inconvenience. Direct communication such as that can go a long way in smoothing ruffled feathers.

Also, in addition to whatever sort of actions your company takes to make up for a customer's suffering, consider what you might do on a personal level to compensate for the difficulties. Even a small gesture acknowledging that a customer was inconvenienced is usually much appreciated.

> **BE CAREFUL**
>
> Don't be an alarmist. Customers don't want to hear about every potential difficulty. Don't trouble them unless you know that a given situation is a true problem.

Keep your perspective. Just as in the train-engine example at the start of this dialog, we sometimes need to be reminded that few things are matters of life and death. This doesn't mean that you can afford to take your customers' problems lightly. Of course, they'll be grateful if you *do* act like their problems are a matter of life and death, but in terms of your own state of mind, you'll do well to keep your perspective intact.

Ask Yourself

- Am I proactive in trying to prevent problems?

- When I don't know the answer to a question, am I quick to say so?

- Do I make a point of finding the answers to such questions and getting back to the customer with the relevant information as soon as possible?

- Am I careful to think through any backup plans I offer?

- Do I ever see problems as opportunities that can actually strengthen my relationships with my customers?

- When have I encountered a problem as a customer that I thought was handled well?

- What could I apply from that experience to my own customer-relations practices?

Dialog 6

Handle Complaints Personally

Scenario

Perhaps even worse than discovering, in advance, that a problem is going to negatively affect a customer, is being informed by a customer about a problem that has already occurred. In this scenario, a customer calls to tell you that a product she ordered got shipped to the wrong address. Instead of going to their East Coast operation, it went to their West Coast operation, and the error has completely messed up their schedule. It's clear to you that your shipping department made a mistake, but rather than lay blame elsewhere or redirect the call, you hear out this customer and embrace her problem as if it were your own.

INSIGHTS

"Service is often the art of making good on somebody else's mistake."

—Cavett Robert

BE CAREFUL

Don't make matters worse by promising to fix a situation with something you can't ultimately deliver. Identify what you'll *try* to do for a customer and report back quickly with a go-ahead on your initial plan or some alternative options.

Strategies

It's inevitable that human error will affect some of your sales transactions. Customers will naturally be upset when such things happen to them. You may be equally upset when a customer brings such issues to your attention. In order to rectify such situations and make your relationships with customers last, you'll use the LAST strategies: **Listen, Acknowledge, Seek-Suggestions,** and **Take-Initiative.**

The Listen strategy, of course, means *listening* thoroughly to your customer's complaints so that she feels completely heard. In the Acknowledge strategy, you'll *acknowledge* and empathize with her feelings so that she feels completely understood. You'll utilize the Seek-Suggestions strategy so that you can have her input on any corrective measures you might take, Finally, you'll utilize the Take-Initiative strategy to go the extra mile in trying to rectify this situation.

Handle Complaints Personally

Customer: … And another thing, those ingredients were perishable, and we had to toss them. So, because of your delay, we not only incurred additional labor expense and disgruntled customers, but also got hit with the cost of supplies gone bad. We're just furious around here!

Listen Strategy

You: Is there anything else that transpired that you'd like me to know about?

Customer: I'm sure I'll think of something.

Notes: You employed one of the most important practices in customer-repair work. First, you listened thoroughly to everything the customer had to say. You didn't make defensive comments or try to cut her off in any way. In fact, you asked her to elaborate and talk more (not less) about all the consequences and complications of the problem and the feelings it generated. The important part of this phase is to let the customer vent till she's spent and to allow her to feel completely heard.

Acknowledge Strategy

You: I completely understand your feelings. I'd be furious, too, given the problem itself and all its ripple effects. It looks like we've really complicated your life and contributed to the animosity your own customers are feeling. I apologize sincerely.

Notes: You acknowledged the customer's feelings by repeating them back to her and indicating that you understood her reaction. You empathized by stating that her reaction made sense to you and that you'd feel the same way if you were in her shoes.

Seek-Suggestions Strategy

You: Again, I want you to know how sorry I am about this and I want to know what you might have us do to help make this situation right.

Customer: Well, for starters, you could contact the three customers of ours who were hurt by this and explain what happened.

You: Consider it done. If you'll just e-mail me their contact information, I'll personally call them today and follow up with a handwritten note. I'll also include a gift certificate for each of them, redeemable on our Web site.

Customer: *(Softening a bit.)* That's a good start. But the other problem I have with this is that you made me look bad with my boss.

You: That's distressing. I don't want something that was our fault to reflect badly on you. How would you feel if I called him about it?

Customer: He's hard to reach. You could e-mail him, though.

continues

Handle Complaints Personally (continued)

Seek-Suggestions Strategy

You: Will do. I'll send you a blind carbon copy of the e-mail, too.

Notes: You sought suggestions on what the customer would like you to do to rectify this situation. This is an important step. Sometimes all that customers want is a simple acknowledgment. Other times, they might want monetary compensation. The important point is to find out what would be meaningful to them. Doing so will help them feel satisfied with how you ultimately handled the situation. It might also save you from overcompensating them.

Take-Initiative Strategy

Customer: Then there's the issue of our out-of-pocket costs. They amounted to a couple thousand dollars.

You: That's something I want to address with my superiors. Although I'm not in a position to give immediate approval to such a request, it is something I want to raise with them. Could I trouble you to e-mail me a list of the expenses you incurred so I can show it to them? I want to fight for you on this.

Customer: I appreciate that. Sure, I'll send a list out today.

You: Is there anything else you want to tell me?

Notes: You finish up this conversation by indicating the initiative you're going to take to personally handle this problem. You'll offer anything that your company allows you to offer, and you'll let the customer know that you'll try to get approval on anything else she's seeking. After a few more pleasantries, you hang up and start making the calls and writing the correspondence you promised to provide. You also take some money from your discretionary budget to have an apology gift sent immediately to your customer and her boss, along with an appropriate note.

Further Considerations

Communication breakdowns are at the heart of many problems that arise in business. Think about what you might do on your own and within your company to improve communication-related breakdowns.

Be clear about how much latitude you have in terms of deciding how to make things right for a customer who's been wronged. Some companies set strict limits on what they're willing to let you do; others empower you to do whatever it takes to make the customer happy.

If you're ever tempted to just let a customer go, consider the following questions. What kind of time, effort, and money did it take to get the customer in the first place? Are you willing to let all that go down the drain? How much in sales might this person generate over the years if you can make her a life-long customer? How much might it cost you and your company if she remains dissatisfied and spreads her bad opinion of you and your company to your current or potential customers? When looking at the big picture, it's rarely worth letting a customer go.

After you've sorted out the problem, consider whether it might be useful for the head of your company (or some other higher-up) to write a letter of apology to the wronged customer in order to smooth out relations. Apologies sometimes mean more when they come straight from the top. If you decide to go this route, make it easy for your superior by writing out the letter in advance and having it ready for her signature, if she agrees to it. You'll stand out for going the extra mile and so will your company.

Decide whether this "infraction" warrants your visiting this customer to deliver a personal apology and perhaps a gift to make amends.

> **WHAT THE EXPERTS SAY**
>
> Studies show that a customer who has had a bad experience with a business is 20 times more likely to talk about it to others than someone who has had a good experience.

> **WHAT THE EXEMPLARS DO**
>
> Henry Ford had this to say about customer service: "The trouble with a great many of us in the business world is that we are thinking hardest of all about the dollar we want to make. Now that is the wrong idea from the start. I'll tell you the man who has the idea of service in his business will never need to worry about profits. The money is bound to come. This idea of service in business is the biggest guarantee of success that any man can have."

Ask Yourself

- Do I make follow-up calls after a problem has been settled, just to make sure everything's okay?

- As an alternative, do I send a follow-up note or e-mail card?

- What can I do to try to prevent mistakes from happening in the first place?

- Do I study various complaints that I see within my company to try to identify any patterns or larger issues that need to be addressed?

Dialog 7

Sell After the Sale

Scenario

Most sales people would agree that current customers are more valuable than potential customers. By definition, current customers are those you've already established a relationship with, those who are already convinced of the benefits that you and your products can provide. While relationships with current customers need to be maintained and nurtured, of course, those efforts are relatively simple compared with the work it takes to find new prospects and convert them into customers. Given the fact that you have more to gain by selling to current customers than to new prospects, you aim to do everything you can to maximize sales with your current customers before seeking new ones.

> **BE CAREFUL**
>
> If an old account was severed on very bad terms, it may not be worth all the repair work needed to revive it. Check with your superiors before approaching a former account. There may be reasons why your company doesn't want to pursue it.

Strategies

The strategies you might follow in your attempts to sell after the sale include those found in the acronym PLUS:

- **Product-Line strategy.** Sell the products that accessorize, supplement, or complement the original item purchased. This technique applies to everything from dresses to computers. Emphasize the fact that you offer these "attachments" to better serve your customer by providing the convenience of one-stop shopping. If discounts are applied to sales totaling over a certain dollar figure, point out the savings to be had by buying the additional items. If applicable, consider a service and/or maintenance agreement as part of the sale, too.

Sell After the Sale

You: So, Rachel, I know you're going to be thrilled with this postage machine. It's going to make your life so much easier and start saving you money immediately.

Customer: I just hope it's not going to jam up or be difficult for my staff to operate.

Product-Line Strategy

You: Well, you know we have an unconditional one-year guarantee, so you're covered. But one of the things that will help keep the machine operating smoothly is this conditioning oil that is recommended by the manufacturer. Just put in a few drops once a week and you should be problem-free. I can give you a dozen bottles at an introductory price of $10.95 each. If you agree to use some each week, the manufacturer will extend the warranty an additional year.

Customer: Why can't I just use an over-the-counter oil?

You: Well, you could. But that's not what the manufacturer recommends. If you choose that route, you'll lose the option of extending the guarantee. Using the recommended oil will be worth it in the long run. Over-the-counter oil is not that much cheaper.

Customer: Okay, I'll take a dozen.

You: Fine. And here's a handy calendar to put next to the machine as a reminder for the conditioning oil. Just place a checkmark here each time you do it. Now the only other thing the manufacturer recommends for keeping the machine trouble-free is using this brand of self-adhesive postage paper. It's $34.75 a ream.

Customer: Okay, I'll take a ream of that.

Lost-Customers Strategy

You: Hello, Ms. Swank. Jeremy Shipman here of Z-Best Company. I've been going through our records and noticed that we did a lot of business together for a long time and then it suddenly dropped off.

Ms. Swank: That's right. We stopped using your company about two years ago.

You: Ms. Swank, I'm pretty new here and I'd like to hear from you what transpired to cause that change. May I take you out to lunch so that I can learn about it? No strings attached. I just want to know what the history was here.

Ms. Swank: I guess that'd be okay.

continues

Sell After the Sale (continued)

Upgrade Strategy

Widow: *(At a funeral parlor.)* I'd like to make arrangements for my late husband.

↓

Funeral director: I'm sure your beloved deserves the very best. We could provide a fitting funeral for $10,000.

↓

Widow: Do you have anything a little less fitting?

↓

Funeral director: Well, if you're interested in just the basics, that would cost you $500.

↓

Widow: My husband believed in the basics.

↓

Funeral director: Excellent choice. Now, will you be doing the embalming yourself?

Notes: The routine carries on this way and, by the end, the widow has spent well over $10,000. The above dialog is based on a comedy routine that was frequently performed by Mike Nichols and Elaine May. The routine humorously demonstrates the technique of upgrading.

Scope-of-Users Strategy

You: Jim, you've been a good customer of ours for a long time now. I want to expand the scope of our customers and I'm hoping you'll do a little brainstorming with me for a few minutes.

↓

Customer: Sure.

↓

You: I'm asking each of my customers to think about any other people or places that might be able to use our products. Would you jot down the names of some other departments in your company that I might be of service to? Also, what about your company's different locations? And who would I speak to from your company's catalog department?

Notes: You'll carry on this conversation by providing prompts that will generate a list of names for you to contact. Ask your customer if you may use his name as a reference when calling the people on your list. Carry out this practice with all your customers periodically.

- **Lost-Customers strategy.** The fact is that former (or simply inactive) customers were sold on your company's products at one time. That means you've already won more than half the battle. Investigate why they're no longer with you and consider taking on the challenge of winning them back. Ask around in your company to identify some of the lost customers. Also consider checking old accounting records to find former accounts.

- **Upgrade strategy.** Keep your customers apprised of any new versions of the basic product that they're already sold on. This includes new models, styles, colors, sizes, and other options that weren't available when the original purchase was made.

- Scope-of-Users strategy. Seek each customer's help in identifying other places where the same products might be used, such as different departments in the same company, different geographic locations of the company, and different outlets for the company (Web sites as well as bricks-and-mortar stores).

Further Considerations

Remember that people change jobs often. So, even if someone at a company rejected a sales overture of yours at some point, check from time to time to see if a replacement has taken over who might be more open to your pitch.

In addition to one-to-one sales calls, use other formats to publicize upgrades or new models of your product, such as e-mail (or standard mail) announcements, faxes, or an invitation to visit your Web site for more details.

When seeking someone's help in broadening your scope of users, show that you've done your homework. For example, read corporate literature or visit the company's Web site to learn about other locations or other divisions. Then ask your customer for information on whom to contact at those sites.

> ### WHAT THE EXEMPLARS DO
>
> Jeff Bezos, head of amazon.com, presents a Web site that is a masterpiece in terms of "selling after the sale." Once the customer has logged on to the site and selected an item of interest, Amazon will suggest other items based on that interest, for example, other books on the same topic, other books by the same author, other items purchased by people who bought this same book, and so on. Amazon can even identify best-selling books and other items within a given group of people, depending on where you work or go to school or where you live. This "Purchase Circle" is based on pooled information that is kept anonymous. Amazon can then offer suggestions that might appeal to you as a member of this group. Visit the site at www.amazon.com.

Ask Yourself

- Do I offer lots of suggestions on products that might be useful to my customers?

- Do I keep myself apprised of changes in my customers' businesses to see how I might better serve their needs?

- Do I read my customers' annual reports?

- Do I seek out inactive or lost customers?

- Do I seek the help of satisfied customers in finding prospects?

Dialog 8

Study After the Sale

Scenario

You're a dedicated sales professional looking for ways to improve your skills. You work for a small company that doesn't offer any kind of training beyond an initial orientation program about the company, its products, and its procedures. You've decided that you want to convince your company to take a more active role in providing training. You're going to try to sell your superiors on the value of study.

Strategies

In order to persuade your superiors, you'll look at what factors would be compelling to your particular audience and, accordingly, sell those specific benefits as they apply to your proposal or product. This is the essence of the Sell-Benefits strategy. You'll also tap into the power of numbers by using the Cite-Statistics strategy, providing data that support your case. Finally, you'll offer a variety of acceptable options in order to increase the chances that your superiors will agree to your proposal in some form, with the Offer-Options strategy.

Further Considerations

Knowledge is, of course, transmitted in a wide variety of ways. There are training seminars offered live or online. In addition, lots of valuable material is presented in books, videotapes, CDs, audiotapes, and magazines. Consider, too, the value of mentors and peer-teachers and the resources of organizations such as SCORE (Service Corps of Retired Executives).

INSIGHTS

"Knowledge, know-how, and the ability to apply them are the keys to the twenty-first century. School is never out for the person who sincerely desires to succeed."

—Brian Tracy

INSIGHTS

"If you think education is expensive, try failure."

—John Condry

EXPERIENCE SHOWS

To learn more about online training (also known as e-learning), go to sites such as www.iti4training.com, www.click2learn.com, and www.eduprise.com.

BE CAREFUL

Don't get so steeped in studying that you do it at the expense of actually getting out and selling. Keep an eye on your priorities.

Study After the Sale

You: So, Josefina, the other sales reps and I would really love it if the company could sponsor some training seminars for us.

↓

Boss: Well, money is really tight right now.

↓

Sell-Benefits Strategy

You: That's the very reason we need training. I'm sure that the reps could be making a lot more sales and the company a lot more profit if we could attend a quality training program.

↓

Boss: I can't afford to send all of you off to some seminar for a week. Who'd cover the territories?

↓

You: We wouldn't have to go all at once. We could stagger it.

↓

Boss: Well, maybe so, but I'm not so sure these things work.

Notes: Like any good salesperson, you considered your audience and appealed to her self-interest when making your pitch. You tailored your comments to reflect benefits that would be meaningful to her.

↓

Cite-Statistics Strategy

You: It's true that some training courses are better than others. But if you look at this data I pulled together, you'll see that, overall, training is the single most effective way to improve the performance of a sales staff.

↓

Boss: *(After studying the chart.)* Well, these numbers are pretty impressive. But I still don't want to take the time away from the workday.

Notes: Your case is made even more compelling by using research figures.

Offer-Options Strategy

You: There are ways we could get training without interfering with our work schedules. Some out-of-town seminars are offered on weekends. Or maybe we could bring in someone to do on-site training on weeknights. We could even do online training individually over the Internet, which would be available 24/7. I've prepared a list of some alternatives and what the costs would be.

↓

Boss: Well, you've clearly done your homework. I'm sold! So well, in fact, that it seems as if you don't need any training.

↓

You: Thanks for the compliment!

↓

Boss: No, thank *you* for bringing all this to my attention. Let me talk it over with my partners, but I promise you'll get your training somehow.

Notes: You recognize a buying signal when you see it and seize this moment in your conversation to begin offering some acceptable alternatives.

Sales newsletters, such as those offered by publishers like LRP, give up-to-date information on specific areas of interest for the sales professional and others. To learn more, check out its Web site at www.lrp.com.

For a daily dose of business news, visit sites such as www.businessweek.com, www.wsj.com, and www.cnn.com.

WHAT THE EXPERTS SAY

Supporting the "use it or lose it" theory, studies show that education helps protect brain function. The more education you have, the less likely that you'll suffer memory loss with age.

WHAT THE EXEMPLARS DO

David Rockefeller, when articulating a formula for success, listed training as the first ingredient. "Success in business requires training and discipline and hard work."

Ask Yourself

- What would I estimate to be the "shelf life" of my current sales knowledge?

- What steps do I take to update that knowledge regularly?

- Do I take full advantage of any training opportunities that my company provides?

- Have I investigated online training possibilities?

- Do I make a point of seeking at least a modicum of business information on a daily basis from newspapers, magazines, or the Internet?

Chapter 13

Letting Other Sources Sell You

As a sales professional, you needn't rely solely on yourself to promote your products and services; you can enlist the support of
outside sources for help in generating a buzz. Those sources include
other people, places, and things that can help sell you and all that you
have to offer.

People who could help sell you include your current customers. The
first two dialogs in this chapter cover ways in which you might ask
current customers for internal as well as external business. Later in the
chapter, we explore such sources as competitors and "complementors"
(those who sell products or services that complement your own), as
well as organizations, associations, and formal and informal business
networks.

Places that could help sell you include those as near as the businesses
right next door and as far-reaching as the new realms of cyberspace.
The final dialog in this chapter is devoted to some of the destinations
on the Internet that could help promote you and your products.

Things that could help sell you include compelling sales materials,
such as testimonials from satisfied customers (both unsolicited and
actively sought out). In addition, a number of other "pass-alongs" are
discussed as possible tools that could help sell you and your products;
such sources include tip sheets, columns, and newspaper articles.
These and other ideas are presented in the dialogs titled "Put Out
Material" and "Take In Material."

Once you set the wheels in motion for other sources to sell you, you can (under ideal circumstances) just sit back and passively reap the rewards they'll bestow in terms of promoting you and your products and services. No additional effort on your part is necessary. Of course, any such arrangements need to be given routine maintenance or perhaps even major overhauls every now and then, but after they're up and running you can often allow them to be self-perpetuating, taking on a life of their own. (We are not suggesting that you approach every facet of your career in this way, only the systems you establish for letting other sources sell you.)

On a final note, remember the power of your reputation as something that continuously sells you (or not!). Word-of-mouth is certainly one of the most effective and least expensive means of promotion. A great product, a killer application, and an outstanding reputation are all prime features that are easily promoted through good word-of-mouth. Consider what kind of word-of-mouth you're likely generating as a sales professional. Imagine the actual words others might typically use when referring to you. Then ask yourself if that's the kind of reputation you want to have. If not, seek to change it.

"Reputation is made every day and every minute."

—Christopher Ruel

Dialog 1

Ask for Internal Business

Scenario

You're a sales rep for office products.

You're looking at ways that you can enlist other sources to help sell you. Your attention naturally turns to your current customer base. You're fortunate enough to have developed a large number of satisfied customers, so you'll try to tap into this highly valuable source for selling you and your services. Every satisfied customer is a potential walking commercial for you! Word-of-mouth is a potent force: what others say about you carries much more weight than anything you could say about yourself.

Strategies

To generate more business for yourself, you're going to enlist the help of current customers, asking them where else in their company you might be of service. You will thereby let other sources sell you in the form of current customers who recommend prospects employed elsewhere in their companies, including other divisions of the company; other locations throughout the city, state, nation, and world; any sort of intranet on which you could do internal advertising; and partner companies or affiliate organizations. This is the essence of the Others strategy.

You may find that a customer is reluctant to help you sell your products elsewhere in his organization. Perhaps he doesn't want to take time out of his busy schedule to call his colleagues for you. If you sense this is the case, use the Take-No-Time strategy and offer to call or e-mail those contacts yourself.

> ### INSIGHTS
>
> "Tell everyone what you want to do and someone will want to help you do it."
>
> —W. Clement Stone

> ### EXPERIENCE SHOWS
>
> Remember to phrase questions carefully in order to generate the best response. If you ask a yes-or-no question ("Do you know anyone else who might use my products?"), you're likely to invite a yes-or-no response. However, if you start your question with "who," "whom," or "what," followed by specific references ("Whom do you know in the R and D division that could use my products?"), you're more likely to generate a response that includes a list of possibilities.

Ask for Internal Business

You: Thanks for this order, Gunther. I've been getting raves on this new line of stick-ums. Customers find that they're so useful!

Customer: They really are!

Others Strategy

You: I'd love to be able to introduce this item to others in your organization. What other departments in the university could use these?

Customer: Well, really all the offices could, and I'll order some more after this trial run. But you know what? I think this product would be useful in the science labs, as well.

You: You're right. I can see lots of ways these might be used in a science lab. Who handles procurement for the labs?

Customer: That would be Lydia Perez.

You: Would you be willing to give her a call on my behalf?

Customer: Sure.

You: Great! Thanks so much.

Take-No-Time Strategy

Customer: That would be Lydia Perez.

You: Would you be willing to give her a call on my behalf?

Customer: To be honest, I'd rather not take the time to do that. Lydia's hard to reach.

You: No problem! I can track her down. But when I do, may I say that you sent me and that you're a satisfied customer?

Customer: Absolutely! She can even call me if she wants additional details. I just don't want to have to try to reach her.

You: I understand completely. You know, it sounds as if I might have better luck reaching her through e-mail. Do you happen to have her e-mail address?

Customer: Sorry, I don't.

You: That's okay. I'll get it from her office. Thanks again for this suggestion, Gunther.

continues

Ask for Internal Business (continued)

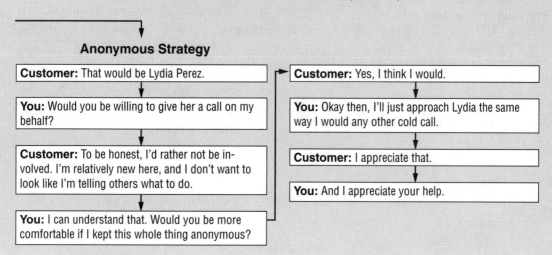

Anonymous Strategy

Customer: That would be Lydia Perez.

↓

You: Would you be willing to give her a call on my behalf?

↓

Customer: To be honest, I'd rather not be involved. I'm relatively new here, and I don't want to look like I'm telling others what to do.

↓

You: I can understand that. Would you be more comfortable if I kept this whole thing anonymous?

Customer: Yes, I think I would.

↓

You: Okay then, I'll just approach Lydia the same way I would any other cold call.

↓

Customer: I appreciate that.

↓

You: And I appreciate your help.

Your customer may be reluctant to get involved in your sales overtures for a number of other reasons. Perhaps interpersonal relationships or the dynamics of office politics make your customer hesitant to appear to be promoting your products elsewhere in the company. In such a situation, utilize the Anonymous strategy and offer to keep your customer's leads *anonymous*.

BE CAREFUL

Referencing the name of your current customer when you contact a lead will lend momentum to your overture. But be sure you have your customer's permission to mention his name as the source of the lead.

Further Considerations

Companies that put out internal newsletters are often looking for articles and other relevant information to include. If you can offer any pertinent content, consider writing an article or providing information for your customers' newsletters as a way to promote yourself or your products more broadly within a customer's company.

WHAT THE EXPERTS SAY

"Ask and ye shall receive, seek and ye shall find."

—Matthew 7:7

If you have product samples or ad specialties that would work well as "favors," consider offering them to your customer for internal gatherings, such as corporate retreats and company-wide picnics; you might even offer them for corporate charity events.

353

You might be able to access an internal list of e-mail addresses from a company's Web site. You could then send an e-mail message to everyone on the list, telling them about a special offer or some other "newsworthy event." Or, you might prepare an e-mail message for your contact to send out company-wide, if the person is willing to do so. If he is, he would be helping to sell you with simply the click of a button.

Ask Yourself

- How often do I ask my current customers for internal business?

- Is it often enough?

- Do I keep a record of such requests so that I can know with certainty when I last asked for referrals?

- Has anyone in my own company "sold me" on the products or services that he uses?

- When? How?

- What can I take from that experience to apply to my own sales practices?

- Do I keep current on internal personnel changes within my customer's company so that I'm aware of potential new prospects who've come onto the scene?

- Do I regularly update the organizational charts that I keep for all of my customers' companies?

Dialog 2

Ask for External Business

Scenario

In an effort to expand your markets, you're approaching the customers who know and love you best and asking for referrals outside their companies. You'll seek to tap into your customers' universe of connections, which might include their suppliers, distributors, acquaintances, competitors, colleagues, and neighboring businesses.

Strategies

You'll be selective about which of your customers you approach in seeking new business, knowing that your best chances for success will be among the customers with whom you have the best relationships. You'll approach selected customers and ask them to consider a pool of prospects from among their many contacts outside their company. You'll provide a written Prospect-Pool list for your customer that names *prospect* categories to help jog the memory. Your list will leave space to jot down the names of any prospects that come to mind. You'll retrieve the list at an appropriate time to follow up with the contacts he has listed. You'll repeat the process again at some point in the future, (perhaps 6 or 12 months later) to tap into any new contacts. This is the basis of the Prospect-Pool strategy.

You'll make it easy for your customers to pass along information about you to others by utilizing a Contact-Info strategy. This strategy recommends that you include all *contact info* on your business cards, including mailing address, e-mailing address, Web site address, phone and fax numbers, etc. In addition, you'll seize any opportunities that arise to help get your name "out there" by including similar information on brochures, catalogues, and other printed matter.

INSIGHTS
"If you don't expect the unexpected, you'll never find it."
—Jurgen Moltmann

BE CAREFUL
Besides being selective about whom you ask to supply outside contacts, be selective about how often you ask for such referrals. And, as always, get permission before revealing your source.

Ask for External Business

You: So, David, I think our company has proven itself over the years in its business relationship with yours. It's probably fair to say that you count on us to deliver great service on high-quality goods at a reasonable price.

Customer: Absolutely. You're the best around.

You: I'm glad you feel that way, and I'm grateful to have had the opportunity to supply your entire company with our products.

Customer: The pleasure's been ours.

Prospect-Pool Strategy

You: David, I'm looking to expand my scope at this time. I'd like to know if you'd be willing to assist me in reaching contacts you have outside your organization.

Customer: Sure.

You: That'd be great! Everybody needs office supplies! What I've done is prepared a "Prospect Pool," a list of categories to help us come up with names that could be contacts. If you'll take a moment to review it with me, we can write down any names that come to mind. The list is handy because it helps to jog and jot: It helps jog the memory and it's a handy place to jot down relevant info.

Customer: That *is* handy.

Contact-Info Strategy

Customer: *(Looking at the list.)* Two names come to me right off the top of my head because I'm having lunch with these people today: Ian McAlister and Mifune Williams.

You: That's great. Let me give you a few of my business cards for your wallet or briefcase. They have my phone number, e-mail address, and even my Web site address on them. Your contacts could take a look at what I offer right on my home page and then I can follow up with them.

Customer: Happy to do it. In fact, if you give me a few extra cards, I'll put them out at our booth when we go to that trade show next week.

You: If you like, I can do better than that. I can bring a box of our company notepads down there. You could distribute them as a freebie to those who visit your booth. And if some people call me after seeing my number on the pads, that would be great.

Customer: It's a deal.

You: I really appreciate all this help. And I'll leave my "Prospect Pool" list with you. If you would just jot down names on the list as you think of them, I'll get back to you in a week or so to see where we are.

Customer: Great.

Notes: You're trying to capitalize on her willingness to help by making it easy for your customer to promote you.

Further Considerations

If you can present a seminar in your community that would be of general interest, consider doing so and asking your customers to invite their external contacts.

Think of what items you might give current customers to distribute in order to help sell you. They might put some of your brochures or other literature in their lobbies or waiting rooms. They might post your business cards or other information about you or your products on their public bulletin boards. Perhaps they would be willing to give away free samples of what you're selling.

When preparing your own Prospect-Pool list, leave enough room next to each category so that your customer can make notes. Make it clear that you're not asking her to supply someone for every category but rather that you're giving this list simply to help identify individuals to whom she might be comfortable referring you. Consider including the following categories:

- Friends, acquaintances

- Family

- Individuals connected with schools

- Church or other religious groups

- Neighborhood contacts, such as other families or nearby businesses

- Any place where you are "a regular," such as restaurants, dry cleaners, gas stations

- Community groups

- Hobby groups

- Recreational sports groups

- People who provide services, such as doctors, lawyers, accountants, real estate brokers, bankers, barbers, hairdressers, manicurists, and travel agents

> **WHAT THE EXPERTS SAY**
>
> Studies show that a referred prospect who has a sense of confidence in your company is approximately 80 percent more likely to become a customer.

- People you know from "another life," such as former high school or college contacts

- Colleagues at other local companies

- Contacts at companies on the Internet

- Other businesses sharing this office space

- Friends in other businesses

- Suppliers

- Customers, clients

- Vendors, distributors

- Competitors

- Members of the same organization, such as Chamber of Commerce, SCORE, industry associations, and Toastmasters

WHAT THE EXEMPLARS DO

The following example illustrates the importance of asking for business, even when you think it's obvious that you would like to have that business. The story is about an insurance agent whom Henry Ford had known for a long time on a personal basis. Despite that fact, the agent never got any business from Ford. When the agent asked Ford why that was so, Ford is said to have responded simply, "You never asked me."

Ask Yourself

- Do I try to help develop "external business" for others?

- When was the last time someone referred me to one of his "external sources"?

- How did that situation come about? How could I get it to happen again?

- Am I aware of any techniques that other salespeople use to broaden their base of contacts?

- Could I adopt any of those techniques?

- Do I make it easy for customers to pass along relevant information about me to their contacts?

Dialog 3

Put Out Material

Scenario

Advertising is the practice of selling without salespeople. It's a passive way to sell but an active way to get out a message. Once a piece of promotional material is created, it can be taken in by an unlimited number of people, an unlimited number of times. It can be circulated again and again without any additional effort on the part of the creator. For this reason, advertising is a powerful and efficient tool. In this scenario, you are a salesperson for a line of unfinished furniture. You're looking at ways to tap into the power and efficiency of advertising by examining some no-cost or low-cost ways of promoting your products and yourself through materials you distribute or otherwise get publicized.

Strategies

You'll consider every possible way you could put out material that helps promote your name and your message. Options include everything from simple flyers to tip sheets, booklets, newspaper articles, and features for company newsletters. You'll also consider interactive materials such as surveys, true/false quizzes on relevant topics, personality tests, and even restaurant-type children's place mats with pictures, games, and puzzles on them. Perhaps you'll decide to put out your own newsletter to send to your customers or to create a Web page for them to visit.

> **INSIGHTS**
>
> "Good business leaders create a vision, articulate the vision, passionately own the vision, and relentlessly drive it to completion."
>
> —John Welch

You'll then seek help in getting such materials distributed in a variety of ways. You'll ask *customers* to *distribute* relevant materials in the Customer-Distributor strategy. You'll also ask your *complementors*, people who sell products or services that complement your own, to help *distribute* your material with a Colleague/Complementor-Distributor strategy. Finally, you'll look at various other *contacts* you have who might serve as *distributors* for your materials, thereby employing the Contact-Distributor strategy.

Put Out Material

You: Hi, Leonardo. How are things?

Customer: Same old, same old. What's new with you?

Customer-Distributor Strategy

You: Well, I've got some new materials I've been sending out.

Customer: Really? Like what?

You: One item is a tip sheet on how to achieve specific decorative effects, such as washes and glazes, and how to use sponging techniques.

Customer: Well, if your other customers are anything like me, they'd welcome that.

You: I'm offering to send a stack of the tip sheets to each of my customers and asking them to distribute the sheets to others who have similar interests. At the bottom of the sheet is my contact information in case anyone has questions or would like to order some unfinished pieces.

Customer: Sounds great to me!

Notes: In an attempt to broaden your business base, you sought the help of a current customer by providing a useful sheet of information that is likely to be distributed. You thereby employed a Customer-Distributor strategy.

A similar approach can be taken with material that would be geared toward colleagues and co-workers or complementors (those who sell products or services that complement your own).

Colleague/Complementor-Distributor Strategy

You: That's why I've prepared this brochure to explain my Web site—how to get there, what you'll see there, and so on. I'm sure your customers would find the site really valuable.

Complementor: *(Who sells paint.)* What, in particular, would they find valuable about it?

You: First of all, I put up some interesting photos of the best examples I've seen of how our unfinished furniture has been painted. I've got shots from all around the country and even a couple from foreign countries. They're quite inspiring, and I add new ones all the time. Also, I provide information about what I think are the best paints to use and the best finishes, too. All of which your store carries, I might add.

Complementor: Well, I like that!

You: I figured you would. There's more in the site, too. You should visit it yourself and see. In the meantime, though, I'd like to ask you to put a stack of these out for your customers. They're good for the customers, good for you, and good for me.

Complementor: You're on.

continues

Put Out Material (continued)

Contact-Distributor Strategy

You: So, Etta, having sent my children to this school for the past five years, I know that many parents are interested in painting furniture for their children's rooms, especially when they're preparing nurseries for newborns or updating the look of an older child's room.

Contact: Oh, yes. Parents talk about their decorating projects all the time.

You: Well, there are some things that parents should know before they begin, for example, what paints are the safest for children and what finishes are best for kids' furniture.

Contact: In terms of safety issues?

You: Yes, there are some safety issues. Certain paints and finishes could be toxic. I've prepared this booklet on safety measures that should be taken when painting children's furniture. But the booklet also includes some tips on making aesthetically pleasing choices.

Contact: Sounds like it could be valuable.

You: I think so. While safety was my primary interest in producing it, I'm also hoping, of course, that I'll generate some business through these booklets; that's why I've included my contact information. Would you be willing to send home one booklet with each child?

Contact: I'd be happy to.

Further Considerations

Ad specialties and premiums are effective ways of getting a simple message out. Distribute them generously.

There are companies that offer the service of posting and/or distributing flyers around a given city. Decide whether such a service might be of use to you.

Writing a regular column for a local newspaper is a great way to keep publicizing yourself and your products. Syndicating the column to appear in numerous newspapers works even better.

Remember that the materials you distribute are a reflection of you—and sometimes they are the *only* information someone has to judge you by. Think about what image your materials create and if that is the image you want to represent you.

EXPERIENCE SHOWS

If you've got a lot to say about a certain subject, you may want to get the material published for distribution in the form of a pamphlet or a book. Electronic publishers will even publish just a single copy of a book you write. For more information, visit sites such as www.fatbrain.com or www.iuniverse.com.

Consider ways in which you could boost circulation of your materials by asking people to pass them along. Some newsletters print that very request at the top of their front page.

Consider ways in which you might do good works with your skills and, at the same time, help promote yourself by putting out relevant material.

Ask Yourself

- Companies use mottoes and logos to brand themselves in a short and simple statement. If I had to come up with a personal motto, what would it be? Should I include that statement on my business cards or on any other materials that represent me?

- Am I comfortable participating in the kind of high-visibility activities that often get written up in the newspaper?

- If not, how could I affiliate with such activities in other ways?

- Do I circulate newspaper articles and other kinds of publicity I've received?

- Have I noticed what kinds of materials and activities other salespeople use to promote themselves and their products?

- Does that give me any ideas for things I might try?

- Do I try to maximize distribution of my materials? If I'm mailing out something anyway do I try to include additional material, if appropriate, that will help promote me or my products?

Dialog 4

Take in Material

Scenario

You're a sales professional who has received a lot of positive feedback over the years. You want to start making a practice of collecting, or "taking-in" these positive comments and compliments and turning them into a tangible form that can be shared with others. You know that when such endorsements and testimonials appear in written form they can serve a number of purposes. They can work as a letter of introduction to a new prospect or contact, and they can illustrate your fine customer-service practices or other strengths. Additionally, they can help you overcome objections in your sales presentations and can show why a particular customer was glad to have switched to you from a competitor. Such materials can be enclosed with your other sales tools and with any proposals you submit.

INSIGHTS

"The purpose of business is to create and keep a customer."
—Theodore Leavitt

Strategies

The best time to ask for an endorsement is the moment when you're given a compliment. You can seize the value of such moments by formalizing compliments on the spot, with the On-the-Spot strategy.

Even if you fail to take advantage of the moment, though, you can always go back to a customer after the fact to get quotes based on past compliments. In doing so, you'll be utilizing the Past-Praise strategy.

EXPERIENCE SHOWS

A simple list of customers who are high-profile individuals or who represent well-recognized companies creates a powerful endorsement in and of itself, without any particular testimonial attached. Even if you don't deal with those customers directly, you can reference them if they are part of your company's pool of customers.

Take in Material

You: I'm glad this product trial worked out for you.

Customer: I'm not surprised it did. I've come to rely on your recommendations. And your follow-up service is the best I've seen in the industry.

You: Thanks very much.

On-the-Spot Strategy

You: Thanks for the compliment! May I quote you on that sometime?

Customer: Of course.

You: *(Writing down the quote on a piece of paper for future reference.)* I'm not sure where or when this may come in handy, but if I plan to use it in my sales literature, I'll be sure to let you know.

Customer: That's not necessary. Feel free to use it at your discretion.

Notes: You seized the moment in trying to capture this quote. However, if it were not an appropriate moment in which to write down a quote, you would simply make mental note of it. Then, at some other time, you'd seek to formalize the quote with a Past-Praise strategy.

Past-Praise Strategy

You: Martina, you once told me I was the best idea-person you had ever met and that you found our brainstorming sessions about your business very useful. Do you remember that?

Customer: I certainly do. It's true!

You: May I quote you on that in some of my sales literature?

Customer: Of course!

Make-It-Easy Strategy

You: I've been making an effort to get down on paper some of the testimonials I've received from my valued customers. I'd love to include a letter from you in my compilation.

Customer: I'd be happy to give you one.

You: Given the nature of our relationship, I was hoping you might be inclined to do so. In order to make it easy for you, I've prepared a short letter that I think accurately reflects what you like best about me and my company. I'll leave it with you to look over. If you agree with what it says, you're welcome to simply sign it and return it to me in this self-addressed stamped envelope. However, if there's anything you'd like to say differently, please feel free to rewrite the letter before you send it back to me.

More elaborate testimonials can come in the form of requests to customers for letters of recommendation that focus on one or more particular issues. When you're seeking such letters from customers with whom you've had a long relationship, you can even prepare the letters in advance. You'll try to accurately reflect customers' feelings about you and your company in the letters and offer them as a sample of what you might like to have mentioned. Make it clear, though, that customers are free to use the letters verbatim or to change them completely. It is entirely at their discretion. The idea is to save your customers time and effort in fulfilling this request of yours, hence is called the Make-It-Easy strategy.

Further Considerations

Consider other sources from which you might capture customer compliments, including customer comment cards, customer surveys, guest books, unsolicited letters, and e-mails that have been sent to the company's Web site.

Think about how you might use testimonials on your Web site. Possibilities include posting letters (in part or in whole) and audio or video testimonials that visitors can play. If some of your clients are open to it, you might even have a list of satisfied customers, complete with their e-mail addresses, in case a prospect would like to have direct contact with them. (Of course, you must get explicit permission from customers to include their personal information on such a list.)

If you organize all of your testimonial material according to the issue it addresses, you'll create a handy file for dealing with various objections. For example, if a customer's letter refers to your superb service and your reasonable prices, make two copies of the letter and put one in each of those categories for future use.

Check to see if your testimonial letters are current enough or whether they should be updated. If a customer has been kind enough to write

> **EXPERIENCE SHOWS**
>
> Endorsements from charities carry a different sort of weight. They generate goodwill with customers because they say that you care. If you or your company has helped with a charitable cause, include that information in your testimonial materials.

> **EXPERIENCE SHOWS**
>
> Awards and citations represent another form of endorsement. If you or your company has received any such honors, be sure to include them in your endorsement materials, along with any flattering articles that may have been written on the topic.

> **BE CAREFUL**
>
> It's imperative to seek permission from your sources before using them or their materials as references. And as a courtesy before you "go to press," allow them to see any printed material that mentions them.

a testimonial letter in the past, she'll probably be willing to give you an updated version.

You can even use fictitious testimonials in promoting your products and services—as long as it's obvious they're fictitious. Doing so can add a humorous touch to your sales materials. For example, if you're selling catering services, you might include a statement such as this: "They can even make spinach taste good!" David, age 8.

Ask Yourself

- Do I seize endorsement opportunities?

- When did an endorsement convince me to buy a particular product or service? Why?

- What endorsement tools have other reps used that I find to be particularly effective?

- Knowing that a picture is worth a thousand words, do I look for meaningful photo opportunities that I might use as part of my testimonial materials?

- If any corporate letters or articles reference me personally, do I make a point of putting copies into my personal files for future use in selling myself?

Dialog 5

Turn to Your Competitors

Scenario

Competitors can help sell you in a different sort of way. They're not likely to pass along your business cards or refer people to your Web site, but competitors can help sell you by allowing you to contrast yourself with them. In this scenario, you decide to face the competition head-on by approaching (rather than avoiding) customers who are already being served by someone else. You'll seek to establish relationships with your competition's customers because you like challenges. You find appealing the philosophy expressed here:

> "Do not follow where the path may lead. Go instead where there is no path and leave a trail."
>
> —Anonymous

Strategies

You'll seek to determine how you are different from the competition. By using the Like-Best/Like-Least strategy, you'll obtain information from your competition's customers about what they like best and least about them. This will help you define your own competitive advantage, immediately or in the long run. If you clearly have an advantage over the competition in an area in which a customer feels dissatisfied, you can act immediately to establish why it would be better to do business with you. But even if you're not superior to your competitor on a particular issue at the moment, you can focus on that issue as an area to improve upon in the future. At a later date you can contact your prospect with evidence of the superiority you've achieved.

This exercise can even help you isolate weaknesses that you need to work on. With the Spot-What's-Not strategy, you'll ascertain ways in which you are different from your competitors. You'll spot what you "are" and what they're "not," what you "have" and what they "don't." This strategy will help you highlight your superior features by contrasting them with your competitor's position in your sales presentations.

INSIGHTS

"Of all the powers operating on the affairs of mankind, none is greater than that of competition."

—Henry Clay

BE CAREFUL

Tread carefully on the territory of competitors. Be prepared for the fact that you may be on the receiving end of similar practices.

Turn to Your Competitors

You: *(Making a cold call.)* So, Germain, that's why I'd like to come in and show you what we have.

Prospect: Sorry, we already have a supplier we're satisfied with.

Like-Best/Like-Least Strategy

You: Well, actually, I've done my homework and know that you're currently dealing with L-M-N Company. What is it about them that you're most satisfied with?

Prospect: Their prices are low and their service is high.

You: That's sure to please a customer. I can understand your overall satisfaction. No one is perfect, though. If you had to name just one area where you'd like to see better performance from your current supplier, what would that be?

Prospect: Well, I'd love to see our orders filled more quickly, but I don't think any supplier could do that.

Spot-What's-Not Strategy

You: Actually, I think we could provide faster delivery on a few of the products you currently use. We've automated our supply chain and can provide direct delivery from some of our suppliers by using the Internet. I've looked at our competitors' operations, and they're not up to speed in this area. I'd like to stop by and show you a comparison of our two operations in terms of how quickly we can supply delivery on these items.

Notes: Because you've done your homework, you've been able to determine that, for certain products, you probably can provide faster delivery than your competitors. You present this information to your prospect as you carry on your dialog.

Just-This-Once Strategy

Prospect: Gee, I don't know. It doesn't seem very loyal.

You: I can understand your reaction. Your sense of loyalty reflects well upon you, but I think you deserve to know the reality of how we are different. If you try us out on a few items just this once, you can have a better basis for comparing how we operate and then you can decide which of us would be better for your company. It seems to me that you owe it to yourself and your company to get faster delivery when it can be provided.

The Just-This-Once strategy helps customers feel more comfortable making a change from another salesperson to you. By limiting their commitment to a one-time trial and not a permanent change, customers are more likely to be willing to give you a try. Once you've proved yourself, you have a better chance of turning them into permanent customers.

Further Considerations

Get as much information as you can on your competitors, including articles, corporate literature, annual reports, and catalogs. Visit their Web sites regularly. Go to their showrooms. Check them out at trade shows. The more informed you are, the better you'll be able to delineate your differences.

When you do sales presentations, use the competitor's very own literature to help your cause and make your case. Use it to show how you're different from them. Paste up sections of their sales brochures against yours on a display board. Create charts and graphs. Print pages from their Web site and compare and contrast them with your own materials on specific measures (for example, we offer a five-year guarantee while theirs is only a two-year one).

As an exercise, put yourself in the position of your competition and consider how they would look at you. What would they see as your strengths and weaknesses? How would they illustrate them? How would they compare themselves with you in a sales presentation to a prospect? How can you use this exercise to strengthen your own competitive position?

WHAT THE EXPERTS SAY

Competition is not just an individual issue—it's a national issue as well. The Council on Competitiveness aims to keep the U.S. economy and workforce competitive in the world by focusing on issues such as innovation, workforce development, and the benchmarking of national economic performance. To learn more, visit its Web site at www.compete.org.

WHAT THE EXEMPLARS DO

Dr. Alan Goldberg, an expert in the field of performance psychology and sports psychology, defines mental toughness as a set of learned skills that include goal setting, stress management, self-confidence, "reboundability," concentration, imagery, and visualization. His Web site is at www.competitivedge.com.

Ask Yourself

- What do I admire most about my competitors?

- What can I learn from them?

- As a consumer, when was the last time I switched to a different provider of a particular product or service? Why?

- What would I define as my unique competitive advantage, as a salesperson and in terms of the products or services I offer?

- What would my universe of potential customers really like to have that is not being given to them? Why is that thing not being provided? How could I provide it in some fashion?

Dialog 6

Turn to Your Complementors

Scenario

Complementors are people who sell products or provide services that complement your own or who somehow represent a group of people whose demographics match your target market. Complementors can be a highly useful resource in your efforts to let others sell you. In this scenario, you're a sales rep for a line of musical instruments.

Strategies

You'll brainstorm to come up with a list of possible complementors. You'll consider complementary products, complementary services, and complementary activities and then devise ways in which you might align with those sources to cross-promote your products.

INSIGHTS
"It is through cooperation, rather than conflict, that your greatest successes will be derived."
—Ralph Charell

Using Complementary-Products strategy, you'll focus on the *products* that *complement* your own in any way, such as a store that sells sheet music. You might also look at places that provide musical accessories, such as music stands, metronomes, etc.

Turn to Your Complementors

You: *(On the phone.)* I'd like to stop by and show you our line of musical instruments, Ms. Blackfeather.

↓

Prospect: Sorry, we don't sell musical instruments, just tapes, CDs, and sheet music.

↓

You: Okay. Thanks, anyway.

↓

Complementary-Products Strategy

You: *(Making a sales call.)* Thanks for taking the time to meet with me, Ms. Blackfeather. I think you run a wonderful music shop here.

↓

Prospect: Thank you.

↓

You: I'd like to make a suggestion that I think would make it even better.

↓

Prospect: What's that?

↓

You: Well, in addition to offering this wonderful array of tapes, CDs, and sheet music, I think a great way to round out your product line and increase profits is to start offering musical instruments as well, for purchase or rental.

↓

Prospect: I'm not sure I want to get into that, especially the rental part. That seems like it would be a nightmare.

↓

You: Well, we offer either purchase or rental options or a combination of the two to stores like yours.

↓

Prospect: Tell me more.

You: First of all, our minimums are low. If you want to buy just a couple of instruments to carry in your shop, that's fine. And if you'd rather not be involved in the rental side, we can take care of that separately when your customers contact us directly. We could put this small informational display on one of your shelves, and it would give your customers all the details on how to contact us for instrument rental. Your customers will appreciate your having all the information right here for them. And we'll appreciate it, too! Whenever someone rents from us and mentions your name, we'll give you 5 percent of the initial rental fee.

↓

Prospect: It sounds like a good deal.

Complementary-Services Strategy

You: Claudine, I've put together this one-year calendar/practice schedule along with this handy list of music vocabulary terms and inserted them in this plastic folder. You see my name and number on the cover, along with a list of the instruments we rent and sell, in case parents are interested in getting instruments for their children. The music teachers I work with say the students and parents find this folder a really useful tool to help with scheduling practice sessions at home.

→

continues

Turn to Your Complementors (continued)

Complementary-Activities Strategy

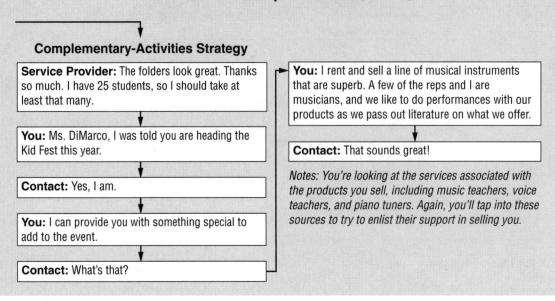

Service Provider: The folders look great. Thanks so much. I have 25 students, so I should take at least that many.

You: Ms. DiMarco, I was told you are heading the Kid Fest this year.

Contact: Yes, I am.

You: I can provide you with something special to add to the event.

Contact: What's that?

You: I rent and sell a line of musical instruments that are superb. A few of the reps and I are musicians, and we like to do performances with our products as we pass out literature on what we offer.

Contact: That sounds great!

Notes: You're looking at the services associated with the products you sell, including music teachers, voice teachers, and piano tuners. Again, you'll tap into these sources to try to enlist their support in selling you.

A Complementary-Services strategy, in this case, would direct your endeavors toward music teachers, voice teachers, piano turners, and perhaps music repair shops. You'll seek ways in which to promote yourself through these kinds of venues.

Turning to the Complementary-Activities strategy, you'll look at any activities associated with your musical instruments including musical performances, such as concerts by school bands and orchestras, municipal band concerts, and parades. Knowing that most of your end users are school-aged children, you also look at places where they gather (such as children's festivals and sporting events) and try to tie in your product offerings at these gatherings. You'll use active tie-ins (music demonstrations, staffed booths) as well as passive tie-ins (displays of your sales literature or perhaps your logo printed on signs and in brochures) to help promote yourself and your products.

Further Considerations

One way to identify complementors is to consider demographics. Look at the profile of your target market. Then ask yourself where people in that demographic would typically spend their money—and you'll be looking at possible complementor sources. For example, if you're trying to reach upscale singles to draw them to your retail Web site, you might arrange to provide paper coasters and/or napkins printed with relevant information at the local upscale bars and restaurants in your area.

Think of how you might entice a complementor's customers by offering them a free sample related to what you sell. The example in this dialog focused on music, so anything connected with music would be appropriate, such as a guitar pick or a reed for a wind instrument. If you sell medical supplies and equipment, you might set up a booth for free screenings at hospital health fairs or related trade shows and conventions.

Geographic proximity is another way to tap into complementors. Look at neighboring businesses to see if you might cross-promote each other in any way.

Web sites often provide links to other sites that offer related products or information. This is another way to tap into complementors.

Ask Yourself

- Am I always on the lookout for different kinds of complementors?

- What kinds of complementary relationships have I noticed among businesses and individuals?

- Do those examples give me any ideas about complementary relationships that I might establish?

- What are other ways to get my name "out there"?

- To whom might I be of service as a complementor? Am I interested in offering my help to these people?

- What are the best examples I've seen of synergy at work?

> **WHAT THE EXPERTS SAY**
>
> The phenomenon of **synergy** occurs when two or more forces combine or interact and produce a result that is greater than the sum of their individual effects. Synergistic alliances can compound your efforts far beyond what you could do independently.

Dialog 7

Develop a Network

Scenario

As a salesperson, you're taking a look at your professional network. In our personal lives, most of us form networks quite naturally. For example, if you look at your entire personal support system, you could call it your personal network. It would include family members and friends; neighbors; religious organizations; and the people who provide services to you, such as doctors, teachers, and counselors. In short, your personal network includes anyone who helps you maintain your life and all those to whom you turn to celebrate your victories or share your defeats and sorrows.

You may think of your professional network only as a collection of business contacts who might want to buy what you're selling. But it could be so much more than that. If your professional network matched the scope of your personal network, it might include the following:

- Those who help you maintain your professional life
- Those who help you develop it further
- Those with whom you can share your defeats and sorrows
- Those with whom you can celebrate your victories
- Those whom you can turn to when in need of "repair"
- Those to whom you can turn for inspiration
- Those to whom you yourself could be of help

Develop a Network

You: Hi, Jamal. Elizabeth here. Did you have a good holiday?

Contact: It was great. How about you?

Care Strategy

You: Really good, thanks. You know, I started thinking about New Year's resolutions and I decided that there's only one thing I want to strive for this year.

Contact: What's that?

You: I want to help others more.

Contact: That's nice of you.

You: Thanks. Anyway, I had two specific ideas I wanted to discuss with you in that regard. First of all, I tried to think of all the people I know who might buy books at your bookstore. I've come up with a list of about 30, so I'd like to get a bunch of your business cards to pass out. Also, I know you're very involved with the literacy group here in town, and I wanted to offer my services there. I can give only an hour a week, but if I could be of service, I'd like to help out.

Contact: Wow! This all sounds great!

Notes: You've tapped into your altruistic side to see where you could broaden your contacts simply by the giving of your time and talents. Another way to enlarge your network is to look to your peers and employ a Share strategy.

Share Strategy

You: David, I've been thinking we should promote each other.

Colleague: How?

You: Well, I know I have contacts who could use what you sell, and I know you must have contacts who could use what I sell. I think that we should expand our monthly lunches with each other to include such contacts. Every month we could each bring one new person to eat out with us. Nothing high pressure, just a way for us to expand our scope, and share our resources.

Colleague: I think that's a great idea. Let's do it.

You: Yeah, and let's brainstorm about other ways in which we could help each other out.

Dare Strategy

You: So, Ciaccia, because you've had a long-standing relationship with Mr. Dickerson and me, I'm wondering if you would be willing to introduce us.

Contact: I'm going to be out of town for the next month, but I'll tell you what I'll do in the meantime. I'll write a letter to him, introducing you and telling him you'll follow up with a phone call to discuss your proposal.

You: That's great. I'm grateful that you're willing to do this.

The people who might fill these roles on a professional level include co-workers, colleagues, peers, mentors, personal coaches, advisers, trainers, educators, counselors, consultants (live, on tape, or in books), team members, bosses, subordinates, and community and/or professional organizations that could benefit from your particular skills, and vice versa. Try to cast a wide net in defining your professional network and use all the resources available to you. The stronger your support system, the further you'll be able to go.

Strategies

In attempting to build your network, you'll look first at people you'd like to help out because you care about them or their causes. This is the focus of the Care strategy.

Utilizing the Share strategy, you'll look at those who are on a par with you, such as the peers with whom you could share networking practices. Accordingly, you'll develop a plan in which you can help promote each other by sharing resources.

Finally, employing the Dare strategy, you'll aim to connect with those prospects who are not yet within your reach but with whom you'd like to establish a business relationship. You'll dare yourself to think big and find a way to connect with these prospects. You'll consider the places they go, the things they do, and the people you may know in common as a means of connecting with them.

Further Considerations

Think of ways to keep yourself "on the radar screen" of the people in your network. Such ways could include newsletters, holiday greeting cards, clipped articles, e-mails, and informal handwritten notes.

Make yourself known to the people in your community who are in a formal position to recommend your products and services, such as members of your local Chamber of Commerce or your SCORE chapter.

Maximize your networking efforts at trade shows and conventions. For lists of upcoming events and other information, visit the Web site of Trade Show Central at www.tscentral.com or the site of WhereWhen at www.wherewhen.com.

> **WHAT THE EXEMPLARS DO**
>
> Marshall Field, the eminently successful owner of the department store bearing his name, was an innovator in his retailing business practices. He had this to say about the importance of developing feelings of goodwill in others: "Goodwill is the one and only asset that competition cannot undersell or destroy."

Ask Yourself

- How wide a net have I cast in my networking practices up until now?

- Am I satisfied with its size?

- If not, have I established clear networking goals for the future?

- What are the best examples I've seen of the impact of networking?

- Do they inspire me to broaden my network?

- Who is the best networker I know? What can I learn from him or other sources?

- How would others describe my networking abilities?

- When was the last time I passed along information to help promote someone else?

- What do I do that generates feelings of goodwill in others?

- How does my personal network compare with my professional network?

Dialog 8

Develop an "Internet-Work"

Scenario

As a sales professional, you're looking at ways in which you might use the Internet as a tool for boosting your business. You're considering how you could connect with customers via cyberspace. In this scenario, you represent several artists who produce high-quality, handmade works of art that range from functional (such as clocks) to purely decorative.

Strategies

In addition to creating your own Web site (which you promote every chance you get), you'll look at ways to align with other relevant outlets on the Internet.

With an Offer-Content strategy, you'll provide an article or some other form of written *content* that someone might post on his Web site. Most people are really eager for new content in order to keep their sites fresh and interesting. If you *offer* the content for free, you'll make it even more enticing. What you'll get back in return is exposure for your name or products and services on that person's Web site.

If your source isn't interested in the content you're offering, however, you might suggest an affiliation by *linking* to each other's Web site. This way, visitors to one site can, with the click of a button, visit the other's site. That's what's behind a Link strategy.

Develop an "Internet-Work"

> **You:** Yeah, J. B., I think your Web site is great! I've noticed the content doesn't change very often, though.

> **Clock parts supplier:** It's hard to come up with new content all the time, even though I know that's what keeps a site fresh and keeps customers coming back. What do they call that? Stickiness?

Offer-Content Strategy

> **You:** Yeah. Listen, I've written up what I think is an interesting article that the visitors to your Web site would enjoy. In a way it's a plug for me and the products I represent, but that's not what the bulk of the article is about. Here's a copy. Let me know what you think. I'd love to include it on your site. All I would ask in return is to have my name and Web site address listed at the bottom of the article.

Notes: You offered material that helps this source and helps you, too, because it has the potential of reaching a pool of prospects you might not otherwise have had access to. You offered this article to a supplier for his Web site, but you could offer such material to other sources as well, including relevant arts education sites, distributors, and related nonprofit groups.

Link Strategy

> **Customer:** Well, I'm thinking I really want to keep writing all the content myself, even if it takes me a while to get around to it.

> **You:** That's fine. But maybe we could help each other in another way.

> **Customer:** How's that?

> **You:** We could each put a small banner for the other on our site, and then visitors to my site could simply click through to yours, and vice versa.

Further Considerations

As an exercise, think of yourself as "a product." What are the features, assets, and benefits of this product? How would you promote those features to someone interested in buying this product? Now consider how you would present that information on the Internet.

If you have a method for capturing the e-mail addresses of current or prospective customers, use it and send out customized e-mails to promote your products and/or your Web site when appropriate.

INSIGHTS

"In the knowledge economy (1995–2020), the best strategy is to over invest in connecting power. Competitive advantage accrues to those who invest more than their competitors to connect to more people and share knowledge faster and farther."

—Dr. James Botkin, author of *Smart Business: How Knowledge Communities Can Revolutionize Your Company*

If material you write gets placed on a particular Web site, let your customers and others know of its presence, and direct them to the site.

Ask Yourself

- Have I taken the time to explore what the Internet has to offer me as a sales professional?

- In what ways have other sales professionals used the Internet to their advantage?

- Do I have any sort of a presence in cyberspace?

- Should I have a presence?

- If I already have visibility in cyberspace, what sort of image does that presence reflect?

- Are there other ways to maximize that presence and draw more people to it?

EXPERIENCE SHOWS

Study the following for more cyber info:

- You can build a free Web page quickly and easily at many sites on the Web, including www.homestead.com and America Online at www.aol.com. Also look at www.fwpreview.com

- To register a domain name, try www.register.com, www.igoldrush.com, or www.netnames.com.

- Use message boards to provide information of special interest on the Internet. To learn more about message boards, go to sites such as www.excite.com/boards and www.insidetheweb.com.

- Newsgroups are online discussion groups whose members often welcome relevant information sent via e-mail. Details regarding newsgroups are available from sites like www.cyberfiber.com, www.liszt.com, and www.newsville.com.

- To keep abreast of developments in technology and cyberspace, go to www.cnn.com/tech and www.internet.com.

Be aware that many sites will allow you to join their "affiliates program" wherein you provide a link to their site on yours, and vice versa. Other affiliate arrangements include the possibility of a "micropayment" to you for any visitors and/or customers who come to their site directly from your site. Company Web sites often provide information on their affiliate programs at the bottom of their home page.

Index

Symbols

1-2-3 strategy, 224

3-A strategies, 301

3-P strategy (people, products, and places of business), 35

3M Corporation, Post-it Notes, 75

5-P strategy, 35

A

Abraham, Jay, 149

Act-Now strategy, 71

Add a Personal Touch dialog, 326-330

Add strategy, 55

Admit strategy, 149

Adore the Gatekeeper dialog, 266-269

advertisements, 155

Affirm strategy, 315

Afterglow strategy, 275

Age of Paradox, 196

Alessandra, Anthony, 181, 139, 176

altavista.com, 20

Amend strategy, 12

analysis, questioning, 90

anecdotes, 219

annual reports, Web sites, 81

Another-Life strategy, 3

Answer-with-a-Question strategy, 305

Anticipation strategy, 149, 274

Apology strategy, 278

application, questioning, 90

Arnold, Oren, 194

Ash, Mary Kay, 269

Ask Analysis Questions dialog, 102-105

Ask Application Questions dialog, 98, 101-102

Ask Attitude Questions dialog, 113-115

Ask Comprehension Questions dialog, 95-98

Ask Evaluation Questions dialog, 109, 112-113

Ask for External Business dialog, 355, 357-358

Ask for Internal Business dialog, 351, 353-354

Ask for the Order dialog, 313-316

Ask Knowledge Questions dialog, 92-94

Ask strategy, 92

Ask Synthesis Questions dialog, 105, 108

Ask Yourself dialog, 115, 119

Assistance strategy, 128

assistants, 268

Associated-Word strategy, 17

Assure strategy, 149

At-This-Point strategy, 85

awards, 365

B

Bachrach, Bill, 92

Back strategy, 193

Backup strategy, 68

Backup-Plan strategy, 334

Bait strategy, 176

Baldrige, Letitia, 260

Ball, Lucille, 131

Becker, Hal, 113, 167

Become a Problem-Solving Pro dialog, 20, 23

Ben Franklin strategy, 71

benchmarking, 325

Bencin, Richard L., 228

Best strategy, 190

Best-Efforts strategy, 255

Bezos, Jeff, 345

Bierce, Ambrose, 184

Bind strategy, 235

Blackstone, Lee, 94

blame, 125

Bloom, Benjamin, 89

body language, 5
   signals, 174

book jackets, inspiration, 3

Boress, Allan, 154

Botkin, James, 379

Bovo, M. J., Dr., 248

bragging, offensiveness, 8

Brainstorm strategy, 231

Branson, Richard, 49

brevity, 5

Build Trust dialog, 207, 209-210

Building Long-Term Relationships dialog, 24, 26-27

Bundling strategy, 79

Bush, George H., 13

Bushnell, Nolan, 188

business cards, 241
   exchanging, 266

Butler, Samuel, 92

By-Product-Benefits strategy, 73

C

Canfield, Bertrand, 149

Care strategy, 376

Carlzon, Jon, 282

Carnegie, Andrew, 38

Caruso, Michael Angelo, 178

Cates, Bill, 60

Caudill, Donald W., 128

Cement strategy, 157

charity issues, 285

Chimpanzee strategy, 116

choices, presentations, 198

Chrysler, Walter, 241

Cinderella strategy, 271

Circumventing Obstacles dialog, 155, 158

citations, 365

Cite-Statistics strategy, 346

Clarify strategy, 182

Clear strategy, 107

Clement, Margaret L., 248

cold calling, 29-30
   strategies, 31

Colleague/Complementor-Distributor strategy, 359

Collins, Harry, 85

Collins, Jim, 125

companies, referencing, permissions, 38

Complementary-Activities strategy, 372

Complementary-Products strategy, 370

Complementary-Services strategy, 372

complementors, 370

comprehension, questioning, 90

Confirm strategy, 55

Congratulate strategy, 157

congratulations, prospects, 155

Connect strategy, 144

Contact-Distributor strategy, 359

Contact-Info strategy, 355

contracts, 308

control, 152

Coolidge, Calvin, 308

Correct strategy, 144

cost, mentioning, 95

Could You Send Something in the Mail? dialog, 82-84

Cox, Marcelene, 125

Create Credibility dialog, 35, 37-38

Creative Selling Today, 304, 315

critical sales, analyzing, 166

CUE strategies, 95

Culberson, Ron, 278-279

Culligan, Matthew, 210, 301, 316

Customer-Distributor strategy, 359

Customer-Meeting strategy, 288

customers, needs, 127

Customized-Creation strategy, 57

D

dailyfix.com, 8

Dare strategy, 376

Davis, Colle, 307

Dawson, Roger, 228

Deal strategy, 137

Dealing with Problems dialog, 334-337

Dean, Dizzy, 6

debsfunpages.com, 8

Decide strategy, 137

decision makers, 76

Deflect strategy, 127

Deliver Drama dialog, 272-276

Demonstrate Confidence dialog, 42

Denial strategy, 10

depersonalization, 215

Design the Show strategy, 274

desirable trait studies, 136

Detect strategy, 40

Develop a Network dialog, 374-377

Develop an "Internet-Work" dialog, 378

Develop Rapport dialog, 213, 216

dialogs

    Add a Personal Touch, 326-330

    Adore the Gatekeeper, 266-269

    Ask Analysis Questions, 102-105

    Ask Application Questions, 98-102

    Ask Attitude Questions, 113-115

    Ask Comprehension Questions, 95-98

    Ask Evaluation Questions, 109-113

    Ask for External Business, 355-358

    Ask for Internal Business, 351-354

    Ask for the Order, 313-316

    Ask Knowledge Questions, 92-94

    Ask Synthesis Questions, 105, 108

    Ask Yourself, 115, 119

    Become a Problem-Solving Pro, 20, 23

    Build Trust, 207-210

    Building Long-Term Relationships, 24-27

    Circumventing Obstacles, 155, 158

Could You Send Something in the Mail?, 82-84

Create Credibility, 35-38

Dealing with Problems, 334-337

Deliver Drama, 272, 275-276

Demonstrate Confidence, 42

Develop a Network, 374-377

Develop an "Internet-Work," 378

Develop Rapport, 213, 216

Directing the Sales Interaction, 152-155

Do Well by Doing Good, 283-286

Embrace Challenges, 235-238

Empathize, 159, 161, 299-302

Empower Employees, 249-252

End on a Positive Note, 53-56

Establish a Relationship, 31-34

Flex Your Flexibility, 38-41

Forestalling Objections, 149-151

Generate Leads, 49

Get and Give Definitions, 139-142

Get Your Foot in the Door, 269-272

Go Virtual, 286-290

Goal Setting Through One-Person Dialogs, 231-234

Guide the Sales Exchange, 137-139

Handle Complaints Personally, 338-341

Handling Awkward Situations, 11-13

Harness Humor, 276, 279

Hear "Possible" When Others Say "Never," 131-133

Hook the Prospect, 203, 207

I Don't Believe This, 188, 191

I Have to Talk It Over With, 76-78

I Need to Think About It, 69-72

I'll Get Back to You, 85-87

I'm Bored, 182-185

I'm Lost, 191-194

I'm Not Getting My Questions Answered, 194-197

I'm Ready to Buy, 198-200

I'm Scared, 185-188

Keep Their Interest, 219-222

Know the Motivators, 245-248

Leading the Way to a Successful Sale, 164-167

Let Exemplars Inspire You, 239-242

Let Those at the Top Hear from You, 128-130

Listen for Opportunities Embedded in Challenges, 125-128

Listen to What Moves You and Your Prospect, 134-136

Listen to Yourself, 123-125

Make a Promise, 302-305

Make Unexpected Calls, 330-333

Motivate Your Customers, 257-260

Offer Reassurance, 311-313

Offset Negatives in the Selling Equation, 167-170

Perk Up Your Sales Staff, 253-256

Plan for Spontaneity, 222-225

Position Your Product, 210-212

Practice "Picturing", 319-322

Price Is Too High, 63-66

Prospect for Prospects, 263-265

Put Out Material, 359-362

Regard Closings as Openings, 322-326

Respond to a Question with a Question, 305-307

Sell After the Sale, 342-345

Sell Steak and Sizzle, 225-228

Study After the Sale, 346-348

Substantiate Your Product-Claims, 170-172

Take In Material, 363-366

Take the Blame, 14-16

Tell a Story, 216-219

The Short "Self-Script," 3-8

Think of No as Maybe, 296-299

Thinking on Your Feet, 17-19

This Is Taking Too Long, 176-178

Turn Around the Objection, 161-164

Turn to Your "Complementors," 370

Turn to Your Competitors, 366

Uncover Needs, 45-49

Use an Example, 308-310

Use Rejection as a Spur, 242-244

Use Trials, Avoid Tribulations, 293-296

Use Unconventional Wisdom, 280-282

We Have Everything We Need Right Now, 73-75

We Haven't Budgeted for This, 79-81

We're Happy with Our Current Supplier, 66-69

When the Customer Speaks, the Employee Listens, 142-145

Win with Wit, 8-11

You Must Leave a Message, 57-60

You're Talking Too Much, 179-181

Dickie, Jim, 157

Direct strategy, 137

Directing the Sales Interaction dialog, 152-155

Direction strategy, 249

Disraeli, Benjamin, 184, 296

Do Well by Doing Good dialog, 283-286

domain names, registering, 380

Don't-Pause strategy, 305

Done strategy, 170

Dotson, Larry, 193

Dreams strategy, 231

dress rehearsals, 275

Drive strategy, 92

Drucker, Peter, 72

E

e-mail cards, 68

economic trends, researching, 152

Edelston, Martin, 107

Edify strategy, 101

Edison, Thomas, 241

Educate strategy, 92, 166

education, mentioning, 8

Einstein, Albert, 131, 176

Elevate strategy, 12

Elicit strategy, 293

Eliminate strategy, 63

Elsea, Janet, 315

Embrace Challenges dialog, 235-238

emotions, signals, 173

Empathize dialog, 159, 161, 299-302

Employee Relationship Report Benchmark, 256

Empower Employees dialog, 249-252

Encyclopedia of Telemarketing, 228

End on a Positive Note dialog, 53-56

Endorsement strategy, 257

endorsements, 366

Enthusiasm strategy, 323

enthusiasm, showing, 170

Ericksen, John, 131

Establish a Relationship dialog, 31-34

Ethos strategy, 311

evaluation, questioning, 91

Excel strategy, 187

Exception strategy, 79

Exchange strategy, 22

excite.com, 20, 56

Explore strategy, 207

Express strategy, 55

F

face-to-face meetings, evaluating necessity of, 115

Features strategy, 221

Feel-Felt-Found strategy, 63

females, communication styles, 72

feng shui, 123

Field, Marshall, 377

Finalize strategy, 315

Find strategy, 235

Fitzgerald, F. Scott, 130

flattery, 310
    strangers, 3

Flex Your Flexibility dialog, 38-41

focus groups, 144

Ford, Henry, 172, 247, 358

Forestalling Objections dialog, 149-151

Four-Minute Sell, The, 315

Frank, Milo, 182

Franklin, Benjamin, 136

friendlieness, 108

Fuller, Alfred C., 137

Fun strategy, 170

Future-Focus strategy, 26

G

Gallagher, Richard, 87

Game of Humor: A Comprehensive Theory of Why We Laugh, The, 279

Gazelle strategy, 116

gender, communication styles, 72

Generate Leads dialog, 49

Get and Give Definitions dialog, 139-142

Get Your Foot in the Door dialog, 269-272

Get-Definition strategies, 141

Getting Back to the Basics of Selling, 301, 316

Giannini, A.P., 362

Gilman, Charlotte, 219

Girard, Joe, 265

Gird strategy, 163

Give-a-Group strategy, 52

Gladstone, William, 184

Gliner, Art, 11, 278-279

Glory strategy, 216

Go Virtual dialog, 286-290

Goal Setting Through One-Person dialog, 231-234

Goldberg, Alan, 369

Goldstein, Mark, 104

Graceful-Exit strategy, 331

Graham, John R., 164

Gratify strategy, 182

Greenberg, Herbert, 141

Gretzky, Wayne, 131

Gruner, Charles R., 279

guarantees, 200

Guare, John, 263

Guide the Sales Exchange dialog, 137, 139

Guiducci, Joan, 179

Guinness Book of World Records, The, 265

H

Hall, David, 115

Handle Complaints Personally dialog, 338-341

Handling Awkward Situations dialog, 11-13

Handy, Charles, 196

Harness Humor dialog, 276, 279

Hayes, James, 17

Hear "Possible" When Others Say "Never" dialog, 131, 133

Heed strategy, 210

Help-You-Succeed strategy, 323

Herd strategy, 163

Hession, Matt, 225

High-Octane-Words strategy, 3

Hillary, Edmund, 235

Hitch strategy, 194

Hook the Prospect dialog, 203, 207

Hopkins, Tom, 163, 215, 305

Hot-Button strategy, 257

How To Get Your Point Across in 30 Seconds, 182

How to Master the Art of Selling, 215

Hubbard, Elbert, 242

Hubbard, Wendy, 34

humor
    copyright, 10
    questionable, 10
    use of, 279

Humor strategy, 249

humorous Web sites, 8

humorproject.com, 10

I

I Don't Believe This dialog, 188, 191

I Have to Talk It Over With … dialog, 76-78

I Need to Think About It dialog, 69-72

I'll Get Back to You dialog, 85-87

I'm Bored dialog, 182-185

I'm Lost dialog, 191-194

I'm Not Getting My Questions Answered dialog, 194-197

I'm Ready to Buy dialog, 198-200

I'm Scared dialog, 185-188

icebreakers, 169

Ignore strategy, 207

inanities, 163

Indirect-Benefits strategy, 268

Induct strategy, 166

Inexpensive strategy, 179

Inflate strategy, 152

Infotrack online service, 33

iNova Corporation, 34

Inquiry strategy, 157

Inside Intel, 13

insincere questions, avoiding, 203

Inspect strategy, 40

Integrate strategy, 134

Interest strategy, 179

International Customer Service Association, 24

International Listening Association, 127

interrupters, 321

Invade strategy, 179

Involve strategy, 221

"It's My Job" strategy, 76

Itch strategy, 194

J–K

Jackson, Tim, 13

James, John Henry, 239

James, William, 115

Jonovic, Donald J., 228

Just-This-Once strategy, 369

Just-You strategy, 76

Kaiser, Henry J., 112, 354

Keep Their Interest dialog, 219-222

Keep-Current strategy, 24

Kelly, Joe, 221

Key strategy, 331

Keyed strategy, 210

Kiam, Victor, 239

Kieran, John, 209

Kimball, Bob, 95

Know strategy, 298

Know the Motivators dialog, 245-248

knowledge, questioning, 90

Knowledge strategy, 128

Kossen, Stan, 304, 315

Kroc, Ray, 69

L

lagniappes, 191, 323

Lamb strategy, 116

Larger-Loyalty strategy, 68

LAST strategies, 338

Late strategy, 176

Lauder, Leonard, 234

Laugh-Line strategy, 315

Leacock, Stephen, 248

Leading the Way to a Successful Sale dialog, 164-167

Leading-Nowhere Leads strategy, 52

Leading-Somewhere Leads strategy, 52

learning styles, 275

Lee, Gerald Stanley, 82

Lehrer, Tom, 191

Less and More strategies, 213

Lessen strategy, 22

Let Exemplars Inspire You dialog, 239-242

Let Those at the Top Hear from You dialog, 128-130

Levitt, Theodore, 187

Lighten-Load strategy, 259

Like-Best/Like-Least strategy, 367

Link strategy, 378

Listen for Opportunities Embedded in Challenges dialog, 125-128

Listen strategy, 92

Listen to What Moves You and Your Prospect dialog, 134-136

Listen to Yourself dialog, 123-125

Listen-List strategy, 327

listening, 121
    retention rates, 136

Logos strategy, 311

Lombardi, Vince, 131

Long-Range Plans strategy, 323

Lost-Customers strategy, 344

love
    usage of the word, 5

Lyet, Jean Paul, 241

M

Mackay, Harvey, 101, 159, 219, 298

Maison-Rouge, Jacques, 26

Make a Promise dialog, 302-305

Make Unexpected Calls dialog, 330-333

Make-It-Easy strategy, 365

Make-It-Memorable strategy, 239

males, communication styles, 72

Maltz, Maxwell, 147, 293

Manipulative strategy, 159

mapquest.com, 56

Marine, Joshua J., 235

Marriott, Bill, 249

Marshall, Jeanie, 248

Maslow, Abraham, 75

Mason, Jackie, 128

Maximal strategy, 283

Maybe strategy, 298

McCormack, Mark, 109, 212, 291

McGuire, Joe, 239

meetings, virtual meetings, 289

Memorialize strategy, 275

Memorized-Line strategy, 17

message boards, 380

metaphors, 276

Miller, George, 119

Miller, Steve, 272

mind-sets, changing, 238

Minimal strategy, 283

Misner, Ivan R., 376

mistakes, reviewing, 119

Moine, Donald, 184

Montgomery, Robert, 158-161

Moock, Harry G., 201

Morrow, William, 298

Motivate strategy, 134

Motivate Your Customers dialog, 257-260

motivation, 229

multipart objections, 188

Multiple-Role strategy, 203

My-Fault strategy, 12

N-O-P

Narrate strategy, 176

National Secretaries Week, 268

Nayak, Ranganath, 94

Need strategy, 210

negativity, 108
    expressing as positive, 224

Nelson, Bob, 256

nesgroups, 380

networking associations, 376

Neuro-Linguistic Programming (NLP), 197

newspaper articles, self-promotion, 2

newspapers, sales opportunities, 8

NLP (Neuro-Linguistic Programming), 197

Non-Manipulative Selling, 181

Nonmanipulative strategy, 159

Nonsales-Call strategy, 24

novelty seeking, 282

Noyce, Robert, 249

Nullify strategy, 101

Object strategy, 144

objections
  multipart objections, 188
  overcoming, 61

Offer Reassurance dialog, 311, 313

Offer-Content strategy, 378

Offer-Info-First strategy, 263

Offer-Options strategy, 346

Offset Negatives in the Selling Equation dialog, 167-170

"Okay But Refer Me" strategy, 73

Onassis, Aristotle, 245

Oppositize strategy, 20

Others strategy, 351

Overstreet, H. A., 137

Oxley, Philip, 286

paralanguage, 115

Partial-Invitation strategy, 57

Past-Praise strategy, 363

Pathos strategy, 311

Pause strategy, 305

pauses, allowing, 198

Penney, J.C., 41

people, referencing, permissions, 38

Perhaps-You-Feel strategy, 63

Perignon, Dom, 228

Perk Up Your Sales Staff dialog, 253-256

Perk-Up strategy, 255

permissions, sources, 365

personal anecdotes, 219

Persuade strategy, 302

Peters, Tom, 185

phone, smiling, 179

Picturing strategy, 319

Piggyback strategy, 193

Plan for Spontaneity dialog, 222-225

Plato, 151

Plea strategy, 302

pledges, 234

Polite strategy, 55

Position Your Product dialog, 210, 212

positions, reversing, 97

Positive-Viewpoint strategy, 123

Post-it Notes, 75

posture, 5

Powell, Colin, 6, 311

Practice "Picturing" dialog, 319-322

preliminary work, 141

presentations
  choices, 198
  preparing, 193
  virtual presentations, 288

Price Is Too High dialog, 63-66

prices, undercuts, investigating, 128

Priority Statements, 233

Proactive-Problem-Prevention strategy, 334

product knowledge, 161

Product-Line strategy, 342

professionalism, maintaining, 108

Promise strategy, 302

Props strategy, 278

Prospect for Prospects dialog, 263-265

Prospect-Meeting strategy, 288

Prospect-Pool strategy, 355

prospects
  best times to reach, 101
  congratulating, 155
  fear, 134

proxemics, 179

public service work, self-promotion, 2

Put Out Material dialog, 359-362

Q-R

Quarry strategy, 216

questioning, 89, 227
  analysis, 90
  application, 90
  comprehension, 90
  evaluation, 91
  insincere questions, avoiding, 203
  knowledge, 90
  phrasing, 351
  synthesis, 90

quips, collecting, 251

Rackham, Neil, 20

realism, 233

Realize strategy, 169

Rebel strategy, 187

Recognize strategy, 169

Recovering-Attorney strategy, 10

Redford, Robert, 207

reducing down-time, 109

Reduction strategy, 79

Reference Recent Events strategy, 33

referrals, 357

Reflect strategy, 127

Regard Closings as Openings dialog, 322-326

rehearsals, 275

Reitmann, John H., 130

rejections, 166

Relate strategy, 134, 152

Relegate strategy, 157

Remarkable-Results strategy, 42

Remind strategy, 236

Request strategy, 169

Respond to a Question with a Question dialog, 305-307

Restate strategy, 55

Restore strategy, 207

retention rates, listening, 136

Rethinking the Sales Force, 20

Revson, Charles, 73, 101

Richardson, Linda, 172, 301

Rid strategy, 23

Ringlein, David, 159

Robinson, Parkes, 238

Rockefeller, David, 348

Roth, Charles, 141

Rouse the Senses strategy, 274

Ruel, Christopher, 350

Ruettgers, Mark, 14

Rusk, Dean, 127

Russell, Walter, 105

S

sales pitches, triteness, 169

Sales-Tool strategy, 278

salesforce.com, 24

saleslobby.com, 24

Satisfactions Strategy, 66

Save strategy, 20

scheduling, 319

Schuller, Robert, 62

Schwarzkopf, Norman, 13

Scope-of-Users strategy, 345

Scott, Joyce, 307

Scott, Walter Dill, 295

scripts

    Add a Personal Touch, 326-330

    Adore the Gatekeeper, 266-269

    Ask Analysis Questions, 102-105

    Ask Application Questions, 98-102

    Ask Attitude Questions, 113-115

    Ask Comprehension Questions, 95-98

    Ask Evaluation Questions, 109-113

    Ask for External Business, 355-358

    Ask for Internal Business, 351-354

    Ask for the Order, 313-316

    Ask Knowledge Questions, 92-94

    Ask Synthesis Questions, 105-108

    Ask Yourself, 115, 119

    Become a Problem-Solving Pro, 20-23

    Build Trust, 207-210

    Building Long-Term Relationships, 24-27

    Circumventing Obstacles, 155-158

    Could You Send Something in the Mail?, 82-84

    Create Credibility, 35-38

    Dealing with Problems, 334-337

    Deliver Drama, 272-276

    Demonstrate Confidence, 42

    Develop a Network, 374-377

    Develop an "Internet-Work," 378

    Develop Rapport, 213, 216

    Directing the Sales Interaction, 152-155

    Do Well by Doing Good, 283-286

    Embrace Challenges, 235-238

    Empathize, 159, 161, 299-302

    Empower Employees, 249-252

    End on a Positive Note, 53-56

    Establish a Relationship, 31-34

    Flex Your Flexibility, 38-41

    Forestalling Objections, 149-151

    Generate Leads, 49

    Get and Give Definitions, 139-142

    Get Your Foot in the Door, 269-272

    Go Virtual, 286-290

    Goal Setting Through One-Person Dialogs, 231-234

    Guide the Sales Exchange, 137-139

    Handle Complaints Personally, 338-341

    Handling Awkward Situations, 11-13

Harness Humor, 276-279

Hear "Possible" When Others Say "Never," 131-133

Hook the Prospect, 203, 207

I Don't Believe This, 188-191

I Have to Talk It Over With ..., 76-78

I Need to Think About It, 69-72

I'll Get Back to You, 85-87

I'm Bored, 182-185

I'm Lost, 191-194

I'm Not Getting My Questions Answered, 194-197

I'm Ready to Buy, 198-200

I'm Scared, 185-188

Keep Their Interest, 219-222

Know the Motivators, 245-248

Leading the Way to a Successful Sale, 164-167

Let Exemplars Inspire You, 239-242

Let Those at the Top Hear from You, 128-130

Listen for Opportunities Embedded in Challenges, 125-128

Listen to What Moves You and Your Prospect, 134-136

Listen to Yourself, 123-125

Make a Promise, 302-305

Make Unexpected Calls, 330-333

Motivate Your Customers, 257-260

Offer Reassurance, 311-313

Offset Negatives in the Selling Equation, 167-170

Perk Up Your Sales Staff, 253-256

Plan for Spontaneity, 222-225

Position Your Product, 210-212

Practice "Picturing," 319-322

Price Is Too High, 63-66

Prospect for Prospects, 263-265

Put Out Material, 359-362

Regard Closings as Openings, 322-326

Respond to a Question with a Question, 305-307

Sell After the Sale, 342-345

Sell Steak and Sizzle, 225-228

Study After the Sale, 346-348

Substantiate Your Product-Claims, 170-172

Take In Material, 363-366

Take the Blame, 14-16

Tell a Story, 216-219

The Short "Self-Script," 3-8

Think of No as Maybe, 296-299

Thinking on Your Feet, 17-19

This Is Taking Too Long, 176-178

Turn Around the Objection, 161-164

Turn to Your "Complementors," 370

Uncover Needs, 45-49

Use an Example, 308-310

Use Rejection as a Spur, 242-244

Use Trials, Avoid Tribulations, 293-296

Use Unconventional Wisdom, 280-282

We Have Everything We Need Right Now, 73-75

We Haven't Budgeted for This, 79-81

We're Happy with Our Current Supplier, 66-69

When the Customer Speaks, the Employee Listens, 142-145

Win with Wit, 8-11

You Must Leave a Message, 57-60

You're Talking Too Much, 179-181

Scully, John, 272

search engines, 378

secretaries, 268

Secrets of Closing the Sale, 66

See strategy, 330

segues, 92

Select strategy, 40

self-promotion
  newspaper articles, 2
  public service work, 2
  Web pages, 2

self-scripts. *See* scripts

Seligman, Martin, 44, 244

Sell After the Sale dialog, 342-345

Sell Steak and Sizzle dialog, 225-228

SELL strategies, 104

Sell strategy, 187, 293

Sell-Benefits strategy, 346

Sell-Myself-First strategy, 239

Selling by Phone, 301

Selye, Hans, 152

Sena, Frank, 302

Send-Something strategy, 271

Seriousness strategy, 128

Service strategy, 109, 280

Set-Up strategy, 278

settings, 319

Shakespeare, William, 125

Share strategy, 376

Shutterbug strategy, 329

Sign strategy, 308

signals
body language, 174
emotions, 173
recognizing, 173

Silent-Dialog strategy, 288

Simplify strategy, 101

Situation strategy, 334

six degrees of separation, 263

Skinner, B.F., 333

smiling on the phone, 179

Smoothing strategy, 334

Snyder, Mike, 252

Sobczak, Art, 8, 191

Socrates, 89

Sold-Out strategy, 280

SOLVER strategy, 20

Some strategy, 308

Soon strategy, 308

sources, permissions, 365

Speaker, Tris, 131

special touches, 321

splashnet.com, 24

Spot-What's-Not strategy, 367

SPUR strategies, 133

Steer strategy, 108

"Stop It Some More" strategy, 10

stories, 276
refining, 218

Story strategy, 216

strategies
1-2-3 strategy, 224
3-A strategies, 301
3-P strategy (people, products, and places of business), 35
5-P strategy, 35

Act-Now strategy, 71

Add strategy, 55

Admit strategy, 149

Affirm strategy, 315

Afterglow strategy, 275

Amend strategy, 12

Another-Life strategy, 3

Answer-with-a-Question strategy, 305

Anticipate strategy, 149

Anticipation strategy, 274

Apology strategy, 278

Ask strategy, 92

Assistance strategy, 128

Associated-Word strategy, 17

Assure strategy, 149

At-This-Point strategy, 85

Back strategy, 193

Backup strategy, 68

Backup-Plan strategy, 334

Bait strategy, 176

Ben Franklin strategy, 71

Best strategy, 190

Best-Efforts strategy, 255

Bind strategy, 235

Brainstorm strategy, 231

Bundling strategy, 79

By-Product-Benefits strategy, 73

Care strategy, 376

Cement strategy, 157

Chimpanzee strategy, 116

Cinderella strategy, 271

Cite-Statistics strategy, 346

Clarify strategy, 182

Clear strategy, 107

Colleague/Complementor-Distributor strategy, 359

Complementary-Activities strategy, 372

Complementary-Products strategy, 370

Complementary-Services strategy, 372

Confirm strategy, 55

Congratulate strategy, 157

Connect strategy, 144

Contact-Distributor strategy, 359

Contact-Info strategy, 355

Correct strategy, 144

CUE strategies, 95

Customer-Distributor strategy, 359

Customer-Meeting strategy, 288

Customized-Creation strategy, 57

Dare strategy, 376

Deal strategy, 137

Decide strategy, 137

Deflect strategy, 127

Denial strategy, 10

Design the Show strategy, 274

Detect strategy, 40

Direct strategy, 137

Direction strategy, 249

Don't-Pause strategy, 305

Done strategy, 170

Dreams strategy, 231

Drive strategy, 92

Edify strategy, 101

Educate strategy, 92, 166

Elevate strategy, 12

Elicit strategy, 293

Eliminate strategy, 63

Endorsement strategy, 257

Enthusiasm strategy, 323

Ethos strategy, 311

Excel strategies, 187

Exception strategy, 79

Exchange strategy, 22

Explore strategy, 207

Express strategy, 55

Features strategy, 221

Feel-Felt-Found strategy, 63

Finalize strategy, 315

Find strategy, 235

Fun strategy, 170

Future-Focus strategy, 26

Gazelle strategy, 116

Get-Definition strategies, 141

Gird strategy, 163

Give-a-Group strategy, 52

Graceful-Exit strategy, 331

Gratify strategy, 182

Heed strategy, 210

Help-You-Succeed strategy, 323

Herd strategy, 163

High-Octane-Words strategy, 3

Hitch strategy, 194

Hot-Button strategy, 257

Humor strategy, 249

Ignore strategy, 207

Indirect-Benefits strategy, 268

Induct strategy, 166

Inexpensive strategy, 179

Inflate strategy, 152

Inquiry strategy, 157

Inspect strategy, 40

Integrate strategy, 134

Interest strategy, 179

Invade strategy, 179

Involve strategy, 221

"It's My Job" strategy, 76

Itch strategy, 194

Just-This-Once strategy, 369

Just-You strategy, 76

Keep-Current strategy, 24

Key strategy, 331

Keyed strategy, 210

Know strategy, 298

Knowledge strategy, 128

Lamb strategy, 116

Larger-Loyalty strategy, 68

LAST strategies, 338

Late strategy, 176

Laugh-Line strategy, 315

Leading-Nowhere Leads strategy, 52

Leading-Somewhere Leads strategy, 52

Less and More strategies, 213

Lessen strategy, 22

Lighten-Load strategy, 259

Like-Best/Like-Least strategy, 367

Link strategy, 378

Listen strategy, 92

Listen-List strategy, 327

Logos strategy, 311

Long-Range Plans strategy, 323

Lost-Customers strategy, 344

Make-It-Easy strategy, 365

Make-It-Memorable strategy, 239

Manipulative strategy, 159

Maximal strategy, 283

Maybe strategy, 298

Memorialize strategy, 275

Memorized-Line strategy, 17

Minimal strategy, 283

Motivate strategy, 134

Multiple-Role strategy, 203

My-Fault strategy, 12

Narrate strategy, 176

Need strategy, 210

Nonmanipulative strategy, 159

Nonsales-Call strategy, 24

Nullify strategy, 101

Object strategy, 144

Offer-Content strategy, 378

Offer-Info-First strategy, 263

Offer-Options strategy, 346

"Okay But Refer Me" strategy, 73

Oppositize strategy, 20

Others strategy, 351

Partial-Invitation strategy, 57

Past-Praise strategy, 363

Pathos strategy, 311

Pause strategy, 305

Perhaps-You-Feel strategy, 63

Perk-Up strategy, 255

Persuade strategy, 302

Picturing strategy, 319

Piggyback strategy, 193

Plea strategy, 302

Polite strategy, 55

Positive-Viewpoint strategy, 123

Proactive-Problem-Prevention strategy, 334

Product-Line strategy, 342

Promise strategy, 302

Props strategy, 278

Prospect-Meeting strategy, 288

Prospect-Pool strategy, 355

Quarry strategy, 216

Realize strategy, 169

Rebel strategy, 187

Recognize stratgy, 169

Recovering-Attorney strategy, 10

Reduction strategy, 79

Reference Recent Events strategy, 33

Reflect strategy, 127

Relate strategy, 134, 152

Relegate strategy, 157

Remarkable-Results strategy, 42

Remind strategy, 236

Request strategy, 169

Restate strategy, 55

Restore strategy, 207

Rid strategy, 23

Rouse the Senses strategy, 274

Sales-Tool strategy, 278

Satisfactions strategy, 66

Save strategy, 20

Scope-of-Users strategy, 345

See strategy, 330

Select strategy, 40

SELL strategies, 104

Sell strategy, 187, 293

Sell-Benefits strategy, 346

Sell-Myself-First strategy, 239

Send-Something strategy, 271

Seriousness strategy, 128

Service strategy, 109, 280

Set-Up strategy, 278

Share strategy, 376

Shutterbug strategy, 329

Sign strategy, 308

Silent-Dialog strategy, 288

Simplify strategy, 101

Situation strategy, 334

Smoothing strategy, 334

Sold-Out strategy, 280

SOLVER strategy, 20

Some strategy, 308

Soon strategy, 308

Spot-What's-Not strategy, 367

SPUR strategies, 133

Steer strategy, 108

Stop-It-Somemore strategy, 10

Story strategy, 216

Strength-in-Numbers strategy, 3

Stun strategy, 170

Subordinate-Question strategy, 85

Suggest strategy, 190

Switch strategy, 194

Take-No-Time strategy, 351

Tap-Into-Technology strategy, 82

Terminate strategy, 293

Test strategy, 190

There-Before strategy, 42

Tie-Down strategy, 85

Time-It-Takes strategy, 82

Timetable strategy, 231

Track strategy, 193

Tying-Up strategy, 293

Update strategy, 152

Upgrades strategy, 344

Verify strategy, 101, 182

Volumize strategy, 22

We strategy, 331

We-Three strategies, 198

Who/What/Where strategy, 52

Why-Hesitate strategy, 71

Word strategy, 163

X-L (excel) strategy, 6

Zest strategy, 221

Strength-in-Numbers strategy, 3

Study After the Sale dialog, 346-348

Stun strategy, 170

styles, examining, 242

Subordinate-Question strategy, 85

Substantiate Your Product-Claims dialog, 170-172

Suggest strategy, 190

***Swim with the Sharks*, 298**

Switch strategy, 194

synergy, 373

synthesis, questioning, 90

T

Take In Material dialog, 363-366

Take the Blame, 14-16

Take-No-Time strategy, 351

Tap-Into-Technology strategy, 82

Technical Assistance Research Program, 24

technical details, 321

technical jargon, avoiding, 196

Tell a Story dialog, 216-219

Templeton, John Marks, 283

Terez, Tom, 329

Terminate strategy, 293

Test strategy, 190

The Short "Self-Script," 3-8

There-Before strategy, 42

Think of No as Maybe dialog, 296-299

Thinking on Your Feet dialog, 17-19

This Is Taking Too Long dialog, 176-178

Thompson, Charles "Chic," 23

Tie-Down strategy, 85

Time-It-Takes strategy, 82

Timetable strategy, 231

Toastmasters, 265

Track strategy, 193

Trout, Jack, 159

Turn Around the Objection dialog, 161-164

Turn to Your "Complementors" dialog, 366, 370

turn-off behaviors, 113

Twain, Mark, 262

Twenty-Two Keys to Creating a Meaningful Workplace, 329

Tying-Up strategy, 293

U

unconventionality, 280

Uncover Needs dialog, 45-49

unexpected phone calls, 330

universal experiences, 216

Update strategy, 152

Upgrades strategy, 344

Use an Example dialog, 308-310

Use Rejection as a Spur dialog, 242-244

Use Trials, Avoid Tribulations dialog, 293-296

Use Unconventional Wisdom dialog, 280-282

V-W

Verify strategy, 101, 182

Virgin Records, 49

virtual meetings, 288-289

vocabulary, 5

voice
  evaluating, 5
  tone, 221

voicemail messages, 57

Volumize strategy, 22

Von Braun, Wernher, 123

Wagner, Jane, 16

Walton, Samuel, 24

Ward, John, 219

Watson, Frank, 242

Watson, Thomas J., 71, 241

We Have Everything We Need Right Now dialog, 73-75

We Haven't Budgeted for This dialog, 79-81

We strategy, 331

We're Happy with Our Current Supplier dialog, 66-69

We-Three strategies, 198

Web sites
  altavista.com, 20
  annual reports, 81
  building, 380
  dailyfix.com, 8
  debsfunpages.com, 8
  excite.com, 20, 56
  humorproject.com, 10
  Infotrack online service, 33
  iNova Corporation, 34
  International Customer Service Association, 24
  mapquest.com, 56
  salesforce.com, 24
  saleslobby.com, 24
  search engines, 378
  self-promotion, 2
  splashnet.com, 24
  Virgin, 49
  yahoo.com, 56

Welch, Jack, 169

When the Customer Speaks, the Employee Listens dialog, 142-145

Whiting, Percy, 133, 144

Whitley, Joe L., 231

Who/What/Where strategy, 52

Why-Hesitate strategy, 71

Wiley, John, 158

Willingham, Ron, 14

Wilson, Orvel Ray, 158

Win with Wit dialog, 8-11

Word strategy, 163

work, prioritizing, 102

work environments, improving, 123

Wren, William, 19

X-Y-Z

X-L (excel) strategy, 6

yahoo.com, 56

"yes, but ..." phrase, 144

You Must Leave a Message dialog, 57-60

You're Talking Too Much dialog, 179-181

Young, Merv, 116

Youngman, Henny, 315

Zero-Resistance Selling, 293

Zest strategy, 221

Ziglar, Zig, 66